INVENTING HEBREWS

Inventing Hebrews examines a perennial topic in the study of the Letter to the Hebrews, its structure and purpose. Michael Martin and Jason Whitlark undertake a thorough synthesis of the ancient theory of invention and arrangement, providing a new account of Hebrews's design. The key to the speech's outline, the authors argue, is in its use of "disjointed" arrangement, a template ubiquitous in antiquity but little discussed in modern biblical studies. This method of arrangement accounts for the long-observed pattern of alternating epideictic and deliberative units in Hebrews as blocks of *narratio* and *argumentatio* respectively. Thus the "letter" may be seen as a conventional speech arranged according to the expectations of ancient rhetoric (*exordium, narratio, argumentatio, peroratio*), with epideictic comparisons of old and new covenant representatives (*narratio*) repeatedly enlisted in amplification of what may be viewed as the central argument of the speech (*argumentatio*), the recurring deliberative summons for perseverance. Resolving a long-standing conundrum, this volume offers a hermeneutical tool necessary for interpreting Hebrews, as well as countless other speeches from Greco-Roman antiquity.

MICHAEL WADE MARTIN is Professor of New Testament in the Alfred and Patricia Smith College of Biblical Studies at Lubbock Christian University. He is the author of *Judas and the Rhetoric of Comparison in the Fourth Gospel* (2010) and coauthor of *Ancient Rhetoric and the New Testament* (in press).

JASON A. WHITLARK is Associate Professor of New Testament in Baylor University's Honors College. He also serves as the assistant faculty director of the Baylor Interdisciplinary Core. He is the author of *Enabling Fidelity to God: Perseverance in Hebrews in Light of the Ancient Reciprocity Systems of the Ancient Mediterranean World* (2009) and *Resisting Empire: Rethinking the Purpose of the Letter to the "Hebrews"* (2014).

SOCIETY FOR NEW TESTAMENT STUDIES

MONOGRAPH SERIES

General Editor: Edward Adams, *King's College, London*

171

INVENTING HEBREWS: DESIGN AND PURPOSE
IN ANCIENT RHETORIC

SOCIETY FOR NEW TESTAMENT STUDIES

MONOGRAPH SERIES

Recent titles in the series:
160. *Faith and the Faithfulness of Jesus in Hebrews*
    MATTHEW C. EASTER
161. *Covenant Renewal and the Consecration of the Gentiles in Romans*
    SARAH WHITTLE
162. *The Role of Jewish Feasts in John's Gospel*
    GERRY WHEATON
163. *Paul's Political Strategy in 1 Corinthians 1–4*
    BRADLEY J. BITNER
164. *The Pauline Church and the Corinthian Ekklēsia*
    RICHARD LAST
165. *Jesus and the Temple*
    SIMON J. JOSEPH
166. *The Death of Jesus in Matthew*
    CATHERINE SIDER HAMILTON
167. *Ecclesiology and Theosis in the Gospel of John*
    ANDREW J. BYERS
168. *The Book of Revelation and Early Jewish Textual Culture*
    GARRICK ALLEN
169. *The Origin of Divine Christology*
    ANDREW TER ERN LOKE
170. *Romans 7 and Christian Identity: A Study of the 'I' in Its Literary Context*
    WILL N. TIMMINS

Inventing Hebrews

Design and Purpose in Ancient Rhetoric

MICHAEL WADE MARTIN
Lubbock Christian University

JASON A. WHITLARK
Baylor University

CAMBRIDGE
UNIVERSITY PRESS

University Printing House, Cambridge CB2 8BS, United Kingdom

One Liberty Plaza, 20th Floor, New York, NY 10006, USA

477 Williamstown Road, Port Melbourne, VIC 3207, Australia

314–321, 3rd Floor, Plot 3, Splendor Forum, Jasola District Centre, New Delhi – 110025, India

79 Anson Road, #06–04/06, Singapore 079906

Cambridge University Press is part of the University of Cambridge.

It furthers the University's mission by disseminating knowledge in the pursuit of education, learning, and research at the highest international levels of excellence.

www.cambridge.org
Information on this title: www.cambridge.org/9781108429467
DOI: 10.1017/9781108554763

© Michael Wade Martin and Jason A. Whitlark 2018

First published 2018

Printed in the United States of America by Sheridan Books, Inc.

A catalogue record for this publication is available from the British Library.

ISBN 978-1-108-42946-7 Hardback

To Mikeal C. Parsons
our mentor and friend

CONTENTS

Acknowledgements   *page* xi
List of Abbreviations   xiii

1   **Structuring Hebrews: Modern Approaches to an Ancient Text**   1

PART I   LAYING THE FOUNDATION – SYNCRISIS IN HEBREWS   21

2   **Comparing Covenants: The Syncritical Backbone of Hebrews**   23

3   **Choosing the Advantageous: Deliberative Syncrisis & Epideictic Syncrisis in Hebrews**   52

PART 2   ARRANGING THE SPEECH – THE ANCIENT RHETORICAL DESIGN OF HEBREWS   77

4   **Arranging an Ancient Speech: Ancient Compositional Theory and a Proposal for Modern Analysis**   79

5   **Proving the Case: *Argumentatio* in Hebrews**   86

6   **Presenting the Facts Relevant to the Case: *Narratio* in Hebrews**   129

7   **Beginning with Favor: *Exordium* in Hebrews**   193

8   **Ending with Recapitulation and Emotion: *Peroratio* in Hebrews**   222

ix

9   **Putting It All Together: The Rhetorical
      Arrangement and Aim of Hebrews**   250

10   **Examining Implications: Early Christian Sermons
      and Apostasy in Hebrews**   260

      Bibliography   271
      Scripture Index   284
      Ancient Sources Index   292
      Modern Authors Index   300
      Subject Index   303

ACKNOWLEDGEMENTS

We are indebted to many "who at sundry times and in divers ways" have contributed to this study. Our book was born out of two articles that we published with *New Testament Studies* in 2011–2012. We want to thank John Barclay, the editor at that time, and the reviewers of those preliminary studies for helping to sharpen our thinking on this project. We are also grateful to Alan Mitchell who prepared a response to a paper presented in the Hebrews Session at the 2014 SBL Annual Meeting in San Diego. His insights and critiques were most helpful and have shaped this work in a number of ways. Thanks also goes to Paul Trebilco, the series editor of SNTMS, and the reviewer of the completed manuscript for their insights and input. Paul always graciously and promptly responded to our inquiries and nurtured this project from our first contact with him. His encouragement to develop our ideas more robustly greatly improved the book. We are deeply grateful for the team at Cambridge Universtity Press and SPI Global who brought this book to publication: Beatrice Rehl, Eilidh Burrett, Katherine Tengco Barbaro, Divyabharathi Elavazhagan, and Margaret Haywood.

We also wish to thank Baylor University's Honors College for providing Jason a summer sabbatical to aid us in finishing this work in a timely manner. Stephanie Peek, Jon Carman, and Greg Barnhill served as Jason's graduate students over the course of this project. They provided both excellent feedback and adroit compilation of data and resources. We are also thankful for the sabbatical leave Lubbock Christian University awarded Michael for the spring of 2017, and for the summer leave and research stipend granted the same year. This support, funded in large part by generous gifts given by Al and Patricia Smith to the college that now bears their name, was critical to Michael's participation in the project and certainly was most appreciated. We are also both grateful, as always, to our

families and our colleagues at our institutions for their encouragement of this work all along the way.

Finally, out of a sense of deep gratitude and affection we dedicate this volume to Dr. Mikeal C. Parsons. The seeds of this project were planted many years ago in his graduate seminar on ancient rhetoric and the New Testament. It was in that course, as young grad students, we first encountered the patterns of persuasion described in this monograph, as well as the ancient texts that taught them. Apart from that encounter, it is doubtful this book would exist. Furthermore, from our graduate days and into our professional careers, Mikeal has continued to promote and encourage our scholarly endeavors. We are deeply thankful for his mentorship and many years of friendship and hope that this volume is a worthy tribute to Mikeal and his scholarship and teaching.

ABBREVIATIONS

Unless otherwise indicated below, the abbreviations in this book follow *The SBL Handbook of Style for Biblical Studies and Related Disciplines* (2nd ed.; Atlanta: SBL Press, 2014).

Anonymous Seguerianus	M. R. Dilts and G. A. Kennedy, eds., *Two Greek Rhetorical Treatises from the Roman Empire: Introduction, Text, and Translation of the Arts of Rhetoric, Attributed to Anonymous Seguerianus and to Apsines of Gadara* (Leiden: Brill, 1997).
Aphthonius	G. A. Kennedy, *Progymnasmata: Greek Textbooks of Prose Composition and Rhetoric* (Atlanta: SBL, 2003). Page numbers from L. Spengel, ed., *Rhetores Graeci* (3 vols.; Leipzig: Teubner, 1854–56).
Rom. Or.	Aelius Aristides. H. Oliver. "The Ruling Power: A Study of the Roman Empire in the Second Century after Christ through the Roman Oration of Aelius Aristides." *TAPS* 43/4 (1953): 895–907, 982–91.
Fortun.	*C. Chirii Fortunatiani artis rhetoricae libri III.* Pages 79–134 in C. Halm, *Rhetores Latini minores. Ex codicibus maximam partem primum adhibitis* (Leipzig: Teubner, 1863).
Libanius	*Libanius's* Progymnasmata: *Model Exercises in Greek Prose Composition and Rhetoric.* Translated by C. Gibson (WGRW 27; Atlanta: SBL, 2008).
Menander Rhetor	Menander. *Menander Rhetor: Edited with Translation and Commentary by D. A. Russell and N. G. Wilson.* Oxford: Clarendon, 1981.

Nicolaus

G. A. Kennedy, *Progymnasmata: Greek Textbooks of Prose Composition and Rhetoric* (Atlanta: SBL, 2003). Page numbers from J. Felten, ed., *Nicolai Progymnasmata* (Leipzig: Teubner, 1913; reprinted, Osnabrück: Zeller, 1968).

Ps. Hermogenes

G. A. Kennedy, *Progymnasmata: Greek Textbooks of Prose Composition and Rhetoric* (Atlanta: SBL, 2003). Page numbers from H. Rabe, ed., *Hermogenis Opera* (Leipzig: Teubner, 1931).

Rhet.

Apsines. *Ars Rhetorica.* M.R. Dilts and G.A. Kennedy, eds. *Two Greek Rhetorical Treatises from the Roman Empire: Introduction, Text, and Translation of the Arts of Rhetoric, Attributed to Anonymous Seguerianus and to Apsines of Gadara* (Leiden: Brill, 1997).

Theon

G. A. Kennedy, *Progymnasmata: Greek Textbooks of Prose Composition and Rhetoric* (Atlanta: SBL, 2003). Page numbers from L. Spengel, ed. *Rhetores Graeci* (3 vols. Leipzig: Teubner, 1854–6).

1

STRUCTURING HEBREWS
Modern Approaches to an Ancient Text

The Problem of Structuring Hebrews

This book revisits one of the persistent challenges in New Testament interpretation – the structure and argument of the Letter to the Hebrews. One of the essential tasks for understanding any text is to discern how its various parts relate to one another. Addressing this challenge in Hebrews, then, is essential if this enigmatic New Testament text is to be interpreted.

The many excellent surveys of this topic commonly note that very little consensus has emerged regarding the structure of Hebrews.[1] One reason for this lack of consensus is that numerous methods have been developed in an effort to discern the structure of Hebrews. Some approaches attempt to arrange Hebrews intuitively based on thematic or topical indicators.[2] Other approaches make the scriptural quotations or allusions in Hebrews the organizing principle.[3]

---

[1] The history of research on this issue has been well-surveyed. For comprehensive surveys see George H. Guthrie, *The Structure of Hebrews: A Text-Linguistic Analysis* (NovTSup 73; Leiden: Brill, 1994), 3–41; Cynthia L. Westfall, *A Discourse Analysis of the Letter to the Hebrews: The Relationship between Form and Meaning* (LNTS 297; London: T&T Clark, 2005), 1–21; Gabriella Gelardini, *"Verhärtet eure Herzen nicht": Der Hebräer, eine Synagogenhomilie zu Tischa Be-Aw* (BIS 83; Leiden: Brill, 2007), 1–84; Barry C. Joslin, "Can Hebrews Be Structured? An Assessment of Eight Approaches," *CBR* 6 (2007): 99–129.

[2] E.g., Philip E. Hughes, *A Commentary on the Epistle to the Hebrews* (Grand Rapids: Eerdmans, 1977); F. F. Bruce, *The Epistle to the Hebrews* (NICNT; Grand Rapids: Eerdmans, 1990).

[3] E.g., Richard N. Longenecker, *Biblical Exegesis in the Apostolic Period* (Grand Rapids: Eerdmans, 1975), 175–84. Longenecker is followed with modification by R. T. France, "The Writer of Hebrews as Biblical Expositor," *TynBul* 47 (1996): 246–76. See also Jonathan I. Griffiths, *Hebrews and Divine Speech* (LNTS 507; London: T&T Clark, 2014), 28–35. Griffiths's structure is a development of the one proposed by Lawrence Wills, "The Form of the Sermon in Hellenistic Judaism and Early Christianity," *HTR* 77 (1984): 277–83. In many of these proposals, the various expositions of Scripture in Hebrews are only loosely held together when considered as a whole. It is not clear why the author moves from one major block of exposition to the next.

Still other approaches emphasize literary indicators that demarcate the major divisions of Hebrews. Among these latter attempts, the proposals by Wolfgang Nauck and Albert Vanhoye have exerted considerable influence on the present study of Hebrews.

Nauck proposed a tripartite structure that emphasized the parallel exhortations in Heb 4:14–16 and 10:19–23.[4] Accordingly, he divided the discourse of Hebrews into the following sections, each with an overarching hortatory theme:

1:1–4:13	Listen carefully, believing in the Word of God which was delivered to us in the unique Son Jesus Christ who is exalted over the representatives of the cosmos and the old covenant.
4:14–10:31	Come near to God and hold firm to the confession because Jesus Christ has opened the way.
10:32–13:17	Stand firm and follow Jesus Christ who is the author and perfecter of faith.

Additionally, there is also some debate over whether there is a structurally significant and central Old Testament text in Hebrews. Psalm 109:1, 4 (LXX) has been a predominant choice due to its Christological focus and prevalence throughout Hebrews, e.g., see Harold W. Attridge, "The Psalms in Hebrews," in *The Psalms in the New Testament* (ed. Steve Moyise and Maarten J. J. Menken; The New Testament and the Scriptures of Israel; London: T&T Clark, 2004), 197–9; Guthrie, *Structure*, 123–4; Andrew Lincoln, *Hebrews: A Guide* (London: T&T Clark, 2006), 13, 69. A case has also been made for Jer 38:31–34 (LXX), e.g., see Gabriella Gelardini, "From 'Linguistic Turn' and Hebrews Scholarship to *Anadiplosis Iterata*: The Enigma of Structure," *HTR* 102 (2009): 72.

[4] Wolfgang Nauck, "Zum Aufbau des Hebräerbriefes," in *Judentum, Urchristentum, Kirche, Festschrift für Joachim Jeremias* (ed. Walter Eltester, BZNW 26; Berlin: Alfred Töpelmann, 1960), 199–206. Nauck's observations (which developed those initially proposed by Otto Michel in his 1957 commentary on Hebrews) have had considerable influence on the arrangement of Hebrews by modern scholars. See Otto Michel, *Der Brief an die Hebräer* (KEK 12; Göttingen: Vandenhoeck & Ruprecht, 1966), 29–35; Werner G. Kümmel, *Introduction to the New Testament* (trans. H. C. Kee; Nashville: Abingdon, 1975), 390–2; Heinrich Zimmermann, *Das Bekenntnis der Hoffnung: Tradition und Redaktion im Hebräerbrief* (Cologne, Peter Hanstein Verlag, 1977), 18–24; Hans-Friedrich Weiss, *Der Brief an die Hebräer* (KEK 15; Göttingen: Vandenhoeck & Ruprecht, 1991), 42–51; Knut Backhaus, *Der Neue Bund und das Werden der Kirche: die Diatheke-Deutung des Hebräerbrief im Rahmen der frühchristlichen Theologiegeschichte* (NTAbh 29; Münster: Aschendorff, 1996), 63; David A. deSilva, *Perseverance in Gratitude: A Socio-Rhetorical Commentary on the Epistle "to the Hebrews"* (Grand Rapids: Eerdmans, 2000), 72–5; Gerd Schunack, *Der Hebräerbrief* (ZBK NT 14; Zürich: Theologischer Verlag Zürich, 2002), 13–15; Martin Karrer, *Der Brief an die Hebräer: Kapitel 5,11–13,25* (ÖKTNT 20/2; Gütersloh: Gütersloher Verlagshaus, 2008), 379. James W. Thompson, *Hebrews* (Paideia; Grand Rapids: Baker 2008), 19; Gareth Lee Cockerill, *The Epistle to the Hebrews* (NICNT; Grand Rapids: Eerdmans, 2012), 79–81; Kevin L. Anderson, *Hebrews: A Commentary in the Wesleyan Tradition* (New Beacon Bible Commentary; Kansas City: Beacon Hill Press, 2013).

Albert Vanhoye proposed a five-part chiastic structure based on such literary indicators as announcement of the subject, inclusions, variation in genre, transitional hook words, characteristic terms that repeat, and symmetrical arrangements.[5] Vanhoye produced the following structure (D = doctrinal; P = paraenetic):

	1:–4	Exordium	
I	1:5–2:18	A name so different from the name of angels	D
II A	3:1–4:14	Jesus, faithful high-priest	P
B	4:15–5:10	Jesus, compassionate high-priest	D
III	5:11–6:20	Preliminary exhortation	P
A	7:1–28	Jesus, high-priest in the order of Melchizedek	D
B	8:1–9:28	Come to fulfillment	D
C	10:1–18	Cause of an eternal salvation	D
	10:19–39	Final exhortation	P
IV A	11:1–40	The faith of the ancestors	D
B	12:1–13	The necessity of endurance	P
V	12:14–13:19	The peaceful fruit of justice	P
	13:20–21	Peroration	

The continuing influence of Nauck and Vanhoye can be seen in two subsequent and significant efforts by George Guthrie and Cynthia Westfall to explain the structure and argument of Hebrews based on discourse analysis.[6] Gabriella Gelardini's more recent proposal of a five-part, chiastic structure of Hebrews (1:1–2:18; 3:1–6:20; 7:1–10:18; 10:19–12:3; 12:4–13:25) shows the influence of Vanhoye's proposed concentric relationships in Hebrews.[7] Still,

[5] Albert Vanhoye, *La Structure Littéraire de l'Épître aux Hébreux* (2d ed.; Paris: Desclée de Brouwer, 1976). Vanhoye's structural analysis has influenced Harold W. Attridge, *The Epistle to the Hebrews* (Hermeneia; Philadelphia: Fortress, 1989), 19; William L. Lane, *Hebrews 1–8* (WBC 47A; Nashville: Thomas Nelson, 1991), lxxxvii–viii; Paul Ellingworth, *The Epistle to the Hebrews: A Commentary on the Greek Text* (NIGTC; Grand Rapids: Eerdmans, 1993), 58; Alan C. Mitchell, *Hebrews* (SP 13; Collegeville: Liturgical Press, 2009), 21.

[6] Guthrie, *Structure*; Westfall, *Discourse Analysis*. Guthrie's study has been approvingly cited in the commentaries by Lane, *Hebrews 1–8*, xc–xcviii, and adopted by Peter T. O'Brien, *The Letter to the Hebrews* (Pillar New Testament Commentary; Grand Rapids: Eerdmans, 2010), 34; as well as Joslin, "Can Hebrews Be Structured?" 115–22.

[7] Cf. Gelardini, "Linguistic Turn," 51–73; idem, *"Verhätet eure Herzen nicht,"* 83. Gelardini shifts the center of Hebrews from Christ as high priest (9:11) in Vanhoye's arrangement to God's covenant-making in Heb 8. Gelardini's structural arrangement makes Hebrews more theocentric and covenantal. We think that Gelardini rightly emphasizes the overarching covenant theology and theocentricity of Hebrews, although our structure enshrines the covenantal emphasis through the topical arrangement of the epideictic syncrises in Hebrews. For another distinct attempt to arrange Hebrews as a chiasm at the macro- and micro-level see John Paul Heil, *Hebrews: Chiastic Structures and Audience Response* (CBQMS 46; Washington, DC: Catholic Biblical Association of America, 2010).

other hybrid approaches have emerged that attempt to incorporate the insights of Nauck with the ancient categories of rhetorical arrangement.[8] In some cases Nauck's tripartite structure exerts a stronger influence over the articulation of the macro-structure and argument of Hebrews than the rhetorical categories.[9]

Nauck's observations are not easily ignored and draw attention to the primarily hortatory nature of Hebrews. We, in fact, will address their place in structuring the discourse of Hebrews, though we do not adopt an overall tripartite structure for the entire discourse or even its *argumentatio*.

With regard to Vanhoye and those he has influenced, we make three observations. First, one of the problems with chiastic macro-arrangements of Hebrews is that they often make the exposition of Christ's high priesthood or God's covenant-making the focal point of Hebrews; but, as we will argue, the focal point is always the exhortations that follow the expositions in Hebrews.[10] The expository material with its theological and Christological implications is not unimportant to Hebrews, but structurally, this material is always placed in service to the hortatory focus throughout Hebrews, as Nauck's proposal rightly recognizes. We will also show that the considerable material devoted to Christ's priestly deeds has more to do with the rhetorical topic under consideration than with that topic being at the center of the discourse.

Second, Luke Timothy Johnson notes that any chiastic arrangement of Hebrews potentially misses "the linear and cumulative force of Hebrews's argument."[11] Likewise, we will demonstrate that the

---

[8] For example, Weiss, Backhaus, Karrer, Thompson, Cockerill, and Anderson give careful attention to the rhetorical categories of arrangement for structuring Hebrews, but they are also significantly influenced by Nauck's tripartite structure (see the survey at the end of this chapter).

[9] Cockerill, *Hebrews*, 79–81.

[10] Cf. Thompson, *Hebrews*, 15, who states that the focal point in Hebrews is not on Jesus's priestly ministry but on the climactic exhortations that follow. See also Barnabas Lindars, "The Rhetorical Structure of Hebrews," *NTS* 35 (1989): 406. Gelardini ("Linguistic Turn," 72) is willing to identify the climactic exhortations (at least in chapter 12) as the pragmatic-paraenetic center of Hebrews. Yet for Gelardini, Heb 8:7–13 remains the logical, structural center by which the whole discourse is understood.

[11] Luke Timothy Johnson, *Hebrews: A Commentary* (NTL; Louisville: Westminster John Knox, 2006), 12. See also Guthrie, *Structure*, 143, and Westfall, *Discourse Analysis*, 301, who place the climax of Hebrews at 12:18–24 and 12:18–29 respectively. By including the exhortations (vv. 25–29) in the climax, Westfall emphasizes the hortatory character of Hebrews. Craig R. Koester ("Hebrews, Rhetoric, and the Future of Humanity," in *Reading the Epistle to the Hebrews: A Resource for Students* [ed. Eric F. Mason and Kevin B. McCruden; RBS 66; Atlanta: SBL, 2011], 108–9) as

topical arrangement of Hebrews is both linear and cumulative. Additionally, we should recognize that ancient rhetoricians such as Quintilian (a contemporary of the author of Hebrews) instruct that the weakest arguments be placed at the center of the speech whereas the stronger arguments are reserved for the beginning and end of a speech and thus are the speech's focal points (cf. *Inst.* 5.12.14).[12] In fact, the author of Hebrews saves what he admits is the most difficult (not necessarily the weakest) part of his discourse for the more central and lengthier sections of his argument (cf. Heb 5:11).

Third, another problem arises when we consider that many of the literary indicators identified by Vanhoye and others such as hook words, chiasmus, repetition, and inclusions are ancient stylistic rhetorical devices. The discussion of style was taken up along with invention and arrangement as one of the tasks of the ancient rhetorician.[13] One of the virtues discussed under style was ornamentation.[14] As ornamental devices, these rhetorical phenomena do not provide a sufficient foundation for the overall structure and logic of a speech like Hebrews.[15] These stylistic devices are helpful for identifying topics and discreet thought units, but prior understanding of invention and arrangement in ancient rhetoric is necessary to recognize how these stylistic elements are deployed in Hebrews.[16] For

---

well emphasizes the linear and cumulative perspective of Hebrews in his articulation of three series of repetitive but also progressive arguments in Hebrews.

[12] See also Cicero, *De or.* 2.313–14; Rhet. Her. 3.18.

[13] Isocrates, in *Soph.* 16–17, appears to be one of the earliest to comment on these three tasks of composition.

[14] Cf. Cicero, *De or.* 3.37; Quintilian, *Inst.* 8.1.1. Style should be correct, lucid, ornate, and appropriate.

[15] Isocrates (*Soph.* 16–17) sequences compositional tasks starting first with invention, then arrangement, and lastly style: "But to choose from these elements those which should be employed for each subject, to join them together, to arrange them properly, and also, not to miss what the occasion demands but appropriately to adorn the whole speech with striking thoughts and to clothe it in melodious phrase" (Norlin, LCL). Cicero (*De. or.* 1.142) and Quintilian also sequence these activities in the same order: invention (*Inst.* 4–6), arrangement (*Inst.* 7), and style (*Inst.* 8–11.1). Treating style in third place after invention and arrangement alerts us that stylistic devices do not provide a framework for the whole speech or composition. These rhetorical devices enhance and assume prior decisions made for arranging a speech – decisions that are based on the other rhetorical tasks of invention and arrangement.

[16] Cf. Nauck, "Zum Aufbau des Hebräerbriefes," 201–3. The finding and arranging of arguments as well as choice of style were organically related as Catherine Steel ("Divisions of Speech," in *A Cambridge Companion to Ancient Rhetoric* [ed. Erik Gunderson; Cambridge: Cambridge University Press, 2009], 80) notes, "It is impossible to separate entirely the finding of arguments from their arrangement; choice of style depends on judgments about the kinds of arguments which a speech will employ; and delivery must accord with style."

example, the announcement of a subject ahead of time has figured significantly in the discussion of Hebrews for Vanhoye and others.[17] Quintilian discusses this rhetorical figure as a matter of style. "Deferring the discussion of some points after mentioning them" lends charm to the speech (*Inst.* 9.2.63 [Russell, LCL]). This feature by itself does not explain, at least from the perspective of ancient rhetoric, why certain topics are addressed and why they might be taken up in the order that they are. The coherence of these topics must be supplied from elsewhere.[18] Thus, discerning the appropriate intertextual or cultural background is a necessary complement to any structural analysis of Hebrews. Such contextual considerations often illuminate connections, arguments, or logics that are not readily apparent to the modern interpreter but are persuasive to the original audience.[19]

The question still remains: By what method or methods will we identify the structure of Hebrews?

The Approach of This Study

As Gelardini has aptly stated, "it is a method that generates a structure."[20] We begin by asking how the audience of Hebrews

---

[17] E.g., Guthrie (*Structure*, 34) states that "any investigation into the book's structure must consider this phenomenon."

[18] E.g., Gelardini ("Linguistic Turn," 72–3) anchors her logical connections in the intertext of the exodus story from the golden-calf incident to the rebellion at Kadesh Barnea. Gelardini acknowledges that her arrangement based on stylistic, lexical, and thematic considerations did not readily suggest the logical connections between some of the topics of her arrangement until she considered the intertext of the exodus narrative. We acknowledge that the narrative substructure assumed by Hebrews is an important aspect of interpreting Hebrews and is a topic that has been given explicit methodological consideration by Kenneth L. Schenck, *Cosmology and Eschatology in Hebrews: The Settings of the Sacrifice* (SNTSMS 143; Cambridge: Cambridge University Press, 2007). Schenck gives emphasis to Ps 8 quoted and interpreted in Heb 2:5–9 as the foundation of the metanarrative assumed in Hebrews. Interestingly, Schenck's narrative substructure is more universal in scope because he begins with the creation and destiny of humanity in the author's use of Ps 8. For a similar perspective to Schenck's but shaped by an analysis of rhetorical categories, see Koester, "Hebrews, Rhetoric, and the Future," 106, where he identifies Heb 2:5–9 as the *propositio* of the entire discourse.

[19] For additional discussion of these points see Bryan J. Whitfield, *Joshua Traditions and the Argument of Hebrews 3 and 4* (BZNW 194; Berlin: De Gruyter, 2013), 22–47. Whitfield ultimately opts for what he labels as reading practices from the first-century Jewish context to discern the connection between Heb 3 and 4 and between the high priest and the sojourning people of God.

[20] Gelardini, "Linguistic Turn," 58.

(and its author) would have conceived or even articulated the structure of this "word of exhortation." Thus, to solve the riddle of the structure of Hebrews, we adopt an audience-critical approach. This question recognizes, as some of our critiques above indicate, that there were rhetorical and compositional categories and strategies peculiar to the historical context of Hebrews that would have guided the compositional practices of the author and informed the expectations of his audience. Thus, we will propose an arrangement that gives serious consideration to the rhetorical categories of arrangement ubiquitously discussed and practiced in the ancient Mediterranean world.[21] We are helped immensely in our task by the preservation of numerous ancient rhetorical handbooks that embody centuries of instruction as well as numerous extant speeches that exemplify the type of rhetorical training found in the handbooks. The handbooks especially provide us with a metadiscourse on actual rhetorical practices in the ancient world and thus serve as self-conscious reflections and evaluations of living rhetoric.[22] It is within a context informed by this kind of rhetorical training that Hebrews, a first-century speech, was composed.

In regard to our use of the rhetorical handbooks and ancient speeches, we recognize that the rhetorical tradition of the ancient Mediterranean world was not monolithic. Yet it was a tradition that was reflective of an ongoing conversation. George A. Kennedy, in his overview of ancient rhetoric, recognizes both the variation in details among rhetorical instructions and speeches and also that "it is possible to speak of a standard system of classical rhetoric, expounded in the handbooks and illustrated in practice."[23] We, therefore, attempt to discern, when possible, where there was broad agreement among the theorists on a rhetorical topic. Sometimes the theorists themselves will highlight commonly accepted ideas practiced in their time with which they might agree or which they might critique. These areas of consensus or common practices alert us to what ancient audiences anticipated in a speech such as Hebrews. Thus in our analysis of Hebrews, we look for points of contact and

---

[21] For a similar perspective see Peter Lampe, "Rhetorical Analysis of Pauline Texts – Quo Vadit?" in *Paul and Rhetoric* (ed. J. Paul Sampley and Peter Lampe; New York: T&T Clark, 2010), 7.

[22] Cf. Cicero, *De or.* 1.146; Quintilian, *Inst.* 5.10.119–25.

[23] George A. Kennedy, "Historical Survey of Rhetoric," in *Handbook of Classical Rhetoric in the Hellenistic Period, 330 B.C.–A.D. 400* (ed. Stanley Porter; Leiden: Brill, 1997), 6.

convergence. The more that Hebrews reflects broad areas of practice and agreement with the rhetorical tradition of its time, the more it reveals the conventional nature of its arrangement.

Our approach is not new. While rhetorical studies of Paul's letters received new impetus beginning in the 1970s with the Han Dieter Betz's rhetorical study of Galatians,[24] Hermann von Soden's commentary on Hebrews published in 1899 had already acknowledged the value of the ancient handbooks and the rhetorical categories of arrangement for understanding the purpose and organization of Hebrews. There, in fact, have been several attempts after von Soden to understand Hebrews's structure and genre by ancient rhetorical canons. Key distinct proposals of this approach in Hebrews have been listed at the end of this chapter spanning from von Soden into the twenty-first century.[25] A cursory examination of the survey indicates that, even within this focused area of inquiry, little consensus has developed. Furthermore, there have been some critiques of this approach to Hebrews. Many of these critiques have arisen from the fact that Hebrews seems to resist the conventional arrangement of an *exordium* followed by a *narratio* followed by an *argumentatio* followed by a *peroratio*. Thus, any attempt to fit Hebrews into these categories has sometimes been seen as artificial.[26] There have been two primary and discrete reasons offered for this critique:

---

[24] Cf. Hans Dieter Betz's seminal article on Galatians, "The Literary Composition and Function of Paul's Letter to the Galatians," *NTS* 21 (1975): 353–79. Paul's letters afterwards have witnessed a robust application of ancient rhetoric with regard to invention, arrangement, and style. For an overview of the use of ancient rhetoric in Pauline studies see Troy W. Martin, "Invention and Arrangement in Recent Pauline Studies: A Survey of the Practices and the Problems," in *Paul and the Ancient Letter Form* (ed. Stanley E. Porter and Sean A. Adams; Pauline Studies 6; Leiden: Brill, 2010), 48–118. For an excellent introduction to the early scholars who have shaped the contemporary application of ancient rhetoric to the New Testament see Troy W. Martin, ed., *Genealogies of New Testament Rhetorical Criticism* (Minneapolis: Fortress Press, 2014).

[25] There are some who use the rhetorical categories of *exordium* and *peroratio* to identify structural elements in Hebrews, but their overall structuring of Hebrews is based on different considerations than the rhetorical arrangement of ancient discourses (e.g., Albert Vanhoye, *A Structured Translation of the Epistle to the Hebrews* [trans. James Swetnam; Rome: Pontifical Biblical Institute, 1964], 7; deSilva, *Perseverance in Gratitude*, 46; Attridge, *Hebrews*, 17; Mitchell, *Hebrews*, 21).

[26] Cf. Lane, *Hebrews 1–8*, lxxix; Guthrie, *Structure*, 33, 35; deSilva, *Perseverance in Gratitude*, 46; O'Brien, *Hebrews*, 26; Westfall, *Discourse Analysis*, 6–7; Gabriella Gelardini, "Rhetorical Criticism in Hebrews Scholarship: Avenues and Aporias," in *Method and Meaning: Essays on New Testament Interpretation in Honor of Harold W. Attridge* (ed. Andrew B. McGowan and Kent Harold Richards; RBS 67; Atlanta: SBL, 2011), 235.

(1) Hebrews is thought to be patterned after the fringe rhetorical phenomenon of a synagogue homily, and (2) rhetorical handbooks encourage flexibility in arrangement.

According to the first critique, the identification of the Hebrews as a synagogue homily[27] is assumed *necessarily* to preclude identification with Greco-Roman genre categories such as deliberative, epideictic, and judicial. This perspective acknowledges the influence of classical rhetorical practices on Jewish homilies, but it ultimately judges the synagogue sermon to be its own genre, and certainly one whose arrangement cannot be explicated by the categories of pagan oratory.[28] Setting aside the question of whether the Christian sermon developed from the synagogue sermon,[29] we acknowledge that the

---

[27] See Guthrie, *Structure*, 32–3; Gelardini, "Rhetorical Criticism in Hebrews Scholarship," 235. Gelardini ("Hebrews, Homiletics, and Liturgical Scripture Interpretation," in *Reading the Epistle to the Hebrews: A Resource for Students* [ed. Eric F. Mason and Kevin B. McCruden; RBS 66; Atlanta: SBL 2011], 121–41) has argued, rather eloquently, that Hebrews is "the oldest synagogue homily of the (proto-)*petichta* type" that interprets the central scriptural quotations from Ps 94:7b–11 (LXX) and Jer 38:31–34 (LXX). Her more extensive arguments can be found in *"Verhätet eure Herzen nicht,"* passim. For an earlier study that employs Hebrews as a source to determine the form of a Hellenistic-synagogue homily see Hartwig Thyen, *Der Stil der jüdisch-hellenistischen Homilie* (FRLANT; Göttingen: Vandehoeck & Ruprecht, 1955), 16–18.

[28] E.g., Gelardini ("Liturgical Scripture Interpretation," 141) states that the author of Hebrews "incorporates elements of ancient rhetoric ... But I doubt whether deliberative, forensic, or epideictic oratory can do justice to a synagogal context." Also, Harold W. Attridge ("Paraenesis in a Homily [λόγος παρακλήσεως]: The Possible Location of, and Socialization in, the 'Epistle to the Hebrews,'" *Semeia* 50 [1990]: 216–7) identifies Hebrews as a synagogue homily or paraclesis which is "a mutant on the evolutionary trail of ancient rhetoric." See also Folker Siegert, "Homily and Panegyrical Sermon," in *Handbook of Classical Rhetoric in the Hellenistic Period, 330 B.C.–A.D. 400* (ed. Stanley Porter; Leiden: Brill, 1997), 421. Siegert acknowledges that the author of Hebrews might have been a professional orator (431). Similar claims have also been made for Philo's treatises. For example, Thomas M. Conley ("Philo of Alexandria," in *Handbook of Classical Rhetoric in the Hellenistic Period, 330 B.C.–A.D. 400* [ed. Stanley Porter; Leiden: Brill, 1997], 695–713) demonstrates how thoroughly immersed Philo is in the classical rhetorical practices of the first-century – even Philo's exegetical and argumentative strategies from Scripture. Conley, however, believes that we will not find a precise analogy to the standard parts of speech of Greco-Roman rhetoric in Philo's treatises, in part, because these rhetorical techniques are adapted to broad homiletic ends and exegetical activities occurring in the synagogues of Alexandria and the Diaspora.

[29] E.g., Siegert, "Homily and Panegyrical Sermon," 431–3. Alistair Stewart-Sykes (*From Prophecy to Preaching: A Survey for the Origins of the Christian Homily* [VCSup 59; Leiden: Brill, 2001], 15) notes the problem of being able to demonstrate whether the line from the synagogue to the practices of the Christian assembly was direct or "more crooked." He believes that, as Christian assemblies developed, Christian liturgical practices such as reading the Scriptures and preaching were influenced by synagogue practices (6), but he does not think that those influences are seen in the first-generation of Pauline churches (10).

reading and exposition of Scripture (i.e., a sermon or homily) was likely a practice of many of the synagogues in the first century.[30] There is, however, no clear evidence of a regular form that such a sermon took in the synagogue at this time.[31] Most of the evidence for possible synagogue sermons is taken from rabbinic sources, which are late, dating from the third to sixth centuries.[32] Moreover, these rabbinic expositions are clearly redacted and may not even have developed from a liturgical context.[33] Thus, the problem of evidence arises concerning what comparative material counts for discerning a typical form of a synagogue homily in the first century. The critique that Hebrews represents the form of a synagogue homily and not classical rhetorical arrangement is ultimately circular and is often employed based on the apparent lack of consensus among interpreters of Hebrews and not primarily on the evidence of the rhetorical handbooks or extant ancient speeches. In fact, if we look at one of the earliest extant Christian liturgical homilies from the mid-second century, *Peri Pascha* by Melito of Sardis, this example of epideictic oratory indeed conforms, as Alistair Stewart-Sykes has argued, to the standard categories of rhetorical arrangement: *exordium, narratio* with *digressio, probatio,* and *peroratio*.[34] Stewart-Sykes

---

[30] Cf. Stephen K. Catto, *Reconstructing the First-Century Synagogue: A Critical Analysis of Current Research* (LNTS 363; London: T&T Clark, 2007), 116–25. For a brief discussion of the development of preaching in Christian assemblies of the first and second centuries, see Stewart-Sykes, *Prophecy to Preaching*, 14–23.

[31] See the conclusion by Günter Stermberger, "The Derashah in Rabbinic Times," in *Preaching in Judaism and Early Christianity: Encounters and Developments from Biblical Times to Modernity* (ed. Alexander Deeg et al.; SJ 41; Berlin: de Gruyter, 2008), 20.

[32] Cf. William Richard Stegner "The Ancient Jewish Synagogue Homily," in *Greco-Roman Literature and the New Testament* (ed. David E. Aune; SBLSBS 21; Atlanta: Scholars Press, 1988), 51. Most of the evidence used for Christian sermons also begins at the end of the second century, cf. Stewart-Sykes, *Prophecy to Preaching*, 3.

[33] Cf. Stermberger, "Derashah," 7–21; idem, "Response," in *Preaching in Judaism and Early Christianity: Encounters and Developments from Biblical Times to Modernity* (ed. Alexander Deeg et al.; SJ 41; Berlin: de Gruyter, 2008), 45–8; Annette von Stockhausen, "Christian Perception of Jewish Preaching in Early Christianity?" in *Preaching in Judaism and Early Christianity: Encounters and Developments from Biblical Times to Modernity* (ed. Alexander Deeg et al.; SJ 41; Berlin: de Gruyter, 2008), 55–7.

[34] Alistair Stewart-Sykes, *The Lamb's High Feast: Melito, Peri Pascha and the Quartodeciman Paschal Liturgy at Sardis* (VCSup; Leiden: Brill, 1998), 72–92, 113–39 (esp. 114). He structures it as follows:

Exordium	1–10
Narratio	11–45
(Digressio)	(34–43)
Probatio	46–65
Peroratio	66–105

further notes that "rhetoric was bound up to liturgical functions" even among pagan worship and religious festivals.[35] Such evidence cautions us from too quickly characterizing Jewish or Christian oration within a liturgical or worshipping context as "fringe" and thus dismissing the relevance of classical rhetorical arrangement for Hebrews.

Some scholars take a form-critical approach to the question of evidence. Acts 13:14–41 is sometimes taken for early evidence of the form of a synagogue sermon because, in the narrative, the speech is reported to have been delivered in a synagogue gathering for worship. Lawrence Wills, in fact, begins his form-critical analysis of a Jewish or Christian sermon with Acts 13:14–41.[36] Wills believes that the tripartite pattern he discovered in Acts 13 (*exempla*, conclusion, and exhortation) was adapted from Greek rhetoric, yet the liturgical context transformed the rhetorical demands so that the Jewish or Christian sermon no longer retains any correspondence to the anticipated categories of classical rhetorical arrangement. After reexamining Wills's evidence, Clifton Black, however, argues that even Wills's pattern is best located not on the fringes but "within the mainstream of classical rhetoric" with regard to both genre and arrangement.[37] Black's observations are strengthened and advanced by Mikeal Parsons in his commentary on Acts. Parsons demonstrates that the "synagogue sermon" in Acts 13:6b–41 aligns well with the expected categories of rhetorical arrangement – *exordium* (13:6b), *narratio* (13:17–25), *probatio* (13:26–27), and *peroratio* (13:38–41).[38] Not only Acts 13, but many of the speeches in Acts appear to accord with classical rhetorical style, genre, and arrangement.[39]

In sum, we consider Hebrews to be a sermon because it was a speech (though written down and sent to its audience) that would

---

[35] Cf. Stewart-Sykes, *The Lamb's High Feast*, 132.

[36] Wills, "The Form of a Sermon," 277–83. Wills does examine the pattern he discovers in a diverse selection of Jewish and Christian texts outside of Acts. Though Wills attempts to relate Hebrews to his pattern, we do not believe that Wills's pattern best describes the arrangement of Hebrews.

[37] C. Clifton Black II, "The Rhetorical Form of the Hellenistic Jewish and Early Christian Sermon: A Response to Lawrence Wills," *HTR* 81 (1988): 1–18.

[38] Mikeal C. Parsons, *Acts* (Paideia; Grand Rapids: Baker, 2008), 191–6. It is difficult to know if Luke is styling his synagogue addresses on the basis of actual synagogue sermons pre- or even post-70 CE. If he is, then the observations above affirm the presence of classical rhetorical forms and structures that were employed in some synagogues settings.

[39] Cf. Parsons, *Acts*, 8–11.

likely have been delivered in the context of a worshipping Christian community, and because the author attempts to relate sacred text and doctrine to the needs of the community.[40] More to the point, Hebrews is likely the best example we have for a first-century sermon. Hebrews then shows us the possible form an early Christian sermon could take. Moreover, the studies by Black and Parsons on Acts and by Stewart-Sykes on *Peri Pascha* encourage us to examine more closely in Hebrews the expectations associated with arrangement and genre found in classical rhetorical instructions.

According to the second critique, scholars note that ancient speakers were not bound to follow rigidly the instructions set forth in the rhetorical handbooks.[41] Creativity and adaptability are part of the best rhetorical training. For example, Cicero acknowledges both the typical (or commonsense) elements of arrangement in a speech and the speaker's skill in adapting these elements to his or her case. He writes,

> [F]or to make some prefatory remarks, then to set out our case, afterwards to prove it by establishing our own points with arguments in their favour and refuting our adversary's points, then to wind up our case and so to come to our conclusion – this is the procedure enjoined by the very nature of oratory; but to decide how to arrange the statements that have to be made for the purpose of establishing and explaining our case – that is in the highest degree a task for professional skill. (*De or.* 2.307–8 [Sutton and Rackham, LCL])

Certainly adaptability and creativity are characteristic of speeches in the first century, but such adaptation and creativity can only be assessed against the anticipated (even commonsense) elements of rhetorical arrangement. Cicero in the same rhetorical treatise acknowledges that "if I were to call this learning useless, I should be lying. For in fact it contains certain reminders, as it were, for the orator, as to the standard he must apply on each occasion, and must keep in mind, if he is not to wander from whatever course he has set himself" (*De or.* 1.145 [Sutton and Rackham, LCL]). With regard to Hebrews, David deSilva's caution, however, remains warranted:

---

[40] This description is close to the loose definition put forward by Stewart-Sykes: "oral communication of the word of God in the Christian assembly" (*Prophecy to Preaching*, 6).

[41] As correctly noted by Lane, *Hebrews 1–8*, lxxix.

"Thus it seems more prudent to use the rhetorical handbooks only as strictly or as loosely as the text under investigation suggests, rather than insisting on squeezing the text into a mold in which it may not fit."[42] Taking this caution seriously, we will attempt to demonstrate that Hebrews does not have to be forced into a predetermined structure codified in the rhetorical handbooks. Our advancement in this area of inquiry comes from a fresh examination of both Hebrews and the ancient rhetorical handbooks. Some of our evidence from the handbooks has yet to be considered but is pertinent to demonstrating that Hebrews does, in fact, represent traditional practices of arrangement discussed in the rhetorical handbooks. Moreover, the proposed rhetorical arrangement will illuminate the purpose and argumentative strategy of Hebrews.

The Argument and Arrangement of This Study

This study is divided into two primary parts. Part I (Chapters 2–3) will take as its starting point two areas of consensus that have developed in Hebrews scholarship. First, syncrisis is commonly recognized as a key rhetorical feature in Hebrews, though its function is debated. In Chapter 2, we will demonstrate that the five major epideictic syncrises serve as the structural backbone of the discourse by showing what they collectively compare – old and new covenants.[43] Thus we will provide an explanation, based on ancient rhetorical expectations, for why, in Hebrews, topics are raised and addressed in their particular order. In other words, we will show by what rhetorical logic the author selects and connects his topics. Second, Hebrews is characterized by alternating rhetorical genres, epideictic and deliberative.[44] It is this feature in particular that has

---

[42] DeSilva, *Perseverance in Gratitude*, 46.

[43] Keijo Nissilä (*Das Hohepriestermotiv im Hebräerbrief: Eine Exegetische Unter-suchung* [Schriften der Finnischen Exegetischen Gesellschaft 33; Helsinki: Oy Liiton Kirjapaino, 1979]) sees the high-priestly motif as the main point that guides his rhetorical arrangement of the whole discourse of Hebrews (see below). Our structure emphasizes covenant.

[44] It is commonplace among commentators to point out this feature in Hebrews. Alternating genres, however, served as the primary foundation of the structural analysis of Rafael Gyllenberg, "Die Komposition des Hebräerbriefs," *SEÅ* 22–23 (1957–1958): 137–47. Prior to Gyllenberg, F. Büschel ("Hebräerbrief," in *Religion in Geschichte und Gegenwart: Handwörterbuch für Theologie und Religionswissenschaft* [ed. H. Gunkel and L. Zscharnack; 2d ed.; Tübingen: J.C.B. Mohr (Paul Siebeck), 1928], 2:1669–73) proposed a structure for Hebrews based on similar criteria.

often proved most puzzling to interpreters since it seems to defy conventional rhetorical arrangement and categorization. Consequently, some who carefully follow the instructions about rhetorical arrangement assign these hortatory sections, which appear to be the main point of this sermon, digressionary roles because these sections are adapted to a structure that has one *narratio* or *propositio*.[45] In Chapter 3, we will demonstrate that the hortatory sections with their comparative enthymemes depend both topically and logically on their preceding epideictic syncrisis. Thus, the overall deliberative thrust of Hebrews can be substantiated.

In Part II of this study (Chapters 4–9), we will demonstrate that the conclusions reached in Chapters 2 and 3 do indeed enable us to see the structural scaffolding or rhetorical arrangement of Hebrews. In Chapter 4, we will briefly explain our approach, namely why we will start with *argumentatio* in our examination of Hebrews. In Chapters 5 and 6, we will identify the *argumentatio* along with the disjointed *narratio* as the key to recognizing conventional rhetorical arrangement in Hebrews. Among other things, this discussion will highlight two elements that have been overlooked in studies of the arrangement of Hebrews. First, exhortations can function as *propositiones* in the *argumentatio* of deliberative oratory. Once this is recognized, the *argumentatio* of Hebrews is readily discernable. Second, a *narratio* can be disjointed or distributed throughout a speech. One scholar, Frederick J. Long, in his study of 2 Corinthians has already pointed to the importance of distributive *narratio* in demonstrating the unity of 2 Corinthians.[46] This little-discussed convention by New Testament scholars (though not by ancient rhetorical theorists) is, likewise, important to discerning the conventional, rhetorical arrangement of Hebrews. We will then proceed in Chapters 7 and 8 to identify the *exordium* and the *peroratio*. In Chapter 9, we will summarize the results of the entire investigation

---

[45] E.g., Koester, "Hebrews, Rhetoric, and the Future," 113–6, who identifies 2:5–9 as the *propositio* and 2:1–4, 5:11–6:20; 10:26–39, and 12:25–27 as digressions (see below). Cf. Anderson, *Hebrews*, 104–6, 175.

[46] Frederick J. Long, *Ancient Rhetoric and Paul's Apology: The Compositional Unity of 2 Corinthians* (SNTSMS 131; Cambridge: Cambridge University Press, 2004), 78, 81, 84, 156. Long primarily cites evidence of distributive *narratio* from Aristotle, *Rhet.* 3.16.11. Long cites Andocides's *On Mysteries* as an example of a forensic speech from Athens in 399 B.C.E. that also made use of distributive *narratio* (80). Long also points to an earlier study by J. D. H. Amador, "Revisiting 2 Corinthians: Rhetoric and the Case of Unity," *NTS* 46 (2000): 92–111, who proposed multiple sections with *narratio* in 2 Corinthians.

showing that Hebrews is both conventional in its arrangement and deliberative in its overall purpose.[47]

We will conclude our study in Chapter 10 by raising two important implications. First, if Hebrews is our earliest self-confessed Christian speech or sermon, what are the implications for understanding the nature of early Christian preaching in the worshipping assemblies? Second, how does the comparative covenant project and deliberative purpose of Hebrews relate to the type of apostasy opposed by the rhetoric of Hebrews?

Our hope is that this study will move the discussion of the structure of Hebrews forward by demonstrating the valuable insights that careful attention to the ancient rhetorical instructions provides for unlocking this interpretive riddle in the New Testament.

Rhetorical Arrangements of Hebrews

A Survey of Select Proposals

Von Soden, 1899[48]

1. προοίμιον πρὸς εὔνοιαν with the πρόθεσις: 1:1–4:13
2. διήγησις πρὸς πιθανότητα: 4:14–6:20

---

[47] DeSilva (*Perseverance in Gratitude*, 56–7) and Craig R. Koester (*Hebrews: A New Translation with Introduction and Commentary* [AB 36; New York: Doubleday, 2001], 82) have proposed that Hebrews is both epideictic and deliberative in its purpose, depending on the perspective of the various members in the audience. Additionally see also Lane, *Hebrews 1–8*, lxxix, and Johnson, *Hebrews*, 13. For those who argue that Hebrews is primarily epideictic, see Thomas H. Olbricht, "Hebrews as Amplification," in *Rhetoric and the New Testament: Essays from the 1992 Heidelberg Conference* (ed. Stanley E. Porter and Thomas H. Olbricht; JSNTSupp 90; Sheffield: Sheffield Academic Press, 1993), 375–87; Attridge, *Hebrews*, 14, Ben Witherington, *Letters and Homilies for Jewish Christians: A Socio-Rhetorical Commentary on Hebrews, James, and Jude* (Downers Grove: IVP, 2007), 42–53. For primarily deliberative purpose see Walter G. Übelacker, *Der Hebräerbrief als Appell: I. Untersuchungen zu* exordium, narratio, *und* postscriptum *(Hebr 1–2 und 13,22–25)* (ConBNT 21; Stockholm: Almqvist & Wiksell International, 1989), 214–29; Lindars, "The Rhetorical Structure of Hebrews," 382–406; Helmut Löhr, "Reflections of Rhetorical Terminology in Hebrews," in *Hebrews: Contemporary Methods – New Insights* (ed. Gabriella Gelardini; BibInt 75; Atlanta: SBL, 2005), 199–210; Lincoln, *Hebrews: A Guide*, 15–16.

[48] Hermann von Soden, *Hebräerbrief, Briefe Des Petrus, Jakobus, Judas* (Hand-Commentar zum Neuen Testament; Freiburg: J. C. B. Mohr, 1899), 11, 113. Von Soden is followed with slight modification by Theodor Hearing, "Gedankengang und Grundgedanken des Hebräerbriefs," *ZNW* 18 (1917–1918): 145–64, and Hans Windisch, *Der Hebräerbrief: Handbuch zum Neuen Testament* (Tübingen: J.C.B. Mohr [Paul Siebeck], 1931), 8.

3. ἀπόδειξις πρὸς πειθώ: 7:1–10:18
4. ἐπίλογος: 10:19–13:21
5. *Postscriptum*: 13:22–25

Spicq, 1952[49]

1. *Prologue* with a *propositio* or πρόθεσις: 1:1–4
2. διήγησις: 1:5–6:20
3. ἀπόδειξις: 7:1–12:13
4. ἐπίλογος: 12:14–29
5. Appendice: 13:1–19
6. Epistolary Epilogue: 13:20–25

Nissilä, 1979[50]

1. *Exordium*: 1:1–4
2. *Narratio*: 1:5–2:18
3. *Argumentatio*: 3:1–12:29
   Second *Exordium*: 3:1–6
4. *Epilogus*: 13:1–21

Übelacker, 1989[51]

1. *Exordium/Prooemium*: 1:1–4
2. *Narratio*: 1:5–2:18
   Propositio: 2:17–18
3. *Argumentatio* (with *probatio* and *refutatio*): 3:1–12:29
   Second *Prooemium*: 5:11–6:20
4. *Peroratio*: 13:1–21
5. *Postscriptum*: 13:22–25

---

[49] Ceslas Spicq, *L'Épitre Aux Hébreux* (2 vols.; EB; Paris: J. Gabalda, 1952–1953), 1:33–8. Spicq labels 1:1–4 as the prologue and later as the preamble. He claims that in this prologue one finds "an authentic proposition or prothesis according to the canon of the best of ancient rhetoric." Spicq also labels 5:11–6:20 as a long preamble. Spicq, however, seemingly identifies the entirety of chapters 1–6 as the *narratio* without distinguishing 1:1–4 or 5:11–6:20. We have chosen in our representation of Spicq's arrangement to distinguish 1:1–4 from the *narratio* since Spicq draws attention to it in the concluding discussion of his rhetorical arrangement.

[50] Nissilä, *Das Hohepriestermotiv im Hebräerbrief.* Nissilä's comprehensive arrangement is presented in the abstract of the book but a complete argument for the arrangement is not provided in the study. Certain aspects of his proposal are discussed on 5*, 24, 39, 47 (second *exordium*), 68, 109, 167, 194, 215–16, 220–3, 237–9, 245–6.

[51] Übelacker, *Der Hebräerbrief als Appell*, 224. Übelacker's proposal is almost identical to that of Nissilä. Übelacker, however, identifies Heb 5:11–6:20 as an elaborate *prooemium* in the *argumentatio* of Hebrews (226). Cockerill (*Hebrews*, 76–7) follows Übelacker in his rhetorical arrangement, though he never explicitly identifies 3:1–12:29 as *argumentatio*.

Backhaus, 1996[52]
1. *Exordium*: 1:1–4
2. *Narratio*: 1:5–4:13
3. *Argumentatio*: 4:14–10:18
   Propositio: 4:14–16
4. *Peroratio*: 10:19–13:21

Lauri Thurén, 1997[53]
1. *Exordium*: 1:1–2:18
2. *Argumentatio*: 3:1–12:29
3. *Peroratio*: 13:1–25

Koester, 2001[54]
1. *Exordium*: 1:1–2:4 including transitional digression (2:1–4)
2. *Propositio*: 2:5–9
3. Three Series of Arguments: 2:10–12:27
   a. Argument: 2:10–5:10 with transitional as digression (5:11–6:20)
   b. Argument: 7:1–10:25 with transitional digression (10:26–39)
   c. Argument: 11:1–12:24 with transitional digression (12:25–27)

---

[52] Knut Backhaus, *Der Neue Bund*, 58–64. Backhaus's arrangement adapts an earlier proposal by Hans-Friedrich Weiss (*Der Brief an die Hebräer*, 49–51). Thompson (*Hebrews*, 17–20) proposes an arrangement that is almost identical to Backhaus's arrangement except that Thompson begins the *peroratio* at 10:32 and extends it through 13:25.

[53] Lauri Thurén, "The General New Testament Writings," in *Handbook of Classical Rhetoric in the Hellenistic Period, 330 B.C.–A.D. 400* (ed. Stanley Porter; Leiden: Brill, 1997), 590–1. Thurén primarily arranges Hebrews in this manner because he identifies it as epideictic rhetoric in which various topics are amplified. In an earlier study, Thomas H. Olbricht ("Hebrews as Amplification," in *Rhetoric and the New Testament: Essays from the 1992 Heidelberg Conference* [ed. Stanley E. Porter and Thomas H. Olbricht; JSNTSupp 90; Sheffield: Sheffield Academic Press, 1993], 378) puts forward a similar arrangement for Hebrews because he sees Hebrews patterned after a funeral oration, the quintessential occasion for epideictic rhetoric (1:1–4 [*exordium*]; 1:5–13:16 [encomium]; 13:17–25 [final exhortation and prayer]). Likewise, Witherington (*Letters and Homilies for Jewish Christians*, 45–7, 51) states that there is no *narratio* and no *propositio* in Hebrews because Hebrews is epideictic rhetoric, and thus, Witherington arranges Hebrews in a similar fashion to Thurén and Olbricht (1:1–4 [*exordium*]; 1:5–12:17 [*probatio*]; 12:18–29 [*peroratio*]; final paranesis [13:1–21]; epistolary closing [13:22–25]). Witherington's arrangement follows most closely the arrangement put forward by Lincoln, *Hebrews: A Guide*, 24–25 (1:1–4 [*exordium*]; 1:5–12:17 [*argumentatio*]; 12:18–29 [*peroratio*]; epistolary closing [13:1–25]).

[54] Koester, "Hebrews, Rhetoric, and the Future," 101–2. For Koester, there is no *narratio* in Hebrews.

4. Peroration: 12:28–13:21
5. Epistolary Postscript: 13:22–25

Anderson, 2013[55]
1. *Exordium*: 1:1–2:4
2. *Narratio*: 2:5–18
3. Second *Exordium* or *Egressio*: 3:1–4:13
4. *Probatio*: 4:14–10:18
   Digressio: 5:11–6:20
5. *Peroratio*: 10:19–13:25

Summary of Proposals by Rhetorical Category

Exordium

1:1–4	(Backhaus, Lincoln, Olbricht, Spicq, Nissilä, Thompson, Übelacker)
1:1–2:4	(Koester, Anderson)
1:1–2:18	(Thurén)
1:1–4:13	(von Soden)

Narratio

1:5–2:18	(Nissilä, Übelacker)
1:5–4:13	(Backhaus, Thompson)
1:5–6.20	(Spicq)
2:5–18	(Anderson)
4:14–6:20	(von Soden)

Propositio

2:5–9	(Koester as a first order category)
2:17–18	(Übelacker as part of the *narratio*)
4:14–16	(Backhaus, Thompson as part of the *argumentatio*)

Argumentatio

1:5–13:16	(Olbricht as encomium)
1:5–12:17	(Lincoln)
2:10–12:27	(Koester)
3:1–12:29	(Nissilä, Thurén, Übelacker)
4:14–10:18	(Anderson, Backhaus)
4:14–10:31	(Thompson)

---

[55] Anderson, *Hebrews*, 58–61, 82, 104–6, 154, 175, 269–71.

7:1–10:18   (von Soden)
7:1–12:13   (Spicq)

Peroratio
10:19–13:21/25   (Anderson, Backhaus, von Soden)
10:32–13:25   (Thompson)
12:14–29   (Spicq)
12:18–29   (Lincoln)
12:28–13:21   (Koester)
13:1–21/25   (Nissilä, Thurén, Übelacker)

Part 1

Laying the Foundation

Syncrisis in Hebrews

2*

COMPARING COVENANTS

The Syncritical Backbone of Hebrews

In this chapter we will examine one of the key rhetorical features ubiquitously acknowledged by interpreters of Hebrews, syncrisis. There is significant discussion from the ancient handbooks on how syncrises are to be composed and arranged. On the basis of these instructions, we propose that the organizing architectural feature of Hebrews is its employment of a five-part epideictic syncrisis spanning the length of the work and proving the superiority of the new covenant to the old covenant via comparisons of representative figures. The syncrisis is ordered both chronologically and topically, each of the five syncrises taking up headings prescribed for syncrisis in ancient rhetorical handbooks. Evident across the length of this argument is a narrative progression through covenant life, from ultimate origins to ultimate eschatological ends. Such progression, we argue, accords with ancient syncritical theory, which requires that "inanimate things" be contrasted beginning to end, using the headings or topics analogous to those normally used to compare human lives in their entirety. Each stage of the five-part comparison, we argue, can be explained in terms of these topics.

Though this architectural feature has not been identified previously in rhetorical studies, there are important precedents, most notably the studies of Thomas H. Olbricht and Timothy W. Seid, that point to some of the same epideictic syncrises identified in this study and that argue for the use of encomiastic topics as the structuring principle of these individual syncrises.[1] Whereas, however,

* A previous version of this chapter appeared as "The Encomiastic Topics of Syncrisis as the Key to the Structure and Argument of Hebrews," *NTS* 57 (2011): 415–39.

[1] Thomas H. Olbricht, "Hebrews as Amplification," in *Rhetoric and the New Testament: Essays from the 1992 Heidelberg Conference* (ed. Stanley E. Porter and Thomas H. Olbricht.; JSNTSupp 90; Sheffield: Sheffield Academic Press, 1993),

these studies focus on Christ and the various figures of the past with which he is comparatively paired as the primary subjects of the running syncrisis, this study argues that the new and old covenants are the primary subjects, and that Christ and the various past figures are representatives of their respective covenants, as are other paired subjects featured in the comparison (Levitical Priesthood/Melchize-dekian priesthood, Sinai/Zion).[2] As a consequence of this insight, this study is able, in contrast to Olbricht's and Seid's studies, to provide a rhetorical rationale for the arrangement of the overall syncritical project. Only when the covenants are identified as the ultimate subjects of comparison is it possible to see that the project is itself chronologically and topically ordered, as are also some of the individual syncrises that comprise it.

It is important to clarify from the outset that we limit the present analysis to the five *epideictic* syncrises comprising what we will call in this chapter "the syncritical project" (i.e., the syncrisis of the old and new covenants). We do not in this chapter attempt to outline materials outside the project, nor set forth in any way a comprehensive rhetorical outline of the overall argument and structure of Hebrews. Such analysis we leave for subsequent chapters, believing that the outline of the syncritical project's argument is foundational to the outline of the larger argument of Hebrews and, therefore, should be clearly articulated first.

Our present investigation will proceed in two parts. First, we attend to the ancient rules for syncrisis most relevant, in our view, to an analysis of Hebrews. Secondly, we set forth in light of these rules our thesis concerning the argument and structure of the syncritical project in its five parts.

375–87; Timothy W. Seid, "Synkrisis in Hebrews 7: Rhetorical Structure and Analysis," in *The Rhetorical Interpretation of Scripture: Essays from the 1996 Malibu Conference* (ed. Stanley E. Porter and Dennis L. Stamps; Sheffield: Sheffield Academic Press, 1999), 322–6. See, too, the more recent work of Brian C. Small, *The Characterization of Jesus in the Book of Hebrews* (BIS 128; Leiden: Brill, 2014).

[2] The "Christ is superior" motif has been a dominant approach in the history of interpretation. Cf. George H. Guthrie, *The Structure of Hebrews: A Text-Linguistic Analysis* (NovTSup 73; Leiden: Brill, 1994), 1–20. See, however, Gabriella Gelardini, "From 'Linguistic Turn' and Hebrews Scholarship to *Anadiplosis Iterata*: The Enigma of Structure," *HTR* 102 (2009): 60, who notes that Christocentric exclusivity in past Hebrews scholarship is giving way to a more theocentric perspective with an emphasis on covenant theology in Hebrews. She cites such representative scholars of this trend as Attridge, Dunnill, Koester, Backhaus, and herself (see n. 51 in Gelardini's article). The argument in this chapter continues to support aspects of this trend in the study of Hebrews.

Syncrisis in Ancient Rhetorical Theory

The art of epideictic syncrisis was learned by ancient students from the progymnasmata, or "preliminary exercises." These textbooks of composition and rhetoric taught students the basic literary forms considered preliminary not only to the practice of declamation, but also to written composition—a matter about which the rhetorician, Theon, is insistent (Theon 70).[3] Each of the four extant Greek progymnasmata (the textbooks of Theon, Ps. Hermogenes, Aphthonius, and Nicolaus) contains an exercise wholly devoted to the art of syncrisis.[4] Though these progymnasmata lay down a number of rules for conducting syncrisis, four are of particular consequence for an analysis of Hebrews:

(1) Comparisons consider whole subjects according to their parts. On this matter, all four progymnastic theorists agree. Aphthonius provides the rationale for the method, insisting that comparison by parts is more persuasive: "It is not necessary in making comparison to contrast a whole with a whole, for that is flat and not argumentative, but compare a heading to a heading; this at least is argumentative" (Aphthonius 43; cf. Nicolaus 59). Thus one does not simply state that Achilles is superior to Hector, for such a simple or "flat" declarative statement does not argue for or demonstrate what it claims. One must rather select topics from the lives of Achilles and Hector to compare in order to demonstrate who is the superior.

Plutarch's *Parallel Lives* also illustrate the principle well. The project consistently compares the politicians and military leaders of

---

[3] All translations of the progymnasmata are from George A. Kennedy, *Progymnasmata: Greek Textbooks of Prose Composition and Rhetoric* (Atlanta: SBL, 2003); citations for Theon and Aphthonius refer to the page numbers of the critical editions in Leonhard von Spengel, ed., *Rhetores Graeci* (3 vols.; Leipzig: Teubner, 1854–6), citations for Ps. Hermogenes to the page numbers of Hugo Rabe, ed., *Hermogenis Opera* (Leipzig: Teubner, 1931), and citations for Nicolaus to the page numbers of Joseph Felten, ed., *Nicolai Progymnasmata* (Leipzig: Teubner, 1913; reprinted, Osnabrück: Zeller, 1968).

[4] For the recent proposal that Theon's progymnasmata are attributable to the fifth century rhetorician and not the first, see Malcolm Heath, "Theon and the History of the Progymnasmata," *GRBS* 43 (2002/3): 129–60. Though most, if not all, of the textbooks were composed after Hebrews was written, the forms they teach derive from classical Greek literature, and the curriculum they preserve derives from no later than the early Hellenistic period (Kennedy, *Progymnasmata*, xi). More importantly, Quintilian's overview of the progymnasmata (cf. *Inst.* 2.4.21) shows that by the first century CE, syncrisis was an established exercise in the Latin curriculum, which is itself dependent on – and therefore later than – the Greek curriculum.

Greece's glorious past with counterparts from Roman history,[5] with the tacit purpose of showing Plutarch's native Greece to be Rome's equal – despite popular opinion to the contrary – in the political and military realms.[6] As Bernadotte Perrin observes,

> Greece, after passing under Roman sway, lost sight gradually of her great men of action, and contented herself with the glories of her men of thought. Here surely the dominant Romans could not vie with her. It was to prove that the more remote past of Greece could show its lawgivers, commanders, statesmen, patriots, and orators, as well as the nearer and therefore more impressive past of Rome, that the *Parallel Lives* were written.[7]

To read Plutarch's *Parallel Lives* only for the individual syncritical verdicts of the *bios* pairings would be to miss this tacit, overarching purpose of the project.

(2) The parts to be compared are the encomiastic topics employed in praise of a person. On this matter, again, all four theorists agree. Each provides a list of the topics to be taken up in the comparison, and a cursory examination of the lists (see Tables 1a and 1b) shows, moreover, that despite their idiosyncrasies, the lists are in general agreement concerning a core set of topics to be considered.

(3) The encomiastic topics, chronologically arranged, serve as the compositional outline of the syncrisis. On this matter three of the four theorists agree. That is, Ps. Hermogenes, Aphthonius, and Nicolaus arrange the topics chronologically and require students to follow

---

[5] The consensus opinion of Plutarch studies since Hartmut Erbse ("Die Bedeutung der Synkrisis in den Parallelbiographien Plutarchs," *Hermes* 84 [1956]: 398–424) is that comparison is carried out not only in the syncrises attached to the end of the *bios* pairs, but also in the *bios* pairs themselves by virtue of their parallel structure. See, e.g., Tim Duff, *Plutarch's Lives: Exploring Virtue and Vice* (Oxford: Clarendon Press, 2000); David H. J. Larmour, "Making Parallels: *Synkrisis* and Plutarch's 'Themistocles and Camillus'," *ANRW* 33.6:4159, 4162–200; Christopher Pelling, "*Synkrisis* in Plutarch's Lives," in *Plutarch and History: Eighteen Studies* (London: Duckworth, 2002), 349–63; and Joseph Geiger, "Nepos and Plutarch: From Latin to Greek Political Biography," *Illinois Classical Studies* 13 (1988): 245–56.

[6] See, e.g., D. A. Russell, *Plutarch* (New York: Charles Scribner's Son, 1973), 109; idem, "On Reading Plutarch's Lives," in *Essays on Plutarch's Lives* (ed. B. Scardigli; Oxford: Clarendon Press, 1995), 73–98; A. Wardman, *Plutarch's Lives* (Berkeley: University of California Press, 1974), 243; Bernadotte Perrin, *Plutarch's Lives* (LCL; Cambridge: Harvard University Press, 1914–26), 1:xiii.

[7] Perrin, *Plutarch's Lives*, 1:xiii.

Table 1a *Chronological Arrangements of Ps. Hermogenes*,
Aphthonius, and Nicolaus*†

Ps. Hermogenes: Encomion	Ps. Hermogenes: Syncrisis	Aphthonius: Encomion, Invective, Syncrisis	Nicolaus: Encomion, Invective, Syncrisis
		1. Prooemion	Prooemion (not numbered as a heading proper)
		2. Origin	1. Origin
1. National origin		2a. nation	2a. nationality
		2b. homeland	
2. City	1. City		2b. native city
3. Family	2. Family	2c. ancestors	2c. ancestors
		2d. parents	
4. Marvelous Occurrences at Birth	——	——	2. Circumstances of Birth
5. Nurture	3. Nurture	3. Upbringing (=nurture and training)	3. Circumstances of Upbringing (=nurture)
6. Upbringing (=training)	——		4. Activities in Youth (=training)
7. Body	——	4b. body	
8. Mind (=virtues)	——	4a. mind (=virtues)	
9. Pursuits and Deeds	4. Pursuits and Deeds	4. Deeds (referred to all 3 goods)	5. Deeds (referred to virtues)
		4c. fortune	
10. Externals	5. Externals	(=externals)	
11. Time	——	——	——
12. Manner of Death	6. Manner of Death	Not listed, but modeled	——
13. Greatness of the One Who Killed the Subject	——	——	——
14. Events after Death	7. Events after Death	——	——
15. Comparison	——	5. Comparison	6. Comparison
——	——	6. Epilogue	——

* Tables 1a and 1b appeared originally in Martin, "Progymnastic Topics List"
(© 2008 Cambridge University Press), and are reprinted with permission.
† The summational list Ps. Hermogenes provides in his syncrisis exercise differs
from the list he provides in the encomion exercise; thus we include both in
Table 1a.

Table 1b *Theon's Arrangement by Goods*

Prooemion (not numbered as a heading proper)

1. External Goods (arranged chronologically)
  a. good birth (=origin)
    i. city, tribe, constitution
    ii. ancestors and other relatives
  b. education
  c. friendship
  d. reputation
  e. official position
  f. wealth
  g. good children
  h. good death
2. Bodily Goods
3. Goods of the Mind (Virtues), and Actions Referred to Virtues

their lists as a template for their syncrises.[8] Theon, by contrast, arranges topics in the older, traditional (i.e., Platonic; cf. Nicolaus 50) manner according to the three goods of personhood: goods of the mind (i.e., virtues), goods of the body, and goods external to the person.[9] Despite this disagreement concerning order, Theon none-theless agrees with the remaining theorists that the topics serve as a compositional template. The tables above arrange each list side by side so that their commonalities and differences are readily apparent.

The differences among the lists – and especially between Ps. Hermogenes's longer encomion list and his summational syncrisis list – show that the exact number and order of topics was not a matter of wide agreement. Indeed, it appears as though some theorists were drawn to expansion, while others were attracted to brevity. The theorists drawn to brevity, however, assist us in highlighting a core set of topics widely employed in syncrisis, encomion, and invective: origin, upbringing, deeds, and comparison. Examination of the lists for multiple attestations yields an only slightly larger core set of topics: origin, birth, nurture, education, pursuits (= office), deeds

---

[8] Cf. Quintilian, *Inst.* 3.7.10 (Russell, LCL): "Praise of men is more varied. First, there is a chronological division, into times before they were born, their own lifetimes, and (with those who have already passed away) the time after their death."

[9] Cf. Nicolaus's discussion (51) of both arrangements.

(bearing some manner of relationship to the three goods), death, and comparison – a core set widely attested in lists outside the progymnasmata.[10] These are the topics, we argue, generally employed in Hebrews's syncrisis both at the macro-level (the larger syncritical project comparing covenants) and at the micro-level (the five individual syncrises that comprise the project) – excluding, of course, the topic of comparison itself, which the theorists say is to be eliminated when encomiastic topics are used in a full syncrisis. As Aphthonius helpfully explains, "There is no comparison in it, since the whole exercise is a comparison" (43).

Also of note in connection with this third rule is that the theorists advise using the lists flexibly, tailoring them so that only those topics that serve the writer's purpose are featured (cf. Theon 111; Nicolaus 51, 61). Moreover, the theorists clearly envision occasions in which comparison by a single topic will suffice for a syncrisis (cf. Nicolaus 61). In view of these considerations, we should not expect to find in all ancient syncrises a rigid conformity to any list of topics – or even the use of more than a single topic. Nonetheless, the writer of Hebrews, as we shall see, makes fairly consistent use in his comparisons of most of the core topics identified above, and in their expected order.

(4) When comparing things, one employs topics analogous to those used in comparing persons. This is a course that Theon (113–14) advises, that is widely attested (cf. Ps. Hermogenes 16–18, 19; Quintilian, *Inst.* 3.7.26–28; Menander Rhetor 346–7), and that goes back at least to the time of Aristotle, who advises that in examining a commonwealth's origin, one might look, for example, at its founders (cf. *Rhet.* 1.5.5 [1360b]) – or if examining the good children of a commonwealth, one might look at its good young men and their individual qualities, topic by topic (cf. *Rhet.* 1.5.6 [1360b]). Similarly, Ps. Hermogenes teaches that a comparison of plants' origins might consider the gods who gave them (19), or that praise of a city's education might mention how "the people have been taught by the gods" (83). Aphthonius, too, employs the method Theon describes in his model "Encomion of Wisdom," taking up the topics of his own encomiastic topic list as though it were intended for use in the case of

---

[10] Cf. Rhet. Her. 3.6.10–11; Cicero, *Inv.* 1.24.34; 2.59.177; *Part. or.* 74–75; Quintilian, *Inst.* 3.7.10–18; Menander Rhetor 368–77.

things. Thus in praising Wisdom's origin, he declares it a descendent of Zeus (38), and in praising Wisdom's deeds, he praises the deeds of wise armies (the Greeks' capture of Troy) and wise individuals (Odysseus's destruction of the Cyclops's eye; 39). From these examples, it is clear that "analogies of topics" are found by considering a corresponding element from the inanimate thing's "lifespan" – as when founders, inventors, or gods from which the thing derives are considered in place of and analogous to origins. These same four rules govern comparison in the syncritical project of Hebrews, to which we now turn.

The Syncritical Project of Hebrews

There are five epideictic syncrises in Hebrews, each of them comparing and contrasting two subjects and pointing to one as the superior:

I. Angels vs. Jesus (1:5–14)
II. Moses vs. Jesus (3:1–6)
III. The Aaronic High Priests vs. Jesus (5:1–10)
IV. The Levitical Priestly Ministry vs. the Melchizedekian Priestly Ministry (7:1–10:18)
V. Mt. Sinai vs. Mt. Zion (12:18–24)

Several commonalities among these five syncrises suggest that they function together coherently as part of a single syncritical project, advancing a common syncritical presentation of the superiority of the new covenant to the old covenant:

First, each syncrisis juxtaposes an old covenant subject with a new covenant subject, arguing for the superiority of the latter.[11] This is in keeping with rhetorical theory, which requires a writer arguing for the superiority of one subject over another to do so not directly (which would be "flat and not argumentative") but indirectly, juxtaposing "part" to "part" and not "whole" to "whole." To read the five

---

[11] In Aelius Aristides's (second-century) encomium of the city of Rome (an inanimate object), the city becomes a metonym for Rome's imperial rule. In a manner similar to Hebrews, Aristides praises the rule of Rome through representative subjects such as its Princeps (32–3), its citizens (36), its army (72), and its constitution (90). The text and translation consulted here is James H. Oliver, "The Ruling Power: A Study of the Roman Empire in the Second Century after Christ through the Roman Oration of Aelius Aristides," *TAPS* 43/4 (1953): 895–907, 982–91.

syncrises of Hebrews only for their individual syncritical verdicts[12] is to overlook the overarching purpose that binds them together as a project – namely, to show which covenant is greater.

Second, each syncrisis contributes, by virtue of the role it features, to a chronological progression that follows the lifespan of a covenant from beginning to end. To put it simply, there is a chronology to the pairings. The first pairing, in juxtaposing the covenants' heavenly mediators, focuses on the moment of the covenant's ultimate origins in heaven. The second pairing, in juxtaposing the covenant inaugurators and their faithful witness to God's house, focuses on the covenant's beginnings. The third pairing, in juxtaposing the high priests and their respective ministries on behalf of the people, moves beyond covenant beginnings to the life and ministry of the covenant. The fourth pairing, in juxtaposing the priestly ministries of each covenant, continues the focus on the life and ministry of the covenant. As we shall see, however, the focus of the third pairing is on the *training* preparatory for the vocation of priesthood (cf. 5:7–10; cf. 5:11–6:1), while the focus of the fourth pairing is on priestly *deeds* carried out upon entrance into the vocation of priesthood – hence there is even chronological progression within the two syncrises devoted to covenant priests. Finally, the fifth pairing, in juxtaposing Sinai and Zion as contrasting ends to which the people are led by each covenant – Sinai, a shakable *telos* of marginal access to God,

---

[12] As has happened often in the reception history of Hebrews (see n. 2 above). That is, the thesis that the "Christ is superior" motif is key to the structure of Hebrews has dominated the history of interpretation, and undoubtedly because Jesus is featured as the new covenant subject in four of the five syncrises – and as the sole representative in three of the five comparisons. While this thesis is correct in seeing a common purpose among the syncrises, it is too narrowly focused on the several verdicts concerning Jesus's superiority and not on their collective implication for the larger comparison of covenants in which they participate.

Jesus's representative function for the new covenant in the syncrises of covenants via encomiastic topics reflects Theon's instruction concerning the syncrisis of genera. According to Theon, one does not compare genus to genus, but species to species, choosing "one or two of the most outstanding" from each genus for the comparison (114). Thus in conducting a syncrisis of men and women to determine who is the bravest, one might compare Themistocles with Artemisia if the goal were to show men are the braver genus, or Tomyris with Cyrus, if the goal were to show women the braver. In either case, though, it would be a mistake to overlook the implication of the individual verdict for the relative greatness of the genera in question. Likewise, Plutarch, as we have noted, matches representative Greeks with Romans in his *Parallel Lives* on the basis of a correspondence of roles – "lawgivers, commanders, statesmen, patriots, and orators," to quote Perrin's list.

and Zion, an unshakeable (= heavenly and eternal) *telos* of complete access to God – focuses on covenant eschatology, bringing the chronological progression to a close.[13]

Third, each syncrisis contributes, by virtue of the role it features, to a topical progression that follows the lifespan of the covenant from beginning to end. That is, the chronological progression described above is attributable to the syncrisis's topical arrangement: (1) The comparison of heavenly covenant mediators, by virtue of its focus on the moment of covenant origins in heaven, takes up a heading analogous in the lifespan of a covenant to a person's "origins." (2) The comparison of covenant inaugurators in or over God's house, by virtue of its focus on the moment of covenant beginnings, takes up a heading analogous in the lifespan of a covenant to a person's "birth." (3) The comparison of high priests, because of its depiction of training undertaken in preparation for the vocation of priesthood, has taken up a topic analogous in the lifespan of a covenant to "education." (4) The comparison of priestly ministries, because of its focus on deeds performed in connection with the vocation of the priesthood, has taken up a topic analogous in the lifespan of a covenant to a person's deeds. Together, comparisons 3 and 4, by virtue of moving beyond covenant beginnings to covenant life and priestly ministry, take up a topic analogous in the lifespan of a covenant to "pursuits" – comparison 3 examining the education preparatory for covenant priestly ministry and vocation, and comparison 4 examining deeds performed in and through covenant priestly ministry and vocation. Finally, comparison 5, by virtue of its focus on the contrasting eschatological ends to which each covenant leads, takes up a topic analogous in the lifespan of a covenant to "death" and "events after death."

Thus we may outline the syncritical project of Hebrews in terms of topics prescribed for syncrisis, or to be more precise, in terms of topics analogous to those prescribed for use in the syncrisis of persons:

I. Origins: Syncrisis of Covenant Mediators
II. Birth: Syncrisis of Covenant Inaugurators

---

[13] This type of progression is in agreement with Koester's (*Hebrews*, 83) observation that the imagery in Hebrews "moves in a ... linear fashion" by which the audience is directed towards a goal. Koester sees this linear, progression, however, repeated in three major movements (2:10–6:20; 7:1–10:39; 11:1–12:27) and not as a topical progression.

III. Pursuits – Education: Syncrisis of the Priestly Appren-
ticeships of Each Covenant
IV. Pursuits – Deeds: Syncrisis of the Priestly Deeds of
Each Covenant
V. Death/Events after Death: Syncrisis of Covenant
Eschata

Chronological progression such as this – via topics analogous to
those used for persons – is widely prescribed and exemplified by the
theorists for encomia, invectives, and syncrises of "inanimate things"
(Theon's terminology; 112, 113).[14] Thus most educated persons would
have been familiar with the method. Its logic, essentially, was that since
"inanimate things" (such as covenants) have lifespans of sorts, with
beginnings, middles, and ends, they can be lauded, censured, and compared chronologically and topically in the same manner as persons.

The syncritical project as we have outlined it above takes its cue
from the comparison of covenants in Jer 38:31–34 (LXX), which
constitutes the longest scriptural quotation in Hebrews (8:8–12). The
Pauline tradition also provides a precedent (2 Cor 3:1–18), developing Jeremiah's comparison of covenants in ways that anticipate
Hebrews.[15] Both Jeremiah and Paul precede Hebrews, specifically,

---

[14] See, e.g., Theon, on encomion of honey, health, virtue, etc. (112), and on syncrisis
of honey and health (113); Menander Rhetor, on encomion of cities (346.26–367.8); Ps.
Hermogenes, on encomion of dumb animals (17), activities (17), growing things
(17–18), and cities (18), and on syncrisis of plants (19); Aphthonius, on encomion of
things (justice, self-control), occasions (spring, summer), places
(harbors, gardens), dumb animals (horse, ox), plants (olive, vine) (35–36) and of wisdom
(38–40), on invective of things, occasions, places, dumb animals, and growing things
(40), and on syncrisis of things, occasions, places, dumb animals, and plants (42);
Nicolaus, on encomion of activities (57), and on syncrisis of goods, evils, and things
(60–61); and, in the Latin tradition, Quintilian, on encomion of cities (3.7.26). In
Libanius's comparison of seafaring and farming, his syncrisis starts with the beginnings of each activity and concludes with the manner of death of those who participate
in each activity (*Libanius's* Progymnasmata: *Model Exercises in Greek Prose Composition and Rhetoric* [trans. Craig A. Gibson; WGRW 27; Atlanta: SBL, 2008], 343–5).

[15] Paul's comparisons speak of the Mosaic or old covenant as both a covenant "with
glory" and one "of death" and "condemnation." The soteriological deficiency of the old
covenant is, in part, articulated along the lines of external versus internal efficaciousness,
namely, the old is external, written on stones, whereas, the new covenant is internal and
transformational, written on the heart by the Spirit. Paul also articulates the polarities
between the covenants as temporary vs abiding, namely, the Mosaic covenant is a
covenant whose glory is set aside and gives way to the enduring new covenant realities.
These comparative trajectories, as we will see, are distinctively taken up in Hebrews's
own comparative project of the covenants. For further discussion of the role of the new
covenant in Paul's writings see Charles H. Talbert, *Reading Corinthians: A Literary and
Theological Commentary* (rev. ed.; Macon: Smyth & Helwys, 2002), 175–85.

in positing a good-to-great comparison, one that recognizes the glory of the old covenant on the one hand and the surpassing glory of the new on the other. The quotation and explication of Jeremiah's comparison in Hebrews 8 not only makes clear the writer's conscious reliance on precedents in his comparison of covenants, but it also makes *explicit* what up until that point has been consistently, if only implicitly, argued – that the new covenant is superior to the old covenant. Thus it would be a mistake to characterize the quotation of Jeremiah as appearing "quite abruptly without any preparation or further explanation."[16]

In short, we take the five epideictic syncrises of Hebrews as a coherent, chronologically ordered, and topically arranged argument for the superiority of the new covenant to the old covenant, and one that is rooted, in part, in Jeremiah's prophecy itself.[17] The specific manner in which Hebrews's syncritical argument is carried out can be further explicated by attending more closely to each of the five syncrises individually, noting not only the specific manner in which they advance the topically driven argument of the larger syncritical project, but also their own arrangement, which in most cases is, like the larger project, topically ordered.

Origin: Syncrisis of Covenant Heavenly Mediators

According to the theorists, one begins a comparison of persons by contrasting their "origins" – that is, the *people* from whom the subjects derive (fathers, ancestors, families), or the *places* from which the subjects derive (native cities, nations, homelands).[18] Comparison of "inanimate things," according to the theorists, should begin similarly, by contrasting something analogous to the persons or

---

[16] Peter Gräbe, "The New Covenant and Christian Identity in Hebrews," in *A Cloud of Witnesses: The Theology of Hebrews in Its Ancient Context* (ed. Richard Bauckham et al.; LNTS 387; London: T&T Clark, 2008), 121. Cf. Susanne Lehne, *The New Covenant in Hebrews* (JSNTSup 44; Sheffield: Sheffield Academic Press, 1990), 103, who observes that, through the cultic reinterpretation of the covenant, the author of Hebrews makes the covenant motif the organizing principle of his sermon.

[17] Supporting our thesis is the early Christian reception of Hebrews's syncrisis by Chrysostom who not only identifies each of the comparisons of Hebrews as "syncrisis," but also interprets the comparison for their representative value – as comparisons ultimately of the old and new covenants. See *Heb. Hom.* 1.2; 5.1–3; 8.1; 12.1; 13.1, 5; and 32.1 (Philip Schaff, ed., *A Select Library of the Nicene and Post-Nicene Fathers of the Christian Church* [14 vols.; Grand Rapids, MI: Eerdmans, 1889]).

[18] The theorists are consistent in dividing this topic by geography and family. See Theon 110; Ps. Hermogenes 15; Aphthonius 36; Nicolaus 50; cf. Quintilian, *Inst.* 3.7.10; Menander Rhetor 368–70.

places from which the things derive. The theorists' examples of possible analogies, noted above, are illustrative. One could compare as an analogous treatment of the things' "origins" their inventors or founders – or, perhaps, the gods from which they derive.

This is, essentially, what the writer of Hebrews has done. That is, the writer begins the macro-level syncrisis of covenants by first examining the persons from whom the two covenants derive, namely, Jesus and the angels. That the writer thinks of Jesus and angels as the covenants' respective mediators is clear from the exhortation of 2:1–4: whereas the old covenant was "declared through angels," the great salvation of the new covenant was "declared at first through the Lord" (2:3–4).

The comparison is carried out via five topics and juxtaposes Jesus's *exalted and enthroned life in the world-to-come (οἰκουμένη)* with that of angels, arguing under each heading for Jesus's superiority.[19] The topical progression may be mapped as follows:

Origin: Jesus is "begotten" as the "Son" of the "Father" on the day of his enthronement – the angels are not. (v. 5)

Birth: Jesus enters[20] as the "firstborn" in the coming world and is worshipped by angels as such.[21] (v. 6)

---

[19] On the exaltation and enthronement of the Son in the heavenly realm (as opposed to incarnation or Parousia in the earthly realm) as the focus of Heb 1:5–14, see. L. D. Hurst, "The Christology of Hebrews 1 and 2," in *The Glory of Christ in the New Testament: Studies in Christology in Memory of George Bradford Caird* (ed. L. D. Hurst and N. T. Wright; Oxford; Clarendon Press, 1987), 151–64; Kenneth Schenck, "Keeping His Appointment: Creation and Enthronement in Hebrews," *JSNT* 66 (1997): 91–117; idem, "A Celebration of the Enthroned Son: The Catena of Hebrews 1," *JBL* 120 (2001): 469–85; Ardel B. Caneday, "The Eschatological World Already Subjected to the Son," in *A Cloud of Witnesses: The Theology of Hebrews in Its Ancient Context* (ed. Richard Bauckham et al.; LNTS 387; London: T&T Clark, 2008), 28–39; Joshua W. Jipp, "The Son's Entrance into the Heavenly World: The Soteriological Necessity of the Scriptural Catena in Hebrews 1.5–14," *NTS* 56 (2010): 557–75; Jody A. Barnard, *The Mysticism of Hebrews* (WUNT 2/331; Tübingen: Mohr Siebeck, 2012), 144–70, 217–42, esp. 237–42.

[20] James Moffatt, citing Epictetus, notes that εἰσάγειν can refer to birth (*A Critical and Exegetical Commentary on the Epistle to the Hebrews* [ICC; Edinburgh: T&T Clark, 1979], 10), though Jody Barnard is certainly right to note the use of the term in the otherworldly journeys of apocalypses (*Mysticism of Hebrews*, 240–41). The ambiguity or dual sense of the term is potentially operative in 1:6. Jesus's resurrection and ascension (cf. Heb 13:20, where God leads Jesus up [ἀναγαγών] from the dead) is a type of birth into a new, eschatological life.

[21] Based upon our reading, the Son's superior firstborn status is indicated by the angelic worship that God commands the angels to give to him. There is the possibility that αὐτῷ could refer to God as the object of worship so that when he brings his firstborn into the world the angels worship God (esp. if Ps 96 [LXX] is in view where

Pursuits:	The angels are "servants," but Jesus is the "anointed" whose "throne is forever" because he loved righteousness. (vv. 7–9)
Death:	Jesus will have unending dominion in the coming world because he "remains," not angels whose dominion will "perish." (vv. 10–12)
Events after death:	Jesus, not the angels, is exalted to God's right hand until his enemies are subjected to him in the future. (vv. 10–12)

While Hebrews 1:5–14 in its entirety treats the post-mortem exaltation of the Son, that exaltation is depicted as an entrance into a new immortal life in the heavenly world (cf. v. 6: "when he brings the firstborn into the world"). Similar to Hebrews, Acts 13:33 identifies Jesus' resurrection as a type of begetting by God in fulfillment of Ps 2:7 ("You are my Son. Today I have begotten you.").[22] Thus it is possible for the writer to depict this new life from beginning to end, chronologically and topically, starting with Jesus' origin as God's chosen Son and his birth into the new world (resurrection and ascension; cf. Heb 13:20), proceeding to his pursuits in that new world as heavenly king and his *non*-death, which is contrasted with the perishing of the heavens and earth, and ending with the event

---

the establishment of David in the land leads to the angelic worship of the Lord). Though possible, this reading would seem to change the speaker of this summons from God in the two previous statements to the Son. The most natural reading is to see God commanding the angels to worship his firstborn upon entrance into the heavenly realm. The nature of the worship offered is debated. Is this the veneration or obeisance given to God's kingly representative (an exalted human) or is this along the lines of cultic worship that identifies the Son with God himself? For an excellent discussion of these points see David M. Allen, "Who, What, Why? The Worship of the Firstborn in Hebrews 1:6," in *Mark, Manuscripts, and Monotheism: Essays in Honor of Larry Hurtado* (ed. Chris Keith and Dieter Roth; LNTS 528; London: T&T Clark, 2015), 159–75.

[22] Cf. Kenneth L. Schenck, "The Worship of Jesus among Early Christians: The Evidence from Hebrews," in *Jesus and Paul: Global Perspectives in Honor of James D. G. Dunn on His 70th Birthday* (ed. B. J. Oropeza et al; LNTS 414; London: T&T Clark, 2009), 117. If the author of Hebrews is making this association, then it may be that the sentence under the heading of "origins" in 1:5 may refer to the resurrection as an event that precedes the ascension and entrance, i.e, "birth," into the heavenly realm in 1:6. Though the early Christian tradition sometimes treated resurrection and the ascension as one event (cf. *T. Ben.* 9.3), it also sometimes treated them as separate events happening on the same (Fourth Gospel) or different days (Acts). See Charles H. Talbert, *Reading John: A Literary and Theological Commentary on the Fourth Gospel and the Johannine Epistles* (rev. ed.; Macon: Smyth & Helwys, 2005), 260–1.

that comes after the perishing of the heavens and earth, the subjugation of Jesus's enemies at the eschaton.[23]

The comparison then gives way to exhortation in 2:1–4. Beyond that, in 2:5–18, comparative materials juxtaposing Jesus and the angels reappear, only here the focus shifts to the audience. The section is not a demonstration of Jesus's superiority as in 1:5–14, nor is it ordered according to topics of syncrisis. Rather, the section is an amplification of the "so great salvation" (2:3–4) extended to the audience and all saved humanity. Citing Ps 8:5–7 (LXX) as his proof text, the author argues that humanity, though temporarily made lower than the angels, awaits a future of glory, honor, and exaltation over "all things" (including the angels). This destiny is made possible, the author argues, because of Jesus's pioneering work. Though in coming into the cosmos he was temporarily made lower than the angels, in his exaltation he was granted a position above them, so that he is "now crowned with glory and honor because of the suffering of death." Thus Jesus's present superiority to the angels ensures a destiny for redeemed humanity that is likewise superior to that of the angels.[24]

Because 2:5–18 does not function as a straightforward argument for Jesus's superiority to the angels, but is concerned more to amplify the salvation in view in the exhortation of 2:1–4 and thereby heighten the readers' urgency in not neglecting it; and because the unit does not employ topics of syncrisis as in 1:5–14; and because the straightforward argument for Jesus's superiority to the angels in 1:5–14 signals its conclusion in vv. 13–14 with the treatment of the final topic of syncrisis, events after death; and lastly, because 2:5–18 is removed from 1:5–14 by the intervening exhortation of 2:1–4 and only follows logically on the latter, we conclude that 2:5–18 should not be considered part of the syncrisis of 1:5–14. Rather, as an amplification of the exhortation of 2:1–4, it extends those hortatory materials and completes the unit devoted to Jesus and the angels, bringing the audience to the next major section of the speech.

---

[23] *Pace* J. P. Meier, "Symmetry and Theology in the Old Testament Citations in Heb 1,5–14," *Bib* 66 (1985): 529, who attempts to argue that the Christological affirmations of the catena move concentrically from exaltation, back to creation, back to preexistence, forward to preservation, and finally again to exaltation.

[24] Cf. Schenck, *Cosmology and Eschatology in Hebrews*, 54–9.

Birth: Syncrisis of Covenant Inaugurators

Only half the theorists list birth as a topic to be employed in comparison (cf. Ps. Hermogenes 15; Nicolaus 51–2; but cf. Ps. Hermogenes 19)—though it is more widely attested outside the syncrisis exercises in various encomiastic topic lists (e.g., Quintilian, *Inst.* 3.7; Menander Rhetor 368–77). From the theorists' examples, it is clear the topic concerns extraordinary signs or indications attending a subject's birth.[25] In the case of a comparison of inanimate things such as covenants, one would expect the focus to be on something analogous to signs of superior "birth" or beginnings. This is precisely what one finds in 3:1–6, the second epideictic comparison of Hebrews. In this unit, the juxtaposition is of the covenants' inaugurators, Jesus the "son" over God's "household" and Moses the "servant" in the "household," with the implicit point being that the new covenant is "better-born."[26]

The comparison begins by establishing their likeness. It may be said of Jesus that he was "faithful to the one who appointed him, as also was Moses 'in all his house'" (3:2, cf. Num 12:7).[27] Jesus, however, is deserving of greater glory just as the builder of a house deserves greater glory in comparison to the house itself (3:3–4). The analogy has in view the distinction the writer draws next between Moses and Jesus. As Num 12:7 shows, Moses displays faithfulness "*in* the household of God" and as a "servant," and his service takes the form of testimony "to the things that would be spoken later." Jesus, by comparison, displays faithfulness as "a son" and one who is "*over* the household of God." Thus, of these two prominent members of the household of God, Jesus may claim the superior birth status.

In these points of contrast, a syncritical dilemma facing the macro-comparison of covenants is solved. That is, the old covenant could claim to be better-born, deriving as it does from Moses who *preceded* Jesus within the household of God. The writer addresses this problem by exclusively granting firstborn pedigree to Jesus and, by extension, the new covenant. The new covenant alone has its

---

[25] Cf. Ps. Hermogenes 15; Nicolaus 51–2.

[26] In Hebrews Jesus is the mediator of the new covenant (8:6, 9:15, 12:24). The author of Hebrews also understands Moses to be the inaugurator of the first/old covenant (cf. Heb 9:18–21).

[27] We should note here that the author does not denigrate the old covenant by assigning it to a faithless inaugurator.

beginnings with the firstborn son over the house, while the old covenant has its beginnings with the older household servant under his authority. Indeed, the servant had to come before the son, for his "service" was a foreshadowing of the new covenant reality consisting in faithful testimony concerning things to be spoken later (cf. Heb 10:1)—and in syncritical practice, the one witnessed to is always greater than the witness.[28]

Pursuits: Syncrisis of Covenant Priesthoods

Though all the theorists attest in some way to the topic Ps. Hermogenes calls "pursuits" (ἐπιτηδεύματα), they generally treat it in tandem with other topics and not by itself. Ps. Hermogenes, for example, treats it together with deeds. He writes: "After this you will draw on his pursuits; for example, what sort of life he led: Was he a philosopher or an orator or a general? Most important are deeds; for deeds are included among pursuits; for example, having chosen a soldier's life, what did he accomplish in it?" (16). From his illustration of the topic, it is clear Ps. Hermogenes has in mind what Theon calls "office" (110, 113; cf. Cicero's "public offices" in *Inv.* 2.59.177). Aphthonius and Nicolaus, by contrast, treat "pursuits" in connection with their topical equivalents of nurture or education. Aphthonius lists "pursuits" (ἐπιτηδεύματα) as a subheading of "upbringing" (ἀναστροφή). Nicolaus, meanwhile, employs the phrase "pursuits in youth" (ἅπερ ἐν τῇ νέᾳ ἡλικίᾳ ἐπετήδευσεν) as the topical equivalent of education in his list. That is, his illustration of the topic ("for example, did he practice rhetoric or poetry or anything like that"; 52) makes it clear he has in mind training preparatory for pursuits (orator, poet, etc.) such as those listed by Ps. Hermogenes. Interestingly, Hebrews treats pursuits topically in connection with both education *and* deeds, as we shall see.

In Hebrews, we encounter a transitional unit in 4:14–16 introducing the high priestly theme that will be followed through 12:14–17.[29]

---

[28] See, e.g., the numerous comparisons of John the Baptist and Jesus, which assume the principle (Mark 1:7–8; Matt 3:11–12; Luke 3:16–17; John 1:15, 26–34; *Recognitions* 1.60; 3.3).

[29] In Chapters 7 and 8 we interpret Heb 4:14–16 as a secondary *exordium* introducing what we here are beginning to define as the "priestly pursuits" section of Hebrews and Heb 12:14–17 as a secondary *peroratio* that concludes this section.

Additionally, because of its parallelism with the exhortation of 10:19–23, the two texts have been taken together, as we have seen, as an *inclusio* bracketing the exposition in between – an exposition that contrasts the two covenants' respective priestly ministries.

In terms of rhetorical theory, the exposition that falls within these two brackets may be described as a treatment of a topic or heading analogous to pursuits in the life of the covenants, focusing as it does on office or vocation – that is, on the high priestly ministries of the covenants' respective priests. At the level of the macro-comparison of covenants in Hebrews, the priests in this comparative exposition not only represent their respective covenants indirectly as "parts" do "wholes" in rhetorical theory, but their priestly ministries may also be seen more directly as the priestly ministry of the *covenants themselves*, as something analogous in the "lives" of the covenants to their "pursuits."

The exposition between the brackets falls, moreover, into two parts (5:1–10 and 7:1–10:18, which are themselves separated by the exhortation of 5:11–6:20), and these deal respectively with the two topics inherently related to pursuits: education, because it is preparatory for one's deeds, which are accomplished, according to Ps. Hermogenes, in connection with pursuits. Since these syncrises come, respectively, immediately after the opening hortatory bracket and immediately before the closing hortatory bracket and take up the brackets' common priestly theme, they lend some credence to supporting Nauck's *inclusio* thesis, though clearly we do not understand the *inclusio* to provide the structural clue for the whole of Hebrews as did Nauck. In any case, we will treat these syncrises separately under their respective topical subheadings, education and deeds.

Pursuits—Education: Syncrisis of the Priestly Apprenticeships of Each Covenant

According to the theorists, the next topic or topics to be employed in syncrisis after origins and (for those who include it) birth are those pertaining to a person's nurture and/or training.[30] The third syncrisis in Hebrews, in our reading, takes up the subject matter of these topics, highlighting Jesus's apprenticeship of obedience

---

[30] Cf. Theon 16; Ps. Hermogenes 16; Aphthonius 36; Nicolaus 52.

(= education) preparatory for his priestly ministry (= pursuits) as the mark of his superiority.[31]

The syncrisis in 5:1–10, which contrasts the high priesthoods of Aaron and Jesus, is made chiastically and may be mapped as follows:

> **A** Aaronic high priests "offer" (προσφέρῃ, 5:1) to God (1–3):
>
> > **Bi** Aaronic high priests do not take the honor of priesthood (4a),
> >
> > **Bii** but are called by God to their vocation (4b).
> >
> > **Bi′** Jesus does not glorify himself in becoming a high priest (5a),
> >
> > **Bii′** but is glorified/appointed as the Father's begotten Son (5b) to an eternal Melchizedekian priesthood (6).
>
> **A′** Jesus "offers" (προσενέγκας, 5:7) to God (7–10)[32]:
>
> > • he offers ups prays and supplications in the days of his flesh for salvation out of death (7a),
> >
> > • he is heard because of his reverent submission (7b),
> >
> > • he learns obedience through suffering (8),
> >
> > • and having been perfected, becomes a source of eternal salvation as a Melchizedekian priest to those who obey him (9–10).

---

[31] Scholars such as Backhaus (*Der Neue Bund und das Werden Der Kirche* [NTAbh 29; Aschendorff: Münster, 1996], 54) have recognized a chronological and logical progression from 5:1–10:18. Though we think the topic at hand for 4:14–5:10 is not "*die Menschenlickeit des Hohepreisters Jesus*" as Backhaus proposes, Backhaus does see a movement from humanity of the high priest Jesus (4:14–5:10) to his priestly office (7:1–28) then to his priestly ministry (8:1–10:18). These latter two topical progressions describe well what the rhetoricians would label as pursuits (see below).

[32] The sacrificial "offering" parallel to that of the Aaronic high priests in this comparison is not the sacrificial "blood" or "body" of Jesus (as we implied in an earlier version of this article), but rather, the "prayers and supplications" for salvation out of death. Such offering "in the days of his flesh" is *preparatory* for – and not to be conflated with—his subsequent heavenly offering as a Melchizedekian high priest. Jesus's death, meanwhile, is not framed here as an "offering" – neither the preparatory "offering" of prayers and supplications on earth, nor the Melchizedekian "offering" of blood/body/self in the heavenly tabernacle. Rather, the death in this comparison *precedes* the Melchizedekian ministry as education preparatory for it (he learns obedience from what he suffers and so is perfected for his Melchizedekian vocation). Cf. David M. Moffitt, *Atonement and the Logic of Resurrection in the Epistle to the Hebrews* (NovTSup 141; Leiden: Brill, 2011), 285–7. On the death, resurrection, ascension, offering of blood/body/self in the heavenly holy of holies, and exaltation to God's right hand as a *series of distinct events* in Hebrews's Christology, see Moffitt, *Atonement and the Logic of Resurrection*, 42–3, passim.

This arrangement simultaneously introduces points of similarity and points of contrast. The points of similarity derive from the pursuit common to both subjects, the vocation of priesthood: both make offerings to God (A and A') and are called by God to their vocation (B and B'). The points of contrast derive from what makes Jesus's priestly ministry unique and superior, and these points are introduced following a topical outline:

Origin:	Jesus, not Aaronic priests, is appointed as the Father's Son (5).
Pursuits:	Jesus, not Aaronic priests, is appointed to an eternal Melchizedekian priesthood (6).
Deeds:	Jesus, not Aaronic priests, prays in the days of his flesh for salvation out of death (7a) and is heard because of his reverent submission (7b).
Death:	Jesus, not Aaronic priests, learns obedience from what he suffers (8).
Events after death:	Jesus, not Aaronic priests, is perfected and becomes a source of eternal salvation as a Melchizedekian priest to those who obey him (9–10).

While it is possible to view these marks as a topically ordered argument *strictly* for the new covenant's superiority with regard to its pursuits – that is, with regard to its high priestly ministry – the important thing to note is that that the priestly ministry depicted here is that of an *apprentice-priest still in training*, one who learns his vocation at the feet of the Father and whose death serves as the crucial moment of learning that leads to his perfection as a Melchizedekian priest. That is, it is Jesus's priestly apprenticeship – his education – that is being surveyed chronologically and topically, from beginning to end.

First, Jesus is called as a Son by his Father (origin) to his never ending, Melchizedekian vocation (pursuits). In antiquity, sons commonly served as apprentices under their fathers in order to learn their vocations – a perspective reflected in Heb 12:7–8, which calls readers to accept trials as *paideia* from their Father, and a perspective reflected in both Luke (2:40–52) and John (5:19–21; 7:16–18; 12:47–50), which similarly cast Jesus as a son-apprentice learning obediently at the feet of the Father.[33] Given the series of clearly

---

[33] On Luke 2:40–52 as the treatment of the encomiastic topic of "nurture and training" in the life of Jesus, see Michael W. Martin, "Progymnastic Topic Lists: A Compositional Template for Luke and Other *Bioi*?," *NTS* 54 (2008): 18–41. On the

pedagogical images that follow—vv. 7–8 depicts a *son's* education at the feet of the Father and vv. 9–10 his graduation to priestly vocation (see below)—we have good cause to view vv. 5–6, with its summons of the Son to the priestly vocation by the Father, as also reflecting the practices of ancient pedagogy.

Second, Jesus reverently submits to the Father in the days of his flesh (deeds) and learns obedience through what he suffers (death). This cluster of obvious pedagogical images—a Son submitting to and learning obedience from Father—has long been acknowledged in scholarship as a depiction of Jesus's education. David deSilva notes the significance of this depiction in terms of rhetorical theory, stating that the unit of 5:8–10 "focuses on Jesus's 'education' (a topic of encomia in general, even though the specific curriculum of Jesus's education—suffering—was not the norm) and the virtuous fruit his education bore, namely, 'obedience' toward God."[34] We would add, despite deSilva's qualification, that "learning from suffering" is commonly attested as a curriculum of sorts in Greek literature, owing in part to the play on words it entails (μαθ-/παθ-; cf. 5:8 ἔμαθεν ἀφ' ὧν ἔπαθεν).[35] Moreover, Dio Chrysostom identifies two types of education, human and divine, and frames suffering and hardship as the standard curriculum of the latter. It is, in his view, the education of kings or "sons of Zeus" (cf. *Or.* 4.26–31). Seneca likewise states that people are divinely educated through toils, testing, and hardship (*Prov.* 1.5, 2.5). Additionally, Matthew Thiessen has helpfully shown that Hebrews's discussion of training and discipline is, in part, informed by the understanding of Israel's divine training in the wilderness prior to its entry into the promised land.[36] Ancient readers then would have recognized suffering as a well-known curriculum of learning.

Third, Jesus is perfected and becomes a source of eternal salvation as a Melchizedekian priest for those who obey him (events after death). Less often noted is that the image of "being perfected" is

---

texts in John as topical treatment of "nurture and training" in the life of Jesus, see Jerome H. Neyrey, "Encomion Versus Vituperation: Contrasting Portraits of Jesus in the Fourth Gospel," *JBL* 126 (2007): 529–52.

[34] David A. deSilva, *Perseverence in Gratitude: A Socio-Rhetorical Commentary on the Epistle "to the Hebrews"* (Grand Rapids, Eerdmans, 2000), 191.

[35] Cf. Philo, *Mos.* 2.280; *Her.* 73; *Fug.* 138; *Spec.* 4.29; *Somn.* 2.107; Aeschylus, *Ag.* 177; Aesop, *Fab.* 370.

[36] Cf. Matthew Thiessen, "Hebrews 12.5–13, the Wilderness Period, and Israel's Discipline," *NTS* 55 (2009): 366–79.

also drawn from the classroom. More importantly, it is treated in the milieu precisely as it is treated in verse 8, as the ultimate goal of *paideia* or philosophical studies (cf. Epictetus, *Diatr.* 1.4.1, 4, 18–21; Philo, *Post.* 132; *Leg.* 3.159; *Somn.* 2.234–5; and *Vita Pachomii* 2, 28, 43).[37] Philo, for example, speaks of the "progress" of a philosopher-in-training – specifically, the movement from "folly" to "wisdom" and "virtue" – as "advancing toward perfection" (*Somn.* 2.234–5), and elsewhere identifies "perfection" as the end-goal of the more generic "pupil" (*Post.* 132). In a similar fashion, the image of Jesus's "being perfected" brings the portrait of Jesus's apprenticeship to its appropriate conclusion. Perfection, here, is the culmination of his learning, the status that results in his becoming a source of salvation to others (v. 9) as a Melchizedekian priest (v. 10).[38]

Pursuits – Deeds: Syncrisis of the Priestly Deeds of Each Covenant

Ps. Hermogenes, Aphthonius, and Nicolaus all treat deeds immediately after the topic or topics devoted to education – Ps. Hermogenes treating it simultaneously with pursuits (see Ps. Hermogenes 16).[39] The fourth syncrisis in our reading (7:1–10:18), takes up this topic, highlighting Melchizedek's and Jesus's accomplishments (= deeds) as priests as the mark of the new covenant priesthood's superiority. Once again, in the macro-comparison of covenants that spans the sermon, the writer has taken up topics analogous to those used for comparing persons, viewing the covenants' respective priestly ministries and the deeds accomplished in those ministries as something analogous to the covenants' pursuits and deeds.

The comparative argument of this section can be briefly summarized in terms of the deeds contrasted. The unit first juxtaposes the

---

[37] For these citations and further discussion, see Charles H. Talbert, "The Way of the Lukan Jesus: Dimensions of Lukan Spirituality," *PRSt* 9 (1982): 237–49.

[38] "Being perfected" in Heb 5:9 likely carries with it both vocational (graduation to Melchizedekian priesthood) and eschatological (entrance into the immortal heavenly realm) associations, though the pedagogical imagery places emphasis on the vocational aspect of this language. Jesus's sufferings train him to become the faithful and merciful Melchizedekian priest. Thus he moves from a priest-in-training to executing the ministry of his office. Jesus, however, does not take up the execution of his priestly ministry until he enters heaven (cf. 7:25–10:18).

[39] Ps. Hermogenes's treatment of body and mind should be viewed as an expansion of his treatment of nurture and training, which mold the person physically and mentally.

two priestly ministries beginning to end through an examination of representative figures. The significant contrasts lie in the following facts:

- Melchizedek, the progenitor (by type) of the tribe that bears his name, is greater than Abraham and Levi, the progenitors (by type and blood) of the Levitical priesthood (7:1–10).
- Jesus arises through the power of an indestructible life and enables the worshipper to draw near to God, but the Levitical priesthood perfects nothing (7:11–19).
- Jesus takes his priestly office with an oath sworn by God, but the Levitical priests do not (7:20–22).
- Jesus continues forever and thus holds his priesthood permanently, but the Levitical priests die and cannot continue in their office as priests (7:23–24).

Hebrews 7:25–10:18 then proceeds to detail comparatively the accomplishments or actions of each priestly ministry:

- Jesus saves and intercedes for those who approach because he enters the heavenly realm. Levitical high priests must offer sacrifices daily for their own sins (7:25–28).
- Jesus ministers in the true tabernacle and sits at God's right hand. Levitical priests minister on earth in a copy and shadow of the heavenly sanctuary (8:1–13).
- Jesus is like the high priest who goes into the Holy of Holies once to make an offering for sins, but he is not like the ordinary priest (= Levitical priests) who enter the second tent continuously. The Levitical ministry is of limited duration until the time of correction, that is, until Jesus's Melchizedekian priestly ministry, which is enduring (9:1–10).
- Jesus achieves purification of the conscience and new covenant inauguration by his own blood. The Levitical priests offer the blood of goats, calves, and bulls, which only purifies the flesh (9:11–23).
- Jesus brings about the forgiveness of sins once for all time through the offering of himself. The Levitical priests' continual offerings for sins cannot perfect the worshipper but only bring about the yearly reminder of sins (9:24–10:18).

The overall effect of these comparisons is that the new covenant priestly ministry is shown to be superior at every point in its "life" from its very beginnings with Melchizedek to its eternal, never-ending ministry, performed by Jesus in the heavenly realm.[40]

Death/Events after Death: Syncrisis of Covenant Eschata

Of the four theorists who provide syncrisis exercises, only Theon and Ps. Hermogenes include topics pertaining to the end of the life (death and/or posthumous events). Outside the progymnasmata, a similar division is seen: Cicero (*Inv.* 1.24.34; 2.59.177; *Part. or.* 74–5) and Menander Rhetor (368–77) do not include death/posthumous events in their lists; Rhetorica ad Herennium (3.6.10–11) and Quintilian (*Inst.* 3.7.10, 17–18) do. This division is probably not one of opinion but circumstance – namely, whether the list in question is designed primarily for eulogizing someone who is dead or alive. Aphthonius, for example, does not include either death or posthumous events in his topic list, but in his model syncrisis of Achilles and Hector (44) and in his model invective of Philip (42) – deceased subjects all – he nonetheless takes up the topic of death, and even cites it by name in the invective of Philip. The theorists are also divided concerning whether to treat life's end under death, posthumous events, or both.[41] Theon even alternates between two of these methods.[42] What we will see here in Heb 12:18–24 is that the topics of death and events after death are employed in the comparison of two "approaches" to God.

In Hebrews's running comparison of covenants, the final comparison (12:18–24) juxtaposes Sinai and Zion as contrasting destinations of the people's "approach" under the respective covenants.[43] If previous comparisons have focused on the beginnings (covenant mediators and inaugurators) and middle (covenant priestly ministries)

---

[40] As we will demonstrate in Chapter 6, these comparisons can be topically and chronologically arranged. Cf. Seid, "Synkrisis," 326–47, who rightly attempts to identify the encomiastic topics that structure the syncrisis in Heb 7 but does not recognize the chronological progression of the topics therein.

[41] Cf. Theon 110, Quintilian, *Inst.* 3.7.10, 17–18; Rhet. Her. 3.6.10–11; Ps. Hermogenes 19; cf. 16–17.

[42] Cf. Theon 78.

[43] Lincoln (*Hebrews*, 25) in his structural outline identifies 12:18–24 as part of the *peroratio* but also sees these verses as a final comparative exposition which is focused upon the two covenants, old and new. See also Michel, *Hebräerbrief*, 459–61.

of covenant life, this final comparison brings the focus to the end – and, specifically, the eschatological end (see below) – of covenant life. Thus the comparison may be viewed as the treatment of something analogous in covenant life to death/posthumous events – that is, to the headings normally used to treat the end of life in a comparison of persons.

The use of numeric symbolism contributes to the portrait, hinting at the eschatological dimensions of the comparison: rather than employing topics to contrast his two subjects as he has in every other comparison in Hebrews, the writer instead structures the comparison via parallel, seven-part depictions of each mountain – seven being, appropriately, the number of completion and perfection.[44] A literal translation and arrangement illustrate the effect:

You have not come

> [1] to something touched
> [2] and to something that has been burned with fire
> [3] and to darkness
> [4] and to gloom
> [5] and to storm
> [6] and to trumpet sound
> [7] and to the voice of words,
> which (voice) made the hearers beg that no further word be spoken to them, for they could not endure the order that was given, "If even an animal touches the mountain, it shall be stoned to death." Indeed, so terrifying was the sight that Moses said, "I tremble with fear."

---

[44] Michel (*Hebräerbrief*, 462) understands there to be seven old covenant items paralleled to eight (7+1) new covenant items in four pairs. The difference between the numbering of Michel's list and our list lies in whether Mount Zion and the heavenly Jerusalem are counted as one item or two. If we follow Michel's enumeration of the lists here, we might have a case where the superiority of the new covenant is reflected in the numeration ("plus one" being an indication of superiority, cf. *Od.* 9.159–60). Moreover, eight being the number used by early Christians to symbolize resurrection might be used here to reflect the end to which the new covenant leads (for the significance of the number 8 as the number for resurrection see François Bovon, "Names and Numbers in Early Christianity," *NTS* 47 [2001]: 283). Whether we number both lists according to sevens or seven and seven plus one, the author is clearly comparing, via these closely aligned descriptive lists, the approach to God via the old covenant (Sinai) and the new covenant (Zion).

But you have come

[1] to Mount Zion and the city of the living God, to heavenly Jerusalem

[2] and to a myriad of angels in a festal gathering

[3] and to the assembly of the firstborn children enrolled in heaven

[4] and to a judge, the God of all

[5] and to the spirits of the righteous who have been made perfect

[6] and to the mediator of a new covenant, Jesus

[7] and to the sprinkled blood that speaks better than Abel's blood.

That the heavenly Zion together with the heavenly Jerusalem is an *eschatological* destination or *telos* in the theology of the writer is clear from its characterization elsewhere in the sermon as "the abiding city to come" (13:14) and the object of the ancestors' hope (11:13–16).[45] It thus belongs to the "heavenly fatherland" for those who "died in faith" (11:13–14) and the "coming world" in which Jesus has already entered and in which he is enthroned, crowned with glory and honor (1:5–2:9). It is part of "God's resting place" created from the foundation of the world (4:3–6).

In this final syncrisis, there are at least three points of contrast, each of which shapes Sinai symbolically as Zion's eschatological opposite.

First, whereas Sinai is characterized by limited access to God, Zion is characterized by the full and final access depicted earlier in the sermon as an eschatological hope (e.g., 6:19–20).[46] In the preceding syncrisis of priestly ministries, a key point of comparison was the contrasting abilities of the covenants' respective priests to perfect the people so that they might approach God in a perfected state (cf. 7:11). This perspective is continued in the present comparison of

---

[45] Aristides's encomium of Rome ends focusing on the *telos* to which Rome has brought the whole world. The world has achieved its ideal state under Roman rule (94–99), a Golden Age of peace (69, 89, 103, 106). Similarly, in Heb 12:22–24 we have the *telos* to which God leads believers through Jesus Christ and the new covenant he inaugurates. See also Libanius's encomium of righteousness which employs the topic of events after death with regard to those who possess righteousness: "for the just alone, life is good, but the afterlife is better" (*Progymnasmata*, 249).

[46] David Peterson, *Hebrews and Perfection: An Examination of the Concept of Perfection in the 'Epistle to the Hebrews'* (SNTSMS 47; Cambridge: Cambridge University Press, 2005), 162.

Sinai and Zion as contrasting mountains of approach. Whereas at Sinai the people cannot approach God in their unperfected state without being struck down (holiness "preserved by exclusion"[47]), at Zion the readers will approach God not just fearlessly but in festal procession, and they will do this with those have gone before them in faith.[48]

Second, whereas Sinai is earthly and temporary, Zion is heavenly and eternal. Of the seven descriptors of Sinai, only two are not drawn from the Sinai traditions but rather are added by the writer. These are telling redactions and may be taken as clues to the way the writer shapes Sinai as Zion's eschatological opposite. The first of these concerns us presently, the description of Sinai as "something touched" (ψηλαφωμένῳ). The word chosen here by the author is both spatially and temporally significant for the comparison. First, the description, "as something touched," indicates that Sinai belongs to the earthly realm as opposed to the heavenly realm of Zion. Second, Zion cannot be touched because it is not yet manifest or visible to those who will inherit it.[49] That manifestation will come at the final shaking of the cosmos. Unlike the earthly Sinai, because Zion is "heavenly," it will remain after the final shaking as part of God's unshakable kingdom (cf. 12:26–27). Thus, it is fitting that the heavenly Jerusalem in the heavenly Zion is also "a remaining city that is to come" (13:14).[50]

Third, whereas Sinai is a mountain marked by "underworldly gloom" and the fear of death, Zion is a mountain of life beyond death both for the approaching readers and for the deceased righteous. The writer's second telling redaction of the Sinai traditions is the

---

[47] Harold W. Attridge, *A Commentary on the Epistle to the Hebrews* (Philadelphia: Fortress, 1989), 373–4.

[48] This description of the heavenly Zion appears to be a proleptic encounter with the "*ultimate complete company of the people of God*," since we seem to be dealing here with a post-judgment picture of God's people rejoicing with the angelic host before him. Cf. Peterson, *Hebrews and Perfection*, 162. Moffitt (*Atonement and the Logic of Resurrection*, 208–12) sees these spirits as currently awaiting resurrection, the perfection of their bodies, along with the community on earth.

[49] Cf. Ole Jakob Filtvedt, "Creation and Salvation in Hebrews," *ZNW* 106 (2015): 297–8.

[50] See further, Filtvedt, "Creation," 301–2, who concludes "the 'realm of salvation' has been prepared already, and only waits to be inhabited by humans. ... The view in Hebrews does not seem to be that God needs to create things anew, but that all things have been prepared from the foundation of the world, and that the 'realm of salvation' now only waits to be inhabited."

description of Sinai as a mountain of ζόφος, the "gloom of the underworld."[51] Here the writer has likely replaced γνόφος in LXX Deut 4:11 // 5:22 with ζόφος (though it is possible he is in possession of a version of the LXX that has made this substitution). This likely redaction, together with the mention of the fear of death that pervades the approach at Sinai (12:21), is chosen by the writer to contrast with the images of life that pervade the portrait of Zion, and particularly those that correspondingly relate to life beyond death and the earthly realm for humanity: the assembly of the firstborn who have been enrolled in heaven, consisting of both the perfected spirits of the righteous and the approaching readers who will join them.

On the whole, Sinai in the writer's depiction is the very image of where the story of the old covenant would end apart from the new covenant ministry it proclaims[52] – at a *telos* of marginal access to God in a world that is not lasting, a *telos* burdened by the fear of death and shrouded in underworldly gloom. By contrast, Zion in the writer's depiction is the very image of where the story of the new covenant will end, not only for the faithful of the present generation, but also for all the faithful of past generations (11:1–39) who are perfected by Christ not apart from but together with the present generation (11:40; cf. 11:15–16). It is a *telos* of complete and final access to God in a world that is un-shakable and lasting into eternity.[53]

---

[51] Cf. *Od.* 20.356; 2 Pet 2:4, 17. On this redaction, see deSilva, *Perseverence in Gratitude*, 465; cf. Peterson, *Hebrews and Perfection*, 162.

[52] This is a hypothetical *telos* only. The old covenant does not exist, in the view of the writer, apart from the new covenant, since its institutions are a shadow of the heavenly, new covenant realities and patterned on those realities. Thus the writer can speak of the old covenant as typological "good news" (4:2) and of Moses as a witness "to the things that would be spoken later" (3:5).

[53] The choice of representative mountains as covenant ends (death/events beyond death), it should be observed, can only be anticipated from the perspective of Mt. Zion and not Mt. Sinai. The latter only makes sense as a syncritical partner for Zion, its comparative non-eschaton. Mount Sinai is not the place to which the old covenant was intended to lead. If anything, it was a beginning, the place of covenant initiation in the exodus narrative, and the place that the old covenant priestly work leaves the people still apart from the priestly work of Christ it foreshadows. Zion, by contrast, is the natural end, both chronologically and topically, of covenantal life. In the Song of Moses in Exodus 15, the goal of the exodus from Egypt was the enthronement of God on the mountain (i.e., earthly Zion) where God would plant the people after God had conquered all Israel's enemies (vv. 17–18). In the author's view, the people will reach the heavenly Zion when all the enemies of the Son have been made a footstool for his feet. It is the place that the perfected people of God will gather in the heavenly Jerusalem in the presence of God after the final shaking of the cosmos (cf. Kiwoong Son, *Zion Symbolism in Hebrews: Hebrews 12:18–24 as a Hermeneutical Key to the Epistle* [PBMS; Milton Keys: Paternoster, 2005], who also notes the significance of Sinai-Zion motifs throughout Hebrews).

Conclusion

In sum, this chapter has examined epideictic syncrisis in Hebrews, identifying five comparisons that collectively span nearly the full length of Hebrews: the angels vs. Jesus (1:5–14), Moses vs. Jesus (3:1–6), the Aaronic high priests vs. Jesus (5:1–10), the Levitical priestly ministry vs. the Melchizedekian priestly ministry (7:1–10:18), and Mt. Sinai vs. Mt. Zion (12:18–24). These comparisons, we have argued, collectively display an internal coherence evident from their consistent juxtaposition of old covenant and new covenant subjects, their consistent argument for the superiority of the new covenant subject in question, and their common contribution – by virtue of the particular roles featured – to a chronologically ordered progression of topics (origin, birth, pursuits/education, pursuits/deeds, death and events after death) through covenant life. Such internal coherence accords with rhetorical theory and is evident not only among the five syncrises collectively, but also within several of the individual syncrises. Such internal coherence shows, moreover – and especially in the light of rhetorical theory – that the five syncrises should be read not just individually, but collectively, as a single syncritical project that argues for the superiority of the new covenant to the old.

3*

CHOOSING THE ADVANTAGEOUS

Deliberative Syncrisis & Epideictic
Syncrisis in Hebrews

Both modern and ancient commentaries on Hebrews acknowledge the significance of comparison or syncrisis in the rhetoric of Hebrews. How one understands the function of syncrisis in Hebrews plays no small role in determining its rhetorical outline and aim. Syncrisis could be employed in service of any of the species of rhetoric – judicial, epideictic, or deliberative – and currently the debate in Hebrews centers upon whether the decidedly syncritical rhetoric of the letter ultimately has deliberative or epideictic force.[1]

As we demonstrated in the last chapter, the prominence of epideictic syncrises in Hebrews and their liberal use of encomiastic topics (1:5–14; 3:1–6; 5:1–10; 7:1–10:18; 12:18–24) have led many scholars to propose that Hebrews's argument is primarily epideictic in nature. In their view, Hebrews seeks to inculcate community values and commitment to a certain way of life in the present. Thomas Olbricht, for example, likens Hebrews to funeral orations, which employed syncrisis and encomiastic topics to praise the deceased.[2] Olbricht thereby concludes that Hebrews is epideictic

---

* A previous version of this chapter appeared as "Choosing What Is Advantageous: The Relationship between Epideictic and Deliberative Syncrisis in Hebrews," *NTS* 58 (2012): 379–400.

[1] The present debate is also due to the presence of exhortations throughout Hebrews that appear to have epideictic force and of those that appear to have deliberative force. For a discussion of this point see David A. deSilva, *Perseverance in Gratitude: A Socio-Rhetorical Commentary on the Epistle to the Hebrews* (Grand Rapids: Eerdmans, 2000), 47–8. Hermann von Soden (*Hebräerbrief, Briefe des Petrus, Jakobus, Judas* [HKNT 3; Freiburg: Mohr, 1899], 8–11) was an early proponent of studying Hebrews in light of Greek rhetorical structures and genre and advocated for a practical purpose (i.e., deliberative or judicial; "einer regelrechten Rede mit praktischen Zwecken").

[2] Later rhetorical discussion of Pericles's popular funeral oration demonstrates that such conclusions are problematic. For instance, Ps. Dionysius of Halicarnassus in [*Rhet.*] 8.9 indicates that, in his discussion of figured speech, Pericles's funeral oration is not simply an encomium. He notes that Thucydides combines both epideictic and

in its "superstructure."[3] Timothy Seid reaches a similar conclusion because he understands the epideictic syncrises in Hebrews to be the structuring principle of the whole discourse.[4] Ben Witherington has argued that Hebrews is written to shore up faith in the face of persecution. "This act of persuasion is surely epideictic in character, appealing to values and virtues that the audience has already embraced in the past."[5] As with Olbricht and Seid, Witherington points to the use of syncrisis and the implementation of encomiastic topics as evidence of an overall epideictic thrust in Hebrews.[6]

Among those who argue Hebrews is ultimately deliberative in its rhetorical aim,[7] David deSilva offers an extensively argued case.[8] As deSilva points out, deliberative rhetoric urges a particular course of action, and one of its tactics is to point out the consequences of following a certain course of action. In deSilva's view, Hebrews

---

deliberative purpose–to praise the dead and exhort the living to take up arms. Dionysius is acknowledging that speeches have multiple aims often determined by historical contingencies that surround the speech, and in the case of Pericles's funeral oration, the overt epideictic function of the speech as a funeral oration is brought into service of what is considered the primary deliberative aim of the speech, namely, to take up arms. The Greek text of Dionysius consulted here is from *Dionysii Halicarnasei quae exstant* (ed. Hermann Usener and Ludwig Radermacher; Bibliotheca scriptorum Graecorum et Romanorum Teubneriana; vol. 6.; Stuttgart: B. G. Teubner, 1997), 306.

[3] Thomas H. Olbricht, "Hebrews as Amplification," in *Rhetoric and the New Testament: Essays from the 1992 Heidelberg Conference* (ed. Stanley E. Porter and Thomas H. Olbricht; JSNTSupp 90; Sheffield: Sheffield Academic Press, 1993), 378.

[4] Timothy W. Seid, "Synkrisis in Hebrews 7: Rhetorical Structure and Analysis," in *The Rhetorical Interpretation of Scripture: Essays from the 1996 Malibu Conference* (ed. Stanley E. Porter and Dennis L. Stamps; Sheffield: Sheffield Academic Press, 1999), 346–7. For other proponents of epideictic rhetoric for Hebrews see Pamela M. Eisenbaum, *Jewish Heroes of Christian History: Hebrews 11 in Literary Context* (SBLDS 156; Atlanta: Scholars Press, 1997), 12; Harold W. Attridge, *A Commentary on the Epistle to the Hebrews* (Hermeneia; Philadelphia: Fortress Press, 1989), 14.

[5] Ben Witherington III, *Letters and Homilies for Jewish Christians: A Socio-Rhetorical Commentary on Hebrews, James and Jude* (Downers Grove: IVP, 2007), 43–4.

[6] Witherington, *Letters and Homilies*, 46–8.

[7] Knut Backhaus, *Der Hebräerbrief* (RNT; Regensburg: Verlag Friedrich Pustet, 2009), 39–40; Walter G. Übelacker, *Der Hebräerbrief als Appell: Untersuchungenzu exordium, narratio, und postscriptum (Hebr 1–2 und 13,22–25)* (ConBNT 21; Stockholm: Almqvist & Wiksell International, 1989), 214–29; Barnabus Lindars, "The Rhetorical Structure of Hebrews," *NTS* 35 (1989): 382–406. Erich Gräßer (*An die Hebräer: Hebr 1–6* [EKK 17/1; Zürich: Benziger Verlag / Neukirchener Verlag, 1990], 15, 16), however, sees the sole theme of Hebrews to be Christ, the true high priest and thus perceives the deliberative sections in Hebrews as *repeated interruptions (immer weider ... unterbricht)* to this more theoretical discussion.

[8] For the discussion that follows see deSilva, *Perseverance in Gratitude*, 47–56.

adopts such a strategy, highlighting the negative consequences of apostasy and the positive consequences of perseverance in confessional faithfulness and community identification. Two other factors are also critical to deSilva's assessment. First, deSilva believes he can identify several rhetorical topics associated with deliberation in Hebrews: justice, courage, honor, expediency, and security. Second, deSilva argues that epideictic-expositional sections of Hebrews serve to set up subsequent exhortations. Thus, deSilva concludes that Hebrews is "deliberative speech that uses epideictic topics extensively to amplify the significance of making the right choice between remaining firm and turning away."[9]

DeSilva's last point is central to the thesis of this chapter. In the previous chapter we argued that the discourse in Hebrews is structured around five epideictic syncrises which are arranged according to standard encomiastic topics and collectively argue for the superiority of the new covenant to the old. In the present chapter, we propose that these five epideictic syncrises are paired with five corresponding deliberative syncrises that (a) assume the premise established in the epideictic syncrises and (b) take up, together with the hortatory units in which they are situated, the encomiastic topic (e.g., origin, birth, education, deeds, death/posthumous events) of the epideictic syncrises. By demonstrating these relationships, we attempt to further the argument for Hebrews as an occasion of deliberative rhetoric, since we show that the epideictic syncrises are in service both logically and topically to the deliberative syncrises.

The chapter will proceed in two parts. First, we consult the ancient handbooks of rhetoric, noting both the aim of deliberative rhetoric and, with regard to syncrisis, its standard logical forms. Second, in view of this survey, we identify all deliberative syncrises in Hebrews, describing their aim and form in categories derived from the handbooks. It is in the light of this latter analysis that the relationship between epideictic and deliberative rhetoric in Hebrews will emerge.

Deliberative Syncrisis in the Handbooks

According to the theorists, "deliberative syncrisis" is characterized by at least two essential traits:

---

[9] DeSilva, *Perseverance in Gratitude*, 56. Cf. Übelacker, *Der Hebräerbrief als Appell*, 219–20.

1. As deliberative rhetoric, its aim is to show the merit (or lack thereof) of a proposed course of action. In ancient Greek rhetoric, merit was construed strictly in terms of the potential "advantage" to the listener. Aristotle provides the classical statement:

> The end of the deliberative speaker is the expedient or harmful; for he who exhorts recommends a course of action as better, and he who dissuades advises against it as worse; all other considerations, such as justice and injustice, honour and disgrace, are included as accessory in reference to this. (*Rhet.* 1.3.5 [1358b] [Freese, LCL])

In his most mature statement on the matter, Cicero echoes the classical verdict that advantage is the singular aim of deliberation, only he construes advantage more broadly than did Aristotle, as encompassing good things that are "necessary" and "not necessary" (cf. *Part. or.* 83–90). Among the latter he counts things desired for their own sake, things desired for their intrinsic moral value (i.e., honor, understood in terms of the four virtues), things desired for the advantage they confer (i.e., bodily goods and goods of fortune), and means to something of value (i.e., wealth, resources, etc). Rhetorica ad Herennium, too, reflects a broadened understanding of advantage as the single aim, dividing it according to two subtopics, security and honor (3.2). Similarly Quintilian, though drawn to the idealistic view of a younger Cicero that honor is the chief aim of deliberation (cf. *De or.* 2.334; *Inv.* 2.146), ultimately concludes pragmatically that the nature of audiences commends identifying and distinguishing two aims in deliberative rhetoric, expediency and honor (cf. *Inst.* 3.8.1–3).

2. As syncritical argument, it takes one of three logical forms: comparison to the greater, comparison to the lesser, comparison to the equal. Once again, Aristotle provides the classical statement. Surveying topics of arguments he prescribes for use in all three species of rhetoric, he arrives at the topic "from the more and the less" and illustrates three forms of this argument.

> Syncrisis with the greater: "For instance, if not even the gods know everything, hardly can men; for this amounts to saying that if a predicate, which is more probably affirmable of one thing, does not belong to it, it is clear that it does not belong to another of which it is less probably affirmable."

Syncrisis with the lesser: "And to say that a man who beats his father also beats his neighbours, is an instance of the rule that, if the less exists, the more also exists."

Syncrisis with the equal: "Further, if there is no question of greater or less; whence it was said, 'Thy father deserves to be pitied for having lost his children; is not Oeneus then equally to be pitied for having lost an illustrious offspring?'" (*Rhet.* 2.23.4–6 [1397b] [Freese, LCL])

By the Hellenistic period, Aristotle's divisions of this argument were standard.[10] For our purposes, it will be helpful to note Cicero, who paraphrases the logical move of each succinctly:

Syncrisis with the greater: "What is valid in the greater should be valid in the less."

Syncrisis with the lesser: "What is valid in the less should be valid in the greater."

Syncrisis with the equal: "What is valid in one of two equal cases should be valid in the other." (*Top.* 23 [Hubbell, LCL])

Theon, too, provides his own account of the logic and, in addition, actual judicial examples of each:

Syncrisis with the greater: "When we make a syncrisis to something greater we amplify the lesser to show that it is

---

[10] See Cicero, *De or.* 2.40.172; *Inv.*1.28.41; 2.17.55; Ps. Hermogenes 19; Aphthonius 42; Nicolaus 60; cf. Michael W. Martin, *Judas and the Rhetoric of Syncrisis in the Fourth Gospel* (Sheffield: Sheffield Phoenix, 2010), 39–41. There is an interesting correspondence between this comparative rationale demonstrated in the rhetorical handbooks and Hillel's seven rules of Scripture interpretation. The first rule, that concerning *Kal wa-homer* ("light and heavy"), corresponds to syncrisis to the greater and the lesser, granting as it does "[a]n inference drawn from a minor premise to a major and vice versa," while the second rule, that concerning *Gezera Shawa* ("an equivalent regulation"), corresponds to syncrisis to the equal, granting as it does "an inference drawn from analogy of expressions." On this correspondence see David Daube, "Rabbinic Methods of Interpretation and Hellenistic Rhetoric," *HUCA* 22 (1949): 239–64; for the characterizations quoted above, see Edward Earle Ellis, *The Old Testament in Early Christianity: Canon and Interpretation in the Light of Modern Research* (Tübingen: J. C. B. Mohr [Paul Siebeck], 1991), 87–91. See also Burton L. Visotzky, "Midrash, Christian Exegesis, and Hellenistic Hermeneutic," in *Current Trends in the Study of Midrash* (ed. Carol Bakhos; Supplements to the Journal for the Study of Judaism 106; Leiden: Brill, 2006), 120–6; and Philip Alexander, "Quid Athenis et Hierosolymis? Rabbinic Midrash and Hermeneutics in the Graeco–Roman World," in *A Tribute to GézaVermès: Essays on Jewish and Christian Literature and History* (ed. Philip R. Davies and Richard T. White; JSOTSup 100; Sheffield: JSOT Press, 1990), 97–115.

> equal to that; for example, that a thief does as much wrong as a temple robber because both are moved by the single desire of stealing and the thief would not hesitate to rob a temple if he had the opportunity nor would the temple robber hesitate to steal."
>
> Syncrisis with the lesser: "When we make a syncrisis to the lesser we shall speak as follows: 'If the thief is punished for taking men's money, how much the more will this man be punished for looting the possessions of the gods?'"
>
> Syncrisis with the equal: "But when we put an equal beside an equal we shall say that if we do not allow one doing equal wrong to go scot-free, neither is it right to overlook this man's action." (108)

Only Quintilian provides models of the three forms in which *explicitly* comparative language is absent. This is because he does not distinguish between syncrises, which draw distinctions or analogies explicitly, and examples, which do so implicitly, but rather insists that all examples are syncrises and vice versa.

> A reminder of parallels will be useful also in speaking about the future; for example, someone arguing that Dionysius was asking for a personal bodyguard in order to seize absolute power with their help could adduce as an example the fact that Pisistratus attained power in the same way.
>
> But while examples are sometimes complete parallels (like this last one), they are sometimes taken "from greater to lesser" or "from lesser to greater." "If whole cities have been overthrown because of violated marriages, what should be done to an adulterer?" "The pipers, having left the city, were recalled by the authority of the people; how much more should leading citizens who have deserved well of the state, but have been victims of envy, be recalled from exile!" (*Inst.* 5.11.8–10 [Russell, LCL])

Quintilian appears exceptional in this regard among the theorists, who generally treat syncrisis and example as distinct arguments, and so we shall limit our analysis of Hebrews to explicitly comparative language with deliberative aims.[11]

---

[11] It should be noted, though, that several of the syncrises we will identify work in concert with accompanying deliberative *exempla*, making their implicitly comparative

Of particular interest for the study of Hebrews is a recurring "how much more" formula that is frequently employed in syncrisis to the lesser: "if X is true in the case of the lesser, then *how much more* is X true in the case of the greater." This formula is reflected in the language of Aristotle (ἐκ τοῦ μᾶλλον καὶ ἧττον [*Rhet.* 2.23.4 (1397b)]), Theon ("When we make a syncrisis [συγκρίνωμεν] to the lesser we shall speak as follows: 'If the thief is punished for taking men's money how much the more [πόσῳ μᾶλλον)] will this man be punished for looting the possessions of the gods,'" 108), and Quintilian ("The pipers, having left the city, were recalled by the authority of the people; how much more should leading citizens who have deserved well of the state, but have been victims of envy, be recalled from exile!" *Inst.* 5.11.9 [Russell, LCL]). Hebrews also employs a form of this formula for some of its deliberative syncrises in 10:29 (πόσῳ ... χείρονος) and 12:9 (πόλυ ... μᾶλλον) in order to make emphatic its deliberative rationale.[12]

Deliberative Syncrisis in Hebrews

In view of the criteria above, six explicit deliberative syncrises may be identified in Hebrews: 2:2–4; 4:2; 6:13–20; 10:28–29; 12:9; and 12:25.

Syncrisis I   "For if the message declared through angels was valid, and every transgression or disobedience received a just penalty, *how can we escape* if we neglect so great a salvation which was spoken first by the Lord and confirmed to us by those who heard?" (2:2–4)

Syncrisis II   "For we also have heard the good news proclaimed *just as they did* but the message they heard did not benefit these who were not united by faith that was in those who heard." (i.e.: For if the good news given to them did not benefit them because of their lack of faith, how much more will it not benefit us because of our lack of faith?) (4:2)

---

logic explicit. For instance, the wilderness generation is held up as a negative *exemplum* for the present generation in 3:7–4:1. This is followed by a deliberative syncrisis to the lesser (that juxtapose the two generations in 4:2–3). Whereas most theorists would designate only 4:2–3 as comparison, Quintilian would call the entire text comparison.

[12] We also find it in the epideictic section of priestly pursuits in 9:14 (πόσῳ μᾶλλον).

Syncrisis III   "For when God made a promise to Abraham he swore by himself ... Thus, Abraham who patiently endured obtained the promise.... So when God wished to show *even more clearly* [than he did to Abraham] to the heirs of the promise the unchanging nature of his purpose, he guaranteed it by an oath ... so that we who have taken refuge might have strong encouragement to take ahold of the hope set before us ..." (i.e.: If Abraham patiently endured, obtaining the promise, how much more should heirs of the promise, to whom God has shown even more clearly the unchangeable character of his purpose, patiently endure? [cf. 6:11–12]) (6:13–20)

Syncrisis IV   "Anyone who has violated the Law of Moses dies without mercy 'on the testimony of two or three witnesses'. *How much worse* punishment do you think will be deserved by those who have spurned the Son of God, profaned the blood of the covenant by which they were sanctified, and outraged the Spirit of grace?" (10:28–29)

Syncrisis V   "If then we had fathers of our flesh who disciplined us and we respected them, *how much more* should we submit to the Father of spirits and live." (12:9)

Syncrisis VI   "For if they did not escape when they refused the one who warned them on earth, *how much more* will we not escape if we reject that voice which warns from heaven?" (12:25)

(1) Each of these syncrises takes up the classical deliberative aim of advantage/disadvantage, generally arguing that perseverance in the faith is advantageous for the readers/listeners, or that apostasy is disadvantageous. Four of these point to the negative consequences of apostasy primarily (I–II, IV, and VI) and two point to the positive consequences of perseverance in the Christian faith (III and V).[13] (2) Each of these happens to be a syncrisis to the lesser, reflecting the logic of the form as it is described by Cicero: "What is valid in the lesser should be valid in the greater." Several of these employ some

---

[13] The four that warn against apostasy are most explicitly built upon preceding verdicts of superiority in the comparison of covenants. This emphasis upon warning may point to the fact that defection was a real and present danger for several in the community.

variation on the formula, "If X is true in the case of the lesser, then *how much more* is X true in the case of the greater." Even those that do not, however, can be translated in terms of the formula, since they all operate according to the same logic.

The Logical Relationship of Epideictic and Deliberative Syncrisis

Of the six deliberative syncrises identified above, five play a key role in the overall structure and argument of Hebrews. They are 2:2–4, 4:2, 6:13–20, 10:28–29, and 12:25. The evidence of their importance to Hebrews's outline is seen in their relationship to the five-part epideictic syncritical project of Hebrews which we describe in the previous chapter. By way of reminder, we outlined this project as follows:

    I. Angels vs. Jesus (1:5–14)
    II. Moses vs. Jesus (3:1–6)
    III. Aaronic high priests vs. Jesus (5:1–10)
    IV. Levitical priestly ministry vs. Melchizedekian priestly ministry (7:1–10:18)
    V. Sinai vs. Zion (12:18–24)

In view of this outline, the logical relationship of five of the six deliberative syncrises to the project will become apparent. In each deliberative syncrisis, the following rationale can be demonstrated: if a certain course of action results in an advantage or disadvantage in the lesser case (= in old covenant experience), then the consequences for such a course of action are all the more valid in the greater case (= in new covenant experience). In each deliberative syncrisis, the disadvantageous course of action is generally understood to be apostasy while the advantageous course of action is understood to be continued faithfulness. The basis for the rationale is established by the preceding epideictic syncrisis.

In epideictic syncrisis I (1:5–14), *Jesus* (= new covenant mediator) was demonstrated to be the superior heavenly Son with a superior destiny to the *angels* (= old covenant mediator). In deliberative syncrisis I (2:2–4), the lesser case concerns those under the old covenant who transgressed the message declared through *angels*, and the greater case those who might neglect the salvation revealed through *Jesus*. Its argument, made explicit with the "if ..., then how ..." formula in verses 2–3 and the comparative adverb περισσοτέρως in verse 1, is

that what is valid for the lesser case (= the rejection of the angelic message results in "a just penalty") is valid all the more in the greater case. The deliberative syncritical rationale then centers upon the disadvantage of apostasy and is an extension of the preceding syncritical evaluation between Jesus and angels in 1:5–14 where Jesus is demonstrated to be the superior heavenly being.

In epideictic syncrisis II (3:1–6), *Jesus,* the son *over* God's household (= new covenant inaugurator), was demonstrated to be superior to *Moses,* the servant *in* God's household (= old covenant inaugurator). The superiority is grounded not only in the son/servant dichotomy but also in the nature of Moses's service: he gave "testimony to the things that would be spoken later" (3:5). In deliberative syncrisis II (4:2), the author states that the gospel/good news was preached (εὐαγγελίζω) to the audience just as also to those of the wilderness generation. From the immediate context in 4:1, the gospel/good news that was proclaimed would appear to center upon the hope to enter God's eschatological place of rest. The wilderness generation failed to enter it but that hope still remains for the audience of Hebrews.[14] In deliberative syncrisis II, then, the lesser case concerns the proclamation of the gospel to the wilderness generation led by Moses (cf. 3:16), the servant, while the greater case concerns the proclamation of the gospel to the present community led by Jesus, the son (cf. 2:10).[15] The argument of the syncrisis is that if

---

[14] The provocative use of εὐαγγελίζω may be more robust. Christians associated the preaching of the gospel (εὐαγγελίζω) with the proclamation of Jesus's Messiahship and salvation through him (e.g., Acts 5:42). Hebrews 1–2 certainly announces the gospel in Jesus's heavenly enthronement as priest-king. On that basis, Jesus announced the great salvation promised in Ps 8 (God's faithful crowned with glory and honor in the world to come). The author understands the Sinai revelation to contain a shadow of the coming good things but not the reality or manifestation of those events themselves (cf. 10:1). Some of the good things anticipated have come with the priestly ministry of Christ in heaven (cf. 9:11). Some of the good things will come later when Christ returns to bring salvation to those waiting for him (cf. 9:28). Moses saw these coming good things promised and possibly even chose to suffer for the sake of Christ in view of that vision (cf. Mary Rose D'Angelo, *Moses in the Letter to the Hebrews* [SBLDS 42; Missoula: Scholars Press, 1979], 248; but see Craig R. Koester, *Hebrews: A New Translation with Introduction and Commentary* [AB 36; New York: Doubleday, 2001], 326, 502–3, for a nuanced perspective). The old covenant as the divinely ordained anticipation of these new covenant realities can then be said "to preach the gospel," especially through Moses its inaugurator.

[15] Explicit comparison is seen in 4:2: "for we have the gospel preached *just as* (καθάπερ) they"; and possibly "these were not united by faith with those who heard [the present community]" (for this interpretation see Attridge, *Hebrews*, 125–7); and in 4:3: "for we who believe will enter into the place of rest."

faithless hearing (apostasy) of the gospel under the old covenant brought no benefit (= exclusion from God's place of rest), then such a penalty is valid all the more for faithless hearing under the new covenant. Again the deliberative syncritical rationale centers upon the disadvantage of apostasy; the covenant representatives of the preceding epideictic syncrisis are implicitly carried over into the deliberative syncrisis through the communities they lead (i.e., the wilderness generation and the authorial audience); and the deliberative rationale extends the evaluative conclusion of the epideictic syncrisis.

In epideictic syncrisis III (5:1–10), *Jesus*, the Melchizedekian (= new covenant) high priest, is demonstrated to be superior to *Aaron and his line*, the Levitical (= old covenant) high priests. In deliberative syncrisis III (6:13–20), the lesser case concerns the promise and confirming oath given to *Abraham* as evidence of the unchangeable character of God's purpose, while the greater case concerns the promise and confirming oath given to *Jesus* as even clearer evidence of the unchangeable character of God's purpose (the character of his purpose is said "to be shown more clearly," περισσότερον ... ἐπιδεῖξαι). The argument of the syncrisis is that if it was advantageous for Abraham to endure on the basis of the first promise – that is, if he obtained what was promised because of his endurance (cf. 6:12; "inherit what has been promised," NIV, *contra* the NRSV; also 6:15)[16] – then it is certainly advantageous for the present generation ("heirs of the promise")[17] to endure in light of God's more clearly revelatory promise to Jesus.[18]

---

[16] On the preferability of the NIV translation, see Koester, *Hebrews*, 326; and Peter O'Brien, *The Letter to the Hebrews* (PNTC; Grand Rapids: Eerdmans, 2010), 236–7.

[17] We take "heirs of the promise" (6:17) to be a reference to the members of the present community. Cf. Paul Ellingworth, *The Epistle to the Hebrews* (NIGTC; Grand Rapids: Eerdmans, 1993), 341; and Attridge, *Hebrews*, 181.

[18] On the identification of the promise and oath in 6:17 as that of Psalm 109:4 (LXX), see deSilva, *Perseverance in Gratitude*, 250; for the alternative view, that Christians are given the same promise and oath as Abraham (Gen 22:16–17), see Koester, *Hebrews*, 328; William L. Lane, *Hebrews 1–8* (WBC 47A; Nashville, Thomas Nelson, 1991), 152; F. F. Bruce, *The Epistle to the Hebrews* (NICNT; rev. ed.; Grand Rapids: Eerdmans, 1990), 154; and Ellingworth, *Hebrews*, 334. In our view, the former option is preferable primarily for three reasons. First, the writer's claim that Christians are "more clearly" shown the "unchangeable character of [God's] purpose" argues for the granting of a different and better oath rather than the same oath. Second, "the unchangeable character of [God's] purpose" (Heb 6:18) is an allusion to Psalm 109:4's claim that "the Lord ... will not change his mind" concerning what he has sworn. Third, Psalm 109:4 (LXX) is explicitly quoted as part

In what sense does the author understand this second promise to be more clearly revelatory for the readers – that is, to "show even more clearly ... the unchangeable character of his purpose"? In the case of Abraham, the promise (Gen 22:16–17; cf. 15:4–5, 21:12): (a) concerned Isaac; (b) served in the writer's fuller telling of the story in 11:17–19 as a guarantee of Isaac's resurrection beyond his being offered (= put to death) to God;[19] and (c) was realized, according to the writer, figuratively when Abraham "received him [Isaac] back" from the dead (11:19).[20] In the case of Jesus, however, the promise (Ps 109:4 [LXX]): (a) concerns *Jesus himself*; (b) is a guarantee of *Jesus's* resurrection beyond his death; and (c) was realized literally and not figuratively. On the basis of this promise, which was also confirmed by an oath, the readers have an even clearer understanding of the character of God's purpose for his people, and therefore, all the more reason to seize the hope set before them.

Deliberative syncrisis III seems to retain only one of the two figures (Jesus) featured in epideictic syncrisis III (Jesus vs. Aaronic high priests) and appears in this regard to be exceptional compared to the other deliberative syncrises, which consistently retain both figures from the epideictic comparisons with which they are paired. The syncrisis essentially argues: if perseverance on the basis of the promise given to *Abraham* (= the lesser) was advantageous for Abraham, then perseverance on the basis of the promise given to *Jesus the high priest* (= the greater) is advantageous for the audience. What we expect is: if perseverance is shown to be advantageous on the basis of some lesser case involving the *Aaronic high priests*, then it is certainly shown to be advantageous on the basis of some greater case involving *Jesus the high priest*.

We could explain the anomaly as an instance simply of literary license: the writer has chosen to depart from the pattern he generally follows. Though the writer has not seemingly in this scenario retained the old covenant/new covenant polarity seen in the other

of the hortatory argument only two verses later (6:20; cf. 7:21), and in echo of the earlier quotation (5:6) from the accompanying syncritical section.

[19] Cf. O'Brien, *Hebrews*, 237.

[20] Cf. James Swetnam, *Jesus and Isaac: A Study of the Epistle to the Hebrews in the Light of the Aqedah* (AnBib 94; Rome: Biblical Institute, 1981), 92, 185. Like Swetnam, we take the author's interpretation of the binding of Isaac in Heb 11:17–19 to be the controlling context for how we interpret the allusive reference to it in Heb 6:13–16.

deliberative syncrises, he has, nevertheless, most certainly retained the shadow/reality polarity common to all of them and crucial to the logic of syncrisis to the lesser: the promise and confirming oath given to Abraham is a shadowy anticipation of the aforementioned (5:5–6) promise and confirming oath given to the high priest Jesus, since both provide assurance of resurrection (though Jesus experienced the "better resurrection," cf. 11:35); hence, if the former may be taken as a source of assurance, the latter may be all the more. In this scenario, the present community's greater assurance and superior perspective is still grounded on the conclusion of the preceding syncrisis, namely, that Jesus's perfection due to his obedience has made him a source of eternal salvation.

There is evidence suggesting, however, that this syncrisis is not exceptional, that the writer at this point considers Abraham a progenitor both by blood and by type of the Aaronic priesthood and therefore its representative in the comparison. We know from epideictic syncrisis IV that the writer not only thinks of Abraham as the progenitor of the old covenant priests, but on that basis is willing to treat him as a representative of old covenant priesthood in a syncrisis with Melchizedek, who is the progenitor (by type, not by blood) of the new covenant priesthood (7:1–10).

Moreover, we know that the writer considers Abraham to bear a relationship to his priestly descendants that goes beyond blood, that he shares with them a history of faithful priestly service, for the writer frames Abraham's own testing in the near slaying of Isaac as a form of priestly offering in chapter 11:

> By faith Abraham, when he was tested, *offered up* (προσφέρω)[21] Isaac. He had received the promises, yet he was ready *to offer up* (προσφέρω) his only son. God had told him, "Through Isaac descendants will carry on your name," and he reasoned that God could even raise him from the dead, and in a sense he received him back from there. (vv. 17–19)

The fact, then, that deliberative syncrisis III parallels this same story with the story of Jesus's own training for priesthood suggests that the writer already is thinking of Abraham's near slaying of Isaac

---

[21] In the Septuagint, προσφέρω is commonly associated with making an offering or sacrifice to the Lord as prescribed by Leviticus (e.g., Lev 2:1, 4, 11, 14; 7:8, 29, 33; 21:6; cf. 1 Macc 4:56; 7:33; 12:11).

as his own priestly training, and, therefore, of Abraham as the progenitor priest and representative of the lesser Aaronic priesthood.[22] Certainly the parallels are striking:[23]

Jesus, the High Priest	Abraham
Is "tested" (4:15, cf. 5:7) by the prospect of his death	Is "tested" (11:17) by the prospect of his offering of Isaac
Is given a promise and confirming oath (i.e., Ps 109:4 [LXX]; Heb 5:6; cf. 7:17–25)	Is given a promise and confirming oath (i.e., Gen 22:17; Heb 6:13–14; cf. 11:18)
Is given assurance of resurrection by the promise (5:5–7; 6:17–18; cf. 7:11–25)	Is given assurance of resurrection figuratively by the promise (6:13–15; cf. 11:19)
Obediently suffers death on the basis of the promise (5:6–10; cf. 12:2)	Obediently "offers up" Isaac on the basis of the promise (6:13–15a; cf. 11:17–19)
Is saved out of death (5:6–10)	Receives Isaac back from the dead (6:15b; 11.17–19)

Abraham thus "works" in deliberative comparison III as the Aaronic high priest representative because he is viewed by the writer as the progenitor both by blood and by type of the Aaronic priesthood and therefore its representative in the comparison: if perseverance on the basis of the promise given to *Abraham, the proto-Aaronic high priest* (of the lesser/old covenant), was advantageous for Abraham, then perseverance on the basis of the promise given to *Jesus, the Melchizedekian high priest* (of the greater/new covenant), is advantageous, not only for Jesus, but also for the present community of whom he is the forerunner.

---

[22] Philo represents Abraham as a priest performing a sacrifice when he offers up Isaac (cf. *Abr.* 168). The binding of Isaac has a rich interpretive tradition in early Judaism and Christianity of which Hebrews is a part; cf. Jon D. Levenson, *The Death and Resurrection of the Beloved Son: The Transformation of Child Sacrifice in Judaism and Christianity* (New Haven: Yale University Press, 1993), 173–232; Leroy A. Huizenga, *The New Isaac: Tradition and Intertextuality in the Gospel of Matthew* (NovTSup 131; Leiden: Brill, 2009), 75–128; Swetnam, *Jesus and Isaac*, 23–85. One of Swetnam's summary conclusions is that "the Aqedah was regarded from the time of the composition of Gn 22 and all through early Judaism as involving a sacrifice" (77).

[23] See also, David M. Moffitt, *Atonement and the Logic of Resurrection in the Epistle to the Hebrews* (NovTSup 141; Leiden: Brill, 2011), 192–3, who draws parallels between the portrayal of Jesus in Heb 5:7 and Abraham in Heb 11:17–19. Moffitt uses these connections to argue an alternative point, namely that Jesus's deliverance out of death *is* an allusion to his resurrection.

In epideictic syncrisis IV (7:1–10:18), Jesus's *Melchizedekian (= new covenant) priestly ministry* is demonstrated to be superior in its administration of the new covenant to the *Levitical (= old covenant) priestly ministry* and its administration of the old covenant. In deliberative syncrisis IV (10:28–29), the lesser case concerns those who *violate the Law of Moses* – that is, the old covenant code. The greater case concerns those who essentially violate the new covenant – that is, those who deliberately keep sinning (10:26) and thus *spurn the Son of God, profane the blood of the covenant, and outrage the Spirit of grace*. Each of these phrases employs a primary term from 7:1–10:18 related to Jesus's new covenant, priestly ministry (Son, 7:28; blood of the covenant, 9:20; Spirit, 9:14) and thus anchors the warning in the cultic presentation of that ministry.[24] The argument of the syncrisis is that if apostates were put to death under the old covenant on the testimony of two or three witnesses,[25] then "how much worse" punishment will those deserve who under the new covenant spurn three witnesses (Son, blood, Spirit). Thus, deliberative reflection on the relative greatness of the respective offenses logically extends the preceding epideictic syncritical analysis in 7:1–10:18 of the covenants' respective priestly ministries. Again, we have returned to the deliberative argument based upon the disadvantages of apostasy.

In epideictic syncrisis V (12:18–24), the superiority of *Zion* (= the mountain of approach under the new covenant) to *Sinai* (= the mountain of approach under the old covenant) was demonstrated chiefly by the relative access to God that was found at each by virtue of their cosmological location (Zion–heaven/Sinai–earth). In the accompanying deliberative syncrisis (12:25), the warning given to the recipients of the old covenant *on earth at Sinai* is presented as the lesser case, while the warning given to the recipients of the new covenant *from Zion in heaven* is presented as the greater case. Its argument is that what is valid in the lesser case of those warned on earth – namely, that those who ignored the warning were unable to escape judgment – is also valid in the greater case of those warned from heaven. Thus apostasy (= refusing the warning) results in disadvantage (= not being able to escape judgment). The warnings

---

[24] Cf. O'Brien, *Hebrews*, 373.

[25] The quotation from Deut 17:2–6 ("died on the testimony of two or three witnesses") refers to the covenant offense of idolatry, which was representative of the ultimate acts of apostasy under the old covenant.

from earth and heaven deliberatively extend the Sinai–earth and Zion–heaven rationale of the preceding epideictic syncrisis.

In sum, each of these five key deliberative syncrises generally argues that what is valid in the case of old covenant experience is valid in the case of new covenant experience. What makes each a syncrisis to the lesser is that the preceding epideictic syncrisis with which it is paired has clarified (through the representative logic of syncrisis of wholes by parts) that the old covenant is the lesser covenant, and the new covenant, the greater. In short, epideictic syncrisis is logically in service to deliberative syncrisis, establishing the premise on which it proceeds:

Epideictic Syncrisis	Deliberative Syncrisis
The old covenant = the lesser	What is valid in the case of old covenant experience (= the lesser)
The new covenant = the greater	is valid even more so in the case of new covenant experience (= the greater)

Furthermore, a specific relationship is also evident among each of the five epideictic-deliberative syncrisis pairs. That is, the covenant representatives in view in each epideictic syncrisis remain in view in each deliberative syncrisis's juxtaposition of covenant experiences: Jesus/angels (I), Jesus/Moses (II), Jesus/Aaron (III), Melchizedekian priestly ministry/Levitical priestly ministry (IV), and Zion/Sinai (VI).

The remaining deliberative syncrisis (V), Heb 12:9, does not relate new covenant experience to old, the concern that spans the super-structure of Hebrews's outline from chapters 1 to 12, but rather, relates the readers' experience with the heavenly father to their experience with their earthly fathers, a concern that prevails only in the relatively shorter supporting unit of 12:5–11. We exclude it, therefore, from the present analysis.

The Topical Relationship of Epideictic and Deliberative Syncrisis

In addition to taking their logical premise from the epideictic (expository) syncrises with which they are paired, the deliberative syncrises identified above, together with the deliberative (hortatory) units in which they are situated, also derive from these epideictic syncrises their topical theme. In the previous chapter, we argued that

the five-part syncrisis is arranged conventionally by standard headings, or topics, of syncrisis. According to the handbooks, a syncrisis of persons or things is supposed to employ as its basic, compositional outline the epideictic topics used to divide a life in encomia of persons: e.g., families and places of origin, circumstances of birth, upbringing and education, career pursuits and achievements, circumstances of death, posthumous honors – the lists vary, depending on the theorist. Though these topics are better suited for syncrises of persons, in that they follow the contours of a person's life from start to finish, they can be adapted, the theorists say, for use in syncrisis of things: one merely finds something analogous in the life or history of the thing.

The five-part syncritical project in Hebrews, as we argued, adopts just such a method, taking up five commonly employed topics – or, to be more precise, topics analogous to those used for persons – in its comparison of the two covenants. In Chapter 2, we developed the following topical outline:

I. Origins: Syncrisis of Covenant Mediators (Angels vs. Jesus, 1:5–14)
II. Birth: Syncrisis of Covenant Inaugurators (Moses vs. Jesus, 3:1–6)
III. Pursuits – Education: Syncrisis of the Priestly Apprenticeships of Each Covenant (Aaronic high priests vs. Jesus, 5:1–10)
IV. Pursuits – Deeds: Syncrisis of the Priestly Deeds of Each Covenant (Levitical priestly ministry vs. Melchizedekian priestly ministry, 7:1–10:18)
V. Death/Events after Death: Syncrisis of Covenant *Eschata* (Sinai vs. Zion, 12:18–24)

(1) The project's first syncrisis considers a heading analogous to "origins," contrasting the angels and Jesus as the heavenly mediators from which each covenant derives (= covenant mediators). In the tacit argument of the larger project, the idea of this first syncrisis is that the new covenant is superior to the old because it originates with the superior heavenly mediator.

(2) The project's second syncrisis focuses on a topic analogous to "circumstances of birth," contrasting the covenants' respective beginnings via inaugurators with contrasting births themselves in regard to God's household: whereas Moses is a servant in the household, Jesus

is the son over the household.[26] The function of the syncrisis in the larger project is to show that the new covenant is better-born than the old, deriving as it does from the better-born inaugurator. The fact that the old covenant is also shown to serve at its inauguration as a shadowy witness to the new covenant reality only strengthens the argument: though the old covenant came first (a potential marker of superiority with regard to birth), it did so as testimony to the latter, proving the latter is the superior-born.

(3) The third epideictic syncrisis takes up a topic analogous to education, contrasting the Melchizedekian high priest, Jesus, with the Aaronic high priests in terms of the training they have undergone for priestly service. Whereas Jesus undertakes an apprenticeship of suffering from which he "learn[s] obedience" (presumably to his Father) and thereby graduates to "perfection," the Aaronic high priests share in the weakness of the "ignorant and wayward" and sacrifice for their own sins as well as those of the people. The function of the syncrisis is to show that the new covenant has the better-trained high priest.

(4) The fourth syncrisis treats the topic of deeds, comprehensively contrasting all that is done by the Levitical and Melchizedekian priesthoods in their cultic administration of their respective covenants, and showing the former ministry to be but a shadow of the latter. The function of the syncrisis is to show that the new covenant's priestly accomplishments are superior to the old.

(5) The fifth syncrisis takes up a topic analogous to death and posthumous events, juxtaposing Sinai and Zion as contrasting *eschata* of access to God belonging to each covenant. On the one hand, Sinai is depicted as an earthly ("something touched") mountain of

---

[26] In Heb 9:18–21, Moses is said to have inaugurated [ἐγκαινίζειν] the first covenant; on Jesus's similarly foundational role with respect to the new covenant, cf. 7:22; 8:6, 12:24.

limited, historical access to God, a mountain ominously characterized by fire, darkness, underwordly "gloom," tempest, trumpet-sound, and a fear-inspiring "voice" warning of death for those who come too close in their approach to God. On the other hand, Zion is depicted as a heavenly mountain of unlimited eschatological access to God, a heavenly city populated by angels in festal gathering, the assembly of the firstborn, God as judge-of-all, the spirits of the perfected righteous, Jesus, and his sprinkled blood. The divine voice that warns from each mountain becomes the focus of the deliberation that follows. For the writer, the voice at Sinai is proof that the access to God provided by the old covenant was always under the threat of "death" and the pall, even, of underworldly "gloom" – and this in contrast to the voice at Zion promising, through the sprinkled blood of Jesus, salvation and ultimate vindication for the righteous.[27]

When one examines the deliberative materials that follow each of these five epideictic units, the same topical theme is evident. Each deliberative unit features as its central argument a deliberative word of advice and a supporting deliberative syncrisis both of which further reflection on the *topos* at hand. Thus the deliberative syncrises advance the argument begun by the epideictic syncrises not only logically but also thematically.

> (1) The first deliberative unit (2:1–4) retains the preceding epideictic unit's focus on the covenants' respective origins – that is, on the heavenly mediators from which

---

[27] It may be that the reference to Abel in 12:24 is to his murder in Gen 4:10, where Abel's blood is a witness against Cain because Cain did not heed God's warning. By the time of Hebrews, Abel and his blood functioned symbolically as witnesses that testify against the oppression of God's righteous ones and to their future vindication and salvation by God (cf. John Byron, "Living in the Shadow of Cain: Echoes of a Developing Tradition in James 5:1–6," *NovT* 48 [2006]: 271–3). In this case, Jesus's sprinkled blood speaks a better message of salvation. Again, if the reference is to Gen 4:10, it may be that Able's death is the atoning death of the martyr that had limited effect as opposed to the eternal salvation through Jesus (so Attridge, *Hebrews*, 377). It may be that Abel as sacrificer (i.e., proleptic and lesser priest) is the focus of the comparison with Christ. This latter perspective was argued by David M. Moffitt, "But We Do See Abel: Hebrews and the Depiction of Abel's Sacrifice in Some Mosaics of Ravenna," (paper presented at the annual meeting of SBL, San Antonio, Texas, 21 November 2016).

the covenants respectively derive, the angels and Jesus – shifting the emphasis to the reception of each covenant upon its mediation by these heavenly agents. Its counsel is essentially for readers not to reject a message of such great origins. Its supporting syncrisis cites the contrast drawn in the preceding epideictic unit's syncrisis of covenant origins, arguing that if rejecting a message of lesser origins ("declared through angels") resulted in disadvantage, then rejecting a message of greater origins ("declared through the Lord") most assuredly will.

(2) The second deliberative unit (3:7–4:13) retains the second epideictic unit's focus on the covenants' respective births – that is, on their historical inaugurations via Moses and Jesus respectively – juxtaposing the readers' reception of God's address "Today" (3:7, 13) with the wilderness generation's reception of God's address at the time of the rebellion (3:7–8). The wilderness generation is the primary focus of this deliberative section because it is the inaugural recipient of the old covenant, and the writer is treating the historical inauguration of the covenant as something analogous in the life of a covenant to birth. The unit's central counsel is for the readers not to respond with the same hardheartedness and unbelief displayed by that generation (3:8, 12, 13, 15; 4:2, 11) and thereby fail to enter into God's place of rest as did they (4:1, 11). The supporting syncrisis argues that if unbelieving reception of the "good news" resulted in failure to enter God's place of rest for the wilderness generation, then it also will for the present generation (4:1–2).

(3) Though often treated in contemporary scholarship as a digression,[28] the third deliberative unit (5:11–6:20)

---

[28] Ron Guzmán and Michael W. Martin have recently outlined the case against viewing 5:11–6:20 as a digression ("Is Hebrews 5:11–6:20 Really a Digression?" *NovT* 57 [2015]: 295–310); cf., too, Fred B. Craddock, "The Letter to the Hebrews," in *The New Interpreter's Bible* (12 vols.; ed. Leander E. Keck et al.; Nashville: Abingdon Press, 1998), 10:3–173 (66); Cynthia Long Westfall, *A Discourse Analysis of the Letter to the Hebrews: The Relationship between Form and Meaning* (LNTS 297; London: T&T Clark, 2005), 144; and Paul David Landgraf, "The Structure of Hebrews: A Word of Exhortation in Light of the Day of Atonement," in *A Cloud of Witnesses: A Theology of Hebrews in its Ancient Contexts* (ed. Richard Bauckham et al.; LNTS 387; London: T&T Clark, 2008), 19–27. The view that 5:11–6:20 is a digression (whether in the technical rhetorical sense or otherwise) is commonplace in the study of Hebrews; see, e.g., Gottlieb Lünnemann, *Handbuch über den Hebräerbrief*

actually continues the third epideictic unit's reflection on the topic of education, shifting the focus from the superior training of the new covenant's high priest to the training the present community is called to undergo in view of it. Introductory verses (4:14–16)[29] introduce the first pedagogical metaphor, Jesus's *testing*, and are followed by the syncrisis of priesthoods, which continues the pedagogical theme (5:1–10). The subsequent hortatory material begins with a short rebuke that chastises the readers for essentially being untrained and immature. The rebuke features a series of metaphors drawn from Hellenistic *paideia*: the hearers are first accused of being *dull in understanding*, of being *infants in need of milk* rather than *mature* persons in need of *solid food*, of being *unskilled* rather than *trained*, and of needing to be *taught the basic elements*, though they should be *teachers* (5:11–14).[30] The rebuke leads

---

(Göttingen: Vandenhoeck and Ruprecht's, 1864), 212; William Lindsay, *Lectures on the Epistle to the Hebrews* (Edingburgh: William Oliphant, 1867), 309–10; Edgar J. Goodspeed, *The Epistle to the Hebrews* (New York: Macmillan, 1908), 64; Leon Vaganay, "La plan de l'Épître aux Hébreux," in *Memorial Lagrange* (ed. L.-H. Vincent; Paris: J. Gabalda, 1940), 269–77; Otto Michel, *Der Brief an die Hebräer* (KEK 12; Göttingen: Vandenhoeck & Ruprecht, 1966), 231; Linda L. Neeley, "A Discourse Analysis of Hebrews," *Occasional Papers in Translation and Textlinguistics* 3–4 (1987): 1–146 (33); Ellingworth, *Hebrews*, 297; Bruce, *Hebrews*, 133; Guthrie, *The Structure of Hebrews*, 110, 146; deSilva, *Perseverance in Gratitude*, 209–10; Koester, *Hebrews*, 83–6, 89, 306–7; idem, "Hebrews, Rhetoric, and the Future of Humanity," *CBQ* 64 (2002): 102–23; O'Brien, *Hebrews*, 188, 244; Steve Stanley, "The Structure of Hebrews from Three Perspectives," *Tyn Bul* 45 (1994): 245–71; Knut Backhaus, *Der Neue Bund und das Werden der Kirche:die Diatheke-Deutung des Hebräerbrief im Rahmen der frühchristlichen Theologiegeschichte* (NTAbh 29; Münster: Aschendorff, 1996), 54; Marie E. Isaacs, *Reading Hebrews and James: A Literary and Theological Commentary* (Macon: Smyth and Helwys, 2002), 80; Thompson, *Hebrews*, 119. On 5:11–6:12 as digressionary, see Peter S. Perry, *The Rhetoric of Digressions: Revelation 7:1–17 and 10:1–11:13 and Ancient Communication* (WUNT 2.268; Tübingen: Mohr Siebeck, 2009), 180–3; Gabriella Gelardini, *"Verhärtet eure Herzen nicht": Der Hebräer, eine Synagogenhomilie zu Tischa be-Aw* (BibInt 83; Leiden: Brill, 2007), 250–2; cf. Luke Timothy Johnson (an "interruption"), *Hebrews: A Commentary* (NTL; Louisville: WJK, 2006), 152.

[29] We identify 4:14–16 as a secondary *exordium* introducing the "priestly pursuits" sections devoted to education and deeds. See the discussion in Chapter 7. We also identify Heb 12:14–17 as a secondary *peroratio* that concludes the priestly pursuits section and, together with 4:14–16, brackets it. See the discussion in Chapter 8.

[30] On the pedagogical nature of these terms and metaphors, see James W. Thompson, *The Beginnings of Christian Philosophy: The Epistle to the Hebrews* (CBQMS 13; Washington, D.C.: Catholic Biblical Association of America, 1982), 29–30; Attridge, *Hebrews*, 158–61; and deSilva, *Perseverance in Gratitude*, 211–12.

naturally to the central counsel of the section, which is for the readers essentially to be trained like Christ (6:1–20). First, they are exhorted to move on to "perfection," the standard goal of Hellenistic *paideia* and the end to which Christ's curriculum of obedience-learned-through-suffering was said to have led[31] – and, correspondingly, to leave behind "basic teaching" about Christ so that the writer and his fellow teachers do not have to "lay again the foundation" of basic Christian catechesis. Second, the readers are exhorted to engage in the standard pedagogical practice of *mimesis*,[32] imitating others who, like Christ (cf. 4:15), patiently endured testing and so inherited what was promised (6:12). Abraham, a well-known exemplar of successful endurance of "testing"[33] is then cited in the syncrisis supporting this advice: if he could patiently endure the test, the writer reasons, on the basis of the promise and confirming oath given to him, certainly the readers can do the same on the basis of the more clearly revelatory promise and confirming oath given to Jesus in advance of his own testing (4:15; 5:6–10).

(4) The fourth deliberative unit (10:19–12:13) continues reflection on the topic of deeds, shifting the focus from Jesus's Melchizedekian priesthood's superior deeds to the good deeds they enable, those of the readers. If in the previous epideictic syncrisis, Jesus's Melchizedekian priestly service was shown to grant readers (as the writer summarizes it in 10:19–20) "confidence to enter the holy of holies ... through the curtain," now in three parallel, hortatory subjunctives, the writer urges readers to appropriately responsive action: to approach confidently (10:22), to hold fast to the confession (10:23), and finally, to provoke one another to *love and good*

---

[31] On "perfection" as the end goal of one's "progressing" in *paideia* or philosophical studies, see citation of evidence in chapter 2.

[32] On *mimesis* as a practice of the ancient classroom – and one with moral dimensions – see Theon 70–1. The *mimesis* in view in Hebrews takes Christ as its ultimate model.

[33] Cf. *Jubilees* 17:16–17, which records seven tests of Abraham with the seventh and final test being the sacrifice of Isaac. *Jubilees* 19:8, however, indicates that Abraham underwent ten tests, the final one being the death and burial of Sarah.

deeds (10:24). Here the writer arrives explicitly at his topical theme and the primary concern of this section, loving action (understood as ongoing commitment to the faith community, 10:25), rooting it causally in the confident approach enabled by Jesus's priestly mediation. In all the material that follows, the writer may be seen to be either encouraging such loving action or discouraging its opposite, the "sin" (10:26) of community defection (10:25). He warns readers that persistence in such sin will result in no remaining sacrifice for sin (10:26–27). He reasons in the supporting deliberative syncrisis that if apostasy under the old covenant was met with punishment, it will be met with even greater punishment in the case of the new covenant (10:28–30). He reminds readers of their own faithful deeds in the past when they had previously faced suffering, encouraging them to similar confidence and endurance in the present (10:32–39). He describes the many faithful deeds of the elders (11:1–40), upholding them as an example of the "assurance" and "conviction" (11:1) he is encouraging. He summons readers to "run the race with perseverance" (12:1–13), looking to their pioneer and perfecter and the "endurance" seen in his faithful deed (12:2–3), and seeing in their trials the deeds of a Father who is training them for their good (12:5–13).

(5) The sixth deliberative unit (12:25–29) retains the preceding epideictic unit's focus on the topics of death and events after death, continuing the juxtaposition of Sinai–earth and Zion–heaven as contrasting *eschata* of access and, in particular, the juxtaposition of the divine voice deriving from those mountains. The unit's essential counsel is for readers not to refuse God's voice that warns them. Its supporting syncrisis explicitly cites the contrast drawn in the preceding epideictic unit between the voices heard at the two mountains, arguing that if refusing the voice that "warned them on earth" resulted in no escape from the "death" it promised, then refusing the voice that "warns from heaven" will most certainly result in no escape from the final judgment it promises. A deliberative proof follows drawing a further distinction between the two voices: whereas the voice at Sinai

merely shook the earth, the voice speaking from Zion will shake the heavens and earth, so that only that which is not shakable – Zion itself – will remain. The point of the syncrisis is made explicit in the counsel that follows, and again the focus has in view final vindication and salvation (events beyond death): the readers should give awe-filled thanks for what will remain once the heavenly voice speaks, the unshakeable kingdom of Zion that they are receiving.

Conclusion

In view of the analysis above, it is possible to sketch the essential structure of Hebrews's argument in outline form. The previous chapter demonstrated that five epideictic syncrises supply the structuring principle. These syncrises, we argued, function collectively as a comparison of covenants, old and new, pointing to the latter as the superior. These syncrises, moreover, are arranged chronologically according to encomiastic topics analogous to those prescribed for comparing persons in syncritical compositions. What the present chapter has shown is that each of these epideictic syncrises has a corresponding deliberative syncrisis that takes up (a) the former's syncritical verdict as the premise on which the latter logically proceeds and (b) the former's encomiastic topic, which serves as the thematic heading of the entire deliberative unit in which the deliberative syncrisis is situated. The result is that each epideictic-deliberative pairing is tied together (a) logically, with epideictic rhetoric serving what may be seen as Hebrews's ultimately deliberative aim – namely, to encourage perseverance in the faith and, correspondingly, to discourage apostasy – and (b) thematically, with five rhetorical topics functioning conventionally as compositional headings of this "word of exhortation." These relationships are illustrated in the following general outline of Hebrews:[34]

I. Covenant Origins – Angels vs. Jesus
   a. Epideictic (1:5–14): The new covenant has greater origins with the superior mediator.

---

[34] Our analysis has left four units as remainder: 1:1–4, 4:14–16, 12:14–17, and 13:1–25. These we subsequently identify respectively as *exordium*, secondary *exordium*, secondary *peroratio*, and *peroratio*. See the discussions of Chs. 7 and 8.

   b. Deliberative (2:1–18): Pay greater attention to/do
      not neglect the salvation announced by the superior
      covenant mediator.
II. Covenant Births – Moses vs. Jesus
   a. Epideictic (3:1–6): The new covenant has greater
      beginnings via the better-born inaugurator.
   b. Deliberative (3:7–4:13): Do not listen faithlessly to
      the gospel announced "Today" by the better-born
      covenant inaugurator.
III. Covenant Education – Aaronic High Priests vs. Jesus
   a. Epideictic (5:1–10): The new covenant's high priest
      is the better-trained.
   b. Deliberative (5:11–6:20): Undergo the new covenant's
      high priest's better training of faithful endurance
      based upon better promises.
IV. Covenant Deeds – Levitical priestly ministry vs. Mel-
    chizedekian priestly ministry
   a. Epideictic (7:1–10:18): The deeds of the new coven-
      ant's priestly ministry are superior.
   b. Deliberative (10:19–12:13): Enabled by the greater
      deeds of the new covenant priestly ministry, approach,
      hold fast, and provoke one another to loving action,
      not defecting from the covenant community.
V. Covenant Deaths/Events beyond Death – Sinai vs. Zion
   a. Epideictic (12:18–24): The new covenant's mountain
      of eschatological access to God is superior.
   b. Deliberative (12:25–29): Do not refuse the voice
      speaking a better word of final vindication from the
      mountain of better, eschatological access to God.

With these results in view, we are now ready to take up in Part 2 of
this book an analysis of Hebrews's arrangement via the traditional
divisions of *exordium, narratio, argumentatio,* and *peroratio.* Indeed,
key features identified in the study thus far – epideictic syncrisis,
deliberative syncrisis, the logical relationship of one to the other, and
the topical ordering of each – will prove, in the light of ancient
rhetorical theory, to be among several key evidences of arrangement – and arrangement, in turn, among several key evidences of
Hebrews's ultimately deliberative aim.

Part 2

Arranging the Speech

The Ancient Rhetorical Design of Hebrews

4

ARRANGING AN ANCIENT SPEECH

Ancient Compositional Theory and a Proposal for Modern Analysis

In the previous chapters we have put forward an argument concerning the *structure* of Hebrews, outlining the speech in terms of five major sections, each of which begins with epideictic comparison showing the superiority of the new covenant to the old, and each of which proceeds to deliberative comparison showing that if perseverance was advantageous, or apostasy disadvantageous, in the case of old covenant experience, it is all the more so in the case of new covenant experience. We have also put forward an argument concerning the *genre* and *purpose* of Hebrews, that it is a deliberative speech with a classically deliberative aim: to show the advantage of a proposed course of action (namely, perseverance in the faith) and the disadvantage of its alternative (namely, apostasy). In the second part of this book, we put forward an argument concerning the *arrangement* of Hebrews that draws on and incorporates these conclusions. Our thesis is that the sermon is ordered conventionally in accordance with the rules of rhetoric, and that this arrangement lends further, clarifying light to the question of the speech's genre and purpose.

We begin our analysis with an introductory survey of the theory of rhetorical arrangement, noting the traditional headings employed and their traditional order. Moreover, on the basis of this survey we propose a new methodological starting place for any analysis of arrangement. Our argument is that such analysis should begin with identification of the only heading essential to a speech, the *argumentatio* – and not, as has been often proposed, the *propositio*. This chapter thus sets the stage, with regard to both content and methodology, for the analysis of Hebrews that follows.

Arrangement in Ancient Rhetorical Theory

In Hellenistic and Roman rhetorical training, arrangement was considered one of the five tasks of the orator alongside invention,

style, delivery, and memory.[1] Depending on the theorist, there could be four, five, six, or even seven parts by which a speech was arranged.[2] The four-part schema consisted of *exordium* (introduction), *narratio* (statement of facts), *argumentatio* (thesis and proof), and *peroratio* (conclusion). This schema was expanded in various ways primarily by elevating elements of the *argumentatio* – theses, subtheses, proofs for, proofs against – to full heading status. The order and function of the headings were well-established and may be sketched in brief.

The *exordium* (also *principium*, προοίμιον) or introduction served as the "beginning" of the speech. Most theorists agreed its goal was "simply to prepare the hearer to be more favourably inclined towards [the speaker] for the rest of the proceedings" (Quintilian, *Inst.* 4.1.5 [Russell, LCL]).

The *narratio* (also διήγησις), which usually came after the *exordium*, was traditionally a biased exposition of the case itself (e.g., of the crime in a judicial trial). By the first century CE, however, it had come to be understood more broadly to include any kind of opening narrative serving the case (e.g., a narrative incriminating the opposition or amplifying the honor of a party in the case).

The *argumentatio* (also *quaestio/ones*, πίστις, ἀποδείξις) was the heart of the speech, the place where the case was demonstrated. According to Quintilian, *argumentatio* consisted of proofs enlisted in support of a thesis or theses (*Inst.* 3.9.2–3; 4.4.1). Several theorists divided this material under two distinct major headings, the

---

[1] E.g., Rhet. Her. 1.3; Cicero, *De or.* 2.79. For a discussion on the development of these tasks among ancient theorists see Malcolm Heath, "Codifications of Rhetoric," in *The Cambridge Companion to Ancient Rhetoric* (ed. Erik Gunderson; Cambridge: Cambridge University Press, 2009), 59–74.

[2] In *De or.* 2.79, Cicero has Antonius summarize standard elements of rhetorical teaching. Concerning arrangement, Antonius acknowledges that speeches are arranged according to four (e.g., Aristotle *Rhet.* 3.13.4 [1414b]; Cicero, *Part. or.* 4; *Top.* 97–8), five (e.g., Quintilian, *Inst.* 3.9.1), six (e.g., Rhet. Her. 1.4.; Cicero, *Inv.* 1.19), or even seven subdivisions depending on the preference of the authority. Anonymous Seguerianus divides political speeches into four parts (προοίμιον, διηγήσις, πίστις, ἐπίλογος). For further discussion on arrangement see Michael de Brauw, "The Parts of the Speech," in *A Companion to Greek Rhetoric* (ed. Ian Wortherington; Malden: Blackwell, 2007), 187–202; Wilhelm Wuellner, "Arrangement," in *Handbook of Classical Rhetoric in the Hellenistic Period (330 B.C.–A.D. 400)* (ed. Stanley E. Porter; Leiden: Brill, 1997), 51–87; Malcolm Heath, "Invention," in *Handbook of Classical Rhetoric in the Hellenistic Period (330 B.C.–A.D. 400)* (ed. Stanley E. Porter; Leiden: Brill, 1997), 89–119, esp. 103–18.

confirmatio (also *probatio*) or argumentation for one's own case, and the *refutatio* (also *confutatio*, *reprehensio*, προκατάληψις) or argumentation against the opponent's case.[3] Others, however, rejected this division and followed the Aristotelian preference for treating all argumentation under a single heading (πίστις; cf. *Rhet.* 3.13.4–5 [1414b]).[4] Some theorists also treated the thesis, or *propositio* (also *expositio*, πρόθεσις), as a separate heading prior to the *argumentatio* or *confirmatio*. Others furthermore prescribed an additional heading after or in place of the *propositio*, namely the *partitio* (also, *enumeratio*, *divisio*), which was a statement dividing a complex thesis into constituent subtheses. While some theorists thus gave first-order heading status of some kind to the thesis, most shared Quintilian's judgment that thesis and proof are intricately related and therefore best treated under a single heading (see esp. *Inst.* 3.9.2–3).[5]

The *peroratio* (also *conclusio*, επίλογος) was the conclusion of the speech. Here the speaker summarized key arguments and attempted to make the audience emotionally disposed to render the desired verdict.

It is important to note that actual speech-making did not always follow traditional arrangement. All parts except the *argumentatio* were considered optional.[6] Some theorists omit *narratio* or *refutatio*

---

[3] See also Übelacker in Chapter 1 who identifies the *probatio* and *refutatio* as elements of the *argumentatio*.

[4] So too Anonymous Seguerianus 186 – which may suggest the Greek tradition especially gravitated to the Aristotelian model. Quintilian thinks Aristotle and those who follow him are mistaken to make refutation part of proof on the grounds that they serve two different functions in the argument of a speech (cf. *Inst.* 3.9.5). In Rhet. Her. 1.18 and 3.8, proof and refutation are treated together though the theorist assigns them distinct first-level headings in the arrangement of a speech. Again, Cicero in *De or.* 2.307 similarly treats these elements closely together, writing, "for to make some prefatory remarks, then to set out our case, afterwards to prove it by establishing our points with arguments and refuting our adversary's points, then to wind up our case and so come to a conclusion – this is the procedure enjoined by the very nature of oratory" (Sutton and Rackham, LCL). See also Cicero, *Inv.* 1.78. In *Inst.* 4.praef.6, Quintilian brings together confirmation and refutation under the singular heading of proof when he considers "how credibility is achieved in Proofs, either in confirming our own propositions or in demolishing those of our opponents" (Russell, LCL).

[5] A minority of theorists endorsed more elaborate schemes wherein the *digressio* (also *digressus*, *egressio*, *eggressus*, *excursus*, παρέκβασις) served as a fixed element either prior to the *argumentatio* or as a lead-in to the *peroratio*. Most theorists, however, joined Quintilian in defining it as a departure, anywhere, from the basic arrangement of the speech—and so saw the assignment to it of a fixed place in the speech an absurdity (see Ron Guzmán and Michael W. Martin, "Is Hebrews 5:11–6:20 Really a Digression?" *NovT* 57 [2015]: 295–310).

[6] See esp. Quintilian, *Inst.* 5.praef.5. Also see Aristotle, *Rhet.* 3.13.2–4, where the proposition and proof are the essential elements of a speech.

altogether from their schemas. Several theorists, too, commend flexible and innovative use of the handbook templates. As cited in Chapter 1, Cicero instructs readers to adapt arrangement to fit the purpose of the speech (*Part. or.* 11–15; *De or.* 2.307–8) – a practice he himself follows regularly.[7] Rhetorica ad Herennium similarly states:

> But there is also another Arrangement, which, when we must depart from the order imposed by the rules of the art, is accommodated to circumstance in accordance with the speaker's judgement; for example, if we should begin our speech with the Statement of Facts [*narratione*], or with some very strong argument, or the reading of some documents; or if straightway after the Introduction [*principium*] we should use the proof [*confirmatione*] and then the Statement of Facts; or if we should make some other change of this kind in the order.... It is often necessary to employ such changes and transpositions when the cause itself obliges us to modify with art the Arrangement prescribed by the rules of art. (3.17 [Caplan, LCL])

The traditional schemas of arrangement, however, were drawn from the common practice of the day, reinforced as a fixed feature of Greco-Roman education, and prescribed in manuals with more of a practical than pedagogical focus. It is with good cause, then, that we raise the question of whether Hebrews, an ancient speech that consistently displays conventional rhetorical invention and style, also displays conventional arrangement.[8]

---

[7] See D. H. Berry and Andrew Erskine, "Form and Function," in *Form and Function in Roman Oratory* (ed. D. H. Berry and Andrew Erskine; Cambridge: Cambridge University Press, 2010), 1–17.

[8] Scholars routinely point out the copious stylistic features and patterns of argumentation in Hebrews that are found in the rhetorical handbooks. Cf. Ceslas Spicq, *L'Épître aux Hébreux* (2 vols.; EB; Paris: J. Gabalda, 1952–1953), 1:351–78; George H. Guthrie, *The Structure of Hebrews: A Text-Linguistic Analysis* (NovTSup 73; Leiden: Brill, 1994), 33, 39–40; idem., "Hebrews in Its First-Century Contexts: Recent Research," in *The Face of New Testament Studies: A Survey of Recent Research* (ed. Scot McKnight and Grant R. Osborne; Grand Rapids: Baker, 2004), 419–25; Harold W. Attridge *The Epistle to the Hebrews* (Hermeneia; Philadelphia: Fortress, 1989), 20–21; William L. Lane, *Hebrews 1–8* (WBC 47A; Nashville: Thomas Nelson Publishers, 1991), lxxx; David A. deSilva, *Perseverance in Gratitude: A Socio-Rhetorical Commentary on the Epistle "to the Hebrews"* (Grand Rapids: Eerdmans, 2000), 52–8. See also, Hermut Löhr, "Reflections of Rhetorical Terminology in Hebrews," in *Hebrews: Contemporary Methods – New Insights* (ed. Gabriella Gelardini; BibInt 75;

A Methodological Proposal

The theorists' comments concerning flexibility of arrangement warrant caution when attempting to identify any headings of rhetorical arrangement employed in Hebrews. Certainly one should not always expect a traditional outline in its traditional order. Jerome Murphy-O'Connor, citing the passage above from Rhetorica ad Herennium, has criticized interpreters of Paul's letters for taking just such an approach and arriving, as a consequence, at sometimes forced analyses wherein minor paragraphs occupy major components of arrangement.[9]

Our analysis, rather, should proceed with some controls. Murphy-O'Connor, following Benoît Standaert and Jean-Noël Aletti, suggests beginning with identification of the *propositio* (*i.e.*, the thesis), remembering, of course, that rhetoricians allow for multiple theses.[10] This approach has much to commend it. The *propositio*, when present, is the turning point of the speech. It summarizes the claim of the case often just after it has been narrated, and just before it will be argued. And in complex cases, the *propositio* will be subdivided into numerous subtheses, which grant further, valuable insight into the speech's organization.

The problem with such an approach, however, is that not all theorists prescribe – or even mention – the *propositio* as a separate and distinct heading in the outline of a speech. Quintilian, as we have said, counts himself among a majority that subsumes *propositio* under the *argumentatio*.[11] And as Quintilian further observes, the thesis may be multipart, mixed throughout the *argumentatio*, or left unstated because it is obvious to all parties (cf. *Inst.* 4.4.1–4.5.28). For these reasons, the *propositio* as separate and primary category in a rhetorical outline simply cannot serve as a reliable starting point for an analysis of arrangement.

Atlanta: SBL, 2005), 199–210; Brian C. Small, *The Characterization of Jesus in the Book of Hebrews* (BIS 128; Leiden, Brill, 2014). Origen as well acknowledges the rhetorical artistry of Hebrews (cf. Eusebius, *Hist. eccl.* 6.25.11–12).

[9] Jerome Murphy-O'Connor, *Paul the Letter Writer: His World, His Options, His Skills* (Good News Studies 41; Collegeville, MN: Michael Glazier, 1995), 83–4.

[10] Murphy-O'Connor, *Paul the Letter Writer*, 84; Benoît Standaert, *L'évangile selon Marc: Composition et genre littéraire* (Nijmegen: Stichting Studentenpers, 1978) 80; Jean-Noël Aletti, "La présence d'un modèle rhétorique en Romains: Son role et son importance," *Biblica* 71 (1990): 1–24 (esp. 9–12).

[11] Cf. Anonymous Seguerianus 160–1.

We propose, instead, to begin our analysis with identification of the *argumentatio*, which consists of proof enlisted in support of a thesis. The *argumentatio* was, after all, the heart of the speech, and the only essential part as well. Aristotle states that the two necessary parts of a speech are thesis (πρόθεσις) and proof (πίστις).[12] According to Rhet. Her. 1.18, "the entire hope of victory and the entire method of persuasion rests on proof and refutation, for when we have submitted our arguments and destroyed those of the opposition, we have, of course, completely fulfilled the speaker's function" (Caplan, LCL). Quintilian writes, "Lastly, of the five parts into which we divided the forensic speech, any one of the other four may sometimes be unnecessary for the Cause; but there is no dispute which does not need a Proof" (*Inst.* 5.praef.5 [Russell, LCL]). Quintilian recommends that the construction of every speech begin with considering the question at issue and the arguments for and against it. Only then could the other parts of the speech be effectively composed (cf. *Inst.* 3.9.6). Furthermore, he writes, "[A]ll the other things, which are developed more in the continuous sweep of oratory, are devised simply to help adorn Arguments" (*Inst.* 5.8.2 [Russell, LCL]).

The advantage of beginning our analysis with the *argumentatio* is that certain controls can guide our investigation. As we shall see, the individual proofs prescribed for the *argumentatio* have a recognizable form and content, and by rule these are generally – though not absolutely – reserved for the *argumentatio*. In other words, where proofs in support of a thesis constitute the primary mode of discourse, we find *argumentatio*. Identification of these proofs, moreover, will clearly point us to the thesis (or theses) that they support – whether stated under a distinct *propositio* or *partitio*, subsumed together with proof under the single heading of *argumentatio*, or left implied. Identification of proofs also will reveal whether the author has intermingled proof and refutation under a single heading or kept them separate under two distinct headings,

---

[12] Cf. *Rhet.* 3.13.2–4 (1414a–b). Aristotle goes on two delineate a four-part arrangement schema (προοίμιον, πρόθεσις, πίστις, ἐπίλογος). Quintilian states that Aristotle introduces a novelty by putting the thesis (*propositio*, πρόθεσις) in place of the statement of facts (*narratio*, διήγησις). Quintilian explains that Aristotle has done this because he considers the thesis the genius and the statement of facts the species, which is not always necessary (cf. *Inst.* 3.9.5). Some later theorists would elevate the *propositio* to a separate first order heading after the *narratio* (Rhet. Her. 1.4; cf. Cicero, *De or.* 1.143).

probatio and *refutatio*. Further, identification of *argumentatio* makes possible the identification of any other headings logically dependent upon it – the *narratio*, which leads into and serves the *argumentatio* in one of several, prescribed ways, and the *exordium* and *peroratio*, whose functions are determined in large part by the main argument of the speech. For these reasons, we begin our analysis of Hebrews's arrangement with *argumentatio* and allow insights from that chapter to determine the shape of the study thereafter.

5

PROVING THE CASE

Argumentatio *in Hebrews*

The task of the present chapter is to identify any *argumentatio* that may occur in Hebrews. To this end, we survey *argumentatio* as it is described in the handbooks, noting key elements identified by the theorists: the three aims of *argumentatio*, the types of proof it employs, the topics or search headings it takes up, the kind of amplification found within it, and the theses or *propositiones* it supports. The survey attends, in particular, to those aspects of *argumentatio* that will be especially relevant to our discussion of Hebrews. Then on the basis of this survey, and employing its categories, we identify those materials in Hebrews that conform to the theorists' descriptions. Our argument is that the five sections we earlier identified as the deliberative units (2:1–18; 3:7–4:13; 5:11 6:20; 10:19–12:13; 12:25–29) display the essential characteristics of *argumentatio*. That is, they have a characteristic aim of *argumentatio* in that they attempt to show that a proposed course of action is advantageous or disadvantageous, they employ the kind of inductive and deductive proofs prescribed for *argumentatio*, their proofs take up prescribed topics of *argumentatio*, their amplification is argumentative in nature, and they feature the kind of *propositiones* prescribed for *argumentatio*, *propositiones* that are recognizable from the relationship they bear to their proofs and their frequently hortatory form. These factors lead us to the conclusion that the five deliberative units collectively constitute the *argumentatio* of the speech.

Argumentatio among the Theorists

According to the theorists, *argumentatio* consists essentially of proof in support of a thesis or theses. It is the heart of the speech, and the place where the central aims of the speech are accomplished. Naturally, the theorists categorize *argumentatio* first by these aims, distinguishing three that correspond to the three species of rhetoric.

Argumentative Aims

At least as early as the classical period, rhetoricians divided speeches into three primary species: deliberative, judicial, and epideictic. Each of these species has characteristic features and aims, and the *argumentatio* is most centrally where they are displayed. In deliberative speeches, the theorists observe that the *argumentatio* takes as its central task exhortation and dissuasion. In such a speech, the *argumentatio* addresses the audience as a judge facing a decision about the future and enlists proofs to show that a proposed course of action is advantageous or disadvantageous.[1] In judicial speeches, the *argumentatio* takes the form of accusation and blame. It addresses the audience as a judge facing a decision about the past and enlists proofs to show that accusations against a defendant are just or unjust. In epideictic speeches, the *argumentatio* takes the form of praise and blame. In such a speech, the *argumentatio* addresses the audience as a "spectator" (critic) of the orator's skill and does not ask the audience to render a judgment. Thus in its traditional form, at least, it consists of no argumentation *per se* (that is, of thesis and

---

[1] While theorists often spoke of the predominant aim of advantage/disadvantage, some theorists identified multiple aims. Stephen Usher ("Symbouleutic Oratory," in *A Companion to Greek Rhetoric* [ed. Ian Worthington; Blackwell Companions to the Ancient World; Malden: Blackwell, 2007], 220–35) in his analysis of Greek symbouleutic oratory regularly identifies the three topics of justice, expediency, and possibility as the common topics or proposals put forward in the speeches. Cicero also points to the necessary, the honorable, and the advantageous as topics well suited to deliberative causes (*Inv.* 1.96; *De or.* 2.336; cf. Aristotle, *Rhet.* 1.4.2 [1359a]). Quintilian discusses the three main topics or proposals that are common to deliberative oratory: the possible, the honorable, and the expedient (cf. *Inst.* 3.8.22–25). There were also the τελικὰ κεφάλαια ("headings of purpose") for evaluating actions that included such topics as the just (δίκαιον), the expedient (συμφέρον), the noble (καλόν), the possible (δύνατον), the necessary (ἀναγκαῖον), the appropriate (πρέπον), and potential circumstances (ἐκβησόμενον) (see Heinrich Lausberg, *Handbook of Literary Rhetoric: A Foundation for Literary Study* [ed. David Orton and R. Dean Anderson; trans. Matthew Bliss, Annemiek Jansen, and David Orton; Leiden: Brill, 1998], § 375). The τελικὰ κεφάλαια were especially useful to deliberative causes. For example, Hermogenes marshals the topics of justice, expediency, possibility, and appropriateness to deliberate whether to marry (11; cf. Theon 11). In his discussion of argumentative topics for deliberative oratory, Anaximenes of Lampsacus in *Rhet. Alex.* 1 (1421b) lists δίκαιον, νόμιμον, συμφέρον, καλόν, ἡδύ, ῥάδιον, and ἀναγκαῖον (cf. Cicero, *Inv.* 2.156–76). Quintilian lists many of these topics as species of the possible, the honorable, and the expedient (cf. *Inst.* 3.8.26–27). In this study, we follow the quintessential theoretical understanding of deliberative rhetoric in our contention that all of Hebrews's deliberative claims can be consistently understood as arguments for the advantage/disadvantage of a proposed course of action. This is not to deny, however, that in some cases the more elaborate schemes provide *topoi* that capture the particular nuance of the advantage/disadvantage in question.

proof), but rather, only of amplification, or speech showing that something is greater.[2] The theorists observe that while epideictic praise and blame may function as the heart of an epideictic speech, more often it functions as amplification in support of nonepideictic causes (Quintilian, *Inst.* 3.7.1–6).[3] Epideictic praise and blame, then, cannot automatically be interpreted as constituting *argumentatio*. By contrast, deliberative exhortation and dissuasion, and judicial accusation and blame, when demonstrated by supporting proof, can only be interpreted as *argumentatio*, as the theorists do not prescribe for such materials an auxiliary role within speeches of a different species. This observation has obvious implications for Hebrews, which displays a relatively even mixture of deliberative exhortation/dissuasion and epideictic praise/blame. In the present chapter we point to numerous factors that further suggest that the speech's exhortation and dissuasion should be viewed as functioning characteristically as *argumentatio* and reflecting the central aims of the speech, while in the subsequent chapter we highlight numerous factors that further suggest that the speech's praise and blame is functioning in its characteristically subservient fashion, and in a specific auxiliary role commonly assigned to epideictic, the incidental *narratio*.

Argumentative Proofs

Any discussion of the proofs that the theorists consider characteristic of the *argumentatio* must address the shifting meaning of

---

[2] "In epideictic speeches, amplification is employed as a rule, to prove that things are honourable or useful; for the facts must be taken on trust, since proofs of these are rarely given, and only if they are incredible or the responsibility is attributed to another" (Aristotle, *Rhet.* 3.16.3 [1417b] [Freese, LCL]). See the discussion in Lausberg, *Handbook of Literary Rhetoric*, § 61. Though epideictic traditionally dealt in matters that were certain (e.g., the praiseworthiness of a city founder), alternatives emerged wherein the praiseworthiness of a subject was in dispute. In such cases epideictic became biased, like deliberative and judicial, and pursued demonstration via proof. Cf. Quintilian, who while acknowledging that the proper function of epideictic is amplification rather than argumentation, nonetheless allows that epideictic employs "proof" in biased or "practical" speechmaking, and even "semblance of proof" in the kind meant only for "display" (*Inst.* 3.7.1–6).

[3] Cf. Rhet. Her. 3.15: "Nor should this kind of cause [i.e., the epideictic] be the less strongly recommended just because it presents itself only seldom in life. Indeed, when a task may present itself, be it only occasionally, the ability to perform it as skillfully as possible must seem desirable. And if epideictic is only seldom employed by itself independently, still in judicial and deliberative causes extensive sections are often devoted to praise or blame. Therefore, let us believe that this kind of cause must also claim some measure of our industry" (Caplan, LCL).

"proofs" (πίστεις) among the ancient theorists.[4] In traditional rhetoric at the time of Aristotle, the term *proofs* (πίστεις) originally referred to the logical arguments that constituted the part of speech (*partes orationis*) that went by the same name. Aristotle, however, expanded the term to encompass all means of persuasion available to the orator. This included persuasion both intrinsic and extrinsic to the speech, or what Aristotle referred to respectively as *artistic* and *artless* proofs (*Rhet.* 1.2.2 [1355b]).[5] By artless proofs Aristotle meant those forms of persuasion that the orator did not have to create: laws, witnesses, contracts, testimonies from torture, and oaths (cf. *Rhet.* 1.15.2–3 [1375a]).[6] These evidences were extrinsic to the speech in that they were entered into the record before the orator spoke, though of course they could become subject matter in the speech itself. By artistic proofs, Aristotle meant those forms of persuasion created by the rhetorician and intrinsic to the speech in its entirety. These he divided into three types: *ethos*, or persuasion deriving from the character of the speaker; *pathos*, or persuasion that is accomplished through the shaping of the audience's emotions; and *logos*, or logical argumentation (cf. *Rhet.* 1.2.3–6 [1356a–b]). Of these, only *logos* was assigned by Aristotle specifically to the part of the speech (*partes orationis*) known traditionally as the proofs. Aristotle writes, "So then the necessary parts of a speech are the statement of the case and proof [πίστις]. These divisions are appropriate to every speech, and at most the parts are four in number – exordium, statement, proof [πίστις], epilogue" (cf. *Rhet.* 3.13.4–5 [1414b] [Freese, LCL]).[7] That he has in mind only *logical* proofs is evident from the discussion that ensues: the only proofs he mentions are enthymeme and example, his two classes of logical proof (cf. *Rhet.* 3.17.1–16 [1417b–1418b] and below).

The concern of the present chapter is with the narrower and traditional sense of proofs or *logos* according to Aristotle, since

[4] See the programmatic articles by Friedrich Solmsen, "The Aristotelian Tradition in Ancient Rhetoric," *AJP* 62 (1941): 35–50, 169–90.

[5] See Quintilian, *Inst.* 5.1.1, who describes the division as nearly universal. Cf. Anaximenes of Lampsacus, *Rhet. Alex.* 7 (1428a); Cicero, *De or.* 2.116; Anonymous Seguerianus 145. The division is absent, however, in Cicero's early and influential *De Inventione* (see 1.51–77, where the only division attested is that of induction and deduction).

[6] Quintilian's list is similar: previous decisions, rumors, evidence from torture, documents, oaths, and witnesses (*Inst.* 5.1.2).

[7] This statement is in distinction from *Rhet.* 3.1.1 (1403b) where Aristotle talks about proofs (πίστεις) distinct from style and arrangement and means the three types of artistic proofs (ethos, pathos, logos).

virtually all theorists treat these as characteristic of, and prescribe them for, the *argumentatio*. Aristotle, despite broadening the notion of proofs, continues, as we have said, to explicate the section of the speech known as the proofs in terms of logical argumentation. Similarly a young Cicero, in his highly influential *De Inventione*, describes only two classes of proof for the part of the speech that he identifies as the *confirmatio* – the deductive and inductive – and so reflects the traditional narrower understanding of proof as logical argumentation (*Inv.* 1.51–77).[8] Indeed Quintilian, in surveying the state of theory with regard to the proofs as a part of the speech, describes two camps: those theorists who say the sole function of the *argumentatio* is logical persuasion, and those who say it is the primary and essential function (*Inst.* 5.praef.1–5). Without choosing sides, Quintilian declares logical argumentation to be the sole focus of his book on proofs. Given this state of affairs, we take logical proofs as the tell-tale sign of *argumentatio*, and so will focus our efforts on identifying them as such in Hebrews.[9]

According to the theorists, there were two classes of logical proofs, the enthymeme (or deductive argument) and example (or inductive argument).[10] By the second century CE, enthymemes could be broadly characterized by their logic, assumptions, and style – that is, they were deductive, they were adapted to the social location of

---

[8] A more mature Cicero, perhaps influenced by years of experience, attempted to revive *ethos* and *pathos* as means of persuasion on par with *logos* (*De or.* 2.114–15, 128, 310), but his effort had little impact on the field if subsequent extant handbooks are any indication. Cicero's *De Inventione*, though a youthful work dismissed by Cicero himself, remained his most influential rhetorical handbook even into the late middle ages. See James Jerome Murphy, *Rhetorical Theory from Saint Augustine to the Renaissance* (Berkeley: University of California Press, 1974), 108–9.

[9] One could also include artless proofs as a potential sign of *argumentatio*. Quintilian appears to include them along with the logical proofs as subject matter for the *argumentatio* (*Inst.* 5.1.1–7.37). Cicero (*De Inventione*), like Aristotle, does not. In fact, Quintilian acknowledges there are those who would eliminate artless proofs from their discussion of the rules of oratory (*Inst.* 5.1.2). We will therefore treat rational argumentation as the one sure sign of *argumentatio*, while being open to the possibility that artless proofs may function in Hebrews as persuasion generally available in the speech or proofs specific to the *argumentatio*.

[10] In this study we follow the Greek tradition that runs from Aristotle (*Rhet.* 1.2.8–9 [1356a–b]) to Anonymous Seguerianus (146) in speaking of examples (παράδειγμα) and enthymemes (ἐνθύμημα) as the inductive and deductive forms of proofs (πίστεις) respectively; cf. Apsines, *Rhet.* 8.1 (285), who uses the same two terms for rhetorical induction and deduction respectively but under the heading of ἐπιχείρημα, by which he means logical argument. Quintilian, by contrast, attests the use of both enthymeme and epicheireme as terms for deductive argumentation (cf. *Inst.* 5.10.1).

the audience, and they were typically brief.[11] Aristotle emphasized the deductive nature of the enthymeme when he described it as a "syllogism of a kind [συλλογισμός τίς]."[12] Likewise, Cicero describes what Aristotle calls an enthymeme as "a form of argument which draws a probable conclusion from the fact under consideration" (*Inv.* 1.57 [Hubbell, LCL]). Quintilian observes that all authorities had a common understanding of enthymeme "as a reasoning which lends credence to what is doubtful by means of what is certain" (*Inst.* 5.10.8 [Russell, LCL]) – or, as Quintilian later puts it, "proof-giving reasoning, by which one thing is inferred from another, and which confirms what is doubtful by means of what is not doubtful." (*Inst.* 5.10.11–12 [Russell, LCL]).

Enthymemes were also adapted to the social location of the audience. Aristotle explains that the uneducated are often more persuasive than the educated because they "speak of what they know and what more nearly concerns the audience. Wherefore one must not argue from all possible opinions, but only from such as are definite and admitted, for instance, either by the judges themselves or by those whose judgment they approve. Further, it should be clear that this is the opinion of all or most of the hearers" (*Rhet.* 2.22.3 [1395b–1396a] [Freese, LCL]). Quintilian lists the kinds of sure premises from which conclusions could be drawn:

> Now we regard as certain (1) things perceived by the senses, for example what we see or hear (Signs come under this head); (2) things about which common opinion is unanimous: the existence of the gods, the duty of respecting parents; (3) the provision of laws; (4) what has been accepted as moral custom, if not in the belief of all mankind, at least in that of the city or nation where the case is being pleaded – many matters of right, for example, involve custom rather than

---

[11] Manfred Kraus, "Theories and Practice of Enthymeme in the First Centuries B.C.E. and C.E.," in *Rhetorical Argumentation in Biblical Texts: Essays from the Lund 2000 Conference* (ed. Anders Eriksson, Thomas H. Olbricht, and Walter Übelacker; Emory Studies in Early Christianity 8; Harrisburg: Trinity Press International, 2002), 99–100. Kraus lists these elements as the logical, psychological, and stylistic factors which follows Thomas Conley's ("The Enthymeme in Perspective," *QJS* 70 [1984]: 174) three main headings used to describe enthymemes during this period.

[12] Translation of Aristotle follows David E. Aune's suggestion in "The Use and Abuse of the Enthymeme in New Testament Scholarship," *NTS* 49 (2003): 303. Cf. Conley, "The Enthymeme in Perspective," 169, who notes that enthymemes are essentially deductive arguments.

laws; (5) whatever is agreed between both parties; (6) whatever has been proved; (7) lastly, whatever is not contradicted by the opponent. So this is the way in which the Argument will be formed: Since the world is governed by Providence, the state must also be controlled; <it follows that the state must be controlled,> if it is clear that the world is governed by Providence. (*Inst.* 5.10.12–14 [Russell, LCL])

Both Aristotle and Quintilian's comments with regard to item 4 show that premises did not have to have universal consent but could be community-specific. This was especially true in the case of common opinion, provision of laws, and moral custom. Furthermore, Quintilian's observations regarding item 6 show that premises could be considered certain because they had been previously demonstrated by the orator. Thus Anonymous Seguerianus states, "Enthymeme, according to Neocles, is language concerning something that has been posited (προειρημένων) or concerning what is antecedent, and stating the conclusion summarily and compactly when the hearers have some understanding (of the premises)" (157 [Dilts and Kennedy]).[13] We have already seen how this is the case in Hebrews, where deliberative comparisons from the lesser (a form of enthymeme, see below) proceed on the basis of an assumed premise, demonstrated in the immediately preceding epideictic section, concerning which comparative subject is the lesser and which the greater.

Enthymemes, thus, did not have to state explicitly all their premises – or even their conclusions – but in fact often left some of them implied and so were stylistically succinct. Brevity was not an absolute quality. Some, like Cicero, understood that the rhetorical syllogism could be longer and complete (five-part according to Cicero). Cicero also recognized that the syllogism could be reduced to four, three, two, or even one of its parts (*Inv.* 1.57, 67).[14] Simple

---

[13] Anonymous Seguerianus seems to articulate two broad categories, namely, what the author assumed his audience knew or believed (what is antecedent) and what the orator had previously established in the speech (what has been posited). This is very close to a general characterization of Quintilian's sure premises. Cf. Conley, "Enthymeme," 175, who notes that the term "προειρημένων" in the quote from Anonymous Seguerianus indicates that the needed premises were supplied beforehand not by the audience but by the speaker (or his or her opponent).

[14] Cicero's five-part syllogism consisted of a major premise, proof of a major premise, a minor premise, proof of a minor premise, and a conclusion. The truncated syllogism as he describes it could be so simple as to include a single stated premise and conclusion, or even either one by itself with the other implied (though Cicero disapproves, he attests others who do not).

forms were more often advocated: a deductive argument from contraries or from consequences; a maxim with a reason; or even a "consideration."[15] Thus, according to Aristotle, enthymemes often used fewer premises (cf. *Rhet.* 1.2.13 [1357a]; 2.22.1–2 [1395b]). Because of the succinct, audience-oriented, and sometimes truncated character of the syllogism, theorists labeled the enthymeme as a rhetorical or incomplete syllogism.[16] Eventually, in the first and second centuries CE, some theorists would come to define the enthymeme as a syllogism with a missing premise.[17]

Enthymemes took typical forms derived from their deductive character. One common form expressed the premise in a causal since-, because-, or for- clause, and the conclusion in the main clause.[18] Aristotle uses the example, "She has given birth, for she has milk" (*Rhet.* 1.2.18 [1357b] [Freese, LCL]). Quintilian provides an example of this form in his discussion of arguments from causes (which he considers particularly apt for deliberative oratory): "Virtue brings praise, so it should be pursued [i.e., because virtue brings praise, it should be pursued]" (*Inst.* 5.10.83 [Russell, LCL]). Another common form of enthymeme introduced the premise in a conditional if-clause and the deduced conclusion in a then-clause. Aristotle uses the example, "if Hector did no wrong in slaying Patroclus, neither did Alexander in slaying Achilles" (*Rhet.* 2.23.5 [1397b] [Freese, LCL]). Cicero, as well, lists several prescribed topics of deductive proofs that are stated in an "if ... then ..." format (*De or.* 2.167–72).[19] Apsines, in his treatise on rhetoric, commonly introduces his enthymeme by the inferential conjunction γάρ, which is followed by an "if ... then" statement. One example will suffice: "Come now, for (γάρ) if it is illegal to destroy one ship, clearly it is

---

[15] See the survey in Quintilian, *Inst.* 5.10.1–8; cf. the similar list of Demetrius, *Eloc.* 30–3.

[16] Cf. Quintilian, *Inst.* 5.10.3; 5.14.1, 24; Aristotle, *Rhet.* 1.2.8 (1356b); Demetrius, *Eloc.* 32. See also Anaximenes of Lampsacus, *Rhet. Alex.* 10 (1430a).

[17] For a discussion of the development of the elliptical enthymeme, see Kraus, "Theories and Practice of Enthymeme," 107–11. Theon, in his discussion of chreia, explicitly identifies an enthymematic chreia as a statement with a missing premise (5). Conley quotes Minoukianos from the second century CE, "Compressed induction is called an enthymeme when what is missing is mentally supplied by the jurors" ("Enthymeme," 175).

[18] This form is close to Quintilian's second definition of an enthymeme: a maxim supported by a reason (*Inst.* 5.10.1). See also Aristotle, *Rhet.* 2.21.2 [1394b] and Rhet. Her. 4.25. These references are also cited by Aune, "The Use and Abuse," 300, and Kraus, "Theories and Practice," 96.

[19] Cf. *Aen.* 4.347–50 where Aeneas argues using an enthymeme in a similar form.

much worse to destroy a whole fleet" (*Rhet.* 8.2 [285] [Dilts and Kennedy]; cf. 8.10, 11, 13, 15, 17, 19, 24 [288–91]).[20]

The second major category of logical proof, induction or example, has a similarly recognizable form of reasoning as its counterpart, enthymeme. Cicero describes induction as that "form of argument which leads the person with whom one is arguing to give assent to certain undisputed facts; through this assent it wins his approval of a doubtful proposition because this *resembles the facts to which he has assented*" (*Inv.* 1.51 [Hubbell, LCL], emphasis ours). In essence, induction draws inferences from analogous known instances. Aristotle divides inductive argumentation into two broad classes – historical examples and nonhistorical examples.[21] (1) Historical examples were actual analogous situations from the past. For instance, "Xerxes did not attack us until he had obtained possession of that country, but when he had, he crossed over; consequently, if the present Great King shall do the same, he will cross over, wherefore it must not be allowed" (*Rhet.* 2.20.3–4 [1393a–b] [Freese, LCL]). (2) Nonhistorical examples or analogies were invented by the rhetor. These included both (a) similitudes (e.g., "if one were to say that magistrates should not be chosen by lot, for this would be the same as choosing as representative athletes not those competent to contend, but those on whom the lots falls," *Rhet.* 2.20.4 [1393b] [Freese, LCL]) and (b) fables (e.g., Stesichorus's story of the horse, the stag, and the man as an analogy for the people of Himera choosing Himera as dictator, in *Rhet.* 2.20.5 [1393b]). Regardless of the kind of example employed, the orator was encouraged to select and shape those aspects of the example most serviceable to the case (cf. Quintilian, *Inst.* 5.11.6).[22] In deliberative cases, examples were considered preferable, especially historical examples (cf. Aristotle, *Rhet.* 1.9.40 [1368a]; 3.17.5 [1418a]; Quintilian, *Inst.* 3.8.66; 5.11.8).

Argumentative Topics

To assist the orator in finding arguments, the theorists prescribed standard *topoi* or search headings that encouraged a thorough

---

[20] Enthymemes could also take the form of rhetorical questions, cf. Quintilian, *Inst.* 8.9.10. See also Kraus, "Theories and Practice," 103–5.

[21] Cf. Quintilian, *Inst.* 5.11.1–29 where he discusses *exemplum* and uses the same categories that are listed by Aristotle: historical parallels, fables, and similitudes.

[22] See S. Perlman, "The Historical Example, Its Use and Importance as Political Propaganda in the Attic Orators," in *Studies in History* (ed. Alexander Fuks and Israel Halpern; ScrHier 7; Jerusalem: Magnes Press, 1961), 150–66.

investigation of the subject at hand. These "topics" represented standard lines of argumentation generally found in all speeches and that could be expressed in enthymatic form.[23] Aristotle lists twenty-eight *topoi*, but only some continue to appear in the handbooks of later eras – for example, arguments made from opposites, arguments proceeding from definitions of terms, arguments based on division by genus and species, and arguments from consequences (*Rhet.* 2.23.1–30 [1397a–1400b]).[24] Anonymous Seguerianus's discussion, which cites Aristotle, Alexander, Neocles, and Eudemus the Academic, offers a shorter list of "the most typical" *topoi* – definition, division, comparison, correspondence, inclusion, likeness, adjunct, inconsistency, potentiality, and judgment (171) – and briefly defines each.

The tradition Anonymous Seguerianus cites tends to view the *topoi* more narrowly as a set of standard logical moves an orator can make in arguing a case. By contrast, Cicero and Quintilian reflect a more developed topical scheme that, while still encouraging a search for many of these traditional logical moves, is focused more broadly on the case as a whole as a source for arguments. In their presentation of *topoi*, there are two broad classes: persons and things/actions/deeds. Cicero writes, "all propositions are supported in argument by attributes of persons or of actions" (*Inv.* 1.34 [Hubbell, LCL]). Quintilian as well states, "there can be no Topics of Argument not based on the accidents of things or persons, which in turn may be either considered in themselves or related to something else" (*Inst.* 5.8.5 [Russell, LCL]; cf. *Inst.* 5.10.23). In framing the discussion of *topoi* in this manner, these theorists were encouraging a thorough scouring of the case as a whole, both the persons involved, and the actions involved, for arguments that could be made in support of the case.[25] The examination of personhood

---

[23] Cf. Troy W. Martin, "Invention and Arrangement in Recent Pauline Studies: A Survey of the Practices and the Problems," in *Paul and the Ancient Letter Form* (ed. Stanley E. Porter and Sean A. Adams; Pauline Studies 6; Leiden: Brill, 2010), 115.

[24] These topics or lines of argument are in distinction to Aristotle's topics or assumed propositions that were common to all three kinds of speeches: the possible and impossible, whether a thing has or will happen, and magnitude (*Rhet.* 2.18.2–2.19.27 [1391b–1393a]). These topics, Aristotle further delimits to their more appropriate application: amplification to epideictic, the past to forensic, and the possible and future to deliberative (cf. *Rhet.* 2.18.5 [1392a]).

[25] As we will see in the next chapter, the same major headings of person and action are employed in the search for narrative material in the *narratio* – minus, of course, the logical adjuncts, since *narratio* consists simply of a biased, exposition of events rather than in arguments.

involved looking at every detail of the life in view. Toward this end, the theorists commend examining each life via the same *topoi* employed in encomium – i.e., origin, birth, education, death, etc.[26] The theorists then turn to actions and commend a similarly close examination in the search for arguments.[27] Here, two sets of *topoi* are considered. First, there is an examination of *topoi* concerning the deed itself, *topoi* such as "motive, time, place, opportunity, means, method, and the like" (*Inst.* 5.10.23). These *topoi,* taken together with the prior examination of personhood, correspond to the basic exploratory questions one could ask concerning an event: who? (person), what? (the action itself?) where? (place), when? (time), why? (the motive, cause or purpose), and how? (manner and means) (cf. *Inst.* 5.10.32). Second, there is an examination of matters logically adjunct to the events – things that may be deduced from them. Here Cicero and Quintilian incorporate many of the logical *topoi* found in the tradition running from Aristotle to Anonymous Seguerianus.[28]

From Quintilian's concluding list of *topoi*, one may observe the general organization of Cicero's and Quintilian's more developed schema:

> And so, to sum up briefly: Arguments are derived from Persons; Motives; Places, Time (of which we distinguished three phases, Antecedent, Contemporary, and Subsequent); Means (under which we included Instruments); Manner (that is, how something was done); Definition; Genus, Species, and Differentiae; Properties; Elimination; Division; Beginning, Development, and Culmination; Similarities and Dissimilarities; Contradictions; Consequences; Causes and Effects; Outcomes; Conjugates; and Comparison, which is divided into a number of Species. (*Inst.* 5.10.94 [Russell, LCL])[29]

---

[26] Cf. Cicero, *Inv.* 1.34–36; 2.32–34; 2.177; Quintilian, *Inst.* 5.10.23–31.

[27] In encomium, deeds are a sub-*topos* of personhood. But in discussions of the *topoi* of *argumentatio*, it is elevated to a major heading alongside person because of its central importance.

[28] Cicero (*Inv.* 1.37–43) discusses actions under four categories: (1) those that are coherent with the action itself, (2) those that are connected to its performance (place, time, occasion, manner, facilities), (3) those that are adjunct to the action (comparison), and (4) those that are consequent to the action.

[29] Cf. Cicero, *Top.* 71; *De or.* 2.162–72.

Of particular note for Hebrews is the argumentative *topos* of motive (why?), which Quintilian associates with deliberation. Quintilian writes:

> Arguments are therefore drawn (1) from the motives of past or future actions. The material of these motives [which some have called *hylē,* others *dynamis*] falls into two genera, each of which is divided into four species. For the motive of any action is normally to do with the acquisition, increase, preservation, and use of good things, or with the avoidance, riddance, diminution, or tolerance of bad. (These points are also very important in Deliberation.) (*Inst.* 5.8.33 [Russell, LCL])

Anonymous Seguerianus, too, attests a similar set of sub-*topoi* for motive:

> Potentiality (*dynamis*) has eight different forms, consistent with the division of what is advantageous; for the advantageous is derived from (consideration) of the good and the bad and in each case is divided into four forms: from the good (come the topics of) acquisition (κτῆσις), increase (αὔξησις), preservation (τήρησις), and benefit (ὄνησις); from the bad, avoidance (ἔκκλισις), diminution (μείωσις), loss (ἀπόκλισις), and endurance (ὑπόστασις). (180 [Dilts and Kennedy])

As we will see, the *topos* of motive and its subdivisions is an important source of argumentation in Hebrews.

Besides the topic of motive, comparison also has particular relevance to Hebrews. In *Rhet.* 2.23.4 (1397b), Aristotle describes deductive arguments derived from more (μᾶλλον) and less (ἧττον). He then cites as an example, "[I]f not even the gods know everything, hardly can men" (Freese, LCL). Cicero also discusses arguments based on comparison to things of greater, lesser, and equal significance. As a deduction from the greater, Cicero gives the following example: "If good repute is above riches, and money is keenly desired, how far more keenly should fame be desired" (*De or.* 2.172; cf. *Inv.* 1.41; *Top.* 23). Quintilian as well identifies a class of arguments derived from comparison to the greater, lesser, and equal which are also syllogistically expressed (*Inst.* 5.10.87–88). As an example of an argument from the lesser, Quintilian writes, "If it is lawful to kill a nocturnal thief, what about a violent robber?"

(*Inst.* 5.10.88 [Russell, LCL]).[30] Comparative enthymemes such as these, as we have seen and will see, are the most common enthymemes employed in the *argumentatio* of Hebrews.

Like enthymemes, arguments from examples could be developed by comparison to the equal, to the lesser, or to the greater. Quintilian gives the following argument from Cicero's *Mil.* 72 as an illustration of the lesser to the greater:

> "I killed, I killed – not Spurius Maelius, who reduced the price of corn and sacrificed his own fortune, and therefore fell under suspicion of aiming to be king, because he was thought to be courting the plebs too much ..." and so on, and then: "– but (for my client would have the courage to admit it, because he had freed his country from danger) I killed the man whose foul adultery on the sacred couches ..." and then follows the whole attack on Clodius. (*Inst.* 5.11.9.12 [Russell, LCL])

Such inductive arguments based on examples were natural since examples were considered inherently comparative, as previously noted in Chapter 3.[31] As we shall see in Hebrews, the writer frequently cites examples in his argumentation, and often in tandem with deductive comparisons.

Argumentative Amplification

Closely affiliated with enthymeme and example was amplification, or "speech that makes a subject seem greater" (Anonymous Segueria-nus 230). The theorists treat amplification as the counterpart to proof (enthymeme and example) and distinguish the two in terms of both function and location. With regard to the former, Cicero writes, "For [amplification] does not establish propositions that are doubtful but amplifies statements that are certain, or advanced as being certain" (*Part. or.* 71 [Rackham, LCL]; cf. *Part. or.* 53). Aristotle similarly frames amplification and its opposite, diminution, as establishing that a matter is great or small, and in contrast to

---

[30] See also Anonymous Seguerianus 174; Theon 11; Ps. Hermogenes 19; Aphthonius 42; Nicolaus 60.

[31] The comparative nature of examples is highlighted by Cicero who lists *exemplum* as a subcategory of comparison in *Inv.* 1.49. Cf. Quintilian, *Inst.* 5.11.1–2, who discusses Cicero's classification of example as well as notes the comparative nature of examples.

proof, which establishes that a matter is true (*Rhet.* 2.26.1–2
[1403a]). This is the rationale that Quintilian uses to distinguish
comparison as proof from comparison as amplification:

> Let no one think that this [comparison] is the same as the
> topic of Argument in which the greater is inferred from the
> less, though there is indeed a similarity. For in that case we
> are aiming at Proof, here at Amplification. Thus, in the
> passage about Oppianicus [previously cited by Quintilian],
> the object is not to show that he did a bad thing, but that he
> did something worse than the other person. But, different as
> these procedures are, there is an affinity between them.
> (*Inst.* 8.4.12 [Russell, LCL])

This distinction in function drawn by the theorists between proof
and amplification led as well to a distinction in location. Because
amplification does not, like proof, establish that a matter is true, it is
not reserved for the *argumentatio*, but rather, can occur in any
section of the speech (cf. Anonymous Seguerianus 160; Cicero, *Part.
or.* 27). This distinction is of obvious importance to our identification
of *argumentatio* in Hebrews. Whereas proof is the tell-tale sign of
argumentatio, amplification is not. Rather, only those amplifications
of statements *made to prove the case* belong to the *argumentatio*.
Here, as elsewhere in the speech, they will often function to stir the
emotions of the audience (cf. Cicero, *Part. or.* 71; Anonymous
Seguerianus 160). However, as amplifications *of proofs* they will be
"very effective for securing credence, inasmuch as amplification is a
sort of forcible method of arguing" (Cicero, *Part. or.* 27 [Rackham,
LCL]). Such argumentative amplification could be adapted for deliberative argumentation and used to show that the goods derived from
a proposed course of action are comparatively great or less (cf.
Aristotle, *Rhet.* 2.19.26 [1398a]).

Despite these distinctions, amplification nonetheless bore a close
resemblance to proof. As the example from Quintilian above suggests, amplification was understood by the theorists to employ the
same topics as enthymeme. Cicero explicitly says that "[a]mplifica-
tion of facts is obtained from all the same topics from which were
taken the statements to secure credence" (*Part. or.* 55 [Rackham,
LCL]; cf. *Inv.* 1.100). In form, amplification also frequently displayed the syllogistic reasoning of the enthymeme. Again, Quintilian
in the previously cited passage about Oppianicus states the amplificatory comparison in the following form:

How much greater is the punishment Oppianicus deserves for the same offence? That woman [from Miletus], by doing violence to her own body, tortured herself; he has brought about the same outcome by the violence and torture suffered by another person. (*Inst.* 8.4.11 [Russell, LCL])

Indeed, Aristotle states that amplification *is* an enthymeme, despite his strictly distinguishing it from the enthymeme (cf. *Rhet.* 2.26.1–2 [1403a]).[32] For this reason, one cannot take the employment of enthymatic topics and enthymatic form alone as indications of enthymeme in Hebrews. Rather, the question of function – does the deduction establish that a matter is true, or that a matter is greater? – must ultimately determine whether one is dealing with an enthymeme or an amplification. To illustrate the difference, we may cite two passages from Hebrews that bear a close resemblance in topic and form to one another, Heb 9:11–14 and Heb 12:25:

But when Christ came as a high priest of the good things that have come, then through the greater and more perfect tent (not made with hands, that is, not of this creation), he entered once for all into the Most Holy Place, not with the blood of goats and calves, but with his own blood, thus obtaining eternal redemption. *For if the blood of goats and bulls, with the sprinkling of the ashes of a heifer, sanctifies those who have been defiled so that their flesh is purified, how much more will the blood of Christ, who through the eternal Spirit offered himself without blemish to God, purify our conscience from dead works so that we might worship the living God!* (Heb 9:11–14)

See that you do not refuse the one who is speaking; *for if they did not escape when they refused the one who warned them on earth, how much more will we not escape if we reject the one who warns from heaven!* (Heb 12:25)

Both passages end with a sentence that employs both a standard topic of enthymeme (in both cases, comparison from the lesser to the greater) and a clear enthymatic form (in both cases, deductive reasoning from premise to conclusion in the classic "if … then …"

---

[32] Quintilian acknowledges the use of enthymeme as ornamental and not only as proof (cf. *Inst.* 8.5.9–11). In this case the matter under discussion has already been established by other proofs.

form). We interpret the former, however, as amplificatory comparison, and the latter as enthymatic comparison, because of their
differing functions. In the case of the first passage, Heb 9:11–14,
the comparison contributes to the larger amplificatory claim that the
Melchizedekian priestly ministry is superior to the Levitical. Like the
larger context in which it is situated, it argues that a matter is greater.
That is, it reasons that the purifying effect of Christ's sacrifice must
be greater than the Levitical priests', since it encompasses the conscience and not merely the flesh, and since it is Christ's blood and not
merely the blood of goats and bulls and ashes of the heifer that is
offered. By contrast, the second comparison in Heb 12:25 serves to
prove that a matter is true. That is, it serves to establish the deliberative thesis or *propositio* (see below) that apostasy should be avoided
("See that you do not refuse the one who is speaking") because it is
disadvantageous. It reasons that if rejection of God's warning
resulted in death in the lesser case (the wilderness generation, which
was warned of death at Sinai), it is all the more certain to result in
death in the greater case (the present generation, which is warned
from heaven).

Argumentative Propositions

A last point of consideration with regard to the *argumentatio* is the
propositio, or a summary statement or claim demonstrated by proof.
As indicated in the previous chapter, some theorists treat the *propositio* as a first-level heading of arrangement, while others subsume it
under the *argumentatio*. While the former understand the *propositio*
to be a single statement or unit located at the transition between the
narratio and the *argumentatio* (e.g., Rhet. Her. 1.4; Cicero, *Inv.* 1.19;
cf. Quintilian, *Inst.* 4.4.1), the latter allow for greater variation in
location and number. In their view, a single thesis may stand at the
head of the *argumentatio* as a transition from narration to proof
(cf. Quintilian, *Inst.* 4.4.1; Anonymous Seguerianus 163), or several
theses may appear, in multiple forms, throughout the *argumentatio*,
as Quintilian instructs:

> Propositions may be simple, double, or multiple, and this
> happens in more ways than one. (1) Several charges may be
> combined, as when Socrates was accused of corrupting the
> youth and introducing new superstitions; (2) single charges
> may be made up of several, as when Aeschines is accused of

the maladministration of the embassy because (a) he lied, (b) he fulfilled none of his instructions, (c) he wasted time, and (d) he took bribes; (3) a rebuttal also sometimes comprises several Propositions, as in this answer to a claim for money: "Your claim is invalid, for you had no right to act as agent, nor had the person on whose behalf you are litigating the right to have an agent; nor is he the heir of the man from whom I am said to have had the loan; nor again did I owe him the money." These examples can be multiplied at will; it is enough to illustrate what is meant. If these Propositions are put forward one at a time, with the Proofs following, there are several Propositions; if they are massed together, it amounts to a Partition. (*Inst.* 4.4.5–7 [Russell, LCL])

Quintilian, furthermore, understands *propositio* to refer not only to the primary claim of the speech, but also to the claims of individual arguments (cf. *Inst.* 4.4.1).[33] Thus there may be within a speech major propositions belonging to the whole, and minor propositions belonging to individual proofs.

With regard to form, Quintilian observes that a *propositio* may be put forward either "by itself ('I prosecute for murder' or 'I allege theft')" or "accompanied by a reason ('Gaius Cornelius is guilty of *maiestas*, in as much as [*num*], being tribune of the plebs, he read out his bill in person before the assembly')" (*Inst.* 4.4.8 [Russell, LCL]).[34] This latter form of a *propositio* is similar to that described in Rhet. Her. 2.28, where the *propositio* is followed by a reason that is then further supported by proof. According to Rhetorica ad Herennium, reasons are briefly stated and often provide the causal basis for the *propositio*. In Hebrews, we will see that almost all propositions are accompanied by reasons and then further supported by proofs.

---

[33] Cf. Rhet. Her. 2.28 who identifies the *propositio* as the summary statement that is to be proven. It is the first part of a complete five-part *argumentatio* which seemingly either could be one particular argument in a speech or the entire *argumentatio* of a speech if it's the only argument presented.

[34] In form, a proposition with an accompanying reason resembles an enthymeme. For example, a maxim with an attached reason could be considered an enthymeme (cf. Aristotle, *Rhet* 2.21.2 [1394a]). What then distinguishes a proposition with a reason from an enthymeme is the function of the statement in the discourse. Does the statement represent the primary issue of the speech and is the statement further supported by enthymemes and examples?

In deliberative causes, the *propositio* is the advice the speaker wishes for his or her audience to adopt. This advice could take the form of an exhortation. Gilbert Highet, for example, observes that in Cicero's first address against Catiline, Cicero puts forward *propositiones* in the form of exhortations: "Catiline, finish the journey you have begun: at long last leave the city; the gates are open: be on your way ... Take all your men with you ... Cleanse the city" (*Cat.* 1.10 [Macdonald, LCL]).[35] In *Inv.* 1.68, Cicero reframes the major proposition ("It is right, gentlemen of the jury, to relate all laws to the advantage of the state and to interpret them with any eye to the public good and not according to their literal expression") in the form of an exhortation: "[T]hat is, since we are servants of the community let us interpret (*interpretemur*) the laws with an eye to the advantage and profit of the community" (Hubbell, LCL). Cicero indicates that this exhortation functions as a proposition because he follows it with a proof in the form of a similitude that is headed by an inferential conjunction: "For (*nam*) as it is right to think that the art of medicine produces nothing except what looks to the health of the body, since it is for this purpose that medicine was founded, so we should believe that nothing comes from the laws except what is conducive to the welfare of the state, since the laws were made for this purpose" (Hubbell, LCL).

Likewise, in his treatment of the deliberative speeches in Virgil's *Aeneid*, Highet identifies *propositiones* in the form of exhortations.[36] For example, in Ilioneus's speech before Dido, he gives a brief opening *exordium* and then frames his proposals for aid in the form of exhortations or pleas: "[W]ard off the horror of flames from our ships; spare our pious race; and look more graciously on our fortunes" (*Aen.* 1.525–26 [Fairclough and Goold, LCL]). Ilioneus follows these proposals with a statement of facts and then proofs after which he makes a second set of propositions or pleas: "Grant us to beach our storm-battered fleet, to fashion planks in the forest and trim oars" (*Aen.* 1.551–52 [Fairclough and Goold, LCL]). Another example is found in *Aen.* 11.252–93, where Diomedes responds to the Latin embassy that has come to request his aid in the fight against Aeneas. Diomedes begins his counter speech with a brief

---

[35] Gilbert Highet, *The Speeches in Vergil's* Aeneid (New Jersey: Princeton University Press, 1972), 52.

[36] The discussion from the *Aeneid* here is informed by Highet's analysis in *Speeches*, 52–81.

exordium (252–54) and a lengthy *narratio* of the tragic Greek home-comings incidental to the case (255–77). He then introduces a proposition in the form of an exhortation or plea: "Do not, do not urge me to such battles!" (278 [Fairclough and Goold, LCL]). After some argumentation (279–82), he concludes with a second proposition in the form of an exhortation and a warning: "Join hand to hand in treaty, as best you may; but beware your swords clash not with his!" (292–93 [Fairclough and Goold, LCL]). Later in Book 11, the Latin assembly gathers to deliberate its war with the Trojans. The deliberation begins with king Latinus (*Aen.* 11.296–335). He starts with a prayer and exordium (300–4). He then narrates the facts (305–13). He follows the narration with three proposals (two in the form of exhortations):

> Let us name just terms of a treaty and invite them to share in our realm. (321–22 [Fairclough and Goold, LCL])

> [L]et us build twice ten ships of Italian oak ... let us contribute bronze, labour, and docks. (326–29 [Fairclough and Goold, LCL])

> Further to bring news and seal the pact, I would have a hundred envoys go forth ... carrying gifts. (330–34 [Fairclough and Goold, LCL])

From this brief survey, what is particularly noteworthy is that these deliberative speeches have multiple propositions that take the form of exhortations. As we will see shortly, the writer of Hebrews adopts a similar method of exhortation.

There is another peculiar variant of deliberative oratory relevant to our discussion: the battle exhortation or commander's speech.[37] Interestingly, a form of παρακαλεῖν or *cohortatio* is used to describe these speeches, the same term the author of Hebrews uses for his speech (ὁ λόγος τῆς παρακλήσεως, Heb 13:22).[38] Many of these speeches have a brief introduction, which is followed by a proposal that amounts to "be courageous." The proposal is then followed by a series of arguments based on standard topics.[39] For example, in

---

[37] For a discussion of this classification see Juan Carlos Iglesias Zoido, "The Battle Exhortation in Ancient Rhetoric," *Rhetorica* 25 (2007): 152–5.

[38] Highet, *Speeches*, 83; Zoido, "Battle Exhortation," 152 n. 53.

[39] Highet, *Speeches*, 85. Many of the standard topics for battle exhortations were nobility in dying for the fatherland, earning the favor of the gods, and glory in an honorable death (e.g., Quintilian, *Inst.* 12.1.28). These topics were the same as those

Anab. 2.7.3–9, Arrian details Alexander's battle exhortation as his
Greek army is about to face the Persians. Arrian begins by stating
that Alexander gathered his military leaders and "exhorted [them] to
be courageous (παρακάλει θηρρεῖν)." Such a summary statement or
exhortation points to the *propositio* of the speech. What then follows
are the arguments arranged by common topics to support the exhortation. Alexander then concludes with examples of valor both from
the present among his own army (including himself) and from the
past (Xenophon and his Ten Thousand). In Thucydides's history,
Demosthenes opens his battle speech with two exhortations that
function as the speech's theses ("Let no one of you ... seek to prove"
and "Let him rather come to grips," 4.10.1). Then he follows with
numerous proofs to support his exhortations not to despair but to
fight (4.10.2–5). Likewise, Virgil has Aeneas recount a short battle
speech he gave as the Greeks raze Troy. He frames his proposal as a
hortatory exclamation: "Let us die and rush into the battle's midst"
(*Aen.* 2.353 [Fairclough and Goold, LCL]). The battle exhortation of Turnus in *Aen.* 10.279–84 employs typical topics to support
Turnus's proposal, "Let us meet them at the water's edge" (Fair-
clough and Goold, LCL).[40] Again, these examples demonstrate that,
when setting forth a deliberative case, theses or proposals could take
the form of exhortations supported by various proofs taken from
traditional *topoi*.

Summary

In sum, *argumentatio* according to the theorists essentially consisted
in logical exhortation/dissuasion, accusation/defense, or praise/
blame, depending on the species of the speech. Toward that end, it
enlisted proofs, whether enthymemes, examples, or both, in support
of its proposition or propositions. These proofs were drawn from
customary topics related to persons or actions/things. Occasionally,
the proofs could be amplified so as to enhance the argument. The
proposition supported by the proofs could be singular or multiple,
and it could be simply stated or accompanied by a brief reason.
In deliberative causes, the proposition could take the form of

that came to be labeled τελκὰ κεφάλαια (see above). For further discussion of these
points see Zoido, "Battle Exhortation," 142–3, 145–6, and 153–4.
    [40] For further discussion of battle exhortations in the *Aeneid* see Highet, *Speeches*,
86–9.

exhortation or advice. As we will see in the following section, the *argumentatio* of Hebrews is recognizable by these same characteristic features.

Argumentatio in Hebrews

In view of the survey above, we are now in a position to examine Hebrews and identify any material that displays the essential features of *argumentatio*. We begin with our conclusions in Chapter 3, where we identified five deliberative sections (2:1–18; 3:7–4:13; 5:11–6:20; 10:19–12:17; 12:25–29), each with a proof in the form of a deliberative syncrisis. These sections serve a typical deliberative function, exhorting the audience as a judge to make a decision about the future (namely, to persevere in the faith) because of the advantages of doing so, and correspondingly dissuading the audience from choosing the alternative course (namely apostasy) because of the disadvantages. These units thus take up one of the three aims the theorists prescribe for *argumentatio*, exhortation and dissuasion, and so are a good candidate for constituting in whole or in part the *argumentatio* of the speech.

What we will argue in the present portion of the study is that each of these sections reflects the expected form and content of *argumentatio*. That is, each contains the anticipated proofs (enthymeme and example) that are characteristic of deliberative *argumentatio* (arguments for advantage or disadvantage), together with the deliberative claims or *propositiones* (exhortations or advice) that those proofs support. Our analysis leads us to designate the five deliberative units as clear occurrence of *argumentatio* in the speech.

Our analysis will proceed as follows. First, we offer a close examination of the first deliberative unit (2:1–18) and show in detail how the material of that unit conforms to the theoretical parameters the rhetoricians establish for *argumentatio*. Then we offer a more general analysis of the five units collectively, sketching in outline form the same kind of thesis and proof seen in 2:1–18. We then offer some concluding reflections on the implications for the arrangement of the speech as whole.

The First Unit of *Argumentatio*: A Close Examination

Probatio

As we stated in the discussion of methodology above, analysis of arrangement begins with *argumentatio* and specifically proof.

Hebrews 2:1–18 certainly displays this telling feature. Here we encounter the first logical proof of the speech, the deliberative syncrisis of Heb 2:2–4:

> For (γάρ) if the message declared through angels (= the lesser case) was valid, and every transgression or disobedience received a just penalty, how can we escape if we neglect so great a salvation (= the greater case) which, being declared at first through the Lord, was attested to us by those who heard, while God added his testimony by signs and wonders and various miracles, and by gifts of the Holy Spirit, distributed according to his will.

This proof belongs to the deductive class of logical proofs, the enthymeme, as evidenced by several considerations. First, with regard to form, we observe that it begins with the conjunction γάρ and is developed deductively via an "if ... then" construction. Again, the numerous examples of enthymemes listed by Apsines cited above are commonly introduced by γάρ and many of these also adopt the "if ... then" form, which was characteristic, as we said, of enthymatic reasoning.[41] Second, as a syncrisis, Heb 2:2–3 develops its logic from the topic of comparison from the lesser to the greater as Cicero describes it: "What is valid in the less should be valid in the greater" (*Top.* 23 [Hubbell, LCL]). Third, as is often the case with enthymemes, here the audience is asked to supply an unstated premise that was previously demonstrated by the author – in this case, the premise that the Son is superior to the angels, which the author demonstrated in the preceding amplificatory syncrisis of 1:5–14. Fourth, this syncrisis serves to show that a matter is true (that those who neglect so great a salvation are certain not to escape the penalty for apostasy) rather than that a matter is greater; thus it is an enthymatic and not an amplificatory comparison.[42]

---

[41] The word γάρ is a common syntactical marker used for proof in the deliberative sections of Hebrews. For enthymemes see 3:14–15; 4:2, 3; 6:4–6, 13–20; 10:26–27, 30–31, 37–39; 12:25. For similitudes and examples see 3:16–19; 4:12–13; 6:7–8; 11:2–38; 12:3; 12:7b–11.

[42] The preceding epideictic material (1:5–14) is rightly viewed as amplification, not proof. That is, it establishes that a matter is greater (i.e., that the Son is "greater than the angels"; 1:4), and not that a matter is true. Not until 2:1–4 does the reader encounter the first attempt – here, through enthymatic comparison – to establish that a matter is true (i.e., that apostasy is disadvantageous).

Indeed, what we observe in the case of this deliberative syncrisis is true of all the deliberative syncrises that we have previously identified (4:2; 6:13–18; 10:28–29; 12:25) and that appear, accordingly, in the outline of *argumentatio* below. They each move from premise to deduction, often via the standard "if ... then" form. They are comparisons from the lesser to the greater. Several of these take the classic "if ... then how much more" form of comparison to the lesser modeled in the textbooks.[43] Even those enthymemes that do not have this explicit form still exhibit the logic of that form. The premise on which the comparison proceeds is provided by the preceding epideictic syncrisis. And each serves to show that a matter is true rather than that a matter is greater, and so functions as an enthymeme and not an amplification.

While 2:2–4 constitutes artistic proof, integrated within the deductive reasoning is the citation of artless proof and specifically "witnesses." That is, the writer says that the "salvation" in view was first declared by the Lord, then confirmed by those who heard. The writer then observes that God "bore witness together" with these two (συνεπιμαρτυροῦντος—the term frames all three as witnesses) to the same salvation through signs, wonders, and distributions of the Holy Spirit. According to the theorists, witnesses could include divine *testimonia* such as oracles, prophesies, and omens (Quintilian, *Inst.* 5.7.35) as well as the testimony of ancient poets such as Homer (Aristotle, *Rhet.* 1.15.13 [1375b]). Quintilian notes that these types of witnesses carry authority in an argument (*Inst.* 5.11.36–44 esp. 40, 42). Here, the witnesses in question are not enlisted as proof *in addition to* the enthymeme; rather, they are *incorporated* within the deduction of the enthymeme and help complete its logic. This is characteristic of the use of artless proof in Hebrews. Generally, the writer invokes various artless proofs – witnesses, oaths, promises, laws, etc. – within his artistic proofs (and amplifications, as well) and as the subject matter of various deductions or inductions.[44]

---

[43] Other examples of the "if ... then" enthymeme in the deliberative sections of Hebrews are 3:14–15; 6:4–6;10:26–27.

[44] The writer also incorporates artless proofs within various epideictic amplifications – a matter we discuss in the next chapter.

Propositio

The identification of proof leads us to the identification of the *propositio* it supports. Sometimes that *propositio* could be implied, as we have said, by the proof itself, or sometimes it could be stated. Clearly in Heb 2:1–18, it is stated. The inferential conjunction γάρ introducing the enthymeme of Heb 2:2–3a ("For [γάρ] if the message declared through angels was valid …") points to the preceding statement in Heb 2:1 as the claim it supports: "For this reason it is necessary for us to pay greater attention to what we have heard so that we do not drift away." Further, the invocation thereafter of three witnesses to that salvation supports the counsel to "pay greater attention to what you heard." Thus we have in 2:1–4 the quintessential characteristic of *argumentatio*, proof enlisted in support of a proposition or thesis.

In addition to the proofs supporting it, several other considerations point to Heb 2:1 as the *propositio* of 2:1–18. First, Heb 2:1 states in summary form the primary deliberative advice that the author wants his audience to adopt, namely not to commit apostasy. The author even lays emphasis on the *necessity* (δεῖ) of his advice, a common consideration in deliberative cases.[45]

Second, Heb 2:1 occupies the anticipated transitional point between the preceding epideictic material in 1:5–14, which we will argue in the next chapter is *narratio*, and the following deliberative section of 2:2–18, which we are presently interpreting as *argumentatio*. Thus it occupies a location commonly prescribed for the *propositio*. In fact, each of the five deliberative sections we interpret as *argumentatio* in the outline below are headed by counsel or exhortation that functions as deliberative *propositio* (cf. 3:7; 6:1–2; 10:22; 12:25).

Third, the *propositio* in Heb 2:1 has a reason appended to the advice – "lest we drift away." The *propositio* thus adopts the form of a *propositio* accompanied by a reason as Quintilian describes in *Inst.* 4.4.8. Almost all propositions in Hebrews adopt this form of

---

[45] Cf. Quintilian, *Inst.* 3.8.22–25. Quintilian is not in favor of the term *necessity* though he recognizes that others use it to mean the sure outcome of a particular choice: "For example, if a besieged garrison, outnumbered and short of water and food, discusses surrendering to the enemy, and this is said to be 'necessary,' it follows of course that one must understand 'otherwise we die'." Quintilian states that this is technically not "necessity" because "the situation itself does not make surrender 'necessary,' because it is open to them to die." (Russell, LCL).

a *propositio*, and often the reasons attached provide the causal or effective basis for the recommended course of action.[46]

Amplificatio

In addition to *propositio* and *probatio*, there is also *amplificatio* in the first deliberative unit. That is, Heb 2:5–18 functions as an amplification of the argument of 2:1–4. That the material is amplification is evident from two key considerations. First, the section shows that the future destiny of redeemed humanity is even greater than that of the angels. Thus it has the prescribed function of amplification. It is "speech that makes a subject seem greater" (Anonymous Seguerianus 230), and in contrast to proof, not speech establishing that a matter is true. Second, it takes up a common topic of amplification, comparison from the lesser. Indeed, the entire text is devoted to explaining the superior destiny of humanity in comparison to angels, and in two places comparative conclusions are drawn. The first is in 2:5–8, where the author announces on the basis of Ps 8 the superior destiny of redeemed humanity over that of angels. He observes that the coming world (οἰκουμένη), which is not subjected to angels but is already subjected to Jesus, the pioneer of the audience's salvation (cf. 1:6; 2:10), will be subjected to God's children in the future.[47] The second comparative conclusion is stated in 2:16. There the author

---

[46] Formally, most reasons in Hebrews, like 2:1, are dependent clauses, which are introduced by the adverbial conjunctions ἵνα or μήποτε. There are three potential exceptions: 6:10 ("for God is not unjust to forget your work and the love which you have shown for his name by having served and continuing to serve the saints"); 10:23 ("for he who promised is faithful"); and 12:29 ("for our God is a consuming fire"). What is common to each of the reasons is that the clauses are connected to the main propositional statement by the inferential conjunction γάρ, the main verb (εἰμί) is implied, and each highlights some aspect of God's character (just, faithful, or a consuming fire) as the basis for the proposed course of action. Similarly, Quintilian's example of a reason connects the clause to the proposition by an inferential conjunction *nam* (*Inst.* 4.1.8). Hebrews 6:10 and 10:23 are also part of a multiple-form *propositio*. The other *propositiones* in these multiple forms include appended reasons via the typical dependent clause. It stands to reason that the author considers the peculiar clauses in 6:10 and 10:23 in a similar light, as appended reasons to a proposition. The fact that 12:29 adopts the same form also argues for treating this clause in a similar manner to the clauses in 6:10 and 10:23.

[47] We understand the interpretation of Ps 8 by the author of Hebrews not only to be christological but also a statement about redeemed humanity of which Christ is a representative. See Craig R. Koester's discussion of this point in "Hebrews, Rhetoric, and the Future of Humanity," in *Reading the Epistle to the Hebrews: A Resource for Students* (ed. E. F. Mason and K. B. McCruder; SBL Resources of Biblical Studies 66; Atlanta: SBL, 2011), 106–7; Kenneth L. Schenck, *Cosmology and Eschatology in*

observes that Jesus helps "the seed of Abraham" and not angels because Abraham's seed is subjected to mortality and the fear of death (2:14–15). Thus it was fitting for Jesus to be made lower than angels and share in humanity's mortality so that he could "taste death for all" (2:9). Conquering death, he is exalted above the one who wields the power of death (the devil) and is now able to lead humanity to its eschatological goal of rule in the world to come, as laid out in Ps 8 (as the author interprets it). Jesus, the exalted Son (cf. 1:5–14), leads God's many "sons" to glory (cf. 2:10–13).[48]

That the material of 2:5–18 is amplification *of the argument* of 2:1–4 is clear from two interrelated considerations. First, the γάρ at the beginning of 2:5 links 2:5–18 with what immediately precedes it – the argument of 2:1–4. Thus Heb 2:1–4 is not a parenthetical aside that interrupts the epideictic comparison in 1:5–14 only to be resumed in 2:5–18. This is what the NRSV's (mis)translation of γάρ as "now" would suggest. Rather, Heb 2:1–4 functions, as we have already argued, as the goal – the climactic argument for perseverance – toward which the epideictic comparison of 1:5–14 leads, and 2:5–18, as subsequent expansion on that argument.[49] Second, when γάρ is correctly translated, the specific link it establishes becomes apparent in context. In the immediately preceding proofs, the writer has argued for the disadvantage of neglecting "so great a salvation" (2:3–4). Hebrews 2:5–18, introduced by "For ...," explicates the greatness of this salvation, amplifying it as a future destiny greater than that enjoyed by the angels. According to Cicero, *amplificatio* does not establish the cause (the function of 2:2–4) but comes alongside what has already been advanced as certain and enhances it (the function of 2:5–18). Cicero also recommends that amplification (in the form of praise or vituperation) should be closely interwoven with argumentation (cf. *Inv.* 1.97). This is precisely what we have in the move from discouraging the rejection of "so great a salvation" in 2:1–4, to the amplifying (in the form of epideictic comparison) of that salvation's greatness in 2:5–18.

Hebrews: The Settings of the Sacrifice (SNTSMS 143; Cambridge: Cambridge University Press, 2007), 54–9.

[48] For further discussion, see Jason A. Whitlark, *Resisting Empire: Rethinking the Purpose of the Letter to "the Hebrews"* (LNTS 484; London: T&T Clark, 2014), 122–59.

[49] For a similar observation concerning 2:1–4, see Luke Timothy Johnson, *Hebrews: A Commentary* (NTL; Louisville: Westminster John Knox, 2006), 89.

In identifying 2:5–18 as amplification of the opening argument of the speech, we are able to account for two trajectories in scholarship on Hebrews. First, several scholars have tended to read Heb 2:5–18 as constituting the *narratio* of Hebrews, and often as a continuation of 1:5–14.[50] They observe that Heb 2:5–18 picks up the epideictic or demonstrative comparison with angels from the preceding epideictic materials in 1:5–14. They note, too, the expositional character of Heb 2:5–18, that the audience is never directly exhorted, and that the author uses only two first person plural indicative verbs (λαλοῦμεν, 2:2; βλέπομεν, 2:9). While we acknowledge the resumption of epideictic comparison of angels in 2:5–18, we suggest that the focus has shifted from comparison with Jesus, the Son, to comparison with redeemed humanity, God's many "sons" – and furthermore, that this shift is a product of the intervening deliberative argument (2:1–4) by addressing the audience as a part of redeemed humanity and by encouraging its members not to neglect the "great salvation" for which redeemed humanity is destined. While we acknowledge that 2:5–18 shares with 1:5–14 an expositional (not hortatory) and amplificatory (not argumentative) character, we draw a distinction in function: whereas 1:5–18 states facts preliminary to and necessary for the argumentation that follows (2:1–4) and so has a classic aim of *narratio* (see the next chapter), 2:5–18 proceeds from and elaborates a key aspect of the argumentation of 2:1–4 ("so great a salvation") and so has the classic aim of argumentative *amplificatio* or amplification in service to and within the *argumentatio*.

Second, several scholars have tended to read Heb 2:5–18 as a text of foundational significance to the speech. Kenneth L. Schenck considers the passage of central importance to the "story world" of the author.[51] And Craig Koester, who underscores the centrality especially of 2:5–9, interprets it as nothing less than the *propositio* of the entire speech.[52] While we agree with these scholars in their high assessment of the text, we differ with Koester in how its importance is reflected in the arrangement of the speech. Koester's thesis is untenable in our view because *propositio* is supposed to precede its proof and govern it, but 2:5–18 follows the proof of 2:1–4 and, as we

---

[50] From Chapter 1 see Spicq, Nissilä, Übelacker, Backhaus, and Anderson.
[51] See Schenck, *Cosmology and Eschatology*, 51–9.
[52] From Chapter 1 see Koester.

have said, is subordinate to it both grammatically (γάρ) and logically (2:5–18 amplifies "so great a salvation," 2:3). Koester's theory does not recognize, too, that the epideictic syncrisis of 1:5–14 takes as its goal the argumentation of 2:1–4, establishing the premise (that Jesus is greater than the angels) on which the deliberative comparison from the lesser in 2:3 proceeds (if there was no escape for those who neglected the message delivered by angels, how much more is there no escape for those who neglect the great salvation announced by the Lord?). Clearly the deliberative advice of 2:1, the counsel to pay greater attention to, so as not to drift away from, the salvation announced by Christ, represents the main thesis, since it is the first occasion in the speech where logical proof is enlisted to demonstrate that a matter is true. The importance of 2:5–18, in our view, is seen in its relationship to that claim. As argumentative *amplificatio*, Heb 2:5–18 does not depart from, but rather, enhances and elaborates this opening deliberative claim by amplifying its central subject matter, the salvation which the writer hopes the audience will not neglect. The author is not content in his opening argumentation merely to mention this salvation and then move on quickly to other matters. Rather, he pauses at first mention of it to expand upon it, sketch it in full, and amplify its greatness – all in support of the opening exhortation not to abandon it. And he has done so at the very point where rhetoricians say the strongest or most important arguments are to be employed, the beginning of the *argumentatio*, as that is the place where the orator has the attention of most of his or her audience.[53] Indeed, this is the only section of *argumentatio* among five (see the outline below) containing such a lengthy, amplificatory exposition. In short, we believe the importance of Heb 2:5–18 is underscored by its place in arrangement, not as the *propositio*, but as an exceptional and lengthy amplification of what rhetorical theory considered the most important argument of the speech – the first. As such, it is quite appropriately the place where "the story world" of Hebrews is introduced.[54]

---

[53] Cf. Cicero, *De or.* 2.313–14; Rhet. Her. 3:18; Quintilian, *Inst.* 5.12.14

[54] E.g., the author has developed in 2:5–18 a strong eschatological focus characteristic of his outlook throughout Hebrews. He has also introduced the notions of the necessity of suffering and the needed divine help the audience requires – both subjects of importance that are addressed repeatedly in the remainder of the discourse.

The Five Units of *Argumentatio*: An Outline

The same essential content of *argumentatio* – *probatio* and *propositio* – evident upon close examination in 2:1–18 is also apparent in the remaining deliberative sections of this speech (3:7–4:13; 5:11–6:20; 10:19–12:13; 12:25–29). This we sketch in outline form below.

Represented in the outline are artistic, logical proofs in the form of enthymemes and examples. The enthymemes, like the one in Heb 2:2–4 discussed earlier, are recognizable by their form, topic, and argumentative function. Most take up the topics of comparison (usually from the lesser) or motive. Similarly, the examples identified are recognizable because of the inferences they draw from analogous known instances, and from the form of example they take up. That is, most take the form of an historical example (e.g., the wilderness generation, the audience itself, the past heroes of the community, and Jesus), while a few take the form of a nonhistorical example and, specifically, similitude (e.g., agricultural metaphors and educational analogies). The reader will observe that topics of argument govern not only the selection of individual arguments, but also the organization of the *argumentatio* as a whole. That is, five argumentative topics of personhood in their traditional order – origins, birth, education, deeds, death/posthumous events – stand as headings for each of the five units respectively and serve to organize arguments according to the different aspects of covenant experience under consideration. Thus, for example, under the heading of covenant "origins," all argumentation centers on the heavenly mediators from which new and old covenant revelation originated, Jesus and the angels respectively.

Also enlisted in these sections are a number of artless proofs. These include laws (10:28), witnesses or testimony (2:3–4; 3:15; 4:4, 7; 10:29, 30; 11:2, 4; 12:1), oaths (3:11, 18; 4:3, 5; 6:13–18), and promises (4:1; 6:13–18; 10:36; 11:9, 13, 17; 12:26). We list artless proofs here rather than in the outline because they are incorporated within the inductive and deductive reasoning (as in 2:1–4, where the witnesses are mentioned in the deductive clause that completes the enthymeme) rather than being distinct and auxiliary. Artless proofs often shore up argumentation in Hebrews. For example, in Heb 3:14–15, the author incorporates the testimony from Scripture (which he earlier had attributed to the Holy Spirit's own voice) within the if-clause of the enythymeme: "For we have become

sharers in Christ if we hold firm to the end our initial confidence *while it is said, 'Today if you hear his voice do not harden your hearts as in the rebellion '"* (emphasis ours).[55]

In addition to *probatio*, these five sections feature clear occurrences of *propositio*. These are recognizable as such because of the proofs subsequently enlisted in support of their claims. In most cases, like Heb 2:1, they also adopt the form of a *propositio* accompanied by a reason (Quintilian, *Inst.* 4.4.8) – that is, a brief clause that establishes the causal or effective basis of the counsel. In the outline below, all reasons are identified in italics.

Furthermore, like Heb 2:1, the *propositiones* outlined below are recognizable as such because they state in summary form the primary deliberative appeal for perseverance in the faith and/or against apostasy. Whereas Heb 2:1 takes the form of advice, however, most of these *propositiones* take the form of summary exhortations (Heb 3:7, 12, 13; 4:1, 11; 6:1–2; 10:22, 23, 25, 35; 12:1, 5–6, 7, 12–13, 25, 28). As we have already noted, exhortations frequently serve as the major propositions of a deliberative speech, forcefully presenting the recommended course of action for which the speaker argues. This is certainly the case in Hebrews, as virtually all of its exhortations stress in some way the need to persevere or to avoid apostasy. In treating the exhortations of Hebrews collectively as *propositio*, we clearly are assigning them a rhetorically central role. Other interpreters apart from such a rhetorical designation have instinctively seen the importance of exhortations in Hebrews. James Thompson, for example, rightly asserts that they are the essential focus of the discourse.[56]

Finally, in most of the deliberative sections, the *propositiones* are several and, thus, are interspersed throughout the section in which they are found. There are five *propositiones* in 3:7–4:13, three in

---

[55] Other interpreters of Hebrews have identified the use of Scripture with the artless proofs of laws, contracts, witnesses, or oaths. See James W. Thompson, "Argument and Persuasion in the Epistle to the Hebrews," *PRSt* 39 (2012): 369; Thomas H. Olbricht, "Anticipating and Presenting the Case for Christ as High Priest in Hebrews," in *Rhetorical Argumentation in Biblical Texts: Essays from the Lund 2000 Conference* (ed. Anders Eriksson, Thomas H. Olbricht, and Walter Übelacker; Emory Studies in Early Christianity 8; Harrisburg: Trinity Press International, 2002), 359.

[56] James W. Thompson, *Hebrews* (Paideia; Grand Rapids: Baker 2008), 14. See also Floyd V. Filson, *"Yesterday": A Study of Hebrews in the Light of Chapter 13* (SBT 4; Naperville: Allenson, 1967) 16–26.

5:11–6:20, eight in 10:19–12:13, and two in 12:25–29.[57] The *propositiones* also occur in single, double, or multiple form, and so reflect the range attested by Quintilian in *Inst.* 4.4.5. Hebrews 3:12–13, 6:9–12, and 12:5–7 are double while Heb 10:19–25 is triple and the only multiple form thesis of the speech – perhaps an indication of its significance. The rest are single propositions. Additionally, according to Quintilian, an overriding charge or thesis can be communicated in multiple charges or theses (cf. *Inst.* 4.4.5–6). Accordingly, the author repeatedly advises for the necessity of perseverance or against its opposite, apostasy. The frequency with which the author returns to his counsel certainly points to its central "propositional" importance. Clearly the author has not reserved all thesis materials for a single *propositio* or *divisio* section that is separate from and prior to an *argumentatio* (though it *is* true, as we have already said, that each of the five units begins with an introductory *propositio* that stands, like Heb 2:1, in the traditional location of *propositio*, at the transition from *narratio* to *argumentatio*). As we have seen, *propositio* in extant speeches is frequently restated in multiple forms and distributed throughout the *argumentatio*. This is an important observation since some interpreters of Hebrews treat the *propositio* as a separate first-level heading in their outline and identify only one *propositio*[58] By recognizing that the *propositio* can be distributed throughout the *argumentatio* and stated several times in various ways, we have not been forced into choosing one statement near the beginning of the discourse as a *propositio*. Rather, we are able to recognize the numerous encouragements to persevere and admonitions against apostasy for what they are collectively – the thesis of the speech.

These essential and characteristic elements of the *argumentatio* – proofs in the form of enthymemes and examples, and the proposition(s) they support – are highlighted in the following outline via bolding and italics. The reader will observe that these elements are confined to the five deliberative sections of Hebrews and collectively support characteristic aims of deliberative *argumentatio*, exhortation, and dissuasion.

---

[57] We exclude the exhortations in 4:14–16 and 12:14–17 since these belong to a secondary *exordium* or *peroratio* which we will discuss in later chapters.

[58] E.g., in Chapter 1 see Übelacker, Backhaus, Koester, and Thompson.

I. Covenant Origins – Angels vs. Jesus
  a. Epideictic Amplification (1:5–14): The new cove-
     nant has greater origins with the superior heavenly
     mediator.
  b. Deliberative Argumentation (2:1–18): Pay greater
     attention to/do not neglect the great salvation
     announced by the superior covenant mediator.

Deliberative Proposition: Apostasy Discouraged
"Therefore we must pay greater attention to what we
heard *so that (μήποτε) we do not drift away.*" (2:1)

Deliberative Enthymeme
Comparison to the Lesser: Apostasy Disadvantageous

"For (γάρ) if the message declared through angels (= the
lesser case) was valid, and every transgression or disobedience received a just penalty, how can we escape if
we neglect so great a salvation which was spoken first
by the Lord (= the greater case) and confirmed to us by
those who heard while God added his testimony by
signs, wonders, and various miracles and by distributions of the Holy Spirit according to his will." (2:2–4)

Argumentative Amplification
Comparison to the Lesser

The author amplifies the greatness of the salvation
announced to the audience, that it is the same as Jesus's
own destiny and superior to that of angels. (2:5–18)

II. Covenant Births – Moses vs. Jesus
  a. Epideictic Amplification (3:1–6): The new covenant
     has greater beginnings via the better born inaugurator.
  b. Deliberative Argumentation (3:7–4:13): Do not listen
     faithlessly to the gospel announced "Today" by the
     better-born covenant inaugurator.

**Deliberative Propositions: Apostasy Discouraged/
Perseverance Advised**
"Therefore, as the Holy Spirit says, "Today, if you hear
his voice, do not harden your hearts ..." (3:7a)

"See to it, brothers and sisters, *so that (μήποτε) none of
you have an evil heart of unbelief that turns away from*

the living God but encourage one another each day as long as it is called 'Today' *so that (ἵνα) none of you may be hardened by the deceitfulness of sin.*" (3:12–13)[59]

"Therefore, let us fear *so that (μήποτε) none among you seem to fall short while the promise to enter in his resting place remains.*" (4:1)[60]

"Let us, therefore, make every effort to enter that rest *so that (ἵνα) no one may fall through such disobedience as theirs.*" (4:11)

Deliberative Examples
Historical Example: Apostasy Disadvantageous[61]

"as in the rebellion on the day of testing in the wilderness ... so I swore in my anger, 'They will not enter my rest.'" (3:7b–11)

"For (γάρ) who heard and rebelled? ... So we see that they were not able to enter because of unbelief." (3:16–19)[62]

---

[59] This is the first double *propositio*. The individual proposition emphasizes the two complementary sides of the deliberative counsel: do not apostatize (v. 12) and persevere (v. 13).

[60] There are two parts to the reason appended to the general proposition, "let us fear." The first is a warning not to fall away, and the second is a declaration that a resting place still remains. The proofs that follow in 4:2–10 support one of these two parts. The proofs in 4:2–3a function to demonstrate either the disadvantage of unbelief and apostasy via comparison or the advantage of belief and perseverance via contraries. The remaining proofs in vv. 3b–10 function to demonstrate that a resting place remains to be entered. For more on this matter, see the discussion of the deliberative enthymemes below.

[61] The wilderness generation is the historical example cited in these two instances (3:7b–11 and 3:16–19). They apostatized and failed to enter God's resting place. The first citation of exemplary proof is within the quotation of Ps 94 (LXX). These are the words of the Holy Spirit addressed to the audience. The quotation fits the author's form of proposition as an exhortation followed by proof (in this case example). Because it is a quote from Scripture it does not use the more common syntactical markers the author of Hebrews prefers. The second use of the exemplary proof is the author's own construction by which he more closely applies the example of the wilderness generation to his audience through a series of inductive questions (see note below).

[62] The author, in 3:16–19, does not tell the story of apostasy of the wilderness generation but employs a series of rhetorical questions with a conclusion in order to highlight those features in the narrative that are the most pertinent to his audience. A series of such questions could characterize inductive inquiry as seen in Socrates's dialogues. Cf. Cicero, *Inv.* 1.51–53; Quintilian, *Inst.* 5.11.3–5. Narrating an example as proof is also what Apsines calls ἀφήγησις (*Rhet.* 2.3; cf., Nicolaus 15–16). As we will see in the chapter on *narratio*, narratives can take the form of questions.

Similitude: Apostasy Disadvantageous

"For (γάρ) the word of God is living and active and sharper than any two-edged sword and piercing even to the point of dividing soul and spirit and joints and marrow and able to judge the desires and thoughts of the heart. No creature is hidden from his sight but all are naked and exposed to his eyes to whom we have to give an account." (4:12–13)

Deliberative Enthymemes
Motive (Acquisition): Perseverance Advantageous

"For (γάρ) we have become sharers in Christ if we hold firm to the end our initial confidence while it says, 'Today, if you hear his voice do not harden your hearts as in the rebellion.'" (3:14–15)

Comparison to the Lesser: Apostasy Disadvantageous

"For (γάρ) we also have heard the good news proclaimed (= the greater case) just as they did (= the lesser case) but the message they heard did not benefit these who were not united by faith with those who heard." (4:2)

Contraries: Perseverance Advantageous/Apostasy Disadvantageous

"For (γάρ) we who believe are entering that resting place just as he has said, 'As I swore in my anger, "They will never enter my resting place."'" (4:3a)[63]

---

[63] The logic of 4:3a appears to be if God swore that those who disobeyed would not enter his resting place, then we who believe enter that resting place. Thus the enthymeme is based on "contraries" which was one of the most commonly attested *topoi* among the theorists. Quintilian writes, "From Contraries: 'Frugality is a good thing, for luxury is a bad thing'; 'If war is the cause of ill, peace will be the cure'" (*Inst.* 5.10.73 [Russell, LCL]). Notice that Quintilian's last example has the form of "If A leads to B, then A's opposite leads to B's opposite." That's precisely the logic in 4:3a. If A (disobedience) leads to B (non-entrance), then A's opposite (faithfulness) leads to B's opposite (entrance). For the author of Hebrews there is only one resting place for which all of God's people, both past and present, hope. Cf. Jon Laansma, in *"I Will Give You Rest": The Rest Motif in the New Testament with Special Reference to Mt 11 and Heb 3–4* (WUNT 2/98; Tübingen: Mohr Siebeck, 1997), 274–5. See also Laansma, *"I Will Give You Rest"*, 310, and Mathias Rissi, *Die Theologie des Hebräerbriefs: Ihre Verankerung in der Situation des Verfassers und seiner Leser* (WUNT 41; Tübingen: J. C. B. Mohr, 1987), 128, who understand the entrance into God's resting place to be both corporate and ultimate, that is, to occur only at the end of history. It is not for the individual immediately upon death. See also,

III. Covenant Education – Aaronic high priests vs. Jesus
   a. Epideictic Amplification (5:1–10): The new coven-
      ant's high priest is the better trained.
   b. Deliberative Argumentation (5:11–6.20): Undergo
      the new covenant's high priest's better training of
      faithful endurance based upon better promises.[64]

Deliberative Propositions: Perseverance Advised
"Therefore, let us go on toward perfection, leaving behind
the basic teaching about Christ, and not laying again the
foundation: repentance from dead works and faith toward
God, instruction about baptisms, laying on of hands,
resurrection of the dead, and eternal judgment." (6:1–2)

"But we are persuaded, beloved, of better things concerning you, things which have as their end salvation,
*for (γάρ) God is not unjust to forget your work and the
love for his name as you have served and continue to serve
the saints.* And we want each one of you to show the

Paul Ellingworth, *The Epistle to the Hebrews: A Commentary on the Greek Text* (NIGTC;
Grand Rapids: Eerdmans, 1993), 245.

   The enthymemes in vv. 3b–10 function to establish that an eschatological and
celebratory place of rest exists and remains to be entered, as stated 4:1 and reaffirmed
in 4:3a. These enthymemes may be regarded as additional proofs in support of proofs
as Quintilian acknowledges is sometimes needed (cf. *Inst.* 5.12.2). The argument can
be difficult to follow because of the premises assumed in the enthymemes. We briefly
suggest here a way of understanding their argument. Verses 3b–5 establish the link
between Ps 94 (LXX) and Gen 2 arguing that God's resting place is cosmological (i.e.,
from the foundation of the world) and thus not the land of Canaan. This is an
enthymeme of time, specifically antecedent time, i.e., God's resting place existed
before Canaan. Verses 6–10 argue that God's resting place and Sabbath are also
eschatological. Verses 6–8 argue that if God warns through David not to harden
hearts "Today" even after Joshua led the people into Canaan, then the cosmological
resting place remains to be entered and those who disobeyed will not enter it. The
argument is based on subsequent time (i.e., God warns through David about entering
a resting place after the time of Joshua). Verses 9–10 argue that one who enters God's
resting place rests from his or her works. We have not rested from our works; thus a
Sabbath remains for God's people. This argument appears to be based on contraries
(i.e., [A] All who enter God's resting place [B] rest from their works. [B-] We have not
yet rested from our works thus [A-] a Sabbath remains because we have not yet entered
God's resting place). For further discussion of the relationship between the cosmology
and eschatology of Hebrews see Jason A. Whitlark, "Cosmology and the Perfection of
Humanity in Hebrews," in *Interpretation and the Claims of the Text: Resourcing New
Testament Theology* (Waco: Baylor University Press, 2014), 117–30; and Ole Jakob
Filtvedt, "Creation and Salvation in Hebrews," *ZNW* 2015 (106): 280–303.

   [64] Hebrews 5:11–14 is a *digressio*. We will take up its discussion in the next chapter
on *narratio* since it helps to demarcate the preceding section (5:1–10) as *narratio*. The
digression, however, closely identifies with *argumentatio* as it facilitates a transition to
the audience and highlights some of its members' need for further training.

same diligence so as to realize the full assurance of hope to the very end, *so that (ἵνα) you may not become sluggish, but imitators of those who through faith and patience inherit the promises.*" (6:9–12)[65]

Deliberative Example

Similitude: Perseverance Advantageous/Apostasy Disadvantageous

"For (γάρ) ground that drinks up the rain falling on it repeatedly, and that produces a crop useful to those for whom it is cultivated, receives a blessing from God. But if [ground that drinks up the rain falling on it repeatedly] produces thorns and thistles, it is worthless and on the verge of being cursed; its end is to be burned over." (6:7–8)[66]

Deliberative Enthymemes

Motive (Loss): Apostasy Disadvantageous

"For (γάρ) it is impossible in the case of those who have once been enlightened, tasted of the heavenly gift, become partakers of the Holy Spirit, have tasted the good word of God and the powers of the coming age, and commit apostasy, to renew them again to repentance since they are crucifying to their disadvantage the Son of God and holding him up to public contempt." (6:4–6)

Comparison to the Lesser: Perseverance Advantageous

"For (γάρ) when God made a promise to Abraham he swore by himself ... Thus, Abraham who patiently endured obtained the promise.... So when God wished to show even more clearly [than he did to Abraham = (the lesser case)] to the heirs of the promise (= the greater case) the unchanging nature of his purpose, he

---

[65] Here again we have another double *propositio*. The first proposition is not the typical exhortation or advice but a statement that expresses present confidence in his audience's future (i.e., salvation) because of God's character and the community's past and present actions. The implied need for ongoing perseverance is then explicitly stated in the second proposition, which is expressed as deliberative advice recommending perseverance in the audience's present course of action because of its future advantage.

[66] On the similitudes of 6:7–8, see Ron Guzmán and Michael W. Martin, "Is Hebrew 5:11–6:20 Really a Digression?" *NovT* 57 (2015): 295–310, esp. n. 14.

guaranteed it by an oath ... so that we who have taken refuge might have strong encouragement to take ahold of the hope set before us ..." (6:13–20)

IV. Covenant Deeds – Levitical priestly ministry vs. Melchizedekian priestly ministry

    a. Epideictic Amplification (7:1–10:18): The deeds of the new covenant's priestly ministry are superior.

    b. Deliberative Argumentation (10:19–12:13): Enabled by the greater deeds of the new covenant priestly ministry, approach, hold fast, and provoke one another to loving action, not defecting from the covenant community.

Deliberative Propositions: Perseverance Advised/ Apostasy Discouraged

"Therefore, brothers, *because we have confidence to enter the most holy place by the blood of Jesus, by a new and living way which he inaugurated for us through the curtain, that is, through his flesh, and because we have a great high priest over the house of God,* let us approach with a true heart in full assurance of faith *because we have had our hearts sprinkled clean from an evil conscience and our bodies washed with pure water.*
Let us hold fast to the confession of our hope without wavering *for (γάρ) he who promised is faithful.*
And let us consider how to provoke one another to love and good deeds, not neglecting to meet together, as is the habit of some, but encouraging one another, *and all the more as (καὶ τοσούτῳ μᾶλλον ὅσῳ) you see the Day approaching.*" (10:19–25)[67]

---

[67] Here we have a multiple or triple *propositio*. The exhortations are complementary. They move from that which enables perseverance (let us approach) to the exhortations to persevere in the community's confession (let us hold fast) and perseverance in good deeds (let us consider how to spur another ... not abandoning meeting together). Each exhortation is accompanied by reasons. The first exhortation has reasons in the form of participles that give motives for one's approach to God. The second exhortation has a reason connected by an inferential conjunction that again provides the causal motive for the action undertaken. The third exhortation contains a reason that is headed by a coordinating conjunction and provides the motive for heeding the exhortation (i.e., so as to share in God's eschatological promise and not to suffer God's judgment).

"Do not, therefore, abandon that confidence of yours *which (ἥτις) brings a great reward.*" (10:35)

"Therefore, *because we are surrounded by so great a cloud of witnesses,* let us lay aside every weight and the sin that clings so closely, and let us run with perseverance the race that is set before us by looking to Jesus, the author and perfecter of faith, who for the joy set before him endured the cross while despising the shame and has sat down at the right hand of the throne of God." (12:1–2)

"And you have forgotten the exhortation that addresses you as sons and daughters, 'My son, do not regard lightly the training of the Lord and do not grow weary when you are corrected by him, *for (γάρ) the Lord trains the one he loves and chastises every son whom he accepts.* ' Endure trials for the sake of discipline *[because] God is treating you as sons and daughters.*" (12:5–7a)[68]

"Therefore, lift your drooping hands and strengthen your weak knees, and make straight paths for your feet *so that (ἵνα) what is lame may not be put out of joint but rather be healed.* " (12:12–13)

Deliberative Examples
Historical Examples: Perseverance Advantageous

The members of the community themselves. They are to remember their early days after their conversion when they "endured a great contest of suffering" because they knew that they had "a better and lasting possession." (10:32–34)

The elders/heroes of the community. "For (γάρ) by this faith the elders were commended [by God in the Scriptures]." They were commended for persevering faith. Thus God has prepared for them a heavenly city and fatherland. (11:2–38)

---

[68] This is another double *propositio.* The first is a negative exhortation that addresses the audience from Scripture. The exhortation is also accompanied by a reason. The second is the author's positive exhortation that is the converse of the deliberative advice and reason from the Scripture previously cited. The reason in the second exhortation is an independent clause but by beginning the clause with ὡς the conjunction possibly performs a double function of introducing the whole clause as a reason while also developing the analogy between God's training of the audience and a father's training of his son.

Jesus. "For (γάρ) consider him who endured such hostility against himself from sinners so that you may not grow weary and give up." (12.3)

Similitude: Perseverance Advantageous

"For (γάρ) what son or daughter is not trained by a father? ... All education seems for the moment not to be joyful but painful. Afterwards it yields the peaceful fruit of righteousness to those who are trained by it." (12:7b–11)

Deliberative Enthymemes
Comparison to the Lesser: Apostasy Disadvantageous

"Anyone who has violated the Law of Moses (= the lesser case) dies without mercy 'on the testimony of two or three witnesses.' How much worse punishment do you think will be deserved by those who have spurned the Son of God, profaned the blood of the covenant by which they were sanctified, and outraged the Spirit of grace (= the greater case)." (10:28–29)

Motive (Loss): Apostasy Disadvantageous

"For (γάρ) if we willingly persist in sin after having received knowledge of the truth, there is no longer any sacrifice for sins, but a fearful prospect of judgment and a fury of fire that will consume the adversaries.... For (γάρ) we know the one who says, 'Vengeance is mine, I will repay,' and again, 'The Lord will judge his people.' It is a fearful thing to fall into the hands of the living God." (10:26–27, 30–31)[69]

---

[69] Hebrews 10:26–31 is a unit. There are three related enthymemes. The unit has a basic ABA' structure: (A) apostates are subjected to God's judgment; (B) how much more worthy of punishment are apostates under the new covenant experience; and (A') apostates are subjected to God's judgment. In v. 30 the author quotes from Deut 32:35 and 36. The quotes support the conclusion in v. 31 that it is a fearful thing to fall into the hands of God, and thus 10:30–31 is an enthymeme related to 10:26–31. The disadvantage of apostasy is further supported by the implicit warning against idolatry assumed by the context of the quotations from the Old Testament. This implicit warning against idolatry is also present in the reference to the Old Testament law in vv. 28–29. For further discussion concerning how these references function as warnings against idolatry (i.e., apostasy) see Whitlark, *Resisting Empire*, 66–67.

Motive (Acquisition): Perseverance Advantageous

"For (γάρ) yet in a little while the one who is coming will come and not delay. But my righteous one will live by faith, and if he or she shrinks back my soul will not take pleasure in him or her. But we are not those who shrink back to destruction, but those who believe to the preservation of their souls." (10:37–39)[70]

Definition: Perseverance Advantageous

"Now faith is the assurance for what we hope and the conviction of things unseen." (11:1)[71]

V. Covenant Deaths/Events beyond Death—Sinai vs. Zion
  a. Epideictic Amplification (12:18–24): The new covenant's mountain of eschatological access to God is superior.
  b. Deliberative Argumentation (12:25–29): Do not refuse the voice speaking a better word of final vindication from the mountain of better, eschatological access to God.

Deliberative Propositions: Apostasy Discouraged/ Perseverance Advised
"See that you do not refuse the one who is speaking." (12:25)

"Therefore, *because we are receiving a kingdom that cannot be shaken*, let us give thanks, by which we offer

---

[70] Hebrews 10:37–38 is an inflated quote of Isa 26:20 and Hab 2:3–4. The quote forms one seamless argument that takes the form of a typical enthymeme. Thus, the NAS and NET translations do not offset these OT passages in quotation marks. Once, however, the OT passages are identified for this argument, their implicit warning against idolatry strengthens this enthymeme as proof for the advantage of perseverance and the disadvantage of apostasy. See Whitlark, *Resisting Empire*, 67–68.

[71] Quintilian notes that definition asks first what a thing is then whether it is this (*Inst.* 7.3.19; cf. 5.10.54). The author of Hebrews appears to have addressed both issues. The author has proven the advantage of faith in 10:39 where he states, "We are ... those who have faith and preserve their soul." He then gives a definition of faith that saves (what it is) followed by *exempla* of such faith (whether it is this). Hebrews 11:39–40 ("And these all were commended because of their faith yet none received what was promised because had prepared something better for us so that they would be made perfect with us") concludes the chapter by returning to the advantage of such faith that the author has defined and exemplified throughout the chapter.

to God an acceptable worship with reverence and awe, *for (γάρ) indeed our God is a consuming fire.*" (12:28–29)

Deliberative Enthymemes
Comparison to the Lesser: Apostasy Disadvantageous

"For (γάρ) if they did not escape when they refused the one who warned them on earth (= the lesser case), how much more will we not escape if we reject that voice which warns from heaven (= the greater case)?" (12:25)

Motive (Acquisition): Perseverance Advantageous

"Then his voice shook the earth but now he has promised, 'I will once more shake no only the earth but also the heaven.' And the words 'once more' indicates the removing of things which cannot be shaken—that is, created things—so that things which cannot be shaken remain." (12:26–27)[72]

Conclusion

In identifying these five sections of deliberative enthymemes and examples in support of propositions, we gain a crucial clue to the arrangement of Hebrews. The theorists treat proof of this kind, both deductive and inductive, as the essential content of the *argumentatio* – indeed, such proof is, by definition, *argumentatio*. Theorists assign extensive proof of this kind to no other part of the speech,[73] and on occasion explicitly state that it does not occur in other parts of the speech.[74] Furthermore, in extant speeches, it is typically found only in the *argumentatio* (e.g., Cicero, *Leg. man.* 51–68; *Mil.* 32–91;

---

[72] This last proof is a little different from the other proofs. This proof precedes its proposition in vv. 28–29. The causal clause ("because we are receiving a kingdom that cannot be shaken") and the conjunction διό looks back to the previous verses in 26–27 and articulates the fitting conclusion to the argument. The author is then able to conclude the body of his *argumentatio* rather forcefully with an exhortation. It also prepares the audience for the form of exhortation and reason that will characterize much of the following *peroratio* (see Chapter 8).

[73] See the short summations of Rhet. Her. 1.4 and Anonymous Seguerianus 1, which assign proof only to the *argumentatio* (or *confirmatio* and *refutatio*) and other non-argumentative materials to other parts of speech.

[74] E.g., for the exclusion of proof from the *exordium*, *peroratio*, and *digressio* see Cicero, *De. or.* 2.311–12. For the exclusion from the *narratio* (with qualification) see Quintilian, *Inst.* 4.2.53–54, 108–9. It should be noted that *exempla* can occur, on occasion, in the *peroratio*, especially of deliberative speeches (see Chapter 8).

Cael. 3–69).[75] Whatever we say, then, about the materials found before, after, and interspersed among these five units, we must assign the five units themselves to the *argumentatio*, and only the *argumentatio*, of Hebrews (assuming Hebrews is as rhetorically conventional in its arrangement of arguments as it is in its invention of arguments).[76] The topical ties (covenants' orgins, births, education, deeds, and posthumous events) that hold these five units together along with their singular deliberative focus on the advantages of perseverance and disadvantages of apostasy give these five sections the coherence of a single, sustained argument. This coherence only further weighs against breaking portions of these materials from the whole and assigning them, instead, to other nonargumentative portions of the speech.[77]

By recognizing these sections of enthymeme and example as *argumentatio*, we gain clarity about those parts of arrangement intimately bound with *argumentatio*. We have already seen that the exhortations function as *propositiones* since these are directly supported by proofs. They are also subsumed in the *argumentatio* and restated multiple times; thus *propositio* does not occupy a first-order heading in Hebrews as it does in some of the theorists' templates. Moreover, throughout the five sections of *argumentatio*, the author mixes arguments for perseverance (arguments for the thesis) together with arguments against apostasy (arguments against the antithesis).

---

[75] These sections, identified by Berry and Erskine as the *argumentatio* of their respective speeches ("The Form and Function," 1–17, at 8–10), are the only sections containing enthymeme and example. Other parts identified by Berry and Erskine (*exordium, narratio, propositio,* and *peroratio*) altogether lack these proofs.

[76] By beginning our analysis with the identification of thesis and proof, or the essential and exclusive content of *argumentatio*, we have found a fairly even, but interspersed, distribution across nearly the full body of the speech, beginning in 2:1 and ending in 12:29. This observation highlights the problem with most previous proposals of arrangement, which have in common the omission from the *argumentatio* of the early proof materials of 2:1–18 and/or 3:7–4:13. From Chapter 1 see, Von Soden, 7:1–10:18; Spicq, 7:1–12:13; Nissilä, 3:1–12:29; Übelacker, 3:1–12:29; Backhaus, 4:14–10:18; Thurén, 3:1–12:29; Anderson, 4:14–10:18.

[77] As previous proposals from Chapter 1 have done with nearly every section of proof identified above: **2:1–4/18** (*exordium*: Von Soden, Thurén, Koester, Anderson; *narratio*: Spicq, Nissilä, Übelacker, Backhaus); **3:7–4:13** (*exordium*: Von Soden; *narratio*: Spicq, Backhaus; second *exordium* or *eggressio*: Nissilä [3:1–6], Anderson); **5:11–6:20** (*narratio*: Von Soden, Spicq; *digressio*: Koester, Anderson; second *exordium*: Übelacker); **10:19–12:13** (*peroratio*: Von Soden, Spicq, Backhaus, Anderson; *digressio*: Koester [10:26–39]); **12:25–29** (*peroratio*: Von Soden, Spicq, Backhaus; Koester [12:28–29], Anderson; *digressio*: Koester [12:25–27]).

Clearly the writer does not reserve the latter kind of arguments for a *refutatio* distinct from and subsequent to a *confirmatio*.

As the outline above makes apparent, we are still left with the question concerning how to identify the rhetorical function of the five units of epideictic syncrisis dispersed among the five units of *argumentatio*. We have already demonstrated that these epideictic units are closely associated both topically and logically with their subsequent deliberative units that constitute the *argumentatio* of Hebrews. In the next chapter, we will take up the appropriate rhetorical identification of these epideictic syncrises by arguing that they constitute the *narratio* of Hebrews, and specifically a form widely commended by the theorists and employed by orators – the "disjointed" *narratio*.

6

PRESENTING THE FACTS RELEVANT TO THE CASE

Narratio *in Hebrews*

Thus far in our analysis of the arrangement of Hebrews, we have made the case that the five deliberative units (2:1–18; 3:7–4:13; 5:11–6:20; 10:19–12:13; 12:25–29), because they consist of theses and supporting proofs in the form of examples and enthymemes, can only be assigned to the *argumentatio* of the speech. The question remains, however, of how to understand the five units of interspersed materials (1:5–14; 3:1–6; 5:1–10; 7:1–10:18; 12:18–24) which we earlier identified as a unified, epideictic project that demonstrates the superiority not only of individual new covenant representatives but also of new covenant experience generally. In the present chapter we will argue that these materials collectively constitute the *narratio* of the speech. This identification is important not only for the arrangement of Hebrews, but also for its genre and purpose, as it serves to clarify further that Hebrews is *not* an epideictic speech and that praise of Christ and of other subjects serves – but does not constitute – the main purpose of the speech.

The Auxiliary Function of Epideictic Amplification in Hebrews

We begin with a preliminary observation that the five units in question consist wholly of epideictic amplification. That the materials are epideictic, as opposed to deliberative, should be clear by now (see Chapter 2) and in any case is widely accepted.[1] That the

---

[1] Scholars who argue that Hebrews is an epideictic speech generally point to these epideictic materials as central to the purposes of the speech. See, e.g., Harold Attridge, *The Epistle to the Hebrews* (Hermeneia; Philadelphia: Fortress Press, 1989), 14; Thomas Olbricht, "Hebrews as Amplification," *Rhetoric and the New Testament: Essays from the 1992 Heidelberg Conference* (ed. Stanley E. Porter and Thomas H. Olbricht; JSNTSup 90; Sheffield: Sheffield Academic Press, 1993), 375–87; Timothy Seid, "Synkrisis in Hebrews 7: Rhetorical Structure and Analysis," in *The*

materials take as their purpose amplification is also often acknowledged.[2] Several interrelated considerations further this conclusion: (1) the theorists widely affirm that "the proper function [of epideictic] is to amplify" (Quintilian, *Inst.* 3.7.6), in contrast to deliberative and judicial, whose purpose is to prove logically or argue,[3] so it should come as no surprise if both epideictic and deliberative materials in Hebrews have their usual respective functions; (2) the theorists define amplification as "speech that makes a subject seem greater" (Anonymous Seguerianus 230), which is an apt description of these units that heighten the greatness of their subjects: Jesus the enthroned heavenly mediator (1:5–14), Jesus the faithful son over the house (3:1–6), Jesus the high priest (5:11–6:20), the Melchizedekian priestly ministry (7:1–10:18), and Zion (12:18–24); (3) the five units are composed entirely of comparison,[4] and comparison is prescribed by Quintilian as one of four common means of amplification (cf. *Inst.* 8.4.3–14); (4) the comparisons in these units do not establish that something *is true*, but rather, that a matter *is greater*, and so should be viewed as amplificatory comparison rather than enthymatic comparison.[5]

Given that these materials are epideictic amplification and that they are interspersed among deliberative argumentation, we may further observe that the materials cannot constitute the *argumentatio* of an epideictic speech, but rather, must play some auxiliary role within a deliberative speech. This is owing both to the relationship of epideictic to deliberative and the relationship of amplification to argumentation within a single speech. That is, the theorists only prescribe deliberative rhetoric for deliberative speeches and never

---

Rhetorical Interpretation of Scripture: Essays from the 1996 Malibu Conference (ed. Stanley E. Porter and Dennis L. Stamps; Sheffield: Sheffield Academic Press, 1999), 346–7; Pamela Eisenbaum, *Jewish Heroes of Christian History: Hebrews 11 in Literary Context* (SBLDS 156; Atlanta: Scholars Press, 1997), 12; Ben Witherington, *Letters and Homilies for Jewish Christians: A Socio-Rhetorical Commentary on Hebrews, James and Jude* (Downers Grove: IVP, 2007), 43–8.

[2] See esp. Olbricht, "Hebrews as Amplification," 375–87.

[3] See the discussion of Heinrich Lausberg, *Handbook of Literary Rhetoric: A Foundation for Literary Study* (ed. David Orton and R. Dean Anderson; trans. Matthew Bliss, Annemiek Jansen, and David Orton; Leiden: Brill, 1998), §§ 59–61.

[4] See the detailed outline by *topoi* in Argument 8 of this chapter. Every sentence contributes to a *topos*-governed comparison.

[5] See Aristotle, *Rhet.* 2.26.1–2 (1403a); Cicero, *Part. or.* 71, cf. 53; Quintilian, *Inst.* 8.4.12, and the discussion of these texts in the previous chapter under "argumentative amplification."

for some subsidiary function within epideictic. By contrast, the theorists describe two functions for epideictic rhetoric. It may be employed by itself in a strictly epideictic speech (e.g., a funerary oration), or it may be employed in service to pragmatic or none-pideictic (i.e., deliberative or judicial) speeches (cf. Quintilian, *Inst.* 3.7.1–6). Indeed, according to Rhetorica ad Herennium, the second auxiliary function was epideictic's primary use and therefore the main reason for students to learn it:

> Nor should this kind of cause [i.e., the epideictic] be the less strongly recommended just because it presents itself only seldom in life. Indeed when a task may present itself, be it only occasionally, the ability to perform it as skilfully as possible must seem desirable. And if epideictic is only seldom employed by itself independently, still in judicial and deliberative causes extensive sections are often devoted to praise or blame. Therefore, let us believe that this kind of cause must also claim some measure of our industry. (3.15 [Caplan, LCL])

Similarly, the theorists frame *argumentatio* as the central function of a speech and certainly never speak of it playing an auxiliary role within and in service to *amplificatio*:

> [T]his book, the whole of which is concerned with this one area ["the Proof"], will, in these people's eyes, be the most essential of all. Indeed what has already been said about forensic Causes is subsidiary to this. For neither the Prooe-mium nor the Narrative has any function except to prepare the judge for the Proof; and it would be pointless to learn the Issues and consider the matters we discussed above, unless we intended to proceed finally to this. Lastly, of the five parts into which we divided the forensic speech, any one of the other four may sometimes be unnecessary for the Cause; but there is no dispute which does not need a Proof. (Quintilian, *Inst.* 5.praef.3–5 [Russell, LCL])

By contrast, the theorists describe two functions for *amplificatio*. They allow that it can serve by itself apart from any *argumentatio* as the central function of an epideictic speech, since epideictic gener-ally does not demand logical proof (cf. Aristotle, *Rhet.* 1.9.40 [1368a]; 3.17.3 [1417b]). More often, though, the theorists speak of an auxiliary function for *amplificatio*, whether as embellishment of

argumentatio specifically (cf. Rhet. Her. 2.28–30, 46) or any part of the speech (cf. Anonymous Seguerianus 160; Cicero, *Part. or.* 27).

In short, though the fairly even mixture of epideictic amplification with deliberative argumentation in Hebrews has given rise to the debate about whether the work is epideictic or deliberative in genre and purpose, that mixture is, in fact, evidence itself for the deliberative thesis, since epideictic amplification can only serve deliberative argumentation and not vice versa. And indeed, we have shown in Chapters 2 and 3 the specific manner in which epideictic amplification serves deliberative argumentation in Hebrews, establishing the comparative premise on which subsequent deliberative comparison proceeds.

As for the specific auxiliary function of these five epideictic units, it is possible given their interspersing throughout the body of the speech to treat them as expansions within and under the heading of *argumentatio*.[6] In this reading, which is certainly not without merit, the body of Hebrews would consist of one lengthy, deliberative, five-part *argumentatio*, with the epideictic materials functioning as digressionary amplifications within it. The strength of this reading is that it continues to treat deliberative enthymeme and example as *argumentatio*—a "must" in any understanding of arrangement. It also accounts for the remaining epideictic amplificatory materials as subsidiary per their most common function. What gives us initial pause in embracing this reading, however, is the sheer size and prominence of the epideictic materials, not to mention the regularity of their appearance and their coherent, internal topical organization. Does it really do justice to these materials to call them digressionary expansions? Would modern interpreters be so inclined to (mistakenly) treat these materials as the center of the speech if they were merely lengthy, digressionary asides?

In our judgment, an alternative understanding of these materials and their function presents itself that is initially more attractive if only because it assigns them a first-order heading of arrangement that better reflects their prominent status. According to this reading, the five epideictic sections constitute the *narratio* of the speech – and

---

[6] The only two possible locations for these materials, given that they belong to the body of the speech, are *narratio* and *argumentatio*. We have shown that other parts traditionally belonging to the body, *propositio, partitio*, and *refutatio*, are subsumed under *argumentatio* in Hebrews.

specifically, a kind of *narratio* not mentioned often in scholarship, but one discussed by nearly all the theorists: the disjointed *narratio*. This form of *narratio*, rather than being limited to a section distinct from and prior to the *argumentatio*, is instead distributed piecemeal in and among the *argumentatio* in an alternating fashion. Thus it bears a remarkable semblance in form to the epideictic project in Hebrews, which is similarly distributed piecemeal in and among a lengthy deliberative argument. Additional semblances are also apparent, but only upon closer examination of the theorists' discussions of *narratio*, to which we presently turn.

Because of the complexity of our argument, it will be helpful in advance to sketch its main tenets. We will argue that the material comprising the five units of epideictic amplification (1:5–14; 3:1–6; 5:1–10; 7:1–10:18; 12:18–24) identified in previous chapters is best viewed as the *narratio* of Hebrews because

(1) it has a location and structure commonly prescribed for *narratio*;

(2) it fits the parameters of the basic definition of *narratio*;

(3) it is a form of exposition the theorists regarded as especially suitable for *narratio*, namely, παραδιήγησις or "incidental *narratio* " in a deliberative speech;

(4) as amplification it takes the most commonly prescribed subtype of παραδιήγησις;

(5) it employs the major schemas or figures of *narratio*, most notably comparison, but also interrogation, indirect narration, direct discourse, possible direct address, and negation;

(6) it combines two or three temporal subtypes, past and present, in a special comparative figure of *narratio* known as ἀντεξέτασις;

(7) it covers a sufficient range of *topoi* to be classified as a complete *narratio* or διήγησις, as opposed to an incomplete *narratio* or διήγημα;

(8) it employs *topoi* of *narratio* both at the macro- and micro-levels of structure, which serve as structural headings of the outline of Hebrews's *narratio*;

(9) it employs persuasion appropriate for *narratio*;

(10) it is further demarcated as *narratio* by the one occurrence of *digressio* in its traditional, transitional location between *narratio* and *argumentatio*;

(11) it displays all the requisite virtues of *narratio* with one exception, brevity – a lack that likely accounts for the piece's disjointed structure in the first place.[7]

Epideictic Amplification as *Narratio* in Hebrews

Argument 1: Location and Structure of *Narratio*

According to the traditional quadripartite and quinquepartite schemes of arrangement, *narratio* comes after the *exordium* and just before the *argumentatio* (or just before the *propositio* and *confirmatio*, for those theorists who distinguish the two headings). In extant speeches, γάρ often marks the transition to the *narratio*.[8] While all theorists attest this traditional order, some debate whether *narratio* might also appear in other locations in the speech.

Part of the debate appears to turn on confusion of terminology. Διήγησις/*narratio* could refer generally to narrative of any kind, whether in a speech or in other genres, or it could refer as a technical term to the second part of the speech. Further, narrative in a general sense could appear anywhere in the speech; however, most would distinguish it from *the* narrative of the speech as Nicolaus docs:

> Narrative practices us equally in all parts of rhetoric: I mean deliberative, judicial, and panegyrical speech; for we need narrative in all of these. Furthermore, in as much as a political speech is divided into five parts, narrative is, on the one hand, one of the five, but often we also use it in the arguments and especially in proofs based on example, and even in epilogues, whenever we are reminding the audience of what has been said. (15–16 [Kennedy])

Indeed, the theorists would eventually (likely after the first century CE) come to distinguish the two kinds of narration, reserving the traditional διήγησις for the part of speech and coining a new term, ἀφήγησις for the more general kind of narration found anywhere in the speech:

---

[7] Most of these considerations have not informed previous proposals for Hebrews's *narratio* and, furthermore, collectively argue against them in our judgment.

[8] See examples and discussion cited by Frederick J. Long, *Ancient Rhetoric and Paul's Apology: The Compositional Unity of 2 Corinthians* (SNTSMS 131; Cambridge: Cambridge University Press, 2004), 84 esp. n. 8.

Furthermore, it is worthwhile to recognize the following, that a narration (διήγησις) differs from recounting of incidents (ἀφήγησις) in that the narration is a recounting of the things that have happened in the matter of judgement, but a passage recounting some incidents is often also included in the proof when examples are cited or when we introduce a rebuttal of what has happened by means of a narrative figure. (Apsines, *Rhet.* 2.3 [Dilts and Kennedy])

Debate over the location of the *narratio*, however, cannot be viewed strictly as a product of terminological confusion. Anonymous Seguerianus gives us perhaps the clearest overview of opinion on the question and sources, and from his sketch it is apparent that the debate went beyond confusion of terms to encompass genuine disagreement over whether one is allowed to include the part of speech bearing the name *narration* in some place other than its traditional location:

The Apollodoreans allow only one place for the narration, right after the prooemia, saying that there is a sequence after preparing the judge for hearing the case to bring in the narration. But Alexander, son of Numenius, and Neocles do not limit it to a single place but sometimes one place, sometimes another. Sometimes even before the prooemion, whenever the judge has been previously provoked and is in haste to learn the facts. There are also times when it belongs after the proofs, as (Alexander and Neocles) remark that Aeschines has done in *Against Timarchus* and Demosthenes in *Against Meidias*; this is fitting whenever the opponents have rather stongly attacked (each other's) accounts; for the judge will accept the narration more easily when previously softened up by the proofs. In (speeches of) Demetrius of Phaleron they say narration is found in an epilogue and after an epilogue; for such treatment is fitting whenever the judges have been strongly captured by the prosecutors. Alexander says the narration should be arranged before the proofs or among the separate proofs (in the latter case) dividing the arguments, and one should put appropriate arguments first, others in the middle, interspersing the narrative of what is left. But he says one should not ever narrate after the proofs; as we earlier said above, we speak narrations for two reasons, clarity and knowledge. If both of

these have been achieved through the proofs, further narrative is excessive; if not through the proofs, still, it is not right to give a narrative; for if what is stronger and more effective has not persuaded, narrative will accomplish nothing. Since it has been demonstrated that one ought not to have narrations after the proofs, it follows that they should not be put after the epilogue either. (124–131 [Dilts and Kennedy]; cf. Quintilian, *Inst.* 4.2.24–30)

One of the implications of this debate for New Testament scholarship is obviously that one cannot simply go looking expectantly for a *narratio* in its traditional location. Identification of *narratio* should begin, rather, with other more stable characteristics (function, content, schemes, topics, etc.), with location being a consideration only after materials suitable as *narratio* have been identified. If those materials happen to fall immediately after the *exordium* and before the *argumentatio*, then location may have a confirmatory effect for the identification. Atypical location, however, cannot be treated as refutation of the identification.

Complicating matters further is the related discussion of the *narratio*'s structure, a question about which there was little debate. Virtually all theorists allowed that the *narratio* could be presented *en bloc* as a single unit usually before the *argumentatio*, or distributed in piecemeal fashion in and among the *argumentatio*, so that the speech's body would alternate between *narratio* and *argumentatio*, starting with the former. This second structure, rarely discussed in rhetorical studies of the New Testament,[9] is mentioned in nearly all extant theoretical discussions of the structure of *narratio*.

Aristotle describes this kind of *narratio* as the "disjointed" narrative (in contrast to the "consecutive" narrative) and observes that "it is sometimes right not to narrate all the facts consecutively, because a demonstration of this kind is difficult to remember" (*Rhet.* 3.16.1–2 [1416b] [Freese, LCL]). In his concluding remarks Aristotle reiterates the point: "Again, the narrative should be introduced in several places, sometimes not all at the beginning" (*Rhet.* 3.16.11 [1417b] [Freese, LCL]). Similarly, the *Rhetorica ad Alexandrum* prescribes three ways of arranging the *narratio* in a deliberative speech – one of which is the disjointed style: "When the actions are too numerous

---

[9] But see Long, *Ancient Rhetoric*, 78, 81, 84, 156. Long only mentions Aristotle for his evidence of distributive or disjointed *narratio* among the handbooks.

and not familiar, we shall in each case put them in connexion and
prove them" (31 [1438b.14–29] [Rackham, LCL]). Cicero observes
that under certain circumstances "it will be necessary to distribute
the narrative piecemeal throughout the speech" (*Inv.* 1.30). Quintilian argues that "one has to take account of the particular circumstances of the Case in considering whether the Narrative should
be put altogether or divided up" (*Inst.* 4.2.101 [Russell, LCL];
cf. 4.2.85–87; 7.10.11). He further states: "For what is to prevent
us, if it is advantageous to the Cause, from ... subdividing the
Narrative and adding Proofs to individual parts of it, and thus
making a transition to the next section?" (*Inst.* 4.2.82 [Russell,
LCL]). And according to Anonymous Seguerianus, Alexander
Numenius cites lengthy or multipart cases as particularly suitable
for the disjointed *narratio*:

> Certain ones have also raised this question, whether one
> should make the narration a single body or should divide
> it into many? Now some say that the narration should not
> be divided but all of it kept together; for none of the other
> parts are to be divided. But Alexander says the other parts
> should be divided if it is useful, and the narration (should be
> divided) whenever there are many charges. It is necessary
> for us to bring together into a single body those (narrations)
> that combine the facts relative to a single charge, but others
> are scattered in many places; and he says that often, if
> they are long, they should be divided up through the whole
> length (of the speech), in order that we may not give an
> account as in a history. (132–33 [Dilts and Kennedy])

The disjointed *narratio* is well-attested, too, in actual practice.
Without noting the above theoretical discussion, Michael de Brauw
strictly on an observational basis identifies the structure and argues
for origins as old as the *narratio* itself, citing examples from Dionysius of Halicarnassus, *De Isaeo*, and Demosthenes, *Pro Phormione*
and *Contra Lacritum*.[10] We observe, furthermore, that Cicero employs
it in *Pro Cluentio*, where *narratio* and *argumentatio* are mixed

---

[10] Michael de Brauw, "The Parts of the Speech," in *A Companion to Greek Rhetoric*
(ed. Ian Worthington; Malden: Blackwell, 2007), 187–202 (esp. 190, 193–4); see also
Malcolm Heath, "Invention," in *Handbook of Classical Rhetoric in the Hellenistic
Period (330 B.C.–A.D. 400)* (ed. Stanley E. Porter; Leiden: Brill, 1997), 95.

throughout the speech – a fact noted by Quintilian (*Inst.* 4.2.85). Quintilian observes, moreover, his own frequent use of the disjointed *narratio*:

> The practice of placing the Narrative before the Proofs is intended to ensure that the judge is not ignorant of what the matter in question is. Why then, if Proofs and Refutation can be taken point by point, should not this be done also with Narratives? If any weight may be put on my personal experience, I know that I have done this in court, whenever my interest required it, with the approbation both of the learned and of the judges in the case. (*Inst.* 4.2.86 [Russell, LCL])

Turning to Hebrews, the fivefold material that we propose as the *narratio* of the speech, material that we will show to have all key characteristics of *narratio* (function, content, schemes, topics, etc.), displays a "disjointed" structure, distributed piecemeal in and among what we have shown to be a five-part *argumentatio*. Additionally, each unit of *narratio* begins with the expected γάρ in 1:5, 5:1, 7:1, and 12:18. Hebrews 3:1 is the only exception where the adverbial conjunction ὅθεν is used instead of γάρ, likely for stylistic variation. We have already described in Chapters 2 and 3 both the rationale for the fivefold subdivision of this material and the auxiliary relationship of each of the five individual expositions to its corresponding unit of argumentation.

Once the disjointed structure of the *narratio* is recognized, it is apparent that its location is otherwise wholly traditional.[11] That is, the *narratio* comes immediately after the *exordium* of the speech (1:1–4—see Chapter 7) and immediately before the *argumentatio* (albeit in piecemeal form). Thus in every regard, both the location and structure of the *narratio* of Hebrews fall squarely within the mainstream of ancient rhetorical theory and practice.[12]

---

[11] John Chrysostom recognizes the disjointed structure of the comparison of covenants in his comment: Βουλόμενος ὁ Παῦλος τὸ διάφορον δεῖξαι τῆς Καινῆς καὶ τῆς Παλαιᾶς, πολλαχοῦ αὐτὸ διασπείρει ... (Paul wishing to show the difference between the New and Old disperses it everywhere ...) (*Heb. Hom.* 12.1 (PG 63.120a).

[12] All previous proposals for *narratio* in Hebrews locate it *en bloc* at the beginning of the speech in conformity to the school template (Backhaus: 1:5–4:13; Thompson: 1:5–4:13; Cockerill: 1:5–2:18; Anderson: 2:5–16) and apart from consideration of disjointed structure and other regularly prescribed features of *narratio* (functional types, schemas, topics, etc.), with the result that early units of argumentation are included in the identification and/or later units of narration are excluded. *Pace*, Brian C. Small, *The Characterization of Jesus in the Book of Hebrews* (BIS 128; Leiden, Brill,

Argument 2: Definition of *Narratio*

The *narratio*, like the four-part theory of arrangement itself, was developed most closely in connection with judicial rhetoric and is often taught in the handbooks with this connection primarily in view, although always with the caveat that it can be adapted for epideictic and deliberative settings. In judicial contexts, the *narratio* traditionally functioned as a biased exposition of *the case itself* – that is, of the speaker's version of the crime in question. It naturally preceded the *argumentatio*, where the speaker would then attempt to prove that events occurred just as they had been narrated. Over time, however, other kinds of expositions came to be introduced, both in judicial settings, and especially in deliberative and epideictic contexts.[13] Speakers used the *narratio*, for example, to praise a key witness or judge by amplifying his or her good qualities; or to vituperate against an opponent by amplifying his or her dishonorable character; or to narrate history relevant to the case; or to tell fictitious stories wholly irrelevant to the case just to amuse their hearers and thereby win favor at a needed moment. Owing to these newer uses of *narratio*, the theorists refrain from narrowly defining *narratio* as exposition "of the case itself," though they often take this understanding as the starting point for their explanations. Thus Quintilian begins his chapter on *narratio* by stating, "It is most natural, and most frequently the right course, to point out the facts on which the judge is to pronounce soon as he has prepared for it by [the *exordium*]" (*Inst.* 4.2.1 [Russell, LCL]). When Quintilian later formally defines *narratio*, however, he does so broadly so as to account for the full range of potential functions (while acknowledging the traditional, narrower definition as well): "A Narrative is an exposition, designed to be persuasive, of an action done or deemed to be done; alternatively (as Apollodorus defines it) it is a speech instructing the hearer on what is in dispute" (*Inst.* 4.2.31 [Russell, LCL]). Other theorists' definitions are similarly broad:[14]

2014), 131, who identifies the disjointed style of Hebrews as indicative of λαλιά that did not follow the technical rules of arrangement.

[13] DeBrauw, "The Parts of the Speech," 193–4.

[14] The theorists may be contrasted in this regard with Heinrich Lausberg, who defines *narratio* too narrowly as "the (biased) statement of the facts (to be proved in the *argumentatio*) to the judge" (*Handbook of Literary Rhetoric*, § 289); and again, "The *narratio* is thus the detailing, in a manner intended to influence the audience in a particular direction of what can be only soberly and briefly expressed in the *propositio*" (Lausberg, *Handbook of Literary Rhetoric*, § 289). These definitions

The *narrative* is an exposition of events that have occurred or are supposed to have occurred. (Cicero, *Inv.* 1.27 [Hubbell, LCL)

The statement [*narratio*] is an explanation of the facts and as it were a base and foundation for the establishment of belief. (Cicero, *Part. or.* 31 [Rackham, LCL])

Narrative is language descriptive of things that have happened or as though they had happened. (Theon 78 [Kennedy])

[T]he narration in a judicial speech is an exposition of matters pertaining to some proposed question or, by Zeus, an exposition of the circumstances pertaining to some question. (Neocles, acc. to Anonymous Seguerianus 46 [Dilts and Kennedy])

A narration is an exposition of the facts in the hypothesis contributing to the role (in declamation) taken on the part of the speaker. (Zeno, acc. to Anonymous Seguerianus 48 [Dilts and Kennedy])

A narration is an exposition of a subject complete in itself by a bare statement of things that have already happened. (Theodorus, acc. to Anonymous Seguerianus 49 [Dilts and Kennedy])

Narration is an exposition of the circumstances. (Apollodorus, acc. to Anonymous Seguerianus 50 [Dilts and Kennedy])

The authorities want narrative to be an exposition of something that has happened or as if it happened. (Ps. Hermogenes 4 [Kennedy])

correspond only to the type traditionally found in judicial rhetoric, "exposition of the case itself" (for further discussion, see "functional types" discussed in Argument 4 later in this chapter), and do not account for the kind most commonly found in deliberative rhetoric, the incidental *narratio*. Biblical scholarship devoted to Hebrews has typically proceeded with a similarly narrow definition better suited for judicial, despite the fact that most agree Hebrews is not judicial; so, e.g., James W. Thompson, "Argument and Persuasion in the Epistle to the Hebrews," *PRSt* 39 (2012): 361–77 (369): "As Quintilian indicated, the *narratio* is a vital part of the argument insofar as it introduces the argument that will be confirmed in the *probatio*."

Narrative is an exposition of an action that has happened or as though it had happened. (Aphthonius 22 [Kennedy])

Narrative ... is an exposition of things that have happened or as though they had happened. (Nicolaus 11 [Kennedy])

A narration is an exposition and transmission to the hearer of the subject which we are sharing with him. (Alexander, acc. to Anonymous Seguerianus 50 [Dilts and Kennedy])

[N]arrations are an exposition of things that have happened. (Apsines, *Rhet.* 3.1 [Dilts and Kennedy])[15]

From these definitions emerge a few common themes. The theorists generally describe the *narratio* as "exposition" (as opposed to argumentation) of facts or events. They frequently clarify, too, that the exposition in view may be of events that have occurred or of events that are *supposed* to have happened. Presumed in this distinction is that the orator's narration is *biased*, intended as it is to present a version of events that benefits the case and not necessarily one that aims at objectivity or even the truth.[16] This bias is reflected by the frequent references in these definitions to some aspect of the speech that the *narratio* serves – the "question" or "subject" at hand, the "dispute" at the center of the case, the "hypothesis" argued, the "hearer" of the case, and the need for "persuasion."

Upon an initial, cursory examination of the five units of epideictic amplification we have identified in Hebrews, it is clear that these materials fit well within the broad parameters of *narratio* reflected in the theorists' definitions. First and most essentially, these materials are exposition – a fact often noted in Hebrews scholarship, which has

---

[15] While it is true that the progymnastic definitions have in view narrative in the broadest sense and are therefore as applicable to exposition found in myth, history, fiction, and drama as the *narratio* of the speech, it must be remembered that these definitions are specially formulated with preparation for declamation primarily in view, that is, they are "exercises preliminary" to declamation. Thus, their primary purpose is to introduce students to the specific kind of exposition found in a declamation, the *narratio* of the speech. Thus, in textbooks devoted solely to declamation, the supposedly broad progymnastic definitions are repeated without alteration as fitting descriptions of the *narratio* of the speech (e.g., Cicero, *Inv.* 1.27).

[16] Noting Theon's definition ("Narrative is language descriptive of things that have happened or as though they had happened"; 78), Kennedy explains: "I.e., a narrative does not need to be factually true. John of Sardis ... points out that there are many things in the orators that are not true but are regarded as true on the basis of the reputation of the persons who report them" (George A. Kennedy, *Progymnasmata: Greek Textbooks of Prose Composition and Rhetoric* [Atlanta: SBL, 2003], 28 n. 193).

long observed a steady movement back and forth in the speech between exposition and exhortation. Further, we will show that these epideictic amplificatory materials in Hebrews are an especially suitable form of exposition for *narratio* according to the theorists; that is, they employ amplification, a common functional subtype of *narratio*, and more specifically, they employ amplificatory syncrisis or comparison, one of the most commonly prescribed schemes of exposition for *narratio*. So clearly we are dealing with the kinds of exposition the introductory definitions have in view. As for the content of the exposition, these five units certainly focus on "events that have occurred." Specifically, the exposition centers on historical events, the most common subject matter of *narratio* according to several theorists. The presentation of this history, however, is deeply biased, presented as it is by a Christian writer and through the lens of the Christ-event. The exposition found in these five units concerns *salvation* history, and in particular the contrasting of the readers' present experience under the new covenant with the wilderness generation's experience under the old. This comparative exposition functions in a broad sense just as *narratio* is expected to function, presenting a version of events that serves the overall case. Specifically, it amplifies the greatness of new covenant experience in comparison to the old, which in turn serves the argument for perseverance under the new covenant.

Argument 3: Epideictic's Suitability for *Narratio*

In their treatment of the subjects of both *narratio* and epideictic, the theorists make clear that epideictic is not only well-suited for *narratio*, but that it is one of epideictic's chief functions. Further, epideictic appears to have been seen especially by the Roman period as a particularly suitable form of exposition for *narratio* in "pragmatic" cases, or cases where matters were in dispute before judges or political bodies. In such a *narratio*, the speaker would engage in praise or blame of various persons involved in the case – orators, witnesses, parties involved in the circumstances of the case, judges, and hearers.[17] This manner of *narratio* belongs to a functional class we shall survey shortly, παραδιήγησις or "incidental *narratio*," that is, *narratio* related to the case but not the case itself.

---

[17] Quintilian cites as an example of this form of *narratio* Cicero's account of the journey of Verres (*Verr.* 5.26–8), which consists wholly of vituperation.

Already in Aristotle there appears to be awareness of the pragmatic use of epideictic *narratio*. Though elsewhere Aristotle treats epideictic as primarily for display before an audience,[18] in his discussion of deliberative *narratio*, he states, "This [narrative in a deliberative speech] may be done in a spirit of praise or blame," and in that part of the speech "the speaker does not perform the function of the deliberative orator" (*Rhet.* 3.16.11 [1417b] [Freese, LCL]). Aristotle is here imagining a deliberative orator employing the second part of the speech to praise or censure some subject connected to the case. The epideictic *narratio* is attested, too, at least as late as Apsines (third century CE), who observes, "Some [narrations], as I say, are encomiastic and they give a detailed account of good works" (*Rhet.* 3.26 [Dilts and Kennedy]). He furthermore lists "the encomiastic" among his idiosyncratic set of *narratio* subtypes (cf. *Rhet.* 3.26). Quintilian, however, singles out the Roman period in particular as the time when epideictic came to be employed most commonly in service to pragmatic causes, and most of the illustrations that Quintilian cites are what is termed *incidental narratio* in discussions of arrangement:[19]

> I shall begin for preference with the Cause which consists of
> Praise and Blame. Aristotle and, following him, Theophras-
> tus seem to have separated this class completely from the
> practical – that is the "pragmatic" – type, and made the
> audience the sole consideration in the whole affair; this
> indeed is in keeping with its name, which is derived from
> the notion of display. Roman custom, on the other hand,
> has found a place for this function in practical business.
> *Funeral laudations are frequently attached to some public*

---

[18] See *Rhet.* 1.3.3 [1358b2]. Aristotle distinguishes here the audience's role of judge and from its role as spectator. The former role was traditionally assigned to judicial and deliberative cases, where decisions had to be rendered, while the latter to epideictic, where appreciation of the rhetorician's "display" was invited.

[19] Heinrich Lausberg, in his overview of epideictic, observes that one of epideictic's main functions when employed within a nonepideictic cause was as *narratio*. He states: "It is to be noted that an epideictic speech can occur not only independently (for instance, as *funebris laudation* [Quint. *Inst.* 3.7.2]), but also as a part of a speech of another *genus* (*genus iudicile* and *genus deliberativum*; in these instances, even as **digression in narrative** or dramatic poetry) or of the *genus demonstrativum* itself" (*Handbook of Literary Rhetoric*, § 243 [italics Lausberg's, bold emphasis ours]). By "digression in narrative" Lausberg means the incidental narratio, or *paradiegesis* (cf. Cicero, *Inv.* 1.27; see *Handbook of Literary Rhetoric*, § 290). He cites in illustration examples from Quintilian, *Inst.* 3.7.2 and 3.7.24.

> *office and are often entrusted to magistrates by order of the*
> *Senate; to praise or discredit a witness is important in court;*
> *it is a permitted practice to let defendants have people to*
> *praise their character; and finally, the published speeches*
> *against Cicero's fellow candidates, against Lucius Piso,*[20]
> *and against Clodius and Curio, contain invective, and yet*
> *were spoken as formal voting statements in the Senate.* (*Inst.*
> 3.7.1–3 [Russell, LCL]; emphasis ours)

Quintilian's comments illuminate, too, the aforementioned assertion in Rhet. Her. 3.15 concerning epideictic's primarily auxiliary function within nonepideictic speeches. The author of that anonymous work is in all likelihood imagining, in large part, the kind of incidental *narrationes* Quintilian describes.

In short, because the five-part comparative project in Hebrews is epideictic, it is well-suited for *narratio*, and indeed, such a possible function warrants careful consideration since it was among the commonest auxiliary uses of epideictic. Further, the project appears to display the essential characteristics of the epideictic *narratio* as it is most commonly sketched by the theorists. That is, it is employed pragmatically in a deliberative case before an audience that must render a judgment, and it engages in praise of subjects related to the case to influence that decision.

Argument 4: Classification of *Narratio* by Functional Types and Subtypes

According to the theorists, there were three functional types of *narratio*. The first was the *narratio* proper, or exposition of the case itself. This was the aforementioned traditional *narratio* wherein the speaker would narrate what he intended to prove in the *argumentatio*. This form of *narratio* was particularly at home in judicial cases, where it would take the form of an exposition of the alleged crime.

The second kind of *narratio* was known as the παραδιήγησις or the incidental *narratio*. It consisted of exposition related to the case, rather than exposition of the case itself. It was framed by some

---

[20] The invective in question (4.21–16.30), which entails syncrisis with Gabinius, is identified in Luca Grillo's commentary as the *narratio* of the speech (Luca Grillo, *Cicero's De Provinciis Consularibus Oratio* [New York: Oxford University Press, 2015], 97–8). The remaining two examples cited by Quintilian are only extant in fragments.

theorists as a form of *digressio*, since it technically would focus on something other than the case itself. Several theorists list subtypes of incidental *narratio* to illustrate it:

Rhetorica ad Herennium (1.12)
    (a) winning belief
    (b) incriminating an adversary
    (c) effecting a transition
    (d) setting the stage for something
Cicero, *De Invention* (1.27):
    (a) incrimination of opposition
    (b) similitude
    (c) amusement
    (d) amplification
Quintilian, *Institutes* (4.2.17–18):[21]
    (a) narratives told as examples
    (b) narratives intended to dispel some charge irrelevant to the case
    (c) narratives intended for amplification
Anonymous Seguerianus (55):
    (a) to increase belief
    (b) amplification
    (c) for prejudice
    (d) "something else of that sort"

From these examples, it is clear that any exposition that serves the case in some way, so long as it is not an exposition of the case itself, belongs to this category. One observes, too, that epideictic amplification is commonly mentioned as a subtype.

The third type of *narratio* was the exposition unrelated to the case. In rhetorical theory, this was the *narratio* written for practice as a progymnasma, or preliminary exercise. Most maintained it was never employed before judges in actual cases. Quintilian agrees but

---

[21] Quintilian helpfully provides instances from Cicero that illustrate each subtype: "Other Narratives, not belonging to the Cause itself but relevant to it, are (a) Narratives told as examples, for instance, in the speech against Verres, the story of Lucius Domitius, who crucified a shepherd because he confessed that the boar which he had brought as a present to Domitius had been killed with a hunting spear; (b) Narratives intended to dispel some charge irrelevant to the case; for example, in the *Pro Rabirio Postumo*: 'On arrival at Alexandria, members of the jury, the only means of saving his money which the king proposed to Postumus was that he should undertake the control and stewardship, as it were, of royal property'; (c) Narratives intended for Amplification, like the description of Verres' journey" (Russell, LCL).

later in his chapter on *narratio* allows that certain kinds of exposition unrelated to the case could fruitfully be employed in actual cases to arouse the emotions, to relax the audience with humor, or to serve as rhetorical ornamentation (*Inst.* 4.2.19).

In light of the theorists' descriptions of the various types and subtypes of *narratio*, the five units we are identifying as the disjointed *narratio* of Hebrews clearly belong to the second class, παραδιήγησις or incidental *narratio*. First, the materials consist of exposition that is quite relevant to the case while not being of the case itself, material that as Rhetorica ad Herennium puts it "enters into a speech as a means of ... setting the stage for something" (1.12 [Caplan, LCL]). As we have argued in previous chapters, in every case the exposition shows the new covenant representative to be superior to the old, thereby establishing the comparative premise upon which deliberative syncrisis proceeds in each subsequent unit of *argumentatio*.

Second and more importantly, as we argued in the introduction of this chapter, all five units consist of amplification, which as we have just seen is not only listed by the theorists as a subtype of παραδιήγησις, but it is the subtype most commonly attested in their varying descriptions. Further, Quintilian mentions as an example of the amplificatory subtype Cicero's description of Verres's journey (*Verr.* 5.26–8). Notably, this account consists of epideictic amplification (the description is an invective) and functions as incidental *narratio* in a nonepideictic speech – precisely what we have in Hebrews with the five units in question.

Argument 5: Classification of *Narratio* by Schemas

The progymnasmata, which gave students their first exposure to *narratio*, describe several schemas or figures that writers and orators could use to narrate events. These figures could be employed either by themselves or in combination with one another, though some were by their nature mutually exclusive (e.g., the direct declarative and oblique schemas detailed below). Pseudo Hermogenes and Nicolaus list the same five and describe them in remarkably similar terms and with helpful illustrations:

> The figures (*skhêmata*) of narratives are five: direct declarative, oblique (or indirect) declarative, interrogative, asyndetical, comparative. Now direct declarative discourse is, for example, "Medea was a daughter of Aeetes. She betrayed

the Golden Fleece." It is called "direct" because through the whole account, or most of it, it keeps the nominative case. Oblique declarative discourse is, for example, "The story is that Medea, daughter of Aeetes, was infatuated with Jason," and so on. It is called "oblique" because it uses the other grammatical cases. The interrogative figure is, for example, "What dreadful thing did Medea not do? Was she not infatuated with Jason, and did she not betray the Golden Fleece, and did she not kill her brother Apsyrtus?" And so on. Asyndeton occurs, for example, in "Medea, the daughter of Aeetes, was infatuated with Jason, betrayed the Golden Fleece, murdered her brother Apsyrtus," and so on. Comparative (narrative) is such as, "Medea, the daughter of Aeetes, instead of showing self-control, fell in love; and instead of guarding the Golden Fleece, betrayed it; and instead of saving her brother Apsyrtus, murdered him." The direct figure is appropriate for histories, for it is clearer; the oblique is more appropriate for trials; the interrogative is suitable for dialectical debate, the asyndetical for epilogues, for it is emotional." (Ps. Hermogenes 5 [Kennedy]

Thus we practice it [narrative] in different ways; for example, in direct discourse, in indirect discourse, in the form of a question, in comparison, and asyndetically. In direct discourse, for example, "Phaethon was a child of the Sun," and so forth; this is called "direct" because of use of the nominative case. In indirect discourse, which is so called from use of oblique cases: for example, "There is a story that Phaethon, child of the Sun ...." In the form of a question, when we speak as though asking something: "What then? Was not this and that the case about Phaethon?" In a comparison, whenever we say that "instead of being self-controlled, he loved strange things, and instead of controlling his love, he mounted the chariot," and so on. And asyndetically, whenever we proceed to say, "Phaethon longed to mount the chariot; he persuaded his father; he took the reins." Since the exposition takes different forms in this way, we shall use direct discourse for the sake of clarity in historical accounts or where we need clarity, and indirect discourse and questions in the arguments and the

refutations, and asyndeton in epilogues, and the comparative form where occasion allows, for there are many places
in all species of rhetoric and parts of a speech where we need
this treatment. (Nicolaus 15–17 [Kennedy])

Theon (89–91) attests and illustrates a more complex list of schemas
that includes some of these five and several others besides: (1)
straightforward statement; (2) more than a straightforward statement; (3) form of a question; (4) form of enquiry; (5) raising doubts;
(6) making a command; (7) expressing a wish; (8) swearing to
something; (9) addressing the participants; (10) advancing suppos-
itions; (11) using dialogue; (12) negative form; (13) asyndeton; (14)
combination of these. Since Theon's progymnasmata likely belong
to the first century, we may surmise that though the schemas were
taught in the Hellenistic period, Hellenistic education had not yet
settled on the five attested by the later theorists.[22]

Turning to Hebrews, we find that the each of the five sections that
we are interpreting as *narratio* employs across its full length the
schema of comparison as its primary means of exposition. As we
showed in Chapter 2, it is clear that all five units engage not only in
comparison of two subjects, but that together they form a single
coherent comparative project structured by the epideictic *topoi* prescribed for comparison. While interpreters have long acknowledged
the use of comparison in these sections, they have not, to our
knowledge, recognized comparison as a commonly attested schema
of *narratio*. This is, in our judgment, an important omission in
discussions of Hebrews's arrangement, as any ancient educated
person would have recognized *narratio* in part by the schemas that
it employed.

If comparison is the primary schema the author uses to narrate
events in the *narratio*, it is also true that he combines that schema
with others. This is in keeping with Theon's instruction concerning
the use of several figures of narration: "It is possible to combine these

---

[22] The matter is debated. Malcolm Heath has attributed the progymnasmata of
Theon to the fifth century ("Theon and the History of the Progymnasmata," *GRBS* 43
[2002/3]: 129–60), departing from previous scholarly attribution to the Theon of the
first century (Kennedy, *Progymnasmata*, x–xiii). Michael Wade Martin and Bryan
Nash have noted, however, how Theon's listing of encomiastic topics by the three
goods is characteristic of the centuries BCE and is judged the ancient method by
Nicolaus (fifth century CE), cf. "Philippians 2:6–11 as Subversive *Hymnos*: A Study in
the Light of Ancient Rhetorical Theory," *JTS* 66 (2015): 94 n. 16. We would further
note the difference from the later progymnasmata regarding the number of figures.

changes with each other and to create a mixture from two or more, thus to state some of the narrative in the negative, some with asyndeton, some however one wants, in order to make the language varied" (Theon 91 [Kennedy]). We may illustrate the author's method by attending to the first unit of the *narratio*, 1:5–14. This unit, in addition to employing comparison throughout, also employs the schemas of interrogation and indirect discourse.

Comparison

That comparison is employed throughout is evident from the sustained contrast of Jesus with angels topically arranged:

> *Origin* (1:5): Jesus is "begotten" as the "Son" of the "Father" on the day of his enthronement – the angels are not.
>
> *Birth* (1:6): Jesus is the "firstborn" in the coming world and worshipped by angels as such.
>
> *Pursuits* (1:7–9): The angels are "servants," but Jesus is the enthroned "anointed."
>
> *Death* (1:10–12): Jesus will have unending dominion in the coming world because he "remains," and in contrast to the angels, whose dominion will "perish."
>
> *Events after Death* (1:13–14): Jesus, not the angels, is exalted to God's right hand until all his enemies are subjected to him in the future.

Interrogation

Bracketing the comparative narration outlined above are questions, which the author uses to frame the piece as an interrogative *narratio*:[23]

---

[23] Whereas Ps. Hermogenes and Nicolaus speak of a single interrogative figure, Theon distinguishes two, question and enquiry: (1) "If we want to treat this [narrative] as a question, we shall do so as follows: 'Is it really true that a force of Thebans a little over three hundred in number made an armed entry during the first watch into Plataea in Boeotia?' And continue in this interrogative way with the rest of the account"; and (2) "If we want to treat it as an enquiry (we shall ask,) 'Who were the Theban men, a little more than three hundred in number, who made an armed entry during the first watch into Plataea in Boeotia' and phrase the rest as an enquiry" (Theon 88 [Kennedy]). The figure employed in Heb 1:5 and 13–14 may be described in Theonic terms as question.

> For to which of the angels did God ever say, "You are my Son; today I have begotten you"? Or again, "I will be his Father, and he will be my Son"? (Heb 1:5)

> But to which of the angels has he ever said, "Sit at my right hand until I make your enemies a footstool for your feet"? Are not all angels spirits in the divine service, sent to serve for the sake of those who are to inherit salvation? (Heb 1:13–14)

Variation of Inflection ("Indirect Discourse")

Finally, the writer varies the inflection both in terms of case and number so that nominatives are not monotonously used. Pseudo Hermogenes and Nicolaus call this schema indirect discourse and limit it strictly to oblique cases (and in contrast to direct, which they limit to nominatives). Curiously, Theon commends a similar variation of inflection, but through all cases (nominatives included) and numbers. Further, Theon commends such variation as something to be practiced generally (85) rather than as an optional schema. For explanation of the practice, he refers readers to an earlier statement where variation of inflection is also commended, and for the explicit reason that variety is "pleasing."[24] The explanation includes a number of helpful illustrations of the practice:

> Fables should be inflected, like the chreia, in different grammatical numbers and oblique cases, and one should give special attention to the accusative cases, because that is the way the ancients told most of the myths, and very rightly, as Aristotle says; for they do not relate myths in their own person but they attribute them to antiquity in order to excuse the fact that they seem to be saying what is impossible. The original grammatical construction must not always be maintained as though by some necessary law, but one should introduce some things and use a mixture (of construction); for example, start with one case and change in what follows to another, for this variety is very pleasing. An example is the myth by Phaedo the Socratic in

---

[24] As an example of inflection through the four common cases, see Rhet. Her. 4.31. See also the "we petitions" of the Lord's Prayer (Michael W. Martin, "The Poetry of the Lord's Prayer: A Study in Poetic Device," *JBL* 134 [2015]: 347–72).

his (dialogue) *Zopyrus*, for he begins in the accusative: "they say, Socrates, someone (accusative) to have given a lion cub as a present to the youngest son of the king." A little further on he changed the construction to direct discourse: "And, as I understand it, the lion, being brought up with the boy, still followed him wherever he went when he became a young man. As a result, the Persians said he loved the boy," and so on. (Theon 74–75 [Kennedy])

In Heb 1:5–14, we find a variation of inflection with regard to clauses involving ἄγγελος that appears to correspond most closely to Theon's proposed method in that all four common cases, the nominative included,[25] are used, as well as the common numbers. We focus here only on those statements composed by the author and not quoted from the scripture, in order to show that the author's own original exposition engages in a full range of inflection.

Number
v. 5: singular: τίνι γὰρ εἶπεν ποτε τῶν ἀγγέλων
v. 7: plural: πρὸς τοὺς ἀγγέλους
v. 13: singular: πρὸς τίνα τῶν ἀγγέλων
v. 14: plural: οὐχὶ πάντες [ἄγγελλοι] εἰσὶν λειτουργικὰ πνεύματα

Case
v. 5: τίνι (dative) γὰρ εἶπεν ποτε τῶν ἀγγέλων (genitive)
v. 7: πρὸς τοὺς ἀγγέλους (accusative)
v. 13: πρὸς τίνα (accusative) τῶν ἀγγέλων (genitive)
v. 14: οὐχὶ πάντες [ἄγγελλοι] (nominative) εἰσὶν λειτουργικὰ πνεύματα (nominative)

A similar combination of schemas is seen, too, in the other four units of *narratio* in Hebrews.[26] Without attempting an exhaustive analysis, we may note these in brief. The second unit (3:1–6) employs

---

[25] If, however, one limits the author's exposition to sentences that explicitly mention "angels," then the nominatives of verse 14 are excluded, and the author appears to follow the schema as Ps. Hermogenes and Nicolaus have described it, as one limited to the oblique cases.

[26] Brief occurrences of ἀφήγησις or narration can also be seen in parts of a speech other than the *narratio* (see Nicolaus 15–16; Apsines, *Rhet.* 2.3; and the discussion of these above under "Location and Structure"). So, for example, as previously noted in 3:16–18, the writer engages in interrogation to narrate the events of a deliberative example.

the schemas of comparison, variation of case,[27] and possibly address of participants (3:1).[28] The third unit (5:1–10) employs comparison and direct discourse.[29] The fourth (7:1–10:18) employs comparison, direct discourse, and at one point, interrogation (7:11). And the fifth (12:18–24), comparison, direct discourse, and negation.[30]

Argument 6: Classification of *Narratio* by Time

The theorists also classify *narratio* by time, dividing it into expositions devoted to the past, the present, and the future. The author of *Rhetorica ad Alexandrum*, for example, considers the division so basic that he includes it in his introductory description of *narratio*: "After this [the *exordium*] we must either report or remind our hearers of events that have occurred before, or arrange in groups and exhibit the facts of the present, or forecast what is going to occur" (30 [1438a] [Rackham, LCL]). Quintilian reports that the division is common, though he does not think much of its value:

> Then they add that a Narrative may relate to the past (which is the commonest form) or the present (like Cicero's account of the panic of Chrysogonus' friends when his name was mentioned) or the future (which is possible only for prophets, for a Hypotyposis cannot be regarded

---

[27] Occurrences of "Jesus," "Christ," and pronouns referring to him include the accusative (3:1, 2) and the nominative (3:3, 6). References to God via the pronoun occur in the genitive via the expression "his house." References to Moses occur in the nominative (3:2) and accusative (3:3). Also there is an intentional contrast of inflection involving πᾶς with the nominative, masculine, singular (3:4a) employed opposite the accusative, neuter, plural (3:4b).

[28] This schema, which employs the vocative address (cf. 3:1), is noted by Theon. Theon, however, frames it as address of participants in the events narrated; Hebrews addresses the audience members, but these are participants in the events of 3:1–6 in that they belong to "his house."

[29] That is, the exposition is carried by the consistent use of nominatives.

[30] "You have not come to ..." Cf. Theon: "Moreover, when stating the facts, sometimes we use the positive, but it is possible (as an exercise) not only to use the positive but also to produce narrations in negative form. The positive form is the way we said Thucydides produced his narration; a negative version would be, for example, 'Neither did a band of Thebans, a little more than three hundred in number, go under arms about the first watch into Plataea in Boeotia, an ally of Athenians, nor did Naucleides and those with him open the gates,' and so on to the end" (90 [Kennedy]). Apsines illustrates a form of this: "And sometimes we shall introduce attacks with a denial: 'I am *not* saying this or that (but I am saying something else)'" (*Rhet.* 2.28 [Dilts and Kennedy]).

as a Narrative). Let us keep our time for more important matters. (*Inst*. 4.2.3 [Russell, LCL])

Quintilian's comments are valuable not only for the illustrations he offers, but also for his observation that *narrationes* devoted to the past are most common, while *narrationes* devoted to the future are to be avoided. The latter observation has deliberative oratory in view – both its focus on the future and the question of how to narrate events in a speech focused on the future. Quintilian apparently disagrees with *Rhetorica ad Alexandrum* and instead sides with Aristotle, who similarly states, "In deliberative oratory narrative is very rare, because no one can narrate things to come; but if there is a narrative, it will be of things past, in order that, being reminded of them, the hearers may take better counsel about the future. This may be done in a spirit either of blame or of praise; but in that case the speaker does not perform the function of the deliberative orator." (*Rhet*. 3.16.11 [1417b])

In Hebrews, we find *narratio* that on first glance appears to belong to the class most commonly employed, that class devoted to past events. Indeed, the *narratio* of Hebrews seems to be very much what Aristotle is describing: exposition of the past (e.g., the exodus and the Christ-event) in a deliberative speech, conducted in a spirit of praise and blame, and with a view to preparing hearers to take better counsel about the future. Upon closer examination, however, matters are not so simple. While exposition devoted to old covenant experience is focused almost wholly on the past, exposition devoted to new covenant experience is actually most centrally concerned with the present experience of the readers (though certainly that experience, as the writer describes it, has origins in the past and hopes for the future). In essence, what we have in Hebrews is a mixture of temporal subtypes – what may be summarized as a comparative narration of past and present experience.

Such a mixture would seem idiosyncratic were it not for an intriguing paragraph on *narratio* found in Apsines's *Ars Rhetorica* in which Apsines describes a special use of the schema of comparison:

> In questions of result – by "result" I mean where something has come about from a decree or law or something else of the sort having been written or done – it will be fitting for you to introduce your narration from a contrast (*antexetasis*): namely, what happened before and what has happened now, as in the following: Lepsines passed a law (abolishing

exemptions to financial burdens on the basis of unusual service to Athens); Leukon ceases to send grain (from Pontos) and Leptines is brought to trial. It will be fitting for you to say, "Consider the situations, placing that in the past and that now side by side. Now in the past the city was surely flourishing because of the goodwill and reputation of good men and because of the abundance of receipts and all the provisions, to the extent that it had not only enough for day to day needs, but also two hundred talents which Callisthenes managed were left over; but look at what now is happening because of the law." And again in the following: Scythians founded a city, and when they became sick someone suggested they should abandon the city; for there too one should use the (figure) of contrast. (2.7–8)

In view of these comments, it is apparent that Hebrews's comparative narration of past and present experience is hardly idiosyncratic and that, indeed, rhetorical theory prescribed this kind of temporal contrast and gave it a name, ἀντεξέτασις – the contrast of "what happened before and what has happened now." Further, Hebrews employs the figure in the circumstances for which it was suggested in rhetorical theory: "in questions of result ... where something has come about from a decree or law or something else of the sort having been written or done." In the case of Hebrews, the "something that has come about" in the broadest sense is new covenant experience.

Argument 7: Classification of *Narratio* by Degree of Completion

According to Nicolaus, the majority of theorists in the Greek rhetorical tradition distinguished the incomplete or partial species of *narratio* from the complete with the terms διήγμα and διήγησις respectively (though some theorists use the terms for other distinctions):

> Some have said that narrative (*diêgêma*) differs from narration (*diêgêsis*) in that, they say, "narration is the exposition of the matters under debate in the law-courts in a way advantageous to the speaker, while narrative is the report of historical and past happenings." Others have called narration the exposition of true events and narrative that of things as though they happened. The majority, however, say

that narrative concerns a single event, narration a combination of many actions; the difference is the same as that between *poiêsis* and *poiêma*: Homer's subject as a whole is *poiêsis*, but the part about the wrath of Achilles or some similar part is a *poiêma*. (Nicolaus 11–12 [Kennedy])

This distinction is attested too in Quintilian, who reveals it was widespread by the first century CE, and in the remaining extant progymnasmata:

Besides this [the classification of *narratio* by *topos* – e.g., facts, person, place, time, causes], they make a distinction between "complete" and "incomplete" Narratives. Well, everyone can see that! (Quintilian, *Inst.* 4.2.3 [Russell, LCL])

Narrative is language descriptive of things that have happened or as though they had happened. Elements of narration are six: the person, whether that be one or many; and the action done by the person; and the place where the action was done; and the time at which it was done; and the manner of the action; and sixth, the cause of these things. Since these are the most comprehensive elements from which it is composed, a complete narration consists of all of them and of things related to them and one lacking any of these is deficient. (Theon 78 [Kennedy])

A narrative (*diêgêma*) differs from narration (*diêgêsis*) as a piece of poetry (*poiêma*) differs from a poetical work (*poiêsis*). A *poiêma* and a *diêgêma* are concerned with one thing, a *poiêsis* and a *diêgêsis* with many; for example, the *Iliad* is a *poiêsis* and the *Odyssey* is a *poiêsis*, while the "making of the Shield" (*Iliad* 18) and "Descent into the Underworld" (*Odyssey* 22) are *poiêmata*. Again, the *History* of Herodotus is a *diêgêsis*, as is that of Thucydides, but the story of Arion (Herodotus 1.23) or of Alcmeon (Thucydides 2.102) is a *diêgêma*." (Ps. Hermogenes 4 [Kennedy])[31]

---

[31] Pseudo Hermogenes goes on to say the authorities class narrative (the short exposition, and also the exercise) by mythical, fictitious, historical, and political or private (legal narrative in a judicial speech). Thus the *narratio* of the declamation would, by the authorities' reckoning [acc. to Ps. Hermogenes], be a type 4, political/ private "narrative" (partial) – and not a "narration" (complete work). But Quintilian (see below) attests authorities who would say the *narratio* of a declamation may be

Narrative (diêgêma) differs from narration (diêgêsis) as a piece of poetry (poiêma) differs from a poem (poiêsis). The *Iliad* as a whole is a poiêsis, the making of the arms of Achilles a poiêma." (Apthonius, 22 [Kennedy])

Though Quintilian is surely right in judging the distinction to be pedantic, Theon's comments are, for our purposes, illuminating. Theon suggests that the distinction may be discerned via the *topoi* treated. A complete narration or διήγησις in Theon's view treats all the narrative *topoi*, while an incomplete narration or διήγημα does not. The significance of this insight for Hebrews only becomes apparent upon an examination of the topics treated, which we undertake in the next section. What we will show is that, while most of the individual units of *narratio* do not take up the full set of *topoi* prescribed by Theon, the five units collectively do. Thus the five units collectively, in contrast to most of the units individually, may alone be deemed a complete *narratio*. This insight is particularly important in view of the fact that most previous proposals for arrangement limit the *narratio* to exposition in the earlier chapters, where the comparative project focuses solely on the topic of persons (Jesus vs. Angels, Jesus vs. Moses – see the analysis in Argument 8 of this chapter). By Theon's standards, however, these are narrative materials, but they do not constitute a *complete* narration. It is not until the fourth and fifth units of the comparative project that one encounters within these units the treatment of the remaining topics mentioned by Theon, namely, action place, time, manner, and cause (again, see the analysis below). Only with these units is the *narratio* of Hebrews made complete.

Argument 8: *Topoi* of *Narratio*

To assist the orator or writer in the composition of narrative, the theorists prescribe *topoi* (literally, "places") as search headings both for finding and organizing material. In essence, these headings encourage the orator or writer in the telling of the narrative to consider and answer every possible question a listener may have: Who? What? Where? When? Why? and How?

incomplete (focused solely on a person or place or time, etc.) or complete (focuses on person, place, time, etc. together).

Though the theorists vary in their organization of the *topoi* of *narratio*, there is a unity of agreement within the diversity. The simplest system is attested in Rhetorica ad Herennium and Cicero's youthful *De Inventione*. These handbooks divide *narratio* into two broad topical classes – the same division employed for argumentative topics:

> It is subdivided into two classes: one concerned with events (*negotiis*), the other principally with persons (*personis*). (*Inv.* 1.27 [Hubbell, LCL]; cf. Cicero, *Inv.* 1.34)

> Of such narratives there are two kinds: one based on the facts (*negotiis*), the other on the persons (*personis*). (Rhet. Her. 1.12–13 [Caplan, LCL)

In this system, "person" covered a full range of commonly attested sub-*topoi*: origin, birth, pursuits, death, events after death, etc. "Facts," or "events," meanwhile, was construed broadly to cover a number of other sub-*topoi*: action, place, time, cause, etc.

Most other theorists, by contrast, distinguish some or all of the latter sub-*topoi* from the fact/event itself and elevate them to full heading status alongside it:

> In dealing with it [the subject of *narratio*], I shall knowingly pass over the over-subtle divisions made by those who distinguish various types. They want the term to cover not only the exposition of the facts (*negotii*), which are the subject of the inquiry before the judges, but also any account (*expositionem*) (a) of the person (*personae*) involved (e.g., "Marcus Lollius Palicanus, a Picentine of humble birth, loquacious rather than eloquent"); (b) of the place (*loci*) (e.g., "Lampsacus, members of the jury, is a town on the Hellespont"); (c) of the time (*temporis*) (e.g., "In early spring, when on the whitened mountains / The frozen moisture melts"); (d) of causes (*causarum*), which historians very often introduce when they explain how a war or a rebellion or a plague came about. (Quintilian, *Inst.* 4.2.2–3 [Russell, LCL])

> A Narrative will be clear and lucid ... if it gives a distinct view of facts, persons, times, places, and causes. (Quintilian, *Inst.* 4.2.36 [Russell, LCL]; cf. *Inst.* 4.2.55)

> Narrative is language descriptive of things that have happened or as though they had happened. Elements of

narration are six: the person, whether that be one or many; and the action done by the person; and the place where the action was done; and the time at which it was done; and the manner of the action; and sixth, the cause of these things. Since these are the most comprehensive elements from which it is composed, a complete narration consists of all of them and of things related to them and one lacking any of these is deficient. (Theon 78 [Kennedy])

A narration becomes persuasive if (the speaker) tries to make everything he says resemble the truth. This would be the case, he says, if we do not set out bare facts but add the "parts" by which the narration is filled out. The "parts" of a narration are person, thing, place, manner, time, and cause; in addition, if the things said agree with each other and are not dissonant or contradictory; moreover, if we do not simply present the parts but narrate each of them in detail, as in *against Meidias:* "He was strong, dark ...." One should add a reason for all the (actions described); (stating the reason) is most inducive of persuasion. (Anonymous Seguerianus 89–93 [Dilts and Kennedy])

The elements of a narration are six; person, action, place, time, cause, manner. Person is, for example, the one doing something, the person of Demosthenes or of Meidias; action is what is being accomplished, for example, an insult; place is where it took place; for example, in the theater; time is when, for example, during a festival; cause is the reason, for example, hatred; manner is how it is done, for example, by words or by fists. There are some who add a seventh element, the material, separating it from manner and attributing acting illegally and violently to manner and to material the use of a sword, perhaps, or a stone or a spear or something like that. (Nicolaus 13–14 [Kennedy])

One observes that in all of these writers' descriptions, place, time, and cause have first-order heading status alongside person and fact/event. Most also include the *topos* of manner so that the question of how the action occurred is addressed. Nicolaus's comments reveal that, for most theorists, the *topos* of manner encompassed means, though some would later separate means as a distinct *topos*.

We will therefore employ the term *manner* with this broad sense in our analysis, as it would be anachronistic for our period to identify instruments of action with the technically more accurate *means*. Viewed collectively, the *topoi* attested in these accounts may be seen as covering the aforementioned questions any auditor might have concerning an occurrence: person (who?), action/event/fact (what?), place (where?), time (when?), cause (why?), and manner (how?).

One observes, too, from these lists some consistency of order – a matter of no small importance since the *topoi* could serve not only as search but also compositional headings. Every theorist attests a list that begins with person and proceeds then to event/fact (Quintilian's second list is the exception). Most then proceed to place and time, followed by cause. Only the *topos* that answers the question "how?" – manner – has yet to find a consistent place in the list. We would observe, however, that the only first century source attesting the *topos* places it after time and before cause.

In his discussion of order, Quintilian reports that theorists sometimes commend beginning a *narratio* with the *topos* of person. Indeed, Quintilian states that in actual speeches of his day, *narratio* most commonly began with person, and he explicitly notes the epideictic spirit of praise and blame in which the *topos* was handled.

> Some hold that a Narrative should always start from a person (*persona*), praising him from the start if he is on our side or discrediting him if he is on the other. This is indeed the commonest practice, because litigation is between persons. But the person too may *either* (1) be introduced with his attendant circumstances, if this is likely to be to our advantage ("Aulus Cluentius Habitus, this man's father, members of the jury, was a man whose character reputation, and birth made him a leading figure not only in the municipality of Larinum where he came from, but in all the neighbouring region," *or* (2) sometimes without these details ("For Quintus Ligarius, being …"). However, we often begin with a fact (*re*), as Cicero does in the *Pro Tullio* ("Marcus Tullius has a family farm in the territory of Thurium") or Demosthenes in his speech for Ctesiphon ("On the outbreak of the Phocian war …"). (*Inst.* 4.3.129–131 [Russell, LCL])

Quintilian's comments commend treating person as a single *topos* (option 2) or treating it via the *topoi* of attendant circumstances (i.e., origin, birth, etc. – option 1) and fact.[32]

In Hebrews, we find that the author has organized his five-part disjointed *narratio*, both at the macro- and micro-levels of structure, using the *topoi* and sub-*topoi* prescribed by the theorists, and in the general order prescribed by theorists. Indeed, the *topoi* govern every point of contrast in the comparative schema used to narrate the exposition, both with regard to content and order.

The topical progression of the comparative project as a whole we have already described in earlier chapters. The sub-*topoi* belonging to the *topos* of person are used as headings, in their traditional order, to contrast old and new covenant experience.[33] We may sketch the progression in outline form as follows:

Unit 1	Origin	Jesus vs. Angels (1:5–14): The new covenant's heavenly mediator is superior.
Unit 2	Birth	Jesus vs. Moses (3:1–6): The new covenant's inaugurator is better born.
Unit 3	Education	Jesus vs. Aaronic High Priests (5:1–10): The new covenant's high priest is better trained.
Unit 4	Deeds	Melchizedekian vs. Levitical priestly ministry (7:1–10.18). The new covenant's priestly ministry is superior in accomplishment.
Unit 5	Death/Events after Death	Zion vs. Sinai (12:18–24): The new covenant's mountain of approach is superior.

The topical progression of individual units of the *narratio*, too, may be sketched in outline form as follows:

Narratio unit 1: Jesus vs. angels (1:5–14)

The first unit, which we have discussed in earlier chapters, is a contrast of persons that takes up the sub-*topoi* of personhood in a conventional order:

---

[32] Cf. Theon, who similarly commends the treatment of person first and via the encomiastic *topoi* (78).

[33] As previously discussed in Chapter 2, theorists prescribed adapting the sub-*topoi* of personhood for the treatment of "inanimate things" such as cities, virtues, animals, etc. (see Theon 113–14; Ps. Hermogenes 16–18, 19; Quintilian, *Inst.* 3.7; Menander Rhetor 346–7).

Origin	Jesus is "begotten" as the "Son" of the "Father" on the day of his enthronement – the angels are not (1:5).
Birth	Jesus is the "firstborn" in the coming world and worshipped by angels as such (1:6).
Pursuits	The angels are "servants," but Jesus is the "anointed" whose "throne is forever" because he loved righteousness (1:7–9).
Death	Jesus will have unending dominion in the coming world because he "remains," in contrast to the angels, whose dominion will "perish" (1:10–12).
Events after Death	Jesus, not the angels, is exalted to God's right hand until all his enemies are subjected to him in the future (1:13–14).

Narratio *unit 2: Jesus vs. Moses (3:1–6)*[34]

The second unit is a comparison of persons via the sub-*topos* of birth. The unit is concerned to demonstrate Jesus's superior birth status within the household of God—and likely in conscious response to normal syncritical standards, which would have judged Moses superior for being born first. The unit functions ultimately to show that the new covenant is better born, deriving as it does from the better-born inaugurator.

The comparison begins with the subjects' similarity: Jesus was "faithful to the one who appointed him just as was Moses 'in all his house'" (3:2, cf. Num 12:7). But then the two are differentiated by birth status within the household. Jesus is said to "deserve greater glory than Moses" just as a builder of the house is superior to the house itself (3:3–4). How is the analogy applicable to the two? Numbers 12:7 shows Moses displayed his faithfulness "*in* the house of God" and as a "servant," his service taking the form of testimony to the things that would be spoken later (3:5). Christ, by comparison,

---

[34] This section is headed by a summons to "consider (κατανοήσατε)" Jesus. This is an epideictic summons to give consideration to the worth of a subject (ἀξιόω; 3:3). Similar summons can be found in Aspines's illustrations of *narratio*: "It will be fitting for you to say, 'Consider [σκέψασθε] the situations, placing that in the past and that now side by side,'" and, "'Already the greatest part of a war against the Sicilians has been completed; for consider [ἐνθυμήθητε] how badly off are the Lacedaimonians, in whom the Syracusians put their greatest hopes'" (*Rhet.* 3.7, 10 [Dilts and Kennedy]).

displayed his faithfulness "as a son *over* God's house" (3:6).[35] Thus Christ may claim the superior birth status within the household of God, despite Moses having been born first.

Narratio *unit 3: Jesus vs. Aaronic high priests (5:1–10)*[36]

The third unit focuses on persons, arguing via conventionally ordered topics that Jesus is the better high priest who undergoes the superior *paideia*:

Origin	Jesus, not Aaronic priests, is appointed as the Father's begotten Son (5:5).
Pursuits	Jesus, not Aaronic priests, is appointed to an eternal priesthood in the order of Melchizedek (5:6).
Deeds	Jesus, not Aaronic priests, prays in the days of his flesh for salvation out of death and is heard because of his reverent submission (5:7).
Death	Jesus, not Aaronic priests, learns obedience from what he suffers (5:8).

---

[35] Hebrews 3:5–6 is a μέν ... δέ construction that is arranged chiastically:

> On the one hand (μέν), Moses was faithful
> > in God's house
> > > as a servant
> But on the other (δέ), Christ [is faithful]
> > as a son
> > over God's house

[36] As noted in Chapter 2, the full syncritical argument is made chiastically with points of commonality tying corresponding units together. The full argument may be represented as follows:

A Aaronic high priests offer to God (1–3)
> **Bi** Aaronic high priests do not take the honor of priesthood (4a)
> **Bii** but are called by God to their vocation (4b)
> **Bi'** Jesus does not glorify himself in becoming a high priest (5a)
> **Bii'** but is glorified/appointed as the Father's begotten Son (5b) to an eternal Melchizedekian priesthood (6)
A' Jesus offers to God (7–10):
> - he offers prays and supplications in the days of his flesh for salvation out of death (7a)
> - he is heard because of his reverent submission (7b)
> - he learns obedience through suffering (8)
> - and having been perfected, becomes a source of eternal salvation as a Melchizedekian priest to those who obey him (9–10)

Events after Death	Jesus, not Aaronic priests, is perfected and becomes a source of eternal salvation as a Melchizedekian priest (5:9–10).

Narratio *unit 4: The Melchizedekian priestly ministry vs. Levitical priestly ministry (7:1–10:18)*

Whereas the first three units juxtapose persons and therefore take up the encomiastic *topoi* for persons, the fourth unit's much lengthier comparison juxtaposes two priestly ministries and therefore gives consideration to a fuller range of *topoi* prescribed for *narratio*. The unit begins with a contrast of priestly tribes or orders via the persons involved by employing a full set of encomiastic sub-*topoi* belonging to personhood in their conventional order as a source for points of comparison: origin, birth, pursuits, and death (7:1–24). The unit then contrasts the ministries of the priestly tribes under the remaining major headings of *narratio*: action, place, time, manner, and cause (7:25–10:18). The Theonic order of person, action, place, time, manner, and cause is followed perfectly in the overall organization of 7:1–10:18.[37] In viewing the entire piece through the lens of the topics the theorists prescribe for *narratio*, one gains clarity about each point of contrast drawn and the ordering of those points of contrast. Thus the topical lens allows modern readers to grasp more readily the unit's structure, which otherwise might seem repetitive and disorganized, and which in any case has in recent interpretation remained elusive. We may sketch this topical structure as follows:

Person	7:1–24
Action	7:25–28
Place	8:1–13
Time	9:1–10
Manner	9:11–23
Cause	9:24–10:18

Because of the length and complexity of 7:1–10:18 we will provide more extensive discussion of the use of these *topoi*.

---

[37] Rhetorica ad Herennium and Cicero's *De Inventione* would describe the topical progression most simply as an account of persons (origin, birth, pursuits, death, events after death) and facts (action, place, time, means, and cause).

Person: Melchizedekian priests vs. Levitical priests (7:1–24)

The focus on this comparison is not on individuals (e.g., Christ and Levi or Aaron), but rather, on the two priestly *tribes* collectively via various representatives. The topical progression clarifies the collective focus:

(1) Origin (7:1–10). First, the *founders* of the two priestly tribes are compared, Melchizedek and Abraham respectively.[38]

(2) Birth (7:11–19). Then, physical birth as a means of entrance into the Levitical priestly tribe is juxtaposed with resurrection birth as a means of entrance into the Melchizedekian priestly tribe.[39]

(3) Pursuits (office/career) (7:20–22). Next, the manner of "becoming priests" in both tribes is juxtaposed, highlighting the point in time, after one's requisite birth, when the priestly office is entered: for Levitical priests this appointment to office is "without an oath" from God; for the Melchizedekian priest, the appointment to office is attended by the divine oath of Ps 109 (LXX).

(4) Death (7:23-24). Finally, the finitude of the Levitical priestly representatives is juxtaposed with the immortality of the Melchizedekian representative: Levitical priests are "prevented by death" from remaining in office, but Christ "remains a priest *forever*."

One observes, furthermore, that these topically shaped comparisons are demarcated by the repeating μέν … δέ constructions. These occur in 7:5/6 and 8a/8b (origins), 7:18/19 (birth), 7:20/21 (pursuits), and 7:23/24 (death).

We may outline the progression in greater detail as follows:

Origin	Artless Proof (Witness): Gen 14:17–20 (7:1–2a)	
	Encomium of Melchizedek (7:2b–3)	
	Name	means "king of righteousness/ peace"
	Origin	without father, mother, or genealogy
	Birth	having no beginning of days

---

[38] Were this a comparison of Christ himself, Christ's own familial origins would be in view.

[39] Were this a comparison of Christ himself, the focus might be on his earthly birth, or even his *resurrection birth into the world to come* (e.g., 2:6). But what is being traced here is not Jesus's life beginning to end (whether in the present world or the world to come), but rather, the "life" of the priestly tribes, beginning to end. The focus of this topic concerns how one is *born into each tribe*.

	Death	having no end of days
	Comparison	resembling the Son of God
	Events after Death	remains a "priest forever"

Origin   Comparison: Melchizedek is greater than Abraham (7:4–10).

On the one hand (μέν), the Levitical priests receive tithes from the people, but on the other (δέ) Melchizedek collected tithes from Abraham and blessed him (7:5/6).

On the one hand (μέν), tithes are received by those who are mortal but on the other (δέ) by the one of whom it testifies that he lives (7:8a/8b).[40]

Birth[41]   Comparison 1: Jesus "arises" according to the priestly order of Melchizedek (so Ps 109:4 [LXX]). This metaphorical birth (and not his literal birth to the nonpriestly tribe of Judah; v. 14) shows that (a) the Levitical priestly tribe has been abrogated and replaced for its inability to perfect (7:11) and furthermore (b) the law pertaining to the Levitical priesthood has been abrogated (7:11–14).

Comparison 2: Levitical priests become priests through a legal requirement concerning physical descent (they must be born into the tribe), but Christ the Melchizedekian priest "arises" (and becomes a priest) through the power of indestructible life (7:15–17).

Summary: On the one hand (μέν) the law requiring birth in the tribe of Levi is abrogated (Comparison 1), but on the other (δέ) a better hope is introduced (Comparison 2) (7:18–19).[42]

---

[40] Interpreters debate the ontology of Melchizedek. Two major positions argued by scholars concern whether Melchizedek is either a mortal priest or an angelic one. Fred L. Horton (*The Melchizedek Tradition: A Critical Examination of the Sources to the Fifth Century A.D. and in the Epistle to the Hebrews* [SNTSMS 30; Cambridge: Cambridge University Press, 1976], esp. 153–61) is an early influential proponent of the former. But see Eric F. Mason, *"You Are a Priest Forever": Second Temple Jewish Messianism and the Priestly Christology of the Epistle to the Hebrews* [STDJ 74; Leiden: Brill, 2008], esp. 199–203) who makes a recent substantial case for Melchizedek being an angelic figure in Hebrews.

[41] Hebrews 7:11–19 is a distinct unit suggested by not only the topic but also the *inclusio* between τελείωσις and νενομοθέτηται in v. 11 and ἐτελείωσεν and νόμος in v. 19.

[42] The summary comparison highlights the effects (or lack thereof) of the respective births of each priest. The Levitical priesthood and those born to it perfected nothing but the Melchizedekian priesthood of Jesus enables one to draw near to God.

Pursuits   On the one hand (μέν), Levitical priests take office with no oath, but on the other (δέ) Christ the Melchizedekian priest takes office with an oath sworn by the Lord (Ps 109:4b [LXX]) (7:20–21).

Accordingly, Christ has also become the *guarantor* of a better covenant (7:22).

Death   One the one hand (μέν), death prevents Levitical priests from continuing in office, but on the other (δέ) Christ holds priesthood permanently because he continues "forever" (7:23–24).

Action: Christ's Melchizedekian service vs. Levitical service (7:25–28)

Several factors lead us to interpret 7:25–28 as treatment of the topic of action.

(1) The main claim in verse 25 is clearly focused on Christ's priestly action (saving, interceding). Verses 26–28 (introduced by γὰρ) elucidate the action topically via comparison with the Aaronic high priests.

(2) The unit also falls precisely where one would expect the treatment of action: after the treatment of person, and before the treatment of place, time, manner, and cause, where most theorists locate the topic.

(3) It is also possible to interpret 7:25–28 as the author's treatment of the final *topos* of personhood, events after death. Certainly the action narrated in 7:25–28, Christ's priestly salvation and intercession, is an event after death, and its narration comes precisely where one would expect treatment of the *topos*, immediately after the treatment of the *topos* of death in 7:23–24. This view, however, ignores the fact that that the μέν ... δέ constructions employed by the writer to mark the contrast of each topic of personhood in 7:1–24 (origin, birth, pursuits, and death) is now abandoned, with ὅθεν καί signaling the transition to a new claim or topic.

(4) More importantly, this view ignores the larger logic of the narrative unit, and the place of the treatment of action in 7:25–28 within the sixfold, traditional progression of person, action, place, time, manner, and cause. This is not to say the view is without merit.

Indeed, it is possible the author sees the full treatment of Christ's posthumous priestly service – not only the action itself (7:25–28), but also its place, time, manner, and cause (8:1–10:18) – as an extended reflection on events after death, negating the need to treat it at the end of his discourse on personhood.[43]

This section may be outlined in the following manner:

Action   Jesus is able to save those who approach, because he always lives to intercede (7:25).

Amplification of action: Jesus meets the needs of the community[44]

Person   "such a high priest is fitting for us, one who is holy, innocent, undefiled" (7:26a)[45]

Place   "separated from sinners, exalted above the heavens" (7:26b)

---

[43] Our analysis, which takes 8:1–10:18 as posthumous action, is favorable to the thesis argued by David M. Moffitt, *Atonement and the Logic of Resurrection in the Epistle to the Hebrews* (NovTSup 141; Leiden: Brill, 2011), esp. 216–96. Moffitt argues that Jesus's sacrifice should not be reduced to the moment of his death on earth, but rather should be seen as a process that begins with his suffering and death, leads to a resurrection that qualifies him for his Melchizedekian priesthood, and ends with ascension into heaven as high priest where he presents himself before God to complete the atonement – after which he sits at God's right hand. See also the earlier study by Timo Eskola, *Messiah and the Throne* (WUNT 2/142; Tübingen: Mohr Siebeck, 2001), 251–69, that argued for the unity of Christ's exaltation and atonement and thus associated Jesus's resurrection in Hebrews as "a necessary precondition for Christ's entering into the heavenly sanctuary and for the atonement that is made by sprinkling the blood of sacrifice on the mercy seat" (264).

[44] The syncrisis in vv. 26–28 functions both as a comparative explanation of the *topos* of action and as an anticipatory sketch of the place, time, manner, and cause of Christ's priestly action – the subject matter of 8:1–10:18. The comparison from artless proofs (law and oath, 7:28) also serves as a transitional statement to place (perfected εἰς τὸν αἰῶνα, understood spatially; cf. 8:1 which immediately follows) – the *topos* of the next section. Luke Timothy Johnson (*Hebrews: A Commentary* [NTL; Louisville: Westminster John Knox, 2006], 194) notes that the idea of "fitting" (πρέπω) in v. 26 means "what we truly need" in a high priest. This notion of πρέπω is reflected in the NIV translation: "such a priestly truly meets our needs."

[45] The author lists the priestly virtues of Jesus as "holy, innocent, undefiled." Virtues could serve as headings for discussing actions. Menander Rhetor in his discussion on the *topos* of the actions of a king states, "Always divide the actions of those you are going to praise into the virtues (there are four virtues: courage, justice, temperance, and wisdom)" (373 [Russell and Wilson]). See also Nicolaus 52 and Cicero, *Part. or.* 75. In the case of Heb 7:26, the virtues listed uniquely qualify Jesus for his priestly action of saving, interceding, and entering.

Time	"who does not need, like the high priests, day after day" (7:27a)
Cause	"first for his own sins ... then for the sins of the people" (7:27b,d)
Manner	"to offer sacrifices" (7:27c)
Cause	"For this he did" (7:27e)
Time	"once for all time" (7:27f)
Manner	"when he offered himself" (7:27g)[46]
Artless Proof	"For the *law* appoints as priests men who have weakness but the word of the *oath* which came after the law appoints a son who has been made perfect forever." (28)

Place: Christ's Melchizedekian service vs. Levitical service (8:1–13)

Hebrews 8:1–13 is devoted to the topic of place, as is evident for at least four reasons:

(1) The comparison of priestly service in 8:1–5 focuses on place. Hebrews 8:1–2 narrates Christ's priestly service with an emphasis on its location. He is "one who sat down at the right hand of the throne of Majesty in heaven," and he is a minister "in the sanctuary and the true tent that the Lord, not humans, set up." Hebrews 8:3–5 then explicitly compares Christ's service with the high priests', and while three *topoi* are in view (person, action, and place), only the *topos* of place is used to draw points of contrast. Verse 3 states that both are priests (person) who offer gifts and sacrifices (action). Verses 4–5 then draws the distinction of place: if Christ were on earth, he would not be a priest; earthly priests serve in a copy and a shadow of the heavenly things.

(2) The comparison of covenants in 8:6–13 emphasizes place. The key sentence is verse 7, and the key phrase is obscured in many English translations. The writer states, "For if that first (covenant)

---

[46] We are treating the means of the sacrifice under the broader *topos* of "manner" as did the theorists of the early first century CE. Later theorists would more accurately distinguish the means or "material" of the action from the "manner." On "himself" as the means of the offering, see Heb 9:24–25; cf. 9:7; 12. In these passages, the specific instrument of sacrifice is in view, with Christ's blood/himself contrasted with the blood of sheep and goats.

had been blameless, *a place* (τόπος) *for a second* would not have been sought." Here, "place for a second" should be taken literally as a reference to the heavenly sanctuary (e.g., NIV), and not metaphorically as an occasion (e.g., ESV, NAS, NRSV).[47] The writer is arguing that the expectant searching for a superior covenant carried with it, as a corollary, the expectant searching for the superior place where it would be mediated. This interpretation is also commended by the μέν ... δέ construction of vv. 4–6. The focus in the μέν-half of the construction on the Levitical place of service on earth naturally creates the expectation that δέ half will similarly focus on Christ's place of service in heaven. This expectation is only met if we opt for the literal reading of τόπος in verse 7.

(3) The scriptures cited in chapter 8 speak to place. Exodus 25:40 ("See that you make everything according to the pattern shown to you on the mountain") is invoked to show that Christ's "sanctuary" is the heavenly original, and the Levitical priests', an earthly copy. The second, Jer 38:31–34 (LXX), as we have seen is framed by the author as proof that a *"place "* for that covenant was all along "being sought." This claim appears to be encouraged by the larger context of Jer 38, which speaks to the place that the new covenant will lead. Jeremiah's prophecy of the new covenant is followed by a prophecy concerning the rebuilding of Jerusalem that will never again be overthrown (cf. 38:38–40 [LXX]). In Hebrews, the new covenant leads to the place of the indomitable, heavenly Jerusalem, where Jesus the mediator of the new covenant resides (cf. 12:22). The writer also alludes to a third text in 8:1, Ps 109:1 (LXX), which, as we have already observed, points to the place of the exalted Son in the heavenly realm.

(4) Finally, this topic of place is taken up where one would expect the discussion of the topic in a narration. Rhetorical theorists traditionally list the topic of place in a narration after the treatment of person and action but before the treatment of time, manner, and cause. Hebrews 8 follows the topics of person and action in chapter 7 and precedes the topics of time, manner, and cause in chapters 9–10.

One final consideration further commends viewing the present section as a major unit devoted to place, namely, the structure it

---

[47] Cf. Heb 11:8, which employs the spatial meaning, and Heb 12:17, where the metaphorical meaning is used.

has in common with the remaining units devoted, respectively, to time, manner, and cause in 9:1–10:18. These four sections may be seen as four parallel literary panels with a common outline and internal logic. Each one moves from a comparison of service to a comparison of covenants ("A" and "B" respectively in the outlines below).[48] In every case, the comparison of service and covenants focuses attention on the main *topos* of the unit.

We may outline Heb 8:1–13 in the following manner:

A. Place of Service Compared (8:1–5)

Person	"We have such a high priest" (8:1a)
Action	"who sat down" (8:1b)
Place	"at the right hand of the throne of Majesty in heaven" (8:1c)
Person	"a minister" (8:2a)
Place	"in the sanctuary and true tabernacle that the Lord, not humans, set up." (8:2b)
Person	"Every priest"
Action	"is appointed to offer gifts and sacrifices ..." (8:3)
Place	"if he were on earth ... who serve in a copy and shadow of the heavenly ..." (8:4 5)

B. Covenants compared (8:6–13): a **place** (τόπος) for a second covenant

Time: Christ's Melchizedekian service vs. Levitical service (9:1–10)[49]

We identify this unit as a treatment of the *topos* of time for the following reasons:

(1) In this comparison of the ordinary priests' continual service with that of the high priest's once-a-year service, the *topos* of time is now added as the only new *topos* of comparison. The manner and cause of the high priest's action, though narrated at the end of the comparison, are not employed as *topoi* of comparison – that is, there

---

[48] This observation is a modification of Craig Koester's proposal, which posits three instead of four similar movements. See *Hebrews: A New Translation with Introduction and Commentary* (AB 36; New York: Doubleday, 2001), 336.

[49] This section is held together by an *inclusio* with δικαιώματα in 9:1 and 9:10.

is no contrasting treatment of manner and cause of the ordinary priests' action.

(2) The comparison of covenants in verses 8–10 of this section is focused solely on the *topos* of time.[50] The way into the holy of holies was "not yet" (μήπω) revealed as long as the first tent (= first covenant) was standing. The first tent is "a symbol for the present time (παραβολὴ εἰς τὸν καιρὸν τὸν ἐνεστηκότα)." The fleshly regulations of the old covenant were only in force "until the time of correction (μέχρι καιροῦ διορθώσεως)" – that is, until the exaltation of Jesus that brings about the new covenant in the last days. The two phrases in verses 9–10 both explicitly invoke the *topos* of time by the use of the word, καιρός, in their contrasting *temporal* characterizations of the old and new covenants respectively.

(3) The unit comes in the expected location for a treatment of time, after person, action, and place (7–8) and before treatment of manner and cause (9:11–10:18).

This section may be outlined as follows:

    A. Time of service compared (9:1–7)
        Levitical priests' service

        Place   (μέν[51]) The two tents described (9:1–5)
                    (μέν[52]) "into the first tent" (9:6a)

---

[50] Covenant is in view in 9:8–10 for the following reasons: (1) already in 9:2–3, the dividing the tabernacle into "first" and "second" tents makes them amenable to associations with the "first" and "new (second)" covenants (cf. 8:7, 13; 9:1, 15, 18); (2) the mention of the first (πρώτη) tent and of its fleshly regulations (δικαιώματα) echoes 9:1 where the author states that the first (πρώτη) covenant had regulations (δικαιώματα) for service; (3) the first tent and the lack of access it provides to the holy of holies is taken as a "symbol," namely of the first covenant and /or present cosmos to which the first covenant belongs; (4) the regulations of the first tent under the first covenant are framed as being of a limited duration and enforced only until the arrival of "the time of correction" – a sentiment that echoes the end of ch. 8 where the old covenant disappears in light of the arrival of the new; and (5) the "time of correction" recalls 8:7–9 and the fault that is found with the old covenant, namely its inability to perfect the worshipper according to the conscience through its priestly service. For further discussion, see Koester, *Hebrews*, 393–406; David A. deSilva, *Perseverance in Gratitude: A Socio-Rhetorical Commentary on the Epistle "to the Hebrews"* (Grand Rapids: Eerdmans, 2000), 297–303; Kenneth L. Schenck, *Cosmology and Eschatology in Hebrews: The Settings of the Sacrifice* (SNTMS 143; Cambridge: Cambridge University Press, 2007), 96–9, 149–55.

[51] This first μέν in 9:1 anticipates the δέ of 9:11, thus framing the full sketch of Levitical service (both by the priests and the high priest) in 9:1–7 as the first half of the comparison with Christ's priestly service in 9:11–14.

[52] The second μέν in 9:6 anticipates the δέ of 9:7, thus framing 9:6 as the first half of the Levitical priest / high priest comparison.

Time   "continually" (9:6b)
Person   "the priests" (9:6c)
Action   "enter, completing their service." (9:6d)

High priest's service

Place   (δέ) "but into the second tent" (9:7a)
Time   "once a year only" (9:7b)
Person   "the high priest" (9:7c)
Action   (enters)
[Manner]   "not without blood"
[Cause][53] "which he offers for himself and the people's sins of ignorance" (9:7d)

B. Covenants compared (9:8–10): the **time** (καιρός) of the covenants

Manner: Christ's Melchizedekian service vs. Levitical service (9:11–23)

Numerous factors suggest this unit is devoted to the *topos* of manner, which was understood by first-century theorists to include means. In this section, the means of priestly service in view is the sacrifice offered, and most often, the blood of the sacrifice.

(1) The comparative sketch of Christ's priestly service in verses 11–14 employs all six *topoi*, but manner is singled out for special emphasis in a concluding amplificatory comparison in 9:13–14. Further, it receives special emphasis within the six-*topos* sketch as the only *topos* framed with a comparative formula (οὐδέ ... δέ) in verse 12.

(2) The comparison of covenants in verses 15–23 is focused exclusively on manner – that is, on what the blood or sacrifice accomplishes. In the case of both covenants, blood inaugurates and cleanses.

(3) The only text quoted in this unit, Exod 24:8, further underscores blood, the means of the sacrificial service, as the unit's central

---

[53] The manner and cause of the sacrifice are narrated but not made topics of comparison. That is, there is no contrasting manner and cause mentioned as a corresponding item in the μέν clause in v. 6 of the comparison. The mention of manner and cause here in the depiction of the high priest's action is thus anticipatory, foreshadowing the comparison with Christ, the high priest in the next unit.

concern: "This is the blood of the covenant that God has commanded you to keep."

(4) Whereas in the preceding two units, the key word was a *topos* explicitly named ("place" [τόπος], 8:7; "time" [καιρός], 9:9, 10), here the *subject* of the *topos* in view – the "blood (αἷμα)" – receives emphasis as a key word through repetition. Ten of the twenty-two occurrences of the word, αἷμα, in Hebrews appear in this unit (including αἱματεκχυσία in verse 22). The word is also emphasized through the schema of indirect discourse (variation of inflection), as it appears in all four cases.

(5) The unit comes in the expected place, after sections devoted to person, action, place, and time (7:1–9:10), and just before that devoted to cause (9:24–10:18).

This section may be outlined in the following manner:

A. Manner of service compared (9:11–14)

Person	"(δέ[54]) But when Christ came, the high priest of the good things to come," (9:11a)
Place	"through the greater and more perfect tent not made with hands – that is, not of this creation – " (9:11b)
Manner	"(οὐδέ) not with the blood (αἵματος) of goats and calves (δὲ) but with his own blood (αἵματος)" (9:12a)
Action	"entered" (9:12b)
Time	"once for all' (9:12c)
Place	"into the holy of holies," (9:12d)
Cause	"so that he obtained redemption" (9:12e)

Amplification of manner (αἷμα) via cause

Manner	"For if the blood (αἷμα) of goats and bulls and the sprinkling of the ashes of a heifer sanctifies those who have been defiled" (9:13a)

---

[54] This δὲ in 9:11 answers the μὲν of 9:1. Thus the six *topoi* employed in the sketch of Christ's priestly service in 9:11–12 may be seen as *topoi* of comparison, answering six *topoi* of comparison employed in the sketch of Levitical service in 9:1–7 – both the four *topoi* used to contrast the priests' service with the high priest's, and the two *topoi* mentioned as an addendum in the sketch of the latter (see the outline above). Only in 9:11–12, then, does the reason for the mention of those two additional *topoi* become apparent: the writer is anticipating the comparison with Christ in 9:11–14.

      Cause   "for the purification of the flesh" (9:13b)

      Manner   "how much more will the blood (αἷμα) of Christ who offered himself through the eternal Spirit purify our conscience from dead works" (9:14a)[55]

      Cause   "so that we might serve the living God." (9:14b)

B. Covenants compared (9:15–23): the **blood** (αἷμα) of the covenants[56]

Cause: Christ's Melchizedekian service vs. Levitical service (9:24–10:18)

We view 9:24–10:18 as treatment of the *topos* of cause understood broadly, as the theorists frame it, to encompass reasons, motives, or purposes underlying an action. In this unit, the cause in view is the removal or forgiveness of sins and thus the perfecting and sanctifying of God's people. There are several reasons for this identification.

(1) The one recurring and climactic element in every comparison of this unit is the ascription of the cause of the removal of sins to Christ's ministry and not to the Levitical ministry: "for the removal of sin" (9:26); "to bear the sins of many" (9:28); "to remind of sins" (10:3); "unable to take away sins" (10:4); "can never take away sins" (10:11); "for sins" (10:12); "theirs sins and lawlessness I will remember no more ... and where there is forgiveness of these there is no longer an offering for sin" (10:18).

---

[55] See the proposal by Moffitt, *Atonement and the Logic of Resurrection*, 279–80, n. 140, where he argues that the Holy Spirit as the power/agent that resurrects Jesus and thus enables him to present his resurrected life before God.

[56] In this section blood occurs six times in most of its inflected forms: αἷματος; αἷμα *2; αἷματι *2; αἱματεκχυσίας. Here the blood inaugurates the covenants. For those interpreters who see 9:23 as concluding this section see Albert Vanhoye, *La structure littéraire de l'Épitre aux Hébreux* (Paris: Desclée de Brouwer, 1963) 152–4; Hans-Friedrich Weiss, *Der Brief an die Hebräer* (KEK 15; Göttingen: Vandenhoeck & Ruprecht, 1991), 485; Koester, *Hebrews*, 427; Georg Gäbel, *Die Kulttheologie des Hebräerbriefes: Eine exegetisch-religionsgeschichtliche Studie* (WUNT 2/212; Tübingen: Mohr Siebeck, 2006), 295, 425. For a recent discussion of 9:23 and its association with what follows in 9:24–28, see R. B. Jamieson, "Hebrews 9.23: Cult Inauguration, Yom Kippur and the Cleansing of the Heavenly Tabernacle," *NTS* 62 (2016): 569–87.

(2) The comparison of service highlights cause in several ways. First, in 9:24–26, the overall point of the comparison is to answer the question of *why* (the central concern of the *topos* of cause): why Christ did not serve as the Aaronic high priest served, and in contrast to that, why Christ served as he did. Second, because of this overall concern, cause is distinguished from the five other topics in the structure of the argument and ultimately made the singular focus of it. In the opening verses of the comparison, the writer employs the first five topics to say how Christ did *not* serve, and then uses those same five topics to sketch the Aaronic high priest's service by analogy. This is merely review of all preceding comparisons of service in the previous two chapters. Not until the ἐπεί clause of v. 26a, however, does the writer arrive at the point to which he is leading, the matter of *why* Christ did not serve as the high priests served. The answer? He would have had to repeatedly sacrifice himself from the beginning of the creation since "removal of sin" is his aim. This, the cause of Christ's "non-service," is not made a point of comparison with the high priest's service like the other five *topoi*. Rather, it is the one *topos* used solely in the comparison with Christ's "actual service."

(3) The *topos* of cause remains thereafter the consistent matter of focus in the amplifications of 9:27–10:14. Cause is amplified in comparison to human destiny and in view of the time, manner, and action associated with the sacrifices offered.

(4) The primary focus of the comparison of covenants concerns the cause of sin's forgiveness where the new covenant alone forgives sins and lawless deeds, and the old covenant's offering for sin has come to an end.

(5) All scriptures cited in this unit are in some way enlisted to underscore the cause of the removal of sins as the exclusive domain of Christ and the new covenant. In the first amplification of cause, the comparison with human destiny, the only scripture cited (or, perhaps, alluded to) is Isa 53:12 (Heb 9:28), "to bear the sins of many." The scripture speaks climactically to the ultimate question in the comparison of why Christ served as he did. In the following amplifications of cause in Heb 10:1–14, Ps 39:7–9 (LXX) is quoted and interpreted in verses 5–10 to show manner's implications for cause – that animal sacrifice cannot take away sins but has been replaced by the offering of Christ's body, which alone can make

holy.[57] Then Ps 109:1 (LXX) is quoted in Heb 10:12–13 to show action's implications for cause – again, that Christ's sacrifice alone can take away sins. Finally, in the comparison of covenants, Jer 38:33–34 (LXX) is quoted and interpreted (Heb 10:15–18) as proof that the new covenant alone provides forgiveness of sins.[58]

(6) The cause of the removal of sins is underscored as a central theme through the repetition of ἁμαρτία. Twelve of the twenty-nine occurrences in Hebrews are found in this unit (Heb 9:24–10:18).

(7) Finally, this unit falls in its expected rhetorical location, after the preceding treatments of person, action, place, time, and manner (7:1–9:23).

This section may be outlined as follows:

A. Cause of service compared (9:24–10:14)

    Why Christ did not serve like the high priest on earth

Action	"(οὐ γάρ) For entered not" (9:24a)
Person	"Christ" (9:24b)
Place	"into a sanctuary made with hands, the antitype of the true one, (δέ) but into heaven itself, now to appear now in the presence of God for us." (9:24c)

---

[57] If we understand the action of Jesus's priestly ministry and offering of himself in 7:25–10:18 to take place after his death in the heavenly realm (cf. Heb 8:1–13), then the quotation and explanation of Ps 39:7–9 (LXX) likely points to the offering of Jesus's body as a postmortem presentation of his resurrected body (i.e., indestructible life, Heb 7:16) in heaven. For further discussion of this point see Moffitt, *Atonement and the Logic of Resurrection*, 238–47. We further acknowledge with Moffitt that whole of Jesus's life is in view in Heb 10:5–10: "A body was prepared for him and with that body he lived and died with perfect faith, without sin. As such, Jesus become the first to receive the full and perfected inheritance of resurrected life. He was therefore able to take his body into heaven where it was presented before God" (255).

[58] In our understanding, the phrase is intended by the writer to encompass more than the forensic dimension of forgiveness. That is, it encompasses both the internal renewal or "cleansing" that enables obedience and the non-remembrance of past disobedience. This is evident from the fact that in 10:15–17 the writer quotes not only the final part of the Jeremiah passage declaring that God will remember sins no longer, but also the first part of the passage referring to God's internal renewal of the people for covenant fidelity—what the writer earlier summarized as "cleansing of the conscience" (9:14). In 10:18, "forgiveness of sins" is the writer's summation of this twofold work. Cf. Jason A. Whitlark, "Fidelity and New Covenant Enablement in Hebrews," in Charles H. Talbert and Jason A. Whitlark, *Getting "Saved": The Whole Story of Salvation in the New Testament* (Grand Rapids: Eerdmans, 2011), 72–91.

Time   "(οὐδ') nor in order that many times"
              (9:25a)
Manner   "he might offer himself" (9:25b)

The high priest's service

Person   "(ὥσπερ) just as the high priest"
              (9:25c)
Action   "enters" (9:25d)
Place   "the holy of holies" (9:25e)
Time   "year after year" (9:25f)
Manner   "with another's blood." (9:25g)

Cause   "(ἐπεί) Since then it would have been
              necessary for him repeatedly to suffer
              from the foundation of the world."
              (9:26a)

Why Christ served as he did in heaven

Time   "(νυνὶ δέ) But now, once for all time, at
              the completion of the ages" (9:26b)
Action   "he has been revealed" (9:26c)
Cause   "for the removal of sin (ἁμαρτίας)" (9:26d)
Manner   "through the sacrifice of himself." (9:26e)

Amplification of cause from human destiny

Human destiny[59]

          Time   "(καὶ καθ' ὅσον) And inasmuch as it
                        is appointed for humans once"
                        (9:27a)
          Cause   "to die" (9:27b)
          Time   "and after this" (9:26c)
          Cause   "the judgment," (9:27d)

Christ's service

          Time   "(οὕτως καί) so also Christ, once"
                        (9:28a)

---

[59] In this maxim, the two appointed ends in a person's life (death and judgment) are
highlighted to prepare the auditor for the two eschatological times in Christ's life
(exaltation and parousia) that brings about salvation for God's people from judgment
and death.

Cause   "being offered[60] to bear the sins
(ἁμαρτίας) of many," (9:28b)

Time   "a second time" (9:28c)

Cause   "without sin (ἁμαρτίας) will appear
to the ones who eagerly await him
for salvation." (9:28d)

Amplification of cause from sacrifices offered[61]

Introduction

"(γάρ) For the law, having a shadow of the good
things to come but not the true form of the things
themselves," (10:1a)[62]

Comparison 1 (10:1–3): cause and time

Not the cause of old covenant sacrifices: to per-
fect/cleanse[63]

Time   "year after year with the same sacrifices
which they offer continually" (10:1b)

Cause   "is not able to perfect the ones who
approach." (10:1c)

Demonstration from time

Time   "(ἐπεί) Otherwise, would they not
have ceased being offered," (10:2a)

---

[60] The manner of the sacrifice ("being offered") is narrated but not made a *topos* of
comparison in the amplification. The phrase "being offered to bear the sins of a many"
stands as a single unit in juxtaposition with "to die." Both phrases describe deaths, and
both deaths are the causes of the divine action implied by the passive verbs.

[61] This unit consists of three comparisons (vv. 1–3; 4–10; 11–14), each with the
same essential structure: what *is not* the cause is compared with what *is* the cause. In
every case, some *topos* or *topoi* are examined for their implications for cause, and in
every case the conclusion reached is that forgiveness of sins is the exclusive domain of
new covenant sacrifice.

[62] Though we treat it as an introduction, this opening line may be interpreted as
belonging to the treatment of time that follows, insofar as the shadow/true form
juxtaposition is arguably more of a temporal matter than a spatial one.

[63] Because this comparison is focused exclusively on old covenant sacrifice, its
persons (Levitical priests), and their manner (offering of sacrifices) remain the same
in both halves of this comparison and are not *topoi* of comparison; only time (year
after year vs. ceased/once for all time) and cause (not able to perfect/cleanse vs.
reminder of sins) are employed as *topoi* under which contrasts are drawn.

Cause	"since the worshipers, would no longer have had consciousness of sins (ἁμαρτιῶν)," (10:2b)
Time	"since they had once for all time" (10:2c)
Cause	"been cleansed?" (10:2d)

The cause of old covenant sacrifices: to remind of sins

Cause	"(ἀλλά) But in these sacrifices there is a reminder of sins (ἁμαρτιῶν)" (10:3a)
Time	"year after year." (10:3b)

Comparison 2 (10:4–10): cause and manner
Not the cause of old covenant sacrifices: to take away sins

Manner	"(γὰρ) For it is impossible for the blood of bulls and goats" (10:4a)
Cause	"to take away sins (ἁμαρτίας)." (10:4b)

Demonstration from manner

Manner	"(Διό) Therefore when he came into the world he said ..." (10:5a) [Ps 39:7–9 (LXX) cited and interpreted to show that Christ *himself/Christ's body* replaces *sacrifices according to the law* as the manner (or material means) of sacrifice, i.e., "he removes the first to establish the second"; 10:5b–9]

The cause of Christ's sacrifice: to make holy

Cause	"by that will we are made holy" (10:10a)
Manner	"through the offering of the body of Jesus Christ once for all time." (10:10b)[64]

---

[64] The time of the sacrifice – "once for all time" – is narrated but not made a *topos* of comparison. That is, there is no contrasting time mentioned as a corresponding item in the depiction of old covenant sacrifice.

Comparison 3 (10:11–14): cause and action

Not the cause of old covenant sacrifice: to take away sins

Person	"(Καί ... μέν) And on the one hand every priest" (10:11a)
Action	"stands serving" (10:11b)
Time	"day after day (10:11c)
Manner	"and repeatedly the same sacrifices offering," (10:11d)
Cause	"can never take away sins (άμαρ-τίας)," (10:11e)

The cause of Christ's sacrifice: for sins

Person	"(δέ) but this one," (10:12a)
Cause	"for sins (άμαρτιῶν)" (10:12b)
Manner	"offering one sacrifice" (10:12c)
Time	"for all time" (10:12d)
Action	"sat down at the right hand of God from there he waits until his enemies are made a footstool for his feet." (10:12e–13)[65]

Concluding summary

Manner	"(γάρ) For by one sacrifice" (10:14a)
Cause	"he has perfected those being made holy" (10:14b)
Time	"for all time" (10:14c)

B. Covenants compared (10:15–18): the forgiveness of **sins** (άμαρτίαι)[66]

---

[65] The place of Christ's service – "at the right hand of God" – is narrated but not made a *topos* of comparison. It is possible to take τὸ λοιπόν in v. 13 as references either to the time of the action (NASB "waiting from that time onward"; NIV "since that time he waits; NRSV "since then has been waiting") or the place (NLT "there he waits"; CEV "and he will stay there"; NET "where he is now waiting").

[66] In this section sin occurs twice and in the inflected forms that it has appeared in the preceding narration of cause: άμαρτίας and άμαρτιῶν.

Narratio *unit 5: Zion vs. Sinai (12:18–24)*

The final unit draws points of contrast via the topics of action and
(most centrally) place – and in their conventional order:

Action   "But you *have not come* … "
Place   "to … [sevenfold description of Sinai]"
            "to something that can be touched, a blazing fire, and
            darkness, and gloom, and a tempest, and the sound of a
            trumpet, and a voice whose words made the hearers beg
            that not another word be spoken to them. For they could
            not endure the order that was given, 'If even an animal
            touches the mountain, it shall be stoned to death.' Indeed
            the sight was so terrifying that Moses said, 'I am trem-
            bling with fear.'" (18–21)

Action   "But you *have come* …"
Place   "to … [sevenfold description of Zion]"
            "to Mount Zion and to the city of the living God, the
            heavenly Jerusalem, and to innumerable angels in festal
            gathering, and to the assembly of the firstborn who are
            enrolled in heaven, and to God the judge of all, and to
            the spirits of the righteous made perfect, and to Jesus, the
            mediator of a new covenant, and to the sprinkled blood
            that speaks a better word than the blood of Abel."
            (22–24)

In sum, the five epideictic units in question not only employ the
topics prescribed for *narratio* but may be outlined beginning to end
in terms of those topics. Units 1–3 focus exclusively on persons and
taking up the sub-*topoi* in a traditional order. Unit 4 treats person
together with the remaining topics: action, place, time, manner
(construed broadly to encompass means), and cause. In beginning
with persons and moving thereafter to the remaining facts, the
author has ordered these topics of *narratio* as most theorists and
orators did (according to Quintilian), and as most lists prescribe.
These topics are also treated in a traditional order, and specifically,
Theon's order, which locates manner after time and before cause.
Thus, unit 4 in Hebrews corresponds in its topical organization most
closely to the only progymnasmata attributable to the first century
CE. Unit 5 then gives additional attention to the topics of action
and place. In short, the author has put the topics to their fullest

theoretical use, both as search headings for finding comparative-narrative material and compositional headings for organizing it.[67] Such usage obviously lends strong support to identifying the five units as *narratio*.

Argument 9: Persuasion Appropriate for *Narratio*

According to Quintilian, logical proof was reserved for the *argumentatio* and was not allowed as a predominant mode of discourse in the *narratio*. This much is implied in all the handbooks, which assign enthymeme and example to the *argumentatio* and prescribe other, nonargumentative forms of discourse for the *narratio*. Quintilian does note, however, some exceptional occasions when *argumentum* (Quintilian's word for enthymeme; cf. *Inst.* 5.10.1) is nonetheless needed in the *narratio*. Speaking generally, he states:

> Argumentation in Narrative, as I said [cf. *Inst.* 4.2.79], we shall never use; Argument we shall sometimes, as Cicero does in the *Pro Ligario* when he says that his client ruled the province in such a way that peace was in his interest. (*Inst.* 4.2.108 [Russell, LCL])

> It will be useful also to sow some seeds of the Proofs, but in such a way that we never forget that this is still the Narrative, and not the Proof. We may however sometimes confirm an assertion by some Argument, but it must be a simple, short one. Thus in a poisoning case: "he was perfectly well as he drank, but he collapsed immediately, and discoloration and swelling soon followed." The same effect is produced by the preparatory remarks in which a defendant is said to be strong, armed, and ready, and facing opponents who are weak, unarmed, and off their guard. We can in fact give a taste in the Narrative of everything that we shall be treating in the Proof: person, motive, place, time, means opportunity. (*Inst.* 4.2.54–56 [Russell, LCL])

---

[67] Small, *The Characterization of Hebrews*, 131, does not see Hebrews following a traditional outline of encomiastic topics. Small's engaging and thorough analysis of the rhetorical characterization of Jesus in Hebrews, we think, fails to see the ordering of *topoi* because Small works with a rhetorical arrangement of Hebrews proposed by Andrew Lincoln (see Chapter 1) which puts forth no *narratio*. Small then arranges the *argumentatio* around key biblical passages as put forward by John Walters and Ben Witherington (19–20).

We shall also insert a brief defense and reasoned account of
events in a Narrative when the situation demands, for one
should not be telling the story as a witness but as an advocate. The order of facts runs: "Quintus Ligarius went out as
legate to Gaius Considius." But how does Cicero put it?
"Quintus Ligarius, when there was no hint of war, went out
to Africa as legate to Gaius Considius." And elsewhere:
"Not only to no war, but to not the slightest hint of war."
And when it would have been clear enough for the purpose
of giving information to say "Quintus Ligarius did not allow
himself to be implicated in any scheme," he added "because
his mind was on home, and he wanted to get back to his
people." In this way Cicero both made his statement cred-
ible by giving a reason, and also filled it with emotion. (*Inst.*
4.2.109–10 [Russell, LCL])

In the light of Quintilian's comments, it is clear that the five
epideictic units in Hebrews employ persuasion appropriate for the
narratio. As the topical outline of the preceding section illustrates,
the five units employ amplification, and not its counterpart, argumentation (enthymeme and example), as the predominant mode of
persuasion. Thus they conform to Quintilian's rule, "Argumentation
in Narrative ... we shall never use." Further, despite Quintilian's
allowances for the occasional argument or enthymeme in *narratio*,
the outline illustrates how enthymeme is altogether absent in these
units. That is, the outline shows how every sentence serves to establish via a governing *topos* that a matter *is greater* (the function of
amplification) rather than that a matter *is true* (the function of
enthymeme).[68] This distinction is overlooked in recent studies that
claim to identify "enthymemes" or "arguments" in these units.[69] We
attribute the error to the close similarity amplification and enthymeme bear to one another. As we said in the previous chapter,

---

[68] See Aristotle, *Rhet.* 2.26.1–2 [1403a]; Cicero, *Part. or.* 71, cf. 53; Quintilian, *Inst.*
8.4.12, and our discussion under "argumentative amplification" in Chapter 5.

[69] E.g., Thomas H. Olbricht, "Anticipating and Presenting the Case for Christ as
High Priest in Hebrews," in *Rhetorical Argumentation in Biblical Texts: Essays from
the Lund 2000 Conference* (ed. Anders Eriksson, Thomas H. Olbricht, and Walter
Übelacker; Emory Studies in Early Christianity 8; Harrisburg, PA: Trinity Press
International, 2002), 355–72; Thompson, "Argument and Persuasion in the Epistle
to the Hebrews," 361–77.

amplification by rule can take the same premise-conclusion or syllogistic form as enthymeme, and it can employ the same *topoi* (e.g., Heb 9:13–14, which displays the if-then enthymatic form and is governed by the *topos* of comparison to the lesser); but it is always distinguished from enthymeme by its heightening function (Heb 9:13–14 shows the Melchizedekian priesthood's sacrifice to be greater than that of the Levitical).

One might object to our thesis by pointing to occurrences of ethical or emotional persuasion in these units as evidence of argumentation, but *ethos* and *pathos* were prescribed for the entire speech and were not the exclusive domain of the *argumentatio* like enthymeme and example. One may also point to the use of artless proof in these units. In our view, such proof is seen in the citation of laws (7:11–12, 16–21, 28; 9:19–22; 10:1–4, 16), witnesses (3:5; 7:8, 17; 10:15–17 – the number could be greater if we included, in addition to these occurrences explicitly cited as witnesses, all citations of Scripture), covenants (7:22; 8:6–13; 9:1, 15, 16–21; 10:15–18), oaths (7:16–21, 28), and promises (8:6, 9, 15).[70] These occurrences, however, are *without exception* enlisted in support of amplificatory rather than argumentative claims (that something is greater, not that something is true). Thus they can hardly be construed as *argumentatio* in violation of Quintilian's rule.[71] Indeed, it is more accurate to describe them as the kind of "proof" or "semblance of proof" Quintilian prescribes for epideictic, whether by itself or (as is the case here) in support of a pragmatic cause (i.e., as incidental *narratio* in a deliberative speech where the central question is disputed). In either case, Quintilian observes, the orator will need to secure, on occasion, some of his or her epideictic claims, even though the proper function of epideictic is amplification (as opposed to argumentation) (*Inst.* 3.7.1–7).[72]

---

[70] See the helpful discussion in Thompson, "Argument and Persuasion in the Epistle to the Hebrews," 370.

[71] And in any case, inartistic proof for many theorists is not exclusive to the *argumentatio*. Aristotle (*Rhet.* bk. 1) introduces inartistic proof in his treatment of persuasion found generally in the speech (together with artistic proof in the form of *ethos*, *pathos*, and *logos*), but focuses on enthymeme and example (*logos*) in his treatment of the part of speech known as the "proofs" (*Rhet.* bk. 3). Cicero's *De Inventione* (1.51–77) similarly focus solely on artistic, logical proofs as the exclusive domain of the *argumentatio*. Quintilian knows of multiple theorists who exclude technical proofs from the discussion (*Inst.* 5.10.1–3).

[72] Cf. Cicero, *Part. or.* 32.

In short, while the five units of *narratio* in Hebrews are *persuasive*, they strictly abstain from argumentation (enthymeme and example). This restraint is not only fully in keeping with Quintilian's prescriptions concerning *narratio*, but it stands in sharp contrast to the consistent use of logical argumentation in the five interspersed units of *argumentatio*. Indeed, that contrast more than any other factor is arguably what most clearly divides the body of the speech into *narratio* and *argumentatio*.

Argument 10: Demarcation of *Narratio* by *Digressio*

According to the theorists, *digressio* was "the treatment of a theme relevant to the purposes of the cause that branches out from the basic structure" (Quintilian, *Inst.* 4.3.14 [Russell, LCL]).[73] *Digressio* was generally understood to consist of epideictic *descriptio* – that is, laudatory or vituperative description. It would usually focus on persons from the case (speakers, the audience, persons mentioned in argumentation) or on other *topoi* (events, places, etc.). Its purpose was to prepare the audience emotionally to receive the argument favorably and, in turn, to issue the desired verdict. Thus it employed *pathos* (as opposed to *logos*) as its primary means of persuasion. Thus a number of theorists – and "most speakers" – in the first century (according to Quintilian, *Inst.* 4.3.1–13) located it at the transition from the *narratio* to the *argumentatio*, whether as a first-order heading of arrangement between the *narratio* and *argumentatio* (see Quintilian, *Inst.* 4.3.13–14; cf. Mart. Cap. 45–54; Vict. 1), subsumed under *narratio* as its conclusion, or subsumed under *argumentatio* as its introduction (cf. Quintilian, *Inst.* 4.3.6).

On the basis of the theorists' descriptions, one occurrence of *digressio* may in our judgment be identified with certainty in Hebrews – namely, Heb 5:11–14. As Guzmán and Martin observe, this passage displays all the essential characteristics of *digressio*. As a brief word of rebuke, it represents a momentary break from the steady ebb and flow of narration and argumentation for perseverance in the faith. It consists of epideictic *descriptio* – and, specifically, vituperation. It is focused on persons involved in the case and, specifically, the audience. Its purpose is to prepare the audience emotionally to receive well the argument that immediately follows

---

[73] For the following we are dependent upon Ron Guzmán and Michael W. Martin, "Is Hebrews 5:11–6:20 Really a Digression?" *NovT* 57 (2015): 295–310.

for moving to perfection (6:1–20). Indeed, it engages in admonishment of the audience, one of the specific means mentioned by Quintilian for achieving such a purpose. Quintilian says the *digressio* may "serve to refresh, admonish, placate, plead with, or praise the judge" (*Inst.* 4.3.16 [Russell, LCL]). It employs *pathos* – and not *logos* (enthymeme or example) – as its chief means of persuasion. That is, it uses "emollients" mentioned by Quintilian as appropriate for *digressio* – among them, "bursts of indignation, ... hostile comments, reproach" (*Inst.* 4.3.14 [Russell, LCL]). And it employs these "emollients" to produce shame, one of the fifteen emotions, according to Aristotle, sought by *pathos*-based persuasion (*Rhet.* 2.2.11 [1379a]).

Perhaps most importantly for our purposes, the passage is also found in the location assigned to *digressio* by most theorists and speakers alike, at the traditional transition point between *narratio* (5:1–10) and *argumentatio* (6:1–20). Indeed, Quintilian, who generally disapproves of interrupting the two with *digressio*, cites approvingly a particular situation where it is "useful":

> However, though this kind of excursus [i.e., *digressio*] is not always a necessary sequel to the Narrative, it is often a useful preparatory stage before the Question [i.e., the *argumentatio*], especially if this is at first glance unfavourable, or if we are invoking a harsh law or bringing a penal action. (*Inst.* 4.3.9).

Remarkably, the rhetorical situation Quintilian describes is precisely what we have in Heb 5:11–14: the writer's digressionary rebuke of the audience for its immaturity and lack of learning serves as a "preparatory stage" for the argumentation that immediately follows in 6:1–20 for moving beyond immaturity to perfection.[74] Further, that argumentation puts forward what is arguably the most unfavorable word, the harshest law, or the severest penal action for apostasy in the whole of the speech (not to mention the entire New Testament canon), Heb 6:4–6.

Quintilian's instruction, too, highlights the artistry with which the author has employed *digressio* as a transition from *narratio* to *argumentatio*. Quintilian, as we have said, generally disapproves of such

---

[74] Thus we subsume it under *argumentatio* in our outline.

an interruption. He allows it nonetheless, however, if it contributes to the thematic coherency of the *narratio* and *argumentatio*:

> I must admit, however, that this sort of discursive passage [i.e., *digressio*] can be opportunely attached not only to the Narrative but to the Questions (taken either as a whole or, on occasion, individually[75]) when the situation demands or at any rate allows it. I admit too that this is a very important source of lustre and elegance for the speech – but only if it coheres with it and follows naturally, not if it is driven in forcibly like a wedge and splits asunder naturally cohesive elements. (*Inst.* 4.3.4–5 [Russell, LCL])

In Heb 5–6, the transition affected from *narratio* to *argumentatio* by *digressio* is indisputably carried out with thematic coherence under the *topos* of *paideia*. The *narratio* (5:1–10), as we have argued in an earlier chapter, introduces the *topos* in its depiction of the superior *paideia* of suffering and perfection that Jesus undergoes (and in contrast to the Aaronic high priests). The *argumentatio* continues that theme with its argument for the audience to similarly move beyond basic teaching to the pedagogical goal of perfection (6:1–10), and to engage in the *paideia* of *mimesis* (6:11–20). Far from driving a wedge between these two thematically cohesive units, the digressionary rebuke of 5:11–14 takes up in every phrase the pedagogical theme that governs both. Indeed, one may point to Quintilian's one example of such a thematically coherent *digressio* as a remarkable parallel:

> There is nothing that follows more naturally on the Narrative than the Proof. There will therefore sometimes be a place for it [an interrupting *digressio*]; for example, if the end of the narrative has been shocking, we can follow it up with a kind of instant outburst of indignation. (*Inst.* 4.3.5–6 [Russell, LCL])

But for its closer ties to the *argumentatio* (by virtue of its focus on the audience's state of faithfulness), Heb 5:11–14 is precisely this kind of transitional and digressionary outburst of indignation.

---

[75] In this comment Quintilian anticipates precisely the kind of transition found in Hebrews – the transition found within a disjointed structure between one of the units of *narratio* and its corresponding unit of *argumentatio* (one of the Questions "taken individually").

In view, then, of the theorists' accounts of *digressio*, and especially Quintilian's instruction, it is clear that in Heb 5–6 we have a highly conventional movement from *narratio* (5:1–10) to *argumentatio* (5:11–6:20) via a transitional *digressio* (5:11–14) at the beginning of the latter. Thus the theory of *digressio* assists us further in demarcating the *narratio* of the speech. In the case of our proposal, it provides further confirmation that the third unit (5:1–10) we have delineated in Hebrews's five-part, disjointed narratio indeed ends at 5:10 and transitions thereafter to *argumentatio*.[76]

Argument 11: The Virtues of *Narratio*

Nearly every textbook discussion of *narratio* includes a discussion of the good qualities or virtues it should ideally display. Quintilian summarizes well the state of that discussion in the first century.

> Most writers, especially the followers of Isocrates, require that it [*narratio*] should be lucid, brief, and plausible. It does not matter if we say "perspicuous" instead of "lucid," or "probable" or "credible" instead of "plausible." I agree with this division, although Aristotle dissents from Isocrates in one respect, because he ridicules the rule of brevity, as though a Narrative necessarily had to be either long or short and one could never find a middle way; while the followers of Theodorus leave only the last criterion standing, on the ground that it is not necessarily expedient to be brief, and not always expedient to be lucid. This makes it all the more important to go carefully into particular differences, so as to show what is best in any given situation. (*Inst.* 4.2.31–33)

The observation that most writers follow the Isocratean doctrine that a *narratio* is ideally lucid, brief, and plausible is supported by the frequent commendation of the model in other extant handbooks (cf. Rhet. Her. 1.14; Cicero, *Inv.* 1.28–29; *Part. or.* 31–32; Theon 79–85; Anonymous Seguerianus 63; Apsines, *Rhet.* 2.1). These textbooks contain some common-sense instructions concerning how to ensure that a narrative possesses the qualities in question.

---

[76] The four remaining units of *narratio* transition, as Quintilian prefers, immediately to *argumentatio* without any intervening *digressio*. This leads us to believe that our writer does not view *digressio* as a major heading of arrangement. Otherwise we would expect him to employ the transitional *digressio*.

Whether Hebrews adopts a style for its *narratio* that would be deemed plausible is a matter of great subjectivity and a matter beyond the scope of our study. What we can say is that the reception history of the speech, which entailed its preservation, widespread publication, and (ultimately) canonization would suggest the work was widely *received* as plausible in these regards by early Christian audiences.[77]

As for the matter of clarity or lucidity, Theon states that the virtue derives from two "sources": from the subjects that are being described, and from the style of the description of the subjects (81). Theon's instruction concerning the former, like instruction in the handbooks generally, centers on order and sensible arrangement of materials.

> [The *narratio*] becomes clear from the subjects whenever the things being said, unlike those in dialectic and geometry, do not depart from common understanding, or whenever one does not narrate many things together but brings each to its completion.... One should also guard against confusing the times and order of events, as well as saying the same thing twice. For nothing else confuses the thought more than this. (Theon 81 [Kennedy])

A similar emphasis on clear order and chronology is attested among other theorists: "Our Statement of Facts [i.e., the *narratio*] will be clear if we set forth the facts in the precise order in which they occurred, observing their actual or probable sequence or chronology" (Rhet. Her. 1.15 [Caplan, LCL]). "You will also create obscurity if you interrupt the sequence with illogical narrative, and extend some things too long, put other beyond their proper place" (Anonymous Seguerianus 88 [Dilts and Kennedy]). That Hebrews conforms to these standards is evident from our analysis in

---

[77] The fives sections of *narratio* together have a focus on Jesus as the enthroned king and heavenly high priest (especially units 3 and 4), a focus that is peculiar to Hebrews among the NT writings. Hebrews's portrayal of Jesus as high priest certainly had affinity with other second-century Christian texts that present Jesus as the eternal high priest (cf. 1 Clem. 36.1; 63.3; 64.1; Justin Martyr, *Dia.* 33, 34, 36, 42, 86, 96, 113, 115, 116, 118; Ign. *Mag.* 4.1; 7.2; Ign. *Phld.* 9.1; Pol. *Phil.* 12.2). Within those streams of early Christianity, Hebrews's *narratio* would likely have been plausible and even compelling. Cf. Ole Jakob Filtvedt and Martin Wessbrandt, "Exploring the High Priesthood of Jesus in Early Christian Sources," *ZNW* 106 (2015): 96–114, who argue that Hebrews did not invent but presupposes an already existing liturgical tradition in the church that acknowledged Jesus as high priest.

Chapter 2, where we show that chronology is not only carefully guarded in the five units we now call *narratio*, but that it is *the* organizing feature. The five units constitute a comparison of new and old covenant experience ordered by *topoi* of syncrisis in their traditional, chronological sequence (origin, birth, education, deeds, death/events after death).

As for the quality of brevity, the textbooks generally offer commonsense instruction about the need to avoid making a *narratio unnecessarily* long while echoing in some way Aristotle's sneering objection to viewing brevity as an absolute virtue. If the *narratio* of Hebrews is any indication, the writer would appear to be in agreement with Aristotle. Not only is Hebrews's *narratio* lengthy and multipart, but its lack of brevity is very likely the rationale underlying the disjointed structure employed. That is, the theorists prescribe the disjointed structure for a *narratio* of greater length, and as an accommodation to audience memory. Aristotle says of disjointed *narratio*, "it is sometimes right not to narrate all the facts consecutively, because a demonstration of this kind is difficult to remember" (*Rhet.* 3.16.1–2 [1416b] [Freese, LCL]). Similarly, the *Rhetorica ad Alexandrum* states, "When the actions are too numerous and not familiar, we shall in each case put them in connexion and prove them" (31 [1438b 14–29] [Rackham, LCL]). Anonymous Seguerianus, as we have already noted, cites Alexander Numenius's opinion that lengthy or multipart cases as particularly suitable for the disjointed *narratio*:

> Certain ones have also raised this question, whether one should make the narration a single body or should divide it into many? Now some say that the narration should not be divided but all of it kept together; for none of the other parts are to be divided. But Alexander says the other parts should be divided if it is useful, and the narration (should be divided) whenever there are many charges. It is necessary for us to bring together into a single body those (narrations) that combine the facts relative to a single charge, but others are scattered in many places; and he says that often, if they are long, they should be divided up through the whole length (of the speech), in order that we may not give an account as in a history. (132–33 [Dilts and Kennedy])

We may say, then, that the *narratio* of Hebrews not only lacks the "virtue" of brevity, but that it has adopted the strategy prescribed for such a lack, the disjointed structure, and likely for the reason the

theorists prescribe, as an accommodation to audience memory. In presenting the *narratio* in disjointed form, the author of Hebrews does make most of the units brief enough to be readily grasped. The one exception is 7:1–10:18 – and as we will see in the subsequent chapters on *exordium* and *peroratio*, special accommodations are made for its complexity.[78] Had the writer otherwise narrated the full comparative history of old and new covenant experience *en bloc*, it most certainly would have been too much to grasp, and certainly the specific connections to the argumentation that we first outlined in Chapter 3 would have been lost on the audience.

Conclusion

In summation, there are numerous and interrelated reasons for viewing Hebrews's five-part syncritical project (1:5–14; 3:1–6; 5:1–10; 7:1–10:18; 12:18–24) as the speech's *narratio*. It is located immediately after the exordium of the speech (1:1–4, see the next chapter) and it precedes the *argumentatio*, albeit in disjointed form. Thus it has both a location and structure prescribed by virtually all theorists. As a biased exposition of history, it fits the parameters of the theorists' definitions of *narratio*. As epideictic material, it is well-suited for *narratio*. Indeed, it is employed pragmatically in a deliberative case, praising subjects related to the case in order to influence the decision the audience must make; thus it functions as the theorists most commonly imagine epideictic *narratio* functioning. It performs the function of the second class of *narratio*, the παρα-διήγησις or incidental *narratio*, "enter[ing] into a speech as a means of … setting the stage for something." Moreover, it adopts the subtype of exposition most commonly prescribed for παραδιήγησις, amplification. It also adopts prescribed *schemas* of *narratio*: predominantly comparison, but also interrogation, indirect discourse (narration with variation of inflection of case and number), direct discourse (nominative narration), (possible) direct address, and negation. It combines two classes of temporal exposition prescribed for *narratio*, past and present, in a special comparative figure of

---

[78] It might be that 7:1–10:18 is the lengthiest section because of its focus on deeds, which was the most important encomiastic topic (see Chapter 2). It also might be that this is, in part, the difficult material that the author admits he has to explain (5:11), a factor possibly accounting for its length. In any case, breaking it up would have disrupted the topical presentation of the subject.

narratio known as ἀντεξέτασις – the contrast of "what happened before and what has happened now." Further, it has done so in circumstances prescribed for ἀντεξέτασις, in "questions of result" where "something has come about" because of something "written or done" ("in these last days he has spoken to us by a son"). It employs a full range of *topoi* for *narratio* (person, action, place, time, manner, and cause – the six most commonly mentioned) and so may be classified as a complete *narratio*. Further, it enlists the *topoi* and sub-*topoi* of *narratio* in their traditional order as compositional headings governing both the five-part structure of the *narratio* as a whole and the structure of each of the units individually. (Indeed, every point of contrast across the length of the five-part syncritical project may be charted according to the six topics of *narratio* listed by Theon, and usually in the order Theon lists them.) It employs the kind of persuasion appropriate for *narratio*, strictly avoiding the use of enthymeme and example. It is further demarcated as *narratio* by Hebrews's one occurrence of transitional *digressio* in its customary location at the seam of *narratio* and *argumentatio*. Finally, it seems to display virtues commonly prescribed for the *narratio*, clarity and plausibility, and though it lacks the one virtue many theorists question, brevity, it adopts a technique commonly prescribed for addressing that lack, the disjointed structure.[79]

---

[79] We would note here that Chapters 5 and 6 model the two forms of arrangement recommended for ancient *narratio*. Chapter 5 treats *en bloc* the rhetorical materials on *argumentatio* followed by the identification of *argumentatio* in Hebrews. This method of arrangement was adopted due to our belief that the "narration" of the primary evidence was not overly complex and could be grasped *en bloc* and then demonstrated in Hebrews. The present chapter adopted a form for arrangement similar to that of Hebrews. The primary evidence was "narrated" piecemeal or disjointedly so that each particular feature of *narratio* could be easily grasped then demonstrated in Hebrews. We did this in the belief that the discussion of *narratio* and its demonstration in Hebrews was too complex to be "narrated" *en bloc* and then clearly shown in Hebrews.

7

BEGINNING WITH FAVOR

Exordium *in Hebrews*

In the previous two chapters, our analysis has identified the body of
the speech and outlined its five-part, disjointed structure. All that
remains is to give attention to the texts this analysis has left as
remainder, the introductory and concluding materials surrounding
the speech as a whole (1:1–4; 13:1–25), and those surrounding the
third and fourth units devoted to "priestly pursuits" (4:14–16;
12:14–17). These materials, though brief in comparison with other
parts of speech, are not insignificant in function. As we will see, the
theorists have quite a lot to say about the purpose of units such as
these and their relationship to the speech as a whole. Indeed, by
attending closely to these units in the light of rhetorical theory, we
may come to understand better not only the units themselves but the
whole of Hebrews.

In the present chapter we focus on oratorical beginnings, or what
the theorists call the *exordium*, and leave discussion of endings, or
peroratio, for the subsequent chapter. We begin our analysis by
attending to the theory of *exordium* as found in the extant handbooks. Then, aided by this theory, we identify and explicate 1:1–4 as
the primary *exordium* of the speech, and after that, 4:14–16 as a
secondary *exordium*. In both sections, we also give attention to
additional factors contributing to the delineation of these units
as *exordia*.

Exordium among the Theorists

According to the theorists, the *exordium* was merely the beginning of
the speech, and its primary task was strictly to win the audience's
favor (cf. Quintilian, *Inst.* 4.1.5; Anaximenes of Lampsacus, *Rhet.
Alex.* 29; Rhet. Her. 1.6; Cicero, *Inv.* 1.20; Anonymous Seguerianus
10–18). It was not a necessary part of the speech (cf. Aristotle, *Rhet.*
3.14.8 [1415b]; Cicero, *Inv.* 1.21; Quintilian, *Inst.* 4.1.72), and was

commonly omitted in deliberative oratory according to Aristotle (*Rhet.* 3.14.12 [1415b]). According to Quintilian, the *exordium* did not usually introduce the main claims of the speech (cf. *Inst.* 4.1.1–5) but, rather, left such introduction of the claims to the body of the speech.[1] As Quintilian puts it, the goal was "winning over the minds of the judges before they start on the actual case"; and again, "simply to prepare the hearer to be more favourably inclined towards us for the rest of the proceedings" (Quintilian, *Inst.* 4.1.5 [Russell, LCL]). For this reason, Quintilian preferred the Greek's term for the section, *prooimion*, to the Latin *principium* or *exordium*, since "theirs makes it clear that this is the part which precedes the introduction of the subject to be treated" (*Inst.* 4.1.1 [Russell, LCL]).[2] Quintilian's point is worth highlighting. Rather than assuming we will find the main claim of a speech like Hebrews articulated in its opening verses, we should instead expect to find that claim *purposefully withheld*.

We should also expect, accordingly, to find the opening verses engaged primarily in winning favor. This task – and, therefore, the kind of *exordium* needed for it – was determined in ancient rhetorical theory by the overall *defensibility* of the case. The theorists distinguished a range of causes based on their intrinsic defensibility (cf. Cicero, *Inv* 1.20; Rhet. Her. 1.5–11; Quintilian, *Inst.* 4.1.40–41): (1) the *genus honestum* (the honorable cause), (2) the *genus anceps* (the doubtful cause), (3) the *genus humile* (the menial cause), (4) the *genus obscurum* (the complex cause), and (5) the *genus admirabile*, or *genus turpe* (the base or dishonorable cause). The first of these was considered the most defensible, and therefore the easiest kind in which to win favor. The second, third, and fourth occupied a middle ground on the spectrum of defensibility. Doubtful, insignificant, or overly complex causes naturally presented special challenges to winning favor. The dishonorable cause was considered the least defensible (e.g., defending a murderer) and therefore presented the greatest challenge to winning favor.

According to the theorists, cases 1–4 above required the use of a standard *exordium*, known as the *principium*, which sought favor

---

[1] The exception to this rule is complex cases, which do require some introductory enumeration of main points or themes (see the discussion below).

[2] As Quintilian explains, "Now *oimē* means song, and lyre-players gave the name *prooimion* to the short pieces they perform to win favour before they begin the formal competition" (*Inst.* 4.1.2 [Russell, LCL]).

directly through standard means (cf. Cicero, *Inv.* 1.20; Rhet. Her. 1.5–11; Quintilian, *Inst.* 4.1.42). The special challenges of case five, the *genus turpe*, however, required the use of a special *exordium* known as the *insinuatio*, which sought favor unconventionally through more indirect means. It will be helpful to sketch both in greater detail.

Principium

The *principium*, the standard and straightforward kind of *exordium*, was the kind of *exordium* used in most speeches. Indeed, the terms *principium* and *exordium* are sometimes used interchangeably among some theorists, though the former is technically a subtype of the latter in more developed systems like that of Quintilian.

For this manner of introduction, the theorists prescribe winning favor in three essential forms: (1) goodwill, (2) attentiveness, and (3) receptivity (cf. Anaximenes of Lampsacus, *Rhet. Alex.* 29 [1436a–1438a]; Rhet. Her. 1.6; Cicero, *Inv.* 1.20; Anonymous Seguerianus 10–12): "Of course," Quintilian observes, "these aims have to be maintained throughout the pleading, but they are particularly vital in the initial stage, since it is by means of this that we gain admission to the judge's mind so as to make further progress later" (*Inst.* 4.1.5 [Russell, LCL]).

In seeking goodwill, the orator would focus the audience's attention on some favorable aspect of the case – someone or something which the audience might be already inclined to view positively (cf. Quintilian, *Inst.* 4.1.6–33; Aristotle, *Rhet.* 3.14.7 [1415a–b]; Anaximenes of Lampsacus, *Rhet. Alex.* 29 [1436a–1438a]; Rhet. Her. 1.8; Cicero, *Inv.* 1.22; Anonymous Seguerianus 16–18). Quintilian commends three categories of such favorable subjects: (1) favorable persons involved in case – the plaintiff, opponent, judge, or pleader (*Inst.* 4.1.6–7)[3]; (2) some favorable thing in the case – but not the whole, for such introduction "expos[es] the naked harshness of our Questions without having first won [the judge's] sympathy" (*Inst.* 4.1.25 [Russell, LCL]); (3) something adjunct to the case that is

---

[3] Quintilian observes that the traditional threefold division of plaintiff, opponent, and judge used by most theorists is "incorrect" in its omission of the "pleader." As Russell explains, the comment "assumes that the litigant and the advocate are not the same – i.e., [Quintilian] is drawing attention to the difference between Roman and Greek court procedure" (Russell, *Quintilian II: Books 3–5* [LCL 125; Cambridge: Harvard University Press, 2001], 182–3 n. 6).

favorable, including: (a) persons, "not only those nearest and dearest to them, as I said, but also relatives, friends, sometimes even districts and even cities" (*Inst.* 4.1.30 [Russell, LCL]); or (b) external circumstances, such as time, place, public opinion, reputation of the court, or expectations of the people (cf. *Inst.* 4.1.31).

In seeking attentiveness, the orator sought an audience that was alert and emotionally engaged (cf. Quintilian, *Inst.* 4.1.33–9; Rhet. Her. 1.7; Cicero, *Inv.* 1.23; Anonymous Seguerianus 14–15). The main threat to this pursuit was tedium, which could arise especially in the *genus humile*. If an audience considered a cause to be of trivial importance, the orator might gain attention by highlighting and magnifying the importance of the topic at hand, by amplifying the cause to show its global or comprehensive scale (cf. Aristotle, *Rhet.* 3.14.12 [1415b]).

In seeking receptivity, the orator attempted to predispose the audience toward learning. His main obstacle in this pursuit was the complexity of the case (cf. Quintilian, *Inst.* 4.1.34; Rhet. Her. 1.7; Cicero, *Inv.* 1.23; Anonymous Seguerianus 10–13). Thus receptivity was of special concern for the *genus obscurum*. The main device the orator employed in the *principium* when prosecuting especially complex cases was a brief *enumeratio* of points to be covered in the *narratio*. Of course, the use of *enumeratio* in the *principium* assumes the *narratio* was of the case itself and not the incidental kind of *narratio*. The *principium* could, therefore, in complex cases introduce the subject matter of the entire case – but not as an end itself – rather, the end, as always, was the favorable disposition of the audience.

Insinuatio

The *insinuatio*, or subtle approach, was employed when the speaker faced an audience unfavorably disposed toward him or her (cf. Rhet. Her. 1.9–11; Cicero, *Inv.* 1.23–25; Quintilian, *Inst.* 4.1.44–50). This form of *exordium* was prescribed not only for the *genus turpe,* or dishonorable cause, but also in instances when an opponent had already won favor, or when the audience was simply fatigued. Essentially, the *insinuatio* attempted to win over the audience indirectly with material having nothing to do with the case, and in contrast to the more direct methods of the (opponent's) *principium*. Rhetorica ad Herennium suggests a range of materials, especially if the hearers have been fatigued:

"[W]e shall open with something that may provoke laughter: a fable, a plausible fiction, a caricature, an ironical inversion of the meaning of a word, an ambiguity, innuendo, banter, a naïvety, an exaggeration, a recapitulation, a pun, an unexpected turn, a comparison, a novel tale, a historical anecdote, a verse, or a challenge or a smile of approbation directed at someone. Or we shall promise to speak otherwise than as we have prepared, and not to talk as others usually do; we shall briefly explain what the other speakers do and what we intend to do. (1.10 [Caplan, LCL])

Secondary *Exordium*

In addition to the primary *exordium* at the beginning of the speech, the theorists also prescribe the use in some cases of a secondary *exordium* within the speech.[4] Quintilian suggests these may occur before individual units of the speech such as the *narratio* or *argumentatio*, and he observes that they are particularly useful in "complex" speeches where listeners may need occasional introductory assistance (cf. *Inst.* 4.1.73–5; 4.3.9–11; see also Fortun. 2.20 [113, 25]). He cites as examples of the phenomenon Cicero's *Pro Cluentia*, 117–8, and *Pro Murena*, 7. From his comments, one gathers that Quintilian considers any kind of prefatory remark that in some way gains goodwill, attentiveness, or receptivity at the beginning of a section to be a secondary *exordium*.[5]

Exordium in Hebrews

The Primary *Exordium* of 1:1–4

If we remember that the *exordium* usually does not introduce the main subject or thesis of the speech, but rather simply begins the speech in a favor-winning way, then Heb 1:1–4, the passage most commonly proposed as Hebrews's *exordium*, appears to fulfill these expectations fairly well. As an encomiastic piece praising Jesus in

---

[4] Heinrich Lausberg, *Handbook of Literary Rhetoric: A Foundation for Literary Study* (ed. David Orton and R. Dean Anderson; trans. Matthew Bliss, Annemiek Jansen, and David Orton; Leiden: Brill, 1998), § 287.

[5] Quintilian states in his conclusion, "The practice is too common to need illustration" (*Inst.* 4.1.75 [Russel, LCL]).

comparison with other past "messengers," it has obvious thematic connections to the speech as a whole, which frequently engages in encomiastic syncrisis devoted to Jesus. The author, however, in these verses refrains from introducing what our previous analysis has identified as the main concern of the speech, the counsel concerning perseverance. Apart from a knowledge of ancient rhetorical theory, this absence might be taken as evidence against the thesis that Hebrews is a deliberative speech. But in the light of Quintilian's instructions that the main claim be purposefully withheld, the absence is wholly in keeping with that thesis. The author intends to get to his difficult, deliberative claim concerning the need to persevere. Convention restrains him, however, from doing so in the *exordium* of the speech, both because that claim is difficult and likely not to be favor winning, and because that is the *main* claim of the speech – something that is reserved exclusively for the body where it is put forward as a proposition or thesis and then proved in the *argumentatio*.[6] Convention has encouraged the author to focus on more positive matters that are likely to win the audience's favor – in this case, the readers' own superior new covenant experience of God in Jesus Christ.

Specifically, Heb 1:1–4 may be seen as a *principium* crafted by the author to seek favor in two conventional forms, goodwill and attentiveness. Orators were taught to obtain goodwill, as we have said, by giving consideration in the *exordium* to some aspect of the speech that the audience finds favorable – but not the entirety of the cause itself. This could be (1) one of the main persons involved in the case, (2) some aspect of the argument, or (3) persons or circumstances adjunct to the case. In Heb 1:1–4, we find attention given to *favorable persons involved in the case*: first to God, who speaks to his people, and then to Jesus himself, who is praised as the one for whom and through whom the creation was made.[7] Though the writer does

---

[6] The main claim is also put forward in narrated form in the *narratio* so long as the latter is of the traditional and not of the incidental variety. In the case of Hebrews, which employs an incidental *narratio*, the main claim is withheld until the *argumentatio*, where it is put forward, as we have said, in multiple *propositiones*.

[7] In Quintilian's Roman model of "persons of the case" (see n. 3), which distinguishes plaintiff and pleader, the writer of Hebrews would be viewed as the pleader of the case, and God as the plaintiff. That is, while the writer is the one engaged in the actual declamation of the case (cf. Heb 13:22), he frames the case as a deliberation concerning *an address brought by God* "in these last days" (Heb. 1:1–2; see, too, thereafter 2:3; 3:7; 10:30; 12:5–6). Further, since Jesus Christ (Heb 1:1–2; 2:3) and the Holy Spirit (3:7) are also framed in the declamation as bearers of God's address, one may view them as God's co-plaintiffs.

not here introduce his thesis concerning perseverance in the faith, he nevertheless sets the stage for his claim by drawing on the positive feelings the audience still likely has, despite its potentially waning faith for God and Jesus Christ. The unit also gives attention to a favorable *aspect of the case*. In praising the recent revelation through Jesus Christ as comparatively superior to that by messengers of the past, the unit introduces the same general comparative claim found in every subsequent five-part *narratio*, namely, that recent, new covenant experience surpasses old covenant experience. Here again, this is not the difficult call for perseverance, the main thesis of the speech. But it certainly sets the stage for such a claim by aggrandizing what God has done recently in Jesus Christ.

The unit also seeks favor by garnering attentiveness in a standard, prescribed way. We have seen that, in the case of the *genus humile* especially, rhetoricians warn against the danger of an audience succumbing to tedium when it considers a case to be of small significance. In such circumstances, it is incumbent upon the orator to begin the speech in such a way that conveys the great importance (*rerum magnitido*; Quintilian, *Inst.* 10.1.48; cf. 4.1.33; Rhet. Her. 1.7) of what will be discussed – without, of course, introducing the thesis itself. And one of the more common ways this was accomplished, Lausberg notes, was by displaying the sheer scale of the cause in cosmic terms. Lausberg writes:

> Here too belongs the indirect aggrandizement of the speech topic (*rerum magnitido*) through the prooimial use of comprehensive, ideally global, concepts (in the expansion of the temporal, geographical and frequency characteristics of a prooimial expression that is only indirectly connected with the speech topic).[8]

In Heb 1:1–4, we find the author taking just such an approach. Without introducing directly the central claim of the speech, that perseverance is advantageous, the author establishes the scale of the stakes involved in such deliberation by portraying Jesus (a) *in relation to God* as God's "Son," the "reflection of God's glory," and the "exact imprint of God's being," (b) *in relation to creation* as "the heir of all things," "the one through whom he made the universe/ages" and "the one who sustains all things by his powerful word," and (c)

---

[8] Lausberg, *Handbook of Literary Rhetoric*, § 270; cf. Aristotle, *Rhet.* 3.14.12 (1415b).

in relation to both as "the one who sat down at the right hand of the Majesty on high." Such a portrait makes clear the global and historical importance of the person central to the argumentation of the case.[9]

Such an opening, too, is all the more fitting when one remembers the situation of the audience, that for them, Roman wealth, status, and honor have served to relativize the perceived importance of faithful living.[10] Such a situation is, in Aristotle's view, precisely the kind that occasions the rare *exordium* in a *deliberative* speech:

> Deliberative oratory borrows its exordia from forensic, but naturally they are very uncommon in it. For in fact the hearers are acquainted with the subject, so that the case needs no exordium, except for the orator's own sake, or on account of his adversaries, or if the hearers attach too much or too little importance to his idea. Wherefore he must either excite or remove prejudice, and magnify or minimize the importance of the subject. (*Rhet.* 3.14.12 [1415b] [Freese, LCL])

Quintilian echoes this counsel with regard to the deliberative *exordium*, invoking Aristotle by name and with approval: "Aristotle, it is true, holds, and not without reason, that the Prooemium in Deliberative is ... sometimes intended to make the subject seem of greater or less importance than it is" (*Inst.* 3.8.8 [Russel, LCL]). Given the focus of the opening verses of Hebrews, we may characterize the audience's attitudes – or, more precisely, the writer's perception of those attitudes – with Aristotle's language. In the writer's view, the audience has "attach[ed] too ... little importance" to perseverance in its confession of Jesus Christ. Thus the writer begins the speech by "magnify[ing] ... the importance of the subject."

All of this suggests that the author judges his case to be, in terms of its defensibility, of the *genus humile* – a cause deemed menial by the audience because of its waning faith and assimilationist tendencies. The "beginning of the speech" anticipates the problem, garnering

---

[9] Lausberg (a classicist normally dealing in Greco-Roman sources) cites the opening of Hebrews as exemplary in its method of garnering attentiveness: "Especially meaningful and momentous is the use of global ideas in the proem, e.g., in Heb. 1:1, where an overview of world history is used as a means of highlighting the subject treated as the present culmination of this period." See *Handbook of Literary Rhetoric*, § 270.

[10] On this latter point, see Jason A. Whitlark, "The Warning against Idolatry: An Intertextual Examination of Septuagintal Warnings in Hebrews," *JSNT* 34 (2012): 382–401.

both goodwill for and attentiveness to the author's cause through its focus on Jesus and his global, even cosmic, importance.[11]

Additional Factors Demarcating the *Exordium* of 1:1–4

Thus far our analysis has only confirmed what most proposals for arrangement suggest, that the content of 1:1–4 fulfills well the theoretical functions of the *exordium*. In truth the only controversial aspect of our proposal, aside from the additional evidence it supplies for an overall deliberative focus of the speech in its entirety, is the demarcation of the *exordium* at 1:4. In this judgment we are in agreement with a majority of earlier proposals (Backhaus, Lincoln, Olbricht, Spicq, Nissilä, Thompson, Übelacker), but part ways with a minority that view the *exordium* as continuing beyond 1:4 to 2:4 (Koester, Anderson), 2:18 (Thurén), or even 4:13 (von Soden). It is therefore not enough to argue that 1:1–4 fulfills well the theoretical parameters of the *exordium*. Some rationale must be given, additionally, for saying the *exordium* ends at verse 4.

In our view, several factors converge to make a compelling case for just such a delineation. First, there is the delineation of Hebrews's *narratio* and *argumentatio*. The analysis of our preceding chapters already provides a compelling rationale for delineating the *exordium* at 1:4. In Chapter 5, we show that Heb 2:1–4 consists of rational proof enlisted in support of a thesis. By definition, these materials are *argumentatio* and therefore cannot be assigned to the *exordium*, as in the proposals of Koester, Anderson, Thurén, and von Soden.[12] Further, in Chapter 6 we show that 1:5–14, the comparison of Jesus with the angels, is the first of five units of disjointed, comparative *narratio*. Because it fulfills in multiple respects the expectations concerning *narratio*, it too cannot be assigned to *exordium*, as in the proposals of Koester, Anderson, Thurén, and von Soden.

Second, there is the periodic form of 1:1–4. In their discussions of style, the theorists distinguish nonperiodic or "continuous" prose from "periodic" prose and describe settings appropriate for each.[13]

---

[11] In taking such a direct approach to winning the audience's favor, Heb 1:1–4 may be classed as a *principium* (as opposed to the *insinuatio*, with its indirect approach).

[12] See Chapter 1.

[13] See esp. Aristotle, *Rhet.* 3.9 (1409a–1410b); Demetrius, *Eloc.* 1–35; also on the period, Anaximenes of Lampsacus, *Rhet. Alex.* 26–8 (1435b–1436a); Rhet. Her. 4.26–32; Cicero, *Brut.* 33–34, 149, 162; *Or. Brut.* 198–221; *De or.* 3.184–92; Dionysius of Halicarnassus, *Comp.* 2, 9, 22–23; Quintilian, *Inst.* 9.4.19–22, 122–30.

According to Aristotle, nonperiodic prose runs on and on without giving the reader any sense of when it may come to a break, and it is typically "united by connecting particles" (*Rhet.* 3.9.1–2).[14] Periodic prose, by contrast is divided into well-balanced sentences or "periods" with a clear "beginning" and "end in itself" and, therefore, a "magnitude that can be easily grasped" (Aristotle, *Rhet.* 3.9.3–4).[15] Its circuitous form, moreover, is often derived from certain pre-scribed figures – most commonly, the "Gorgianic" figures of antith-esis (opposition of terms and or meaning), parisosis (parallelism of structure), and paromoiosis (beginning and ending assonance).[16] Examples from the theorists illustrate well the circuitous effect of each of these figures:

---

[14] Aristotle describes the nonperiodic style of prose as "that which has no end in itself and only stops when the sense is complete." He states, "It is unpleasant, because it is endless, for all wish to have the end in sight" (Aristotle, *Rhet.* 3.9.1–2 [1409a]). Demetrius, who refers to the nonperiodic style as "disjointed," observes that its clauses "are not closely attached to each other" as in the periodic style, but rather "seem thrown one on top of the other in a heap without the connec-tions or buttressing or mutual support which we find in periods" (*Eloc.* 12 [Roberts and Innes, LCL]). Both Aristotle and Demetrius agree that the nonper-iodic style lacks the circuitous form of the period, and the devices that may lend it that circuitous form.

[15] Demetrius similarly observes, "A period is a combination of clauses and phrases arranged to conclude the underlying thought with a well-turned ending." Citing Aristotle's definition above as "excellent and apt," he adds, "For the very use of the word 'period' implies that it has had a beginning at one point, will end at another, and is speeding towards a definite goal, like runners sprinting from the starting place. For at the very beginning of their race the end of the course is already before their eyes. Hence the name 'period,' an image drawn from paths which go round and are in a circle. In general terms a period is nothing more nor less than a particular arrangement of words. If its circular form should be destroyed and the arrangement changed, the subject matter remains the same, but there will be no period" (Demetrius, *Eloc.* 10–11 [Roberts and Innes, LCL]).

[16] The Gorgianic figures characterized the periodic style as first employed in oratory by its originators, Isocrates, Gorgias (for whom the figures are named), and Alcidamas (see Demetrius, *Eloc.* 12, 15; cf. Cicero, *Brut.* 33–4; Dionysius of Halicarnassus, *Comp.* 33; see, too, the many examples of periods from Isocrates in Aristotle, *Rhet.* 3.9.7–10 [1409b–1410a]). The best modern discussion remains John C. Robertson, *The Gorgianic Figures in Early Greek Prose* (Baltimore: Frieden-wald, 1893); cf. Michael W. Martin, "The Poetry of the Lord's Prayer: A Study in Poetic Device," *JBL* 134 (2015): 347–72. Aristotle accordingly treats them as essential to the periodic style (cf. *Rhet.* 3.9.7–10 [1409b–1410a]), as well – and the schoolmasters continue to introduce the Gorgianic figures in connection with the period (see Rhet. Her. 4.26–32; cf. Anaximenes of Lampsacus, *Rhet. Alex.* 26–28 [1435b–1436a]), thereby implicitly suggesting a close connection to the period's form (see R. A. Fowler, "Aristotle on the Period," *The Classical Quarterly* 32 [1982]: 89–99).

Antithesis[17]

οὐ γὰρ δίκαιον τουτοῦ μὲν τὰ ἐμὰ ἔχοντα πλουτεῖν,
ἐμὲ δὲ τὰ ὄντα προέμενον οὕτω πτωχεύειν.

("It is not fair for my opponent to have my money and be a rich man
while I from parting with my substance am a mere beggar.")
(Anaximenes of Lampsacus, *Rhet. Alex.* 26 [1435b] [Rackham, LCL])

Parisosis[18]

[S]i quantum in agro locisque desertis audacia potest,
tantum in foro atque iudiciis impudentia valeret.[19]

("[I]f shamelessness were as powerful in the forum and in the courts
as audacity is powerful in the countryside and wilderness.")
(Quintilian, *Inst.* 9.3.80 [Russell, LCL])

---

[17] After Aristotle, theorists commonly define antithesis as a juxtaposition in opposed clauses of terms, of meaning, or of both: "A sentence is antithetical when either terminology or meaning, or both at once, are opposite in opposed clauses... Antithesis in both respects, meaning and in terminology, would be most effective, but the two remaining forms are also antithetical" (Anaximenes of Lampsacus, *Rhet. Alex.* 26 [1435b] [Rackham, LCL]); "The antithesis may lie in the content ... or it may be twofold, in content and language ... There are also clauses which have only verbal antithesis" (Demetrius, *Eloc.* 22–3 [Roberts and Innes, LCL]).

[18] Also called *parison* and *isocolon*, the device is characterized by a parallelism of structure that is variously and sometimes vaguely defined: "[E]quality of clauses is parisosis" (Aristotle, *Rhet.* 3.9.9 [1410a] [Freese, LCL]). "Parisosis occurs when a sentence has two equal members. Equality may exist between many small things and a few large things, and between an equal number of things of equal size" (Anaximenes of Lampsacus, *Rhet. Alex.* 27 [1436a] [Rackham, LCL]). "[Isocolon] is when the clauses have an equal number of syllables" (Demetrius, *Eloc.* 25 [LCL, Roberts and Innes]). "We call Isocolon the figure comprised of cola ... which consist of a virtually equal number of syllables. To effect the isocolon we shall not count the syllables – for that is surely childish – but experience and practice will bring such a facility that by a sort of instinct we can produce again a colon of equal length to the one before it ... In this figure it may often happen that the number of syllables seems equal without being precisely so – as when one colon is shorter than the other by one or even two syllables, or when one colon contains more syllables, and the other contains one or more longer fuller-sounding syllables, so that the length or fullness of sound of these matches and counterbalances the greater number of syllables in the other" (Rhet. Her. 4.28 [Caplan, LCL]). Illustrations from these same writers show everything from attached clauses of roughly equal length, to the same with close verbal and syntactical parallelism.

[19] Cicero, *Pro Caecin.* 1.

Paromoiosis[20]

(a) Homoeoteleuton[21]

τί ἂν ἔπαθες δεινόν,
εἰ ἄνδρ᾽ εἶδες ἀργόν

("[W]hat ill would you have suffered,
If you had seen an idle man?")
(Aristotle, *Rhet.* 3.9.9 [1410b] [Freese, LCL])

(b) Homoeokatarkton[22]

δωρητοί τ᾽ ἐπέλοντο
παράρρητοι τ᾽ ἐπέεσσιν.[23]

---

[20] Paromoiosis, or "assonance," occurs according to the theorists either "at the beginning" or "at the end" of associated clauses (*Eloc.* 25), and with the conformity especially in the final syllables of parallel words (Aristotle, *Rhet.* 3.9.9 [1410a]; Anaximenes of Lampsacus, *Rhet. Alex.* 28 [1436a]). Unlike modern rhyme, paromoiosis may entail a looser semblance even of single, final syllables, with correspondence of position or accent evidencing intentionality when the semblance is slight (cf. Robertson, *The Gorgianic Figures*, 20). The device also encompasses numerous subtypes. Aristotle describes and illustrates five different kinds. By the Roman period, these and other kinds were assigned technical names and treated individually rather than as a group, and often with conflicting and overlapping definitions. Our survey reflects the Roman treatment and includes the most common types (others, such as paronomasia [word play] and homoeoptoton [repetition of identical case endings], could also have been included, and in some cases are encompassed by the surveyed devices when broadly construed).

[21] Homoeoteleuton literally means "similarity of ending." Aristotle counts among its types similarity of final syllables, similarity of a single syllable, "inflections of one and the same word" (polyptoton among most later theorists), and "repetition of the same word" (epistrophe among most later theorists). There is a narrowing in later definitions: "Homoeoteleuton is when clauses end similarly, either with the same word [epistrophe among later theorists] ... or with the same syllable" (Demetrius, *Eloc.* 25 [Roberts and Innes, LCL]); "Homoeoteleuton occurs when the word endings are similar, although the words are indeclinable" (Rhet. Her. 4.28 [Caplan, LCL], here distinguishing homoeoptoton). "Similarity of cadence, the same syllables being placed at the end of each clause; this is called *homoeoteleuton*, that is to say, the similar ending of one or more clauses" (Quintilian, *Inst.* 9.3.77 [Russell, LCL]).

[22] We follow Robertson, *The Gorgianic Figures*, 18, in referring to the device as "homoeokatarkton"; ancient theorists describe it without assigning it a technical term; e.g., "At the beginning the similarity [paromoeosis] is always shown in entire words" (Aristotle, *Rhet.* 3.9.9 [1410a] [LCL, Freese]); "There are also clauses with assonance [paromoia]. The assonance is either at the beginning ... or at the end" (Demetrius, *Eloc.* 25 [Roberts and Innes, LCL]).

[23] Homer, *Il.* 9.526.

("[T]hey were ready to accept gifts
and to be persuaded by words.")
(Aristotle, *Rhet.* 3.9.9 [1410a] [Freese, LCL]; also cited
by Demetrius, *Eloc.* 25)

(c) Antistrophe[24]

Σὺ δ᾽ αὐτὸν καὶ ζῶντα ἔλεγες <u>κακῶς</u>
καὶ νῦν γράφεις <u>κακῶς</u>

("[W]hile he lived you spoke ill of him,
Now he is dead you write ill of him.")
(Aristotle, *Rhet.* 3.9.9 [1410a] [Freese, LCL])

(d) Anaphora[25]

<u>Vobis</u> istuc adtribuendum est,
<u>vobis</u> gratia est habenda,
<u>vobis</u> ista res erit honori.

("To you must go the credit for this,
To you are thanks due,
To you will this act of yours bring glory.")
(Rhet. Her. 4.19 [Caplan, LCL])

(e) Polyptoton[26]

ἄξιος δὲ σταθῆναι <u>χαλκοῦς</u>,
οὐκ ἄξιος ὢν <u>χαλκοῦ</u>

---

[24] Also called *epistrophe* and *epiphora*. "Antistrophe is the opposite of epanaphora; for as the latter begins with the same words, so the former ends with the same words" (Alexander, *Fig.* 3.29); "In Antistrophe, we repeat, not the first word in successive phrases, as in Epanaphora, but the last ..." (Rhet. Her. 4.19 [Caplan, LCL]); "A series of clauses may ... end with the same words," (Quintilian, *Inst.* 9.3.30 [Russell, LCL]). Counted as homoeoteleuton by Aristotle and Demetrius (see above), antistrophe is treated as a distinct figure by most later theorists.

[25] Also called *epanaphora*. "Epanaphora is when two or more cola begin with the same expression" (Alexander, *Fig.* 3.20.30); "Epanaphora occurs when one and the same word forms successive beginnings for phrases expressing like and different ideas ..." (Rhet. Her. 4.19 [Caplan, LCL]); "A series of clauses may ... begin with the same words, with great effect and urgency" (Quintilian, *Inst.* 9.3.30 [Russell, LCL]).

[26] Polyptoton is repetition in different inflections – usually case, but also gender and number (the latter two being treated sometimes as a separate device). "The inflexions of one and the same word" (Aristotle, *Rhet.* 3.9.9 [1410a] [Freese. LCL]). "This Figure is formed both with cases alone (it is then called *polyptoton*) and in other ways" (Quintilian, *Inst.* 9.3.36–7 [Russell, LCL]). Most of the theorists' illustrations are anaphoric, but all forms of word repetition are possible (cf. Lausberg, *Handbook of Literary Rhetoric*, § 642.).

("worthy of a bronze statue,
not being worth a brass farthing")
(Aristotle, *Rhet.* 3.9.9 [1410a] [Freese, LCL])

Theorists divide the period into "cola," the clauses or word groups that in Demetrius's definition are coterminous with either a complete thought or a part of a thought (cf. *Eloc.* 1–2). Cola, when divisible, comprise commata ("what is less than a clause"; *Eloc.* 9).[27] Theorists disagree on the number of cola allowed per period. Aristotle prescribes one colon (in which case the "bending back" happens within a single clause) or two (cf., *Rhet.* 3.9.5–6 [1409b]). Demetrius prescribes two to four, but also allows for the single colon period (*Eloc.* 16–17). Cicero and Quintilian insist on a minimum of two cola and affirm an *average* rather than a ceiling of four (Cicero, *Or. Brut.* 221–5; Quintilian, *Inst.* 9.4.125). In examples of the period and related figures from the handbooks, the bi-colon, tri-colon, and quatrant are most commonly represented.

According to Quintilian, periodic prose is especially commendable for the *exordium* of a significant cause: "The period is well suited to the Prooemia of important causes" (*Inst.* 9.4.128 [Russell, LCL]).[28] This is in contrast, in Quintilian's view, to the *narratio*, which employs clauses in a nonperiodic style or, at most, in "loosened up" periods with "less tight knots" (*Inst.* 9.4.127).[29] Based on Quintilian's comments, one would expect to find in *exordia* that conform to his doctrine tight, circular periods, perhaps with Gorgianic figures, and in *narrationes* nonperiodic prose and/or occasional "loose" periods lacking these figures.

---

[27] The triad of period, colon, and comma is widely attested. See the citations in Lausberg, *Handbook of Literary Rhetoric*, § 926.

[28] Lausberg explains, "The reason is that the cyclic structure (cf. § 924) more easily introduces the audience to the matter than a linear (cf. § 921) form of expression, which, in view of its slowness would only be able to introduce them to the matter step by step. Periods of one colon (cf. §§ 924, 933) and of several cola may thus serve as openings" (*Handbook of Literary Rhetoric*, § 947). See, too, the examples Lausberg subsequently cites.

[29] In speaking of "loosened up" periods, Quintilian is likely invoking a broader conception of the period held by some theorists that distinguished "tight" rhetorical or rhythmic periods from those less carefully constructed (Demetrius, *Eloc.* 19–21; Cicero, *Or. Brut.* 198–211). Among these theorists, the figures are not essential to periodic form, but rather, merely lend it a more compact form. This view is to be contrasted with that of Aristotle, who treats the Gorgianic figures as essential to the periodic form.

In Hebrews, we find precisely this. The *exordium* of 1:1–4 features a series of periods tightly constructed with multiple Gorgianic figures, and thereafter, the first *narratio* unit of 1:5–14 features mostly nonperiodic prose that is, as Aristotle says, "strung-on" by "particles." We may arrange the periodic form of 1:1–4 by its constituent periods and cola, noting the various figures that give the section its rhetorical shape:[30]

(1) Πολυμερῶς καὶ πολυτρόπως

This opening line, long recognized for its rhetorical parallelism, is a single colon period formed by homoekatarkton (Πολυ- ...; πολυ- ...), homoeoteleuton (... -ῶς; ... -ως), and parisosis (symmetry of syntax and meaning).[31]

(2) πάλαι   ὁ θεὸς λαλήσας τοῖς πατράσιν ἐν τοῖς προφήταις
    ἐπ' ἐσχάτου τῶν ἐλάλησεν   ἡμῖν   ἐν υἱῷ,
    ἡμερῶν τούτων

A two-colon period, the unit is formed by parisosis (parallelism of grammar, syntax, and meaning) and antithesis (evident in the opposition of πάλαι/ἐπ' ἐσκάτου τῶν ἡμερῶν τούτων).[32]

(3) ὃν ἔθηκεν   κληρονόμον πάντων,
    δι' οὗ καὶ ἐποίησεν τοὺς αἰῶνας·

Another two-colon period, this unit also employs parisosis (symmetry of grammatical structure and meaning). Also, polyptoton (ὃν ...; δι' οὗ ...) and likely homoeokatarkton (ἔθηκεν ...; ἐποίησεν...;) at the opening of both lines fortify the couplet.[33]

---

[30] While the devices and their resulting symmetries of the first four verses are clear, the periodic divisions are less so. Aristotelian analysis, as we have said, allows only for a single- or two-colon period, and one formed strictly by Gorgianic figures, and so would divide the four verses into the following seven units. At the other end of the theoretical spectrum, Cicero and Quintilian reject the single colon period and allow for longer, more complex periods of multiple cola. Analysis in that vein would possibly delineate the following seven figured units as forming three compound periods (vv. 1–2a, 2b, and 3–4), and perhaps as few as two (vv. 1–2, 3–4) or even one (vv. 1–4). In any case, the analysis of the constituent cola and associated figures would remain the same, as would the verdict that this is periodic prose.

[31] Those theorists who do not allow for the mono-colon (Cicero and Quintilian) would likely treat this colon together with the unit below as a single three-colon period.

[32] The phrases ἐν τοῖς προφήταις / ἐν υἱῷ could be antithetical if we see a comparison between the many and the one.

[33] "Likely" because it immediately proceeds on the initial correspondence of the polyptoton, rather than at the very beginning of the cola.

(4) ὃς ὢν ἀπαύγασμα τῆς δόξης καὶ χαρακτὴρ τῆς ὑποστάσεως αὐτοῦ,
φέρων τε τὰ πάντα τῷ ῥήματι τῆς δυνάμεως αὐτοῦ,

This two-colon period is formed by homoeokatarkton (ὃς ὢν ἀπαύγασμα …; φέρων τε τὰ πάντα …), homoeoteleuton (… τῆς ὑποστάσεως αὐτοῦ; … τῆς δυνάμεως αὐτοῦ), and antistrophe (… αὐτοῦ; … αὐτοῦ).

(5) καθαρισμὸν τῶν ἁμαρτιῶν ποιησάμενος
ἐκάθισεν ἐν δεξιᾷ τῆς μεγαλωσύνης ἐν ὑψηλοῖς,

Another two-cola period, this unit is bound together by homoeokatarkton (καθαρισμὸν …; ἐκάθισεν …) and possible homoeoteleuton (… -ος; … -οῖς).[34]

(6) τοσούτῳ   κρείττων γενόμενος   τῶν ἀγγέλων
ὅσῳ   διαφορώτερον   παρ' αὐτοὺς κεκληρονόμηκεν ὄνομα.

The final period of the unit, another two-cola construction, is formed by homoeokatarkton (τοσούτῳ …; ὅσῳ …). There is also a close parisosis (symmetry of grammatical structure and meaning) that is interrupted only by hyperbaton:[35]

Clause A: dative neuter pronoun + comparative adjective + *clause's main verb* + comparative object
Clause B: dative neuter pronoun + comparative adjective + comparative object + *clause's main subject and verb*

The suspended κεκληρονόμηκεν ὄνομα is also longer than its counterpart, γενόμενος, both because the subject is explicit and

---

[34] Unlike modern rhyme, homoeoteleuton can occur among single concluding syllables, and the resemblance can be less precise. See again Robertson, *The Gorgianic Figures*, 20–21; Martin, "The Poetry of the Lord's Prayer," 347–72. What Robertson says of paronomasia might be said of all the sound-based figures: "The precise amount of similarity in sound is not fixed; it is greater in μέλλει … μέλει (Tiber. III 71) than in προσήκει προθύμως (Hermog. II 335)" (*The Gorgianic Figures*, 21).

[35] Hyperbaton, as Quintilian defines it, is the "elegant transposition of words" (Quintilian, *Inst.* 9.3.91 [Russell, LCL]). The placement of γενόμενος between the comparative adjective and genitive noun is the hyperbaton in this colon. It is possibly employed here to bring emphasis to the extended ending of the second colon and thus signaling the end of the *exordium* (see below). For a thorough discussion of hyperbaton in Hebrews see S. M. Baugh, "Hyperbaton and Greek Literary Style in Hebrews," *NovT* 59 (2017): 194–213. Baugh demonstrates the extensive utilization of hyperbaton throughout Hebrews.

the verb has more syllables, with the result that the final clause of the sentence is longer than those immediately preceding it. This is in keeping with the commonly attested doctrine that the final clause of "compound periods" be longer (Demetrius, *Eloc.* 18; so also Theophrastus, cited with approbation by Cicero, *De or.* 3.184–7) – and thus further evidence for delineating the conclusion of the *exordium* at verse 4.

In short, the first four verses are characterized beginning to end by tightly formed, circular periods with clearly discernible constituent cola. Each period bends back on itself and concludes with a satisfying rhetorical resolution. These moments of resolution, rather than "connecting particles," serve to signal transitions from one unit to the next.

One may compare the periodic shape of this prose to that of the *narratio* in 1:5–14. Although the Septuagint passages that the author quotes occasionally display what the Greeks would call periodic form,[36] the writer's own prose in this section becomes decidedly nonperiodic. Transitions from one unit to another are now signaled by the "connecting particles" Aristotle prescribes for nonperiodic or "strung-on" prose: "For ..." (5a), "And again..." (5b), "But when again..." (6), "And..." (7), "But..." (8); "And..." (10); "But..." (13). More importantly, circular form, the essential characteristic of periodic prose according to the theorists, is noticeably lacking beginning in verse 5. The opening clause, "For to which of the angels did he ever say," neither has circuitous form itself, nor does it serve as a protasis in a larger circular structure. The same may be said for most clauses that follow.[37] Furthermore, the figures that typify periodic form are for the most part lacking in verses 5–14 in the author's

---

[36] This is owing to Hebrew parallelism, a feature of Hebrew poetry. On the similarity of Hebrew poetry to Greek periodic prose – and especially the use in both of the Gorgianic figures, see Martin, "The Poetry of the Lord's Prayer," 347–72.

[37] One possible exception is the comparison of vv. 7–8. Its introductory formulae (καὶ πρὸς μὲν τοὺς ἀγγέλους λέγει ...; πρὸς δὲ τὸν υἱόν ...) introducing the contrasting scriptural claims about the angels and Jesus respectively do lend the comparison a broad, circuitous form. The intervening, multiclause scripture citations that follow these formulae, however, prolong the resolution and thus prevent the circuitous form from being "tight." Further, each formula, as we have said, is introduced by particles. Thus in style the comparison is more at home in the *narratio* of vv. 5–14 than in the *exordium* of vv. 1–4.

original prose.[38] In short, beginning in verse 5 we have left behind the exalted periodic prose of the *exordium* and arrived at the body of the speech.[39]

Third, Heb 1:3 introduces a *hymnos* that arrives as its climactic conclusion in v. 4. The thesis that Heb 1:3–4 is a hymn has been argued by others, though the matter is far from settled.[40] In our view,

---

[38] Again, the comparison of vv. 7–8 may be cited as exceptional. The author's introductory formulae serve to frame the comparison as broadly antithetical and lend it a partial parisosis (though the formulae display a brief symmetry of structure, the effect of that symmetry quickly dissipates with the introduction of the lengthier, contrasting proof-texts, which are in no way parallel in form to one another).

[39] This is in keeping with the widely attested doctrine that periodic prose, Gorgianic figures, and/or style consisting of these not be used overly much in an oration (see Aristotle, *Rhet.* 3.1.8–10 [1404a]; 3.3.4 [1407a]; Demetrius, *Eloc.* 12–15; Cicero, *Or. Brut.* 174–6; cf., Dionysius of Halicarnassus, *Lys.* 2–3; *Is.* 19; *Dem.* 25; *Comp.* 23; Diodorus Siculus 12.53.4).

[40] On the hymnic thesis, see Günther Bornkamm, "Das Bekenntnis im Hebräerbrief," in *Studien zu Antike und Urchristentum: Gesammelte Aufsätze, Volume 2* (ed. Günther Bornkamm; BEvT 28; Munich: Kaiser, 1963), 188–203 (see esp. 197–200); Reinhard Deichgräber, *Gotteshymnus und Christushymnus in der frühen Christenheit* (SUNT 5; Göttingen: Vandenhoeck & Ruprecht, 1967), 137–40; Jack T. Sanders, *The New Testament Christological Hymns: Their Historical Religious Background* (SNTSMS 15; Cambridge: Cambridge University, 1971), 19–20; Heinrich Zimmerman, *Das Bekenntnis der Hoffnung: Tradition und Redaktion im Hebräerbrief* (BBB 47; Köln: Hanstein, 1977), 52–60; William R. G. Loader, *Sohn und Hoherpriester: Eine traitionsgeschichtliche Untersuchung zur Christologie des Hebräerbriefes* (WMANT 53; Neukirchen-Vluyn: Neukirchener, 1981), 64–71; Janusz Frankowski, "Early Christian Hymns Recorded in the New Testament: A Reconsideration of the Question in Light of Heb 1,3," *BZ* 27 (1983): 183–94; Walter G. Übelacker, *Der Hebräerbrief als Appel: Untersuchungen zu exordium, narratio, und postscriptum (Hebr 1–2 und 13, 22–25)* (ConB 21; Stockholm: Almquist & Wiksell, 1989), 87; Ben Witherington III, *Letters and Homilies for Jewish Christians: A Socio-Rhetorical Commentary on Hebrews, James, and Jude* (Downers Grove: IVP, 2007), 101–22; idem, *The Indelible Image: The Theological and Ethical Thought World of the New Testament, Vol. 2: The Collective Witness* (Downers Grove: IVP, 2010), 125–27 (Heb 1:2b–4). This thesis is often intertwined with the view that 1:3–4 is source material by a different author and so is often rejected on grounds of authorship (see, e.g., Craig R. Koester, *Hebrews: A New Translation with Introduction and Commentary* [AB 36; New York: Doubleday, 2001], 178–9; James W. Thompson, *Hebrews* [Paideia; Grand Rapids: Baker 2008], 33). There is no compelling reason, once the use of *hymnos* in these verses is recognized, to assume different authorship or a prior life setting (cf. Frankowski, "Early Christian Hymns," 190). *Hymnos* was a form of epideictic composition that was learned by orators primarily for use in *speeches*, including those with practical (deliberative or judicial) aims. Given that Hebrews is just such a speech, and given that our author demonstrates a mastery of other topically ordered epideictic forms like encomium and syncrisis that were closely related to and taught in connection with *hymnos*, we believe that any hymnic text found in Hebrews is most naturally to be assigned to the writer of Hebrews and to be viewed as an organic part of the speech's composition.

the piece most certainly belongs to the genre of *hymnos*. In the rhetorical handbooks, *hymnos* is identified by "four consistently attested generic markers": (1) it is epideictic, (2) it praises a god (whether *divis* or *deus*), (3) it sketches the god's life in multiple clauses (in contrast to *epainos*, which is typically only a single sentence of praise), and (4) it takes its form and content from *topoi* of praise and blame – for some theorists, the same *topoi* employed in praise of humans, for others, *topoi* specially listed for the gods.[41] In view of these markers, one may readily grasp the hymnic nature of Heb 1:3–4. (1) Certainly the piece is encomiastic, praising as it does the life of Jesus. Indeed, epideictic rhetoric, as we have seen, is prescribed for the *exordium*, and especially the *exordium* of a deliberative speech, and especially speeches where the audience may be wavering about the importance of the subject – so it is not surprising that we would find its use at the beginning of Hebrews. (2) Though there is much debate about the Christology of Hebrews,[42] the subject of the praise in 1:3–4 is without question sufficiently divine for the *hymnos* genre. According to Quintilian, even divinized emperors were subjects of *hymnos* ("Some should be praised ... because they earned immortality by virtue, a theme which the piety of our emperor has made the glory of the present age too"; *Inst.* 3.7.9 [Russell, LCL]).[43] Menander Rhetor taught that both gods and

---

[41] The notions about *hymnos* cited in this paragraph are more fully developed in the article by Michael Wade Martin and Bryan A. Nash, "Philippians 2:6–11 as Subversive *Hymnos*: A Study in the Light of Ancient Rhetorical Theory," *JTS* 66 (2015): 90–138.

[42] Some have discerned in Hebrews an epiphany Christology in which the Son has ontological preexistence; e.g., Koester, *Hebrews*, 104–5; Luke Timothy Johnson, *Hebrews: A Commentary* (NTL; Louisville: Westminster John Knox, 2006), 66–9; Richard Bauckham, "The Divinity of Jesus Christ in the Epistle to the Hebrews," in *The Epistle to the Hebrews and Christian Theology* (ed. R. Bauckham et al.; Grand Rapids: Eerdmans, 2009), 15–36. Others have discerned an exaltation Christology with Jesus as the enthroned Son in whom God's creative wisdom indwells and who embodies the purposes God has for his creation from the beginning; e.g., G. B. Caird, "Son by Appointment," in *The New Testament Age: Essays in Honor of Bo Reicke* (ed. W. C. Weinrich.; 2 vols; Macon, GA: Mercer University Press, 1984), 1:73–81; L. D. Hurst, "The Christology of Hebrews 1 and 2," in *The Glory of Christ in the New Testament: Studies in Christology in Memory of George Bradford Caird* (ed. L. D. Hurst and N. T. Wright; Oxford; Clarendon Press, 1987), 151–64; Kenneth L. Schenck, "Keeping His Appointment: Creation and Enthronement in Hebrews," *JSNT* 66 (1997): 91–117.

[43] In his lifetime, Augustus's name was included in the hymn of the *Salii* that praised gods and divinized heroes (cf. *Res ges. Divi Aug.* 10.1).

emperors/kings are "to be hymned [ὑμνεῖν] to the best of our ability" (368 [Russell and Wilson]).[44] Given the exaltation depicted at the end of the piece, its subject may be judged to be at least as divine as divinized men, whatever one makes of his origins. (3) Though brief, the piece depicts Christ via multiple clauses, and so cannot be described as mere *epainos*. And perhaps most importantly, (4) the piece takes up common hymnic *topoi* in the depiction – and it is this generic feature that helps us to see where the hymn both begins (1:3) and ends (1:4). Various theorists' *topos* lists illustrate both the diversity of the *topoi* employed (particularly in lists tailored specifically for the *hymnos* genre) and the unity within it. Further, theorists commonly commend the lists not as rigid templates, but as search headings, and with the caveat that writers only use those topics that serve the rhetorical aims of the writer. Of these lists, Quintilian's (*Inst.* 3.7.7–9) is of particular note:

> Majesty of nature
> Power
> Inventions benefitting humanity
> Actions
> Parents
> Age
> Offspring
> Born immortal/earned immortality by virtue

Evidently, the writer of Hebrews is selecting *topoi* from a list very much like this, as four of these eight *topoi* are employed, and in precisely the same order, to structure the *hymnos*. The only *topoi* used by the writer and not appearing on this list are comparison and names – but these are commonly treated as addenda topics to be used at the conclusion of epideictic pieces.[45] Comparison and names are treated, too, as the final *topoi* of the Christ-hymn of Phil 2, and in connection with the exaltation of Christ over creation.[46] Thus there

[44] The text and translation of Menander consulted here is from *Menander Rhetor* (ed. and trans. D. A. Russell and N. G. Wilson; Oxford: Clarendon Press, 1981, repr. 2004), 76–7.

[45] Theon (112–5), Ps. Hermogenes (18–20), Menander Rhetor (368–77), Aphthonius (35–44), and Nicolaus (47–63) all list Comparison as the final topic. Theon treats "Names, Homonyms, and Nicknames" as an additional consideration (109–12), while Cicero treats "Name" as a prefatory topic (*Inv.* 1.34–6).

[46] Martin and Nash, "Philippians 2:6–11 as Subversive *Hymnos*," 90–138.

is a Christian precedent for the use of these *topoi* as climactic subject-matter in hymnic conclusions.

Using Quintilian's list and these two addenda *topoi*, we may briefly sketch the topical structure of 1:3–4 as follows. The reader will observe that each clause, formed as a colon by the figures surveyed above, corresponds to a single *topos*:

Majesty of nature	ὃς ὢν ἀπαύγασμα τῆς δόξης καὶ χαρακτὴρ τῆς ὑποστάσεως αὐτοῦ,
Power	φέρων τε τὰ πάντα τῷ ῥήματι τῆς δυνάμεως αὐτοῦ,
Actions	καθαρισμὸν τῶν ἁμαρτιῶν ποιησάμενος[47]
Immortality by virtue	ἐκάθισεν ἐν δεξιᾷ τῆς μεγαλωσύνης ἐν ὑψηλοῖς,
Comparison	τοσούτῳ κρείττων γενόμενος τῶν ἀγγέλων
Name	ὅσῳ διαφορώτερον παρ' αὐτοὺς κεκληρονόμηκεν ὄνομα.

Majesty of nature	Who being the radiance of his glory and the imprint of his nature,
Power	and bearing all things by the word of his power,
Actions	having accomplished purification of sins,
Immortality by virtue	he sat down at the right hand of the majesty on high,
Comparison	having become so much greater than the angels,
Name	as much as he has inherited a name more excellent than they.

This topical structure, in our view, settles the debate concerning whether 1:3–4 is a *hymnos*. The writer is praising a divine/divinized person using conventional headings of praise. The invocation of the first *topos* of Quintilian's list *by name* serves to delineate the beginning of the *hymnos*, over and against those who might say it starts in

---

[47] One wonders whether this line treats the immediately preceding *topos* in Quintilian's list, inventions benefitting humanity. We have taken ποιησάμενος, "doing," as a natural fit for the *topos* of actions, but it could be as readily read as beneficial "making."

1:2b.[48] Other factors also suggest the hymn's beginning in 1:3: the use of ὅς, which is employed as an introductory formula in other Christologically focused hymns (cf. Phil. 2:6; Col 1:15; 1 Tim 3:16), and the change in grammatical subject from God in 1:1–2 to Christ in 1:3–4. The continued invocation thereafter of standard *topoi* – one for every colon, often by name, and in a standard topical progression – marks the subsequent divisions. Most importantly for the purposes of the present study, the invocation of two standard concluding *topoi* in 1:4 serves to mark with certainty the conclusion of the *hymnos*. Comparison and names are, as we have said, the most commonly cited concluding *topoi* in the theorist's lists. They are also precisely the same two *topoi* that conclude the *hymnos* of Philippians 2:6–11. Further, the material that immediately follows, a syncrisis of Christ and the angels, begins a new series of *syncritical topoi*, starting with origins – the first *topos* in all syncrises and epideictic lists.[49] All these factors together point to the same conclusion: in 1:4, we have an ending, and in 1:5, a new beginning.

Fourth, there is a transitional link between the last item in Heb 1:1–4 and the material that follows. One factor potentially arguing against 1:4 as an ending is that its claim, that Jesus has become greater than the angels, seems to be of a piece with the extensive, topic-by-topic comparison of Jesus and the angels that follows. This, however, is intentional in our judgment and entirely in keeping with the nature of *exordium*. Quintilian states that the final item in an *exordium* should ideally have some manner of connection to the beginning of whatever section comes next, whether it be a *narratio* or *argumentatio*:

> However, when we *have* used a Prooemium, whether we then pass to a statement of facts or straight to the proofs, the last item in the Prooemium ought to be that to which the beginning of the next section can most conveniently be linked. (*Inst.* 4.1.76–77 [Russell, LCL])

In view of Quintilian's comments, the comparison of Jesus with the angels in 1:4 should unquestionably be viewed as "the last item in the Prooemium."

---

[48] E.g., Witherington, *Letters and Homilies*, 101–22.
[49] See the analysis of the preceding chapters.

The Secondary *Exordium* of 4:14–16

In addition to the main *exordium*, there is also within the speech a secondary *exordium* deserving of our attention. Hebrews 4:14–16 may be seen as the *exordium* for the lengthy section devoted to the topic of pursuits (5:1–12:13), a two-part unit ordered by the subtopics closely associated with pursuits by the theorists, education and deeds. These are the third and fourth *narratio-argumentatio* units, respectively, of our analysis in the preceding two chapters. We may represent the arrangement as follows:

Exordium: covenant priestly pursuits (4:14–16)

III. Covenant priestly pursuits: education – Aaronic high priests vs. Jesus the high priest
   a. *Narratio*
      Epideictic amplification (5:1–10): The new covenant's high priest is the better trained.
   b. *Argumentatio*
      Deliberative argumentation (5:11–6.20): Undergo the new covenant's high priest's better training of faithful endurance based upon better promises.
IV. Covenant priestly pursuits: deeds – Levitical priestly ministry vs. Melchizedekian priestly ministry
   a. *Narratio*
      Epideictic amplification (7:1–10:18): The deeds of the new covenant's priestly ministry are superior.
   b. *Argumentatio*
      Deliberative argumentation (10:19–12:13): Enabled by the greater deeds of the new covenant priestly ministry, approach, hold fast, and provoke one another to loving action, not defecting from the covenant community.

This secondary *exordium* (the only one in the body of the speech), like the *exordium* for the speech itself, seeks primarily to win the audience's favor. Here, though, the primary obstacle to that favor appears to be the complexity of what follows: the topical section it introduces (priestly pursuits) is much longer than the two preceding topical units (origins and birth) and more diverse, falling as it does under two topical subheadings (education and deeds). Complexity, according to the theorists, threatens favor in the form of receptivity, and in cases where complexity is an issue, as we have discussed

previously, the theorists make an exception to the rule about *not* introducing subject matter. That is, in such cases the theorists allow for and encourage a brief enumeration of the main points to be argued subsequently.

Accordingly, what we find in the case of this secondary *exordium* is a brief enumeration of the major points to come in the priestly pursuits section. There is both epideictic praise of Jesus as a great high priest (4:14a and 4:15), the major claim of both *narratio* sections (5:1–10; 7:1–10:18), and deliberative exhortation for the readers themselves to follow their high priest in his path of perseverance and approach to God (4:14b and 4:16), the major thesis of both *argumentatio* sections (5:11–6:20; 10:19–12:17) that follow.[50] Also, major topical motifs from the priestly pursuits section are introduced: from the priestly education section, the educational motif of the high priest's "testing" (4:15); and from the priestly deeds section, an exalted high priest who has gone through the heavens and the specific exhortations to "hold fast" and "approach" in view of God's gracious enablement (4:14b, 16; cf. 10:19–25, where these exhortations are repeated, again in connection with divine enablement, as the opening thesis for the section). Such enumeration is typical of *exordia* that open complex pieces (*genus obscurum*). Here, it serves to transition to the major section of the body of the speech, lays out its key themes, and thereby orients the audience favorably – by fostering greater receptivity – toward the lengthy and diverse material that follows. When, toward the end of the piece, the two exhortations from the *exordium* are repeated as the opening thesis of the deeds deliberative *argumentatio*, the piece is effectively bracketed as a single unit, the *inclusio* signaling that the end of the pursuits unit is at hand.[51]

If receptivity is the major goal, the *exordium* nonetheless also pursues the two remaining dimensions of favor, goodwill and attentiveness, in standard ways. In seeking goodwill, it has focused on two of the three prescribed possible topics: (a) a favorable *person involved*

---

[50] Since the deliberative thesis concerning perseverance has at this point in the speech already been broached in the first two *argumentatio* sections, there is no need to withhold it here, as in the speech's primary *exordium*.

[51] Thus we ultimately agree with Wolfgang Nauck, "Zum Aufbau des Hebräerbriefes," in *Judentum, Urchristentum, Kirche, Festschrift für Joachim Jeremias* (ed. Walter Eltester; BZNW 26; Berlin: Alfred Töpelmann, 1960), 199–206, that that 4:14–16, by virtue of its connection to 10:19–23, plays a role in the structure of Hebrews.

in the case, Jesus – here described as sympathizing with the listeners' weaknesses because of his own experience of testing and, as the high priest who has passed through the heavens, mediating mercy and grace to the listeners; and (b) a favorable *part* of the case, the exhortation to hold fast because of Jesus's sympathy and to approach the throne in order to find mercy and grace in time of need. Only the favorable dimensions of approach are highlighted. Nothing is mentioned presently of the need in the approach to embrace suffering as testing and sacrifice, that is, of the need to bring one's life as an offering to God. This more challenging dimension of the exhortation, with its attendant rebuke and warning, is withheld until the body of the discourse.[52] And in seeking attentiveness, the author once again conveys the great importance (*rerum magnitido*) of what will be discussed by highlighting, in the opening sentence, the cosmic scale of Christ's work: "Since, then, we have a great high priest who has passed through the heavens, Jesus, Son of God."

With regard to style, however, we note that Heb 4:14–16 lacks the concentrated use of Gorgianic figures that was seen in Heb 1:1–4. The unit does open with a loose period where the main clause resolves the tension created by a subordinate clause (ἔχοντες οὖν ἀρχιερέα μέγαν διεληλυθότα τοὺς οὐρανούς Ισοῦν υἱὸν τοῦ θεοῦ |

---

[52] In the "priestly education" section that follows, Christ will be depicted undergoing a priestly curriculum of suffering, learning obedience from that suffering, and arriving at perfection (the goal of *paideia*) through his sacrificial death, thereby entering into the Melchizedekian priesthood to which he was first summoned by the Father. Immediately following this depiction, the audience is severely rebuked for its own lack of maturity and training, is summoned to leave behind basic teachings and move on to perfection, and is exhorted to engage in *mimesis* of Abraham, who (like Jesus) on the basis of God's promise faithfully endured (he offered Isaac and received him back from the dead). The *paideia* this section calls the audience to, essentially, is Christ-like obedience-through-suffering, a curriculum of sacrifice made to God in pursuit of priestly vocation. Similarly, in the "priestly deeds" section that follows, Christ's priestly ministry will be depicted as in every way superior to the one foreshadowing it, a depiction that climaxes with the account of the inner cleansing of conscience and heart that enables approach to the heavenly throne. Immediately following this depiction, the audience is summoned once again, in language repeated from the *exordium*, "to approach" with cleansed hearts and to "hold fast"—only this time, a third exhortation is added: they are to "consider how to provoke one another to love and good deeds, not neglecting to meet together." Here again is the potentially unfavorable (for an immature audience) element of life offered to God as priestly sacrifice – love and good deeds are later recast as the sacrifices the readers bring in their own priestly approach (cf. 13:16). The *exempla* that follow – the readers in their early days (10:32–39), the faithful witnesses (11:1–40), and Christ himself (12:1–3), all further highlight the need to embrace suffering.

κρατῶμεν τοὺς ὁμολογίας).[53] The unit also closes with a brief rhetorical flourish. The final ἵνα clause is a single colon period consisting of two brief commatta held together by chiastic parisosis (parallelism of grammar, syntax, and meaning) and paramoiosis (evident in the parallel, identical verb endings, -ωμεν). The colon also ends with an extending phrase similar to what we saw at the conclusion of 1:1–4:

ἵνα
λάβωμεν ἔλευς
καὶ
χάριν εὕρωμεν[54] εἰς εὔκαιρον βοήθειαν

While such stylistic material is certainly at home in an *exordium*, it does not constitute the high style seen in the primary *exordium* of 1:1–4. The difference is likely attributable to the different contents and functions of the two *exordia*. The theorists recommend that Gorgianic figures and the associated rhythmical or polished style only be used sparingly in a speech and with material with which it is well-matched such as laudatory praise and amplification.[55] Hebrews 1:1–4 consists wholly of such material and is intended to open the speech in exalted, favor-winning praise and *hymnos*. There the polished style is most appropriate. Hebrews 4:14–16, by contrast, consists of equal parts deliberation and praise and serves the more practical function of enumerating for clarity's sake the major points of the complex section to come. This is precisely the kind of material well-suited for the tempered style, which is a mixture of the austere (which lacks Georgianic figures and rhythmical periods altogether) and the polished (which uses them in every clause).[56]

If the content of 4:14–16 in every way conforms with expectations concerning the *exordium* of a complex unit, additional factors serve to delineate this *exordium* at verses 14–16. First, the analysis of the previous chapters identified a second *narratio-argumentatio* unit comprising 3:1–4:13. Clearly this material is bound together not only

---

[53] The author has potentially employed hyperbaton here by placing the attributive participial phrase (διεληλυθότα τοὺς οὐρανούς) between the noun phrase ἀρχιερέα μέγαν and the appositional referent, Ἰησοῦν υἱὸν τοῦ θεοῦ.

[54] The author has employed hyperbaton by placing εὕρωμεν between χάριν and εἰς εὔκαιρον βοήθειαν. By so doing, the author is able to create a chiastic construction with λάβωμεν ἔλεος and emphasize the prepositional phrase as an elongating phrase signaling the end of the *exordium*.

[55] See esp. the discussions of Cicero, *Or. Brut.* 108–211; Dionysius of Halicarnassus, *Comp.* 22–3.

[56] See Dionysius of Halicarnassus, *Comp.* 23.

topically as a treatment of covenant births, as we earlier argued, but also thematically in its consideration of Moses and the wilderness generation. With 4:14–16, those topics and themes come to an abrupt end, and a topical and thematic shift to covenant priestly pursuits is signaled. Indeed, many interpreters acknowledge the verses as both transitional and forward looking in their language and themes – which is what one would expect of a secondary *exordium*.[57] What sets these three verses apart from what follows, however, is the syncrisis of priests that begins in the immediately following verses (5:1–10). This unit is topically ordered and chiastically arranged, as we have seen, so it is clearly a discrete unit.[58] Further, it has all the characteristics of *narratio* and, moreover, takes up the *topos* of education in its expected place within a standard progression. It is paired, too, with an immediately following *argumentatio* devoted to the same *topos* of education (5:11–6:20). Apart from the fact that 4:14–16 has all the characteristics of a secondary *exordium*, its very location between these major units, together with its brevity, naturally commend it as a likely secondary *exordium*.

Second, as we shall see in the next chapter, the priestly pursuits section ends in verses (12:14–17) that display key characteristics of *peroratio* – enough that on their own merit the verses deserve in our judgment the designation of secondary *peroratio*. Since the priestly pursuits section ends with such a secondary conclusion, one would expect the same unit to have a secondary introduction, and indeed, both identifications have a mutually confirmatory effect on one another. They show that the section they bracket has been judged, because of its length and complexity, to be in need of its own introduction and conclusion.

Third, as noted above, Quintilian advises that "the last item in the Prooemium ought to be that to which the beginning of the next section can most conveniently be linked" (*Inst.* 4.1). As in the primary *exordium*, so in the secondary *exordium* of Heb 4:14–16, we find the writer employing just such a transition. The final clause of verse 16, "in order that we might receive mercy and we might find grace in our time of need," serves to transition to the first thought of

---

[57] George H. Guthrie (*The Structure of Hebrews: A Text-Linguistic Analysis* [NovTSup 73; Leiden: Brill, 1994], 23) notes that the function of 4:14–16 is disputed among interpreters. Does it end a section? Does it introduce a section? Or neither? Our analysis strengthens the case of those who see 4:14–16 as introductory.

[58] The chiasm delineating 5:1–10 as a discrete unit is widely acknowledged; see the citations assembled by Koester, *Hebrews*, 292 n. 143.

the subsequent *narratio* (5:1–10) with its comparative depiction of how Aaronic high priests mediate mercy and grace to the people in their need: "Every high priest chosen from among mortals is put in charge of things pertaining to God on their behalf, to offer gifts and sacrifices for sins. He is able to deal gently with the ignorant and wayward, since he himself is subject to weakness; and because of this he must offer sacrifice for his own sins as well as for those of the people" (5:1–3). These comments anticipate the comparison eventually drawn with the high priest Jesus and highlight his superior manner of mediating mercy and grace. Whereas Aaronic high priests share in the weakness and sin of the people, Jesus the great high priest "learns from his suffering" and becomes "a source of salvation" by his obedience and perfection (5:8–10). Thus the secondary *exordium* of Hebrews shares with the primary *exordium* a standard delineating feature, employing its final words as a transitional link to the material it introduces.

Conclusion

Our analyses thus far of the individual units of the Hebrews speech – its *exordia, narrationes,* and *argumentationes* – coordinate well with one another and, though independent of one another, have a mutually confirming effect. In this chapter, we have seen how the primary *exordium* of the speech (1:1–4) leads in prescribed ways to the related narrative and argumentative materials that follow, and similarly, how a secondary *exordium* within the speech (4:14–16) does the same. Further, we have noted how the contents of the primary *exordium* lend additional insight into the speech as a whole. On the one hand, the presence of epideictic generally, and laudatory, comparative *hymnos* to Christ specifically, in these four verses suggests that the speech does *not* pursue an epideictic thesis, since rhetorical theory commends *refraining* from introducing the thesis in the *exordium*.[59] On the other hand, it does suggest a deliberative thesis, not only because that is the only viable alternative to an epideictic thesis in contemporary interpretation, but also because epideictic *exordia* were prescribed *in particular* for deliberative speeches (cf. Aristotle, *Rhet.* 3.14.12 [1415b]; Quintilian, *Inst.* 3.8.8), and especially those

---

[59] This observation calls into question those who would point to the laudatory introduction as evidence the speech is epideictic; e.g., Witherington, *Letters and Homilies,* 97–8.

(like Hebrews) where the audience potentially "attaches too little importance" to the author's "idea" (Aristotle, *Rhet.* 3.14.12 [1415b]; cf. Quintilian, *Inst.* 3.8.8). Indeed, all epideictic in Hebrews, and not just that of the *exordium*, may be explained with reference to the theory of *exordium* as the essential material of the *genus humile* – that is, as the amplification needed in a speech challenged by waning audience commitment.

8

ENDING WITH RECAPITULATION AND EMOTION

Peroratio *in Hebrews*

We come now to the final major heading of arrangement in a speech – the *peroratio* or the conclusion. We begin by first looking at a *peroratio* composed by Thucydides. In the brief deliberative speech by the Peloponnesian commanders on the eve of battle, the commanders end their exhortation to their troops saying

> There is accordingly not a single reason that we can find why we should fail; and as to our earlier mistakes, the very fact that they were made will teach us a lesson. Be of good courage, then, and let each man, both helmsman and sailor, follow our lead as best he can, not leaving the post to which he may be assigned. We shall prepare for the attack at least as well as your former commanders, and shall give no one an excuse to act like a coward; but if anyone should be inclined that way, he shall be punished with the penalty he deserves, while the brave shall be honoured with rewards such as befit their valour. (2.87.7–9 [Smith, LCL])

The *peroratio* begins with a brief recapitulation of the argument. It also appeals to the emotions. It provides a summary exhortation to the troops that stirs up the emotion of courage. It attempts to make the troops favorable toward their commanders, who will be prepared. It also stirs up fear of loss for cowardliness and desire for the benefits of valor. As we will discuss in this chapter, these characteristics are typical of *peroratio* according to the theorists.

But does Hebrews have an identifiable *peroratio* according to first-century expectations? No consensus has developed among interpreters of Hebrews with regard to the identity and limits of the *peroratio* in this sermon. Some interpreters (von Soden, Backhaus, and Anderson) have identified the *peroratio* of Hebrews as a rather lengthy unit extending from 10:19–13:21/25. Our previous analysis has demonstrated that this unit contains a lengthy section of

argumentatio (10:19–12:13) as well as the final *narratio* (12:18–24) with its *argumentatio* (12:25–29). Other interpreters such as Spicq identified 12:24–29 as the *peroratio*. Again, as we have argued, the majority of this unit is the final *argumentatio* that completes the *narratio* of Heb 12:18–24. Nissilä, Übelacker, and Thurén recognized 13:1–21/25 as the *peroratio*. In agreement with the last three scholars, our analysis of Hebrews has, by default, left Heb 13:1–25 as the remaining material to consider for the primary *peroratio* of the sermon.[1] In this chapter, we will argue that Heb 13:1–25, indeed, fits the expectations associated with the *peroratio*. Additionally, we will argue that Heb 12:14–17 can be identified as a secondary *peroratio*. As in the example cited from Thucydides, the *peroratio* could be recognized by some key characteristics: by its location, by its functions, and by its length. In this chapter we will build our case cumulatively, considering each of these elements in turn.

The Location of *Peroratio* and Hebrews

The primary and essential indicator of the *peroratio* was its location. The *peroratio* came at the end of the speech after the *argumentatio*. Aristotle lists the four primary parts of a speech in order as προοίμιον, πρόθεσις, πίστις, and ἐπίλογος (*Rhet.* 3.13.4 [1414b]).

---

[1] Some scholars distinguish Heb 13:22–25 from 13:1–21, identifying the former as an epistolary postscript appended to the sermon with a view to its delivery by proxy. For example, see Martin Karrer, *Der Brief an die Hebräer: Kapitel 5,11–13,25* (ÖTKNT 20/2; Gütersloh: Gütersloher Verlagshaus, 2002), 351; Walter G. Übelacker, *Der Hebräerbrief als Appell: Untersuchungen zu* exordium, narratio, *und* postscriptum *(Hebr 1–2 und 13,22–25)* (ConBNT 21; Stockholm: Almquist & Wiksell, 1989), 197–201; Peter T. O'Brien, *The Letter to the Hebrews* (Pillar New Testament Commentary; Grand Rapids: Eerdmans, 2010), 513. It is possible that Heb 13:22 belongs to the *peroratio* of the speech. Self-conscious reference to one's speech as either an accusation or a defense could be found in the *peroratio* of forensic oratory in Antiphon (*On the Murder of Herodes*, 85) and Lysias (14.46). The reference then functions as the most succinct recapitulation of the entirety of the speech. The author also mentions in v. 22 that his exhortation is written down as a letter. He subsequently adds typical epistolary forms of travel plans, greetings, and a grace wish in vv. 23–25. These elements also have identifiable rhetorical functions consistent with a *peroratio*, that is, to generate good will towards the author and those with him. In light of these considerations, we view the whole of Heb 13 as the *peroratio* of a speech that was sent as a letter, that is, delivered by proxy. The references to Antiphon and Lysias are cited by Frederick J. Long, *Ancient Rhetoric and Paul's Apology: The Compositional Unity of 2 Corinthians* (SNTSMS 131; Cambridge: Cambridge University Press, 2004), 191.

He identifies the ἐπίλογος as the conclusion of the speech (*Rhet.* 3.19.6 [1430a]). Cicero, in his youthful *De Inventione*, writes, "the peroration is the end or conclusion of the whole speech" (1.98 [Hubbell, LCL]; cf. *Part. or.* 52). Quintilian states that the terms ἐπίλογος and *peroratio* "plainly indicate that this is the final conclusion of the speech" (*Inst.* 6.1.55 [Russell, LCL]). Anonymous Seguerianus writes, "An epilogue, according to Neocles, is speech added to previously spoken demonstrations ... According to certain others, however, (it is) the last part of a speech following demonstrations" (198–99 [Dilts and Kennedy]).

Rhetorical theorists also recognized that a *peroratio* or a part of the *peroratio,* recapitulation, could occur within the speech at the boundaries between the parts of arrangement. Rhetorica ad Herennium writes, "We can in four places use a Conclusion: in the Direct Opening, after the Statement of Facts, after the strongest argument, and in the Conclusion of the speech" (2.47 [Caplan, LCL]). Quintilian states that in complex cases there can be a number of passages resembling *peroratio.* Quintilian calls these passages divided *peroratio* or μερκοὶ ἐπίλογοι. Quintilian states that these distributed epilogues are only quasi-conclusions, not the actual conclusion of the whole speech, which occurs at the end of the speech (*Inst.* 6.1.54–55; cf. *Inst.* 4.3.11–12). As we will discuss below, recapitulation or summing up, which was one of the primary functions of the *peroratio,* was acknowledged to occur throughout the speech. Anaximenes of Lampsacus states that recapitulation could be employed both at the end of the whole speech or after a major division in the speech (cf. *Rhet. Alex* 20 [1433b]; 36 [1444b]). Similarly, Anonymous Seguerianus states, "We make a recapitulation not only at the ends (of speeches) but also in the middles" (211 [Dilts and Kennedy]; cf. 236, 239). Apsines writes that recapitulation could come at the end of the speech, between the narration and demonstration, or after a single heading has been demonstrated (*Rhet.* 10.3).

With regard to Heb 13:1–25, this unit obviously occupies the place in the speech where the primary *peroratio* would occur – at the end, after the final *argumentatio* or demonstration. This factor alone does not decide the issue since Aristotle acknowledges that not every speech needs a conclusion, especially when the speech is short and the matter easy to recollect (cf. *Rhet.* 3.13.3 [1414b]). As we have demonstrated, however, the argument in Hebrews is extended, leading the author to choose the method of disjointed *narratio* to present his whole case. Thus, it seems fitting for the author to

conclude this more complex arrangement of his speech with an anticipated *peroratio*.

With regard to Heb 12:14–17, this unit takes up a location at the seam between the longest section of *argumentatio* (10:19–12:13) and the next *narratio* (12:18–24). It is also a seam where the encomiastic topic of covenant deeds transitions to the final topic of covenant death or events beyond death. Thus Heb 12:14–17 comes at a place in the sermon where one would expect to find a quasi-conclusion. Additionally, this unit comes at the end of the extensive central section that spans Heb 5:1–12:13 and covers the topics related to covenant pursuits – i.e., both education (5:1–6:20) and deeds (7:1–12:13). In both sections, the priestly representatives of the old and new covenants along with their ministries are the focus of each *narratio*. This central section began with a secondary *exordium* in Heb 4:14–16. It is fitting then that this long and central unit of covenant pursuits that begins with a secondary *exordium* should also conclude with a secondary *peroratio*.

Both Heb 13:1–25 and 12:14–17 then occupy the expected location of a *peroratio*. We next will consider whether Heb 13:1–25 and Heb 12:14–17 fulfill the anticipated functions of a *peroratio*.

The Functions of *Peroratio* and Hebrews

Theorists discuss typical functions of the *peroratio*. Aristotle identifies four parts or functions of the *peroratio*: to dispose the hearer favorably toward oneself and unfavorably toward one's adversary, to amplify the proofs of the case, to excite the emotions (such as pity, indignation, anger, hate, jealousy, emulation, and strife), and to recapitulate (*Rhet.* 3.19.1–4 [1419b]). Anaximenes of Lampsacus reduces the parts of the *peroratio* to the first and last part of Aristotle's description – to recapitulate and to make the audience favorable toward oneself and unfavorable toward one's opponents (cf. *Rhet. Alex.* 36 [1444b]). Cicero in *Inv.* 1.98 identifies the three parts of the *peroratio* as summing-up, indignation, and pity. Likewise, Apsines follows the same division – reminder, pity, and indignation (cf. *Rhet.* 10.1). Rhetorica ad Herennium lists a slightly modified trio – summing-up, amplification, and appeal to pity (cf. 2.47). Cicero, however, in another rhetorical treatise states that the *peroratio* consists of two parts – amplification and recapitulation (cf. *Part. or.* 52–57). Both Cicero and Rhetorica ad Herennium discuss amplification as a means to stir the emotions of the audience. Quintilian simply

states that the *peroratio* comprises two aspects – facts and emotions through recapitulation and appeal to the emotions (cf. *Inst.* 6.1.1). Anonymous Seguerianus similarly identifies the two parts of the *peroratio* as the practical and the pathetical, which are achieved through recapitulation and appeal to the emotions (cf. 203). From this brief survey, we see that rhetorical theorists commonly identified recapitulation or reminder as a common function of the *peroratio*. The other common function was the appeal to the emotions broadly conceived, whether that was stirring up emotions against one's opponent, or stirring up emotions in favor of oneself, one's client, or one's cause. In this section, then, we will discuss the two common functions of the *peroratio* as recapitulation and appeal to the emotions broadly conceived.

Recapitulation

Among the rhetorical theorists

Recapitulation (*enumeratio, ἀνακεφαλαίωσις, ἀνάμνησις*) involves summarizing the arguments of a speech or enumerating the various headings or topics under which those arguments were made. For instance, Aristotle states that recapitulation in the *peroratio* is "a summary statement of the proofs" (*Rhet.* 3.19.4 [1419b] [Freese, LCL]). Rhetorica ad Herennium also advises that recapitulation should "set forth the points treated in the Proof and Refutation" (2.47 [Caplan, LCL]). Cicero writes that recapitulation is "a passage in which matters that have been discussed in different places here and there throughout the speech are brought together in one place and arranged so as to be seen at a glance" (*Inv.* 1.98; cf. Rhet. Her. 2.47). Likewise, Quintilian notes that recapitulation "places the whole Cause before the [judges] eyes at once" by enumerating the headings of the proofs or facts of the case (*Inst.* 6.1.1–2 [Russell, LCL]).[2] Anonymous Seguerianus states that recapitulation "is a brief exposition of the headings or epicheiremes that have been previously discussed, or, by Zeus, a compact running over of the arguments spoken in detail in order to remind the hearers of them" (210 [Dilts and Kennedy]). The primary focus of these instructions indicate that recapitulation is a summary of the proofs or facts under consideration.

---

[2] Cf. Apsines, *Rhet.* 10.2.

The theorists discuss various techniques for recapitulation. Aristotle states that recapitulation can be achieved either by comparing one's points with those of his or her opponents or by going over the order of one's statements (cf. *Rhet.* 3.19.5 [1420a]). Anaximenes of Lampsacus states that "a summary reminder may be made either by enumerating the points that have been made or in the form of a calculation or by putting questions as to your strongest points and your opponent's weakest, and if you like by employing the figure of a direct question" (*Rhet. Alex.* 36 [1444b] [Rackham, LCL]). Cicero notes that recapitulation may be handled in different ways in order, in part, to avoid boredom. The simplest recapitulation, according to Cicero, was "to touch on each single point and so to run briefly over all arguments" (*Inv.* 1.98 [Caplan, LCL]).[3] Quintilian advises against "straightforward repetition of facts" and advises the use of innumerable figures to enliven the recapitulation (*Inst.* 6.1.2–3 [Russell, LCL]). Anonymous Seguerianus lists four species of recapitulation: hypothesis, stasis, epicheirema, and topic (cf. 214). He also advises that the recapitulation should not be introduced by such obvious statements as "I wish to go through for you from the beginning what I have at the same time been talking about" (219 [Dilts and Kennedy]). Like Quintilian, Anonymous Seguerianus states that *peroratio* utilizes all figures (cf. 221). Apsines lists ten techniques of recapitulation: by headings, by prosopopoeia, by hypotysis, by ethopoeia, by comparison, by introduction of a decree, by γνωσιγραφία, by introduction of laws, by imagining an inscription or likeness or statue or tomb, and by rhetorical question (cf. *Rhet.* 10.4–13).

Recapitulation was recommended for the *peroratio* of all speeches and as mentioned above could be employed at any division in a speech. Anaximenes of Lampsacus writes, "recapitulations should be employed at every part of a speech and with every kind of speech. It is most suitable for accusations and defenses, but also in exhortations and dissuasions" (*Rhet. Alex.* 36 [1444b] [Rackham, LCL]). Quintilian confirms, "What everyone agrees is that a Recapitulation is often useful in other parts of the speech as well, if the Cause is a complex one" (*Inst.* 6.1.18 [Russell, LCL]). Cicero notes some distinctions among the genres of oratory in the use of recapitulation. He writes that recapitulation "in panegyrics is required sometimes and in deliberative speeches seldom, while in judicial oratory it is more

---

[3] Cf. Rhet. Her. 2.47.

often necessary for the prosecutor than for the defendant" (*Part. or.* 59 [Rackham, LCL]).

In Hebrews

When we turn to Heb 13:1–25, do we find recapitulation? Hebrews 13:22 provides the most succinct form of recapitulation when the author summarizes the whole of his speech as a "word of exhortation." Recapitulation, as we will see, is also woven into all that precedes the final summary statement in verse 22. First, Heb 13:1–21 is a series mostly of exhortations (1–19), many with accompanying reasons, and concludes with a benediction (20–21).[4]

- let "brotherly" love remain (v. 1)
- do not neglect hospitality (v. 2a)
  reason: for by this some have entertained angels without knowing (v. 2b)
- remember those in prison and those who are tortured (v. 3)
  reason: as though you too were in prison
  reason: as though you also felt their torment (because you also are in the body)
- marriage is to be honored by all and sex is to be undefiled (4a)
  reason: for God judges the sexually immoral and adulterer (v. 4b)
- your manner of life is to be free from the love of money, being content with your possessions (v. 5a)
  reason: for he has said, "I will never leave or forsake you" so that courageously we say, "the Lord is my helper and I will not be afraid. What can humans due to me." (vv. 5b–6)
- remember your (past) leaders and imitate their faith (v. 7)
  reason: [for] Jesus is the same yesterday, today, and forever (v. 8)[5]
- do not be carried away by various and strange teachings (v. 9a)

---

[4] Cf. A. J. M. Wedderburn, "The 'Letter' to the Hebrews and Its Thirteenth Chapter," *NTS* 50 (2004): 395, n. 18.

[5] For an explanation of the reason v. 8 supplies for the exhortations in v. 7, even though v. 8 has no syntactical connection to v. 7, see David A. deSilva, *Perseverance in Gratitude: A Socio-Rhetorical Commentary on the Epistle "to the Hebrews"* (Grand Rapids: Eerdmans, 2000), 494–6.

    reason: for to have our hearts strengthened by grace is
       better than by foods in which those who walk were not
       benefited (v. 9b)

- we have an altar from which those who serve in the tent
  have no authority to eat (v. 10)
    reason: for the bodies of those animals whose blood was
      brought into the Most Holy Place by the high priest
      were burned outside the camp. For this reason, Jesus
      suffered outside the gates in order to sanctify the people
      by his own blood (vv. 11–12)

- let us, then, go to Jesus outside the camp bearing his
  reproach (v. 13)
    reason: for here we do not have city that remains but look
      for one to come (v. 14)

- let us through him continuously offer up a sacrifice of
  praise to God, this is the fruit of lips which confess his
  name, and do not neglect doing good and sharing
  (vv. 15–16a)
    reason: for God is pleased with such sacrifices (v. 16b)

- obey your (present) leaders and submit to them (v. 17a)
    reason: for they watch over your souls for your benefit as
      those who will give an account (v. 17b)
    reason: so that they may do this with joy and without com-
      plaining, for this would be unprofitable for you (v. 17c)

- pray for us … and I urge you to do this more and more
  (vv. 18a, 19a)
    reason: for we are convinced that we have a good
      conscience, wishing to live honorably in all things
      (v. 18b)
    reason: so that I may be restored to you soon (vv. 19b)

- And may the God of peace, who led up from the dead the
  great shepherd of the sheep by the blood of the eternal
  covenant, our Lord Jesus, equip you with all good things
  to do his will, working in us what is pleasing before him
  through Jesus Christ, to whom is glory forever, Amen.
  (vv. 20–21)

The final exhortations in 13:1–19 resemble the propositions of
the *argumentatio*, many of which, as we previously argued, are
exhortations with appended reasons. These final proposition-like
statements in Heb 13:1–19 are not accompanied by extensive proofs

like we saw in the *argumentatio*, but such a lack of extensive argumentation was recommended for *peroratio*. Thus, Heb 13:1–19, at least in form, resembles a rapid recounting of propositions in Hebrews.

On further consideration, the statements in Heb 13:1–19 only appear to have a loose connection with the previous content of the sermon. It is this loose connection that has led some interpreters to regard Heb 13:1–21/25 as a later addition to the original sermon.[6] Clearly, these final exhortations do not merely rehash in summary form what was previously said. Yet such an observation is in agreement with Quintilian's recommendation that recapitulation should not present a straightforward recounting of proofs, facts, or topics.[7] A more careful examination of Heb 13:1–19 demonstrates that the author does indeed remind his hearers of and develop further the previous content of his sermon. First, in 13:3, the author reminds his audience of their previous sufferings (cf. 10:32–34) and of the sufferings of the faithful witnesses (cf. 11:35–38) in his exhortation to remember those who are imprisoned and tortured. Second, the exhortation to be free from the love of money in 13:5 reminds the audience of Moses who considered the reproach of Christ greater wealth than the treasures of Egypt (cf. 11:26) or of Esau who sold his birthright for one meal (cf. 12:16). Third, in his exhortation to imitate the past leaders' faith, the author harkens back to his exhortation to imitate those who inherit God's promise through faith and patience (cf. 6:12). Fourth, in his declaration of Jesus's unchanging nature (he is the same yesterday, today, and forever), the author recalls his declaration about the enthroned Son in 1:10–12 (he remains and his years will never end) and in 7:28 (Jesus is perfected forever). Fifth, when the author exhorts his audience to avoid varied and strange teachings that are of no benefit to them, he reminds his audience of his earlier exhortation in 2:1–4 to pay careful attention to the message they first heard from their leaders and of the singular word (λόγος) about Christ they had received from them (6:1). Sixth, his exhortations to love, to show hospitality, to do good, and to

---

[6] E.g., Wedderburn, "Thirteenth Chapter," 390–405, represents a more recent challenge to authenticity of Heb 13. Others, who challenge the authenticity of Heb 13, include Simcox, Torrey, Jones, and Buchanan (for references and further discussion see Gareth Lee Cockerill, *The Epistle to the Hebrews* [NICNT; Grand Rapids: Eerdmans, 2012], 673–5 esp. n. 4).

[7] Cf. Übelacker, *Der Hebräerbrief als Appell*, 221: "Die *recapitulatio* soll aber nicht nur aus einer bloßen Wiederholung bestehen, sondern umschrieben."

share recall the general exhortations to continue meeting together and to encourage one another to love and good deeds (cf. 6:10; 10:24–25). Seventh, the exhortation to praise God with one's lips (i.e., confessing loyalty to God through Jesus Christ as a public confession) recalls Jesus who proclaims God's name in the midst of the assembly and also possibly reminds the audience of the severe warning offered in Heb. 6:4–6 where denying Jesus is said to "re-crucify" him for public contempt once again.[8] Additionally, the pleasing (εὐαρεστέω) sacrifices of confessing God's name, beneficence, and sharing allude to the pleasing (εὐαρέστως) worship that is to be offered to God (cf. 12:28). Eighth, in the care that the leaders give to watching over the audience's souls, the author reminds his audience of his previous exhortation to encourage one another every day so as not to be hardened by sin's deceitfulness (cf. 3:13). The author might also be reminding his audience of Moses's task as an overseer of the wilderness generation that was developed in chapters 3–4. That generation grumbled and rejected Moses's oversight and thus failed to enter God's place of rest.

Besides these reminders, there are two additional places in the *peroratio* where recapitulation or reminding is most distinctive. The first place is Heb 13:10–14. Hebrews 13:10–14 is a discrete unit in the conclusion.[9] The unit sets itself apart for three reasons. (1) As we will discuss in a later section, the author departs from his use of asyndeton after verse 10, and (2) after verse 10, the author also departs from his usual pattern of doubling. (3) This unit begins with a declaration and not an exhortation. The primary exhortation comes in verse 13, which builds upon the example of Jesus that was developed in verses 11–12. Additionally, verse 10 takes its point of departure from the reference about foods to state that those who serve in the tent have no authority to eat from the community's "altar." Thus it appears that verses 10–14 are explanatory of verses 7–9.[10] In the cryptic statement that begins this unit, the author

---

[8] Ὁμολέγω in 13:15 is often associated with public acknowledgment or praise (e.g., Ps 18:49 [LXX]; Matt 10:32//Luke 12:8). See also BDAG 708, s. 4.

[9] Cf. Craig R. Koester, "Hebrews, Rhetoric, and the Future of Humanity," in *Reading the Epistle to the Hebrews: A Resource for Students* (ed. Eric F. Mason and Kevin B. McCruden; Resources for Biblical Study 66; Atlanta: SBL 2011), 117, who recognizes verses 10–14 as a distinctive and central unit to the *peroratio*.

[10] It explains what it means to imitate the past leaders' faith, especially if they have been martyred for faithfully bearing Christ's reproach. Also the varied and strange teachings might be ways of allowing the community to avoid bearing Christ's reproach.

returns to the comparative project between the old and new covenant experiences, especially the comparative insights he developed from the old covenant cultic priests and their ministry in 5:1–11 and 7:1–10:18. In 13:11–12, the author parallels an aspect of the Day of Atonement ritual (one of the rituals alluded to in Heb 9) with the death of Jesus – "for after the priests offered the blood of animals in the Most Holy Place, their bodies were burned outside the camp. For this reason, Jesus suffered outside the gates in order to sanctify the people by his own blood."[11] An analogy is not only drawn between Jesus and the sacrificial victims, but possibly there is an implicit comparison of Jesus to the priests who offer the animal's blood and burn their bodies outside the camp. As in 5:1–10, Christ is superior because he underwent suffering and shame in order to sanctify the people, whereas the Levitical priests (or "those who serve in the tent") do not suffer. As the author has done in the previous five epideictic syncrises, the comparative project between the old and new covenant is developed into a deliberative exhortation to persevere by joining Jesus outside the camp in order to bear his reproach (v. 13). Such fidelity was the focus of many of the examples in 10:32–12:3, especially Moses, who bore the reproach (ὀνειδισμός) of Christ. The author concludes his exhortation with a comparative rationale. The audience is to reject identification with Rome ("here we do not have a city that remains"), which claimed to be eternal, for a coming and truly eternal city – the heavenly Jerusalem (cf. 12:22) which has been prepared by God (cf. 11:16).[12] In the same way, Moses rejected identification with the pagan Egyptian empire. Likewise, Rahab rejected identification with her seemingly indomitable, pagan city of Jericho. Thus, the exhortation and comparative imagery in 13:10–14 constitutes a substantial reminding and development of Heb 5:1–12:29.[13]

The second place of distinctive recapitulation or reminding occurs in vv. 20–21, the benedictory prayer.[14] The first part of the prayer

---

[11] The sacrifice of the red heifer in Num 19:1–6 is also in view in the representation of Jesus. Similarly, the red heifer ceremony is conflated with the Day of Atonement, the dedication of the tabernacle, and the covenant ratification ceremony in Heb 9.

[12] For further discussion of this point see Jason A. Whitlark, *Resisting Empire: Rethinking the Purpose of the Letter to "the Hebrews"* (LNTS 484; T&T Clark, 2014), 100–15.

[13] Cf. deSilva, *Perseverance in Gratitude*, 498, who states that Heb 13:10–16 offers a fitting recapitulation of the argument and exhortation of the whole sermon.

[14] Cf. Übelacker, *Der Hebräerbrief als Appell*, 222–3.

("the God of peace who led up from the dead by virtue of the blood of the covenant, our Lord Jesus, the great shepherd of the sheep") recalls many of the points that the author has addressed in chapters 1–2, namely, the enthronement of the Son who will lead many "sons" to glory because of his obedience to undergo suffering and death.[15] The second part of the prayer ("equip you with all things good for doing his will and work in us what is pleasing to him") is a request for divine enablement that is grounded on the author's articulation of new covenant fidelity through the purification of the conscience in chapters 7–10.[16] This recapitulating prayer is also a fitting end to the exhortations of the *peroratio* and even of the entire discourse by appealing to God on the basis of Jesus's exaltation for the divine enablement necessary to live courageously. In effect, the author has exemplified one who boldly approaches the throne of grace for grace and mercy in time of need (cf. 4:14–16).[17]

We now consider whether the possible secondary *peroratio* of Heb 12:14–17 is characterized by recapitulation or reminding. Similar to Heb 13:1–19, the author provides a string of exhortations that are not a simple restatement of topics or propositions previously covered:[18]

- seek peace with all (v. 14a)
- and the holiness (v. 14b)

  reason: without which no one (οὐδείς) will see the Lord (v. 14c)

- see to it that no one (μή τις) falls short of the grace of God
- [see to it] that no one (μή τις) is a root of bitterness that causes trouble by growing up and many become defiled because of it (v. 15)

---

[15] Cf. Jason A. Whitlark, "The God of Peace and His Victorious King: Hebrews 13:20–21 in its Roman Imperial Context," in *Hebrews in Context* (ed. Harold W. Attridge and Gabriella Gelardini; AJEC 91; Leiden: Brill, 2016), 155–78.

[16] Cf. Jason A. Whitlark, "Fidelity and New Covenant Enablement in Hebrews," in Charles H. Talbert and Jason A. Whitlark, *Getting "Saved": The Whole Story of Salvation in the New Testament* (Grand Rapids: Eerdmans, 2011), 72–91. See also Cockerill, *Hebrews*, 714, 718.

[17] Appeals to the gods could also be found in the *peroratio* of speeches. Cf. Cicero, *Dom.* 144–5. Cicero elsewhere notes that to pray or appeal to the gods is an effective figure available to the orator (cf. *Or. Brut.* 138; *De. or.* 3.205). Dio Chrysostom concludes his address to the Nicomedians with an appeal to the gods for enablement to persevere in heeding his advice (cf. *Or.* 38.51).

[18] The participle (ἐπισκοποῦντες) in v. 15 is treated with imperatival force influenced by the opening imperative, διώκετε. The imperatival participle then governs the string of indefinite pronouns (μή τις).

- [see to it] that no one (μή τις) is sexually immoral or worldly like Esau, who sold his birthright for one meal (v. 16)

    reason: For you know that even afterwards when he wanted to inherit in the blessing he was rejected, for he did not find a place for repentance even though he sought it with tears (v. 17)

Do these exhortations then remind the audience of what has gone before especially since the preceding secondary *exordium* in 4:14–16? First, "Seek peace with all" recalls the hostility that the community suffered (and suffers) recounted in Heb 10:32–34. Such a command would appear to prohibit reciprocal hostility or vengeance for persecution suffered.[19] Second, the godward dedication or holiness that the audience is also to seek is not to be compromised by the pursuit of peace. Again, the directive recalls Moses's choice to suffer with God's people over Egyptian riches as well as the list of others who suffered for their faithfulness to God (cf. 11:36–37). Moreover, Moses persevered because he saw the one who is unseen. The reference in 12:14 to the future seeing (ὄψεται) of the Lord may also recall the eschatological hope in Heb 6:19–20 that goes behind the veil into the Most Holy Place with Jesus. Third, the three exhortations to "see to it" that no one falls short of the grace of God, that no one is a root of bitterness, and that no one is sexually immoral or worldly like Esau not only remind the audience of the earlier encouragement in Heb 3:12–13 to watch over each other so as not to fall away from God but also remind the audience of the more recent encouragement in Heb 10:24–31 to provoke one another to love and good deeds, not to give up meeting together, and not to sin deliberately. Additionally, the negative example of Esau is fitting in light of the positive examples derived from the patriarchal period which is a point of emphasis in Heb 11.[20] Esau not only reminds the audience of the apostasy of the wilderness generation in Heb 3, but he also

---

[19] Of interest also is Dio Chrysostom's comment to the Nicomedians in his speech advising them to seek concord or peace with the Nicaeans. He states that all envoys who sue for peace come into military camps unarmed because messengers on behalf of friendship are considered servants of the gods (cf. *Or.* 38.18).

[20] The patriarchal period is covered in vv. 8–22. It is 15 verses out of the 35 verses that cover examples beginning with Abel in v. 4 and concluding in v. 38. Thus, almost 43 percent of the material dedicated to the examples in Heb 11 is focused on the patriarchal period.

recalls the severe warning in Heb 6:4–6 concerning the impossibility of repentance for those who commit apostasy.

In sum, our contention is that Heb 13:1–25 and 12:14–17 fulfill the function of recapitulation typical of a *peroratio*. The author does not simply list his arguments and topics or announce the summation of his discourse. Instead, the author interweaves themes from the *narratio* and *argumentatio* into these concluding exhortations in order to further develop the aims of his sermon.[21] Such a method accords with the instructions of Quintilian and Anonymous Seguerianus noted above. Furthermore, the form of reminding that the author adopts in Heb 13:1–19 and 12:14–17 shares similarities with the instructions in *Rhet. Alex.* 20 [1434a] where to remind (ἀναμιμνήσκειν) is achieved by proposing a course of action (ἐκ προαιρέσεως).[22] This form of recapitulating is fitting for the deliberative focus of Hebrews that encourages perseverance and discourages apostasy.

We would add that the deliberative concluding exhortations, especially in Heb 13:1–19, are more concretely focused on particular aspects of community life than many of the potent but more generally articulated propositional exhortations for perseverance and against apostasy throughout Hebrews.[23] Developing insights from the sociology of knowledge, Knut Backhaus argues that the exhortations in Heb 13:1–19 "construct and secure the symbolic counter-world that may direct and strengthen the cognitive self-affirmation of Christians confronted with the claims of pagan society," and the audience learns "in closing paraenesis which everyday factors may work to ground and to secure the normative referential system of a Christian community model."[24] The primary examples in each *peroratio* support Backhaus's observations. In 13:11–14, the example of Jesus who suffered outside the camp encourages the audience's own solidarity and fidelity over its present urban context in Rome. Conversely, in Heb 12:14–17, the negative example of Esau who sold his birthright for a

---

[21] Cf. Koester, "Rhetoric," 118.

[22] In Demosthenes, ἐκ προαιρέσεως means to act from deliberate choice (cf. *2 Philip.* 16).

[23] Cf. Knut Backhaus, *Der Hebräerbrief* (RNT; Regensburg: Verlag Friedrich Pustet, 2009), 45; Knut Backhaus, "How to Entertain Angels: Ethics in the Epistle to the Hebrews," in *Hebrews: Contemporary Methods – New Insights* (ed. Gabriella Gelardini; Atlanta: SBL, 2005), 149–75; Karrer, *Der Brief an die Hebräer*, 351–2.

[24] Backhaus, "How to Entertain Angel," 160–1.

meal discourages defection to the audience's pagan society for temporary relief.[25]

Appeal to the Emotions

Among the rhetorical theorists

The second major function of the *peroratio* was to appeal to the emotions (πάθος, ἦθος, *adfectus*; cf. Quintilian, *Inst.* 6.2.8–9).[26] While appealing to the emotions could occur throughout a speech, Cicero notes that the most appropriate place for stirring the emotions is in the *exordium* and *peroratio* (cf. *De or.* 2.311–12). Similarly, Quintilian states:

> All these appeals to emotion, though some think their proper home is in the Prooemium and the Epilogue (where indeed we may allow them to be commonest), nevertheless have a place in other parts of the speech as well, though in a shorter form, because the greater part of them must be held in reserve. But here, if anywhere, we are allowed to release the whole flood of our eloquence. If we have spoken the rest well, we shall by now be in possession of the hearts of the judges; having escaped the reefs and shoals, we can spread our sails; and, as the main business of an Epilogue is Amplification, we can use grand and ornate words and thoughts. (*Inst.* 6.1.51–52 [Russell, LCL]; cf. 6.2.2)

---

[25] The "root of bitterness" which is an allusion Deut 28:17 (LXX) warns against idolatry, i.e., defection or assimilation to the pagan culture. The subsequent example of the sexual immorality and worldliness of Esau that results in selling his birthright for a meal complements the warning from Deut 28:17. For further discussion on Hebrews's resistance to the pressures of assimilation coming from the audience's pagan society see Knut Backhaus, *Der Neue Bund und das Werden der Kirche: die Diatheke-Deutung des Hebräerbriefs im Rahmen der frühchristlichen Theologiegeschichte* (NTAbh 29; Münster: Aschendorff, 1996), 264–82; deSilva, *Perseverance in Gratitude*, 483–4; idem, *Despising Shame: Honor Discourse and Community Maintenance in the Epistle to the Hebrews* (SBLDS 152; Atlanta: Scholar's Press, 1995), 145–208, esp. 163; Whitlark, *Resisting Empire*, 49–76.

[26] See the programmatic article by Christopher Gill, "The Ēthos/Pathos Distinction in Rhetorical and Literary Criticism," *The Classical Quarterly* (1984): 149–66, for the development of ethos and pathos in the ancient literary and rhetorical tradition. Gill notes that, in the rhetorical tradition after Aristotle, ethos and pathos were associated with certain types of emotional tenors and distinctive styles. In this section we are concerned with emotional appeal more broadly defined.

Quintilian, again, acknowledges that "the final part of forensic causes consists mainly in emotional appeals" (*Inst.* 6.2.1 [Russell, LCL]). Quintilian also notes that the orator not only wants to excite some emotions but also to assuage other emotions in the *peroratio* (cf. *Inst.* 6.1.11; Cicero, *De. or.* 2.183; *Top.* 98). Similarly, Anonymous Seguerianus states that "the function of the epilogue is to amplify already existing emotions or to create them if they do not exist" (228 [Dilts and Kennedy]).

The importance of the appeal to the emotions in the *peroratio* for Quintilian is demonstrated by that fact that this topic dominates much of Quintilian's discussion of the *peroratio* (cf. *Inst.* 6.1.9–52). The emphasis on the appeal to the emotions is because "[p]roofs may lead judges to *think* our Cause the better one, but it is our emotional appeals that make them also want it to be so; and what they want, they also believe" (*Inst.* 6.2.5 [Russell, LCL]). In fact, Quintilian states that appeals to the emotions are especially necessary in the case of deliberative oratory (cf. *Inst.* 3.8.12). Likewise, Cicero affirms that the favor of the audience is decided by emotion more than reason: "For men decide far more problems by hate, or love, or lust, or rage, or sorrow, or joy, or hope, or fear, or illusion, or some other inward emotion, than by reality, or authority, or any legal standard, or judicial precedent, or statute (*De or.* 2.178 [Sutton and Rackham, LCL]).[27]

As the quote from *De or.* 2.178 shows, the theorists could discuss a range of emotions to which appeals could be made. Aristotle lists hate, pity, emulation, anger, jealousy, and strife (cf. *Rhet.* 3.19.3 [1419b]). Quintilian mentions both exciting and assuaging the emotions of envy, goodwill, dislike, and pity (cf. *Inst.* 6.1.11). Specifically, with regard to deliberative oratory, Quintilian lists anger, fear, ambition, hatred, reconciliation, and pity (cf. *Inst.* 3.8.12). Anonymous Seguerianus mentions grief, fear, desire, and pleasure (cf. 224). No list is exhaustive but is representative of emotions commonly stirred in oratory. The emotions that are stirred are those most appropriate to the situation and goals of the orator.

Appeals to the emotions could focus on three broad areas. There was the appeal to the audience about themselves, to the audience about oneself, one's client or one's cause, and the appeal to the audience concerning one's opponent (cf. *Rhet.* 3.19.1 [1419b]).

---

[27] For a similar list of emotions by Cicero see *Or. Brut.* 131.

Aristotle writes, "[I]t is not only necessary to consider how to make the speech itself demonstrative and convincing, but also that the speaker should show himself to be of a certain character and should know how to put the judge into a certain frame of mind" (*Rhet.* 2.1.2–3 [1377b] [Freese, LCL]). In the *peroratio* by Thucydides at the opening of this chapter, we see the Greek commanders speak to the soldiers about the soldiers' responses – to be courageous and act honorably. They also speak to the soldiers about the commanders themselves – to trust them that they will act wisely and justly.

Aristotle recommends that, especially in deliberative oratory, "the speaker should show himself to be possessed of certain qualities and that his hearers think that he is disposed in a certain way towards them" (*Rhet.* 2.1.3–4 [1377b] [Freese, LCL]). Cicero writes that "to expound one's advice on matters of high importance" is "for a person with the greatest weight of character" (*De or.* 2.333 [Sutton and Rackham, LCL]). Quintilian also echoes this sentiment stating that the speaker's moral character and authority are most important in deliberative oration (cf. *Inst.* 3.8.12–13; 4.1.6–7; 6.1.12). Elsewhere, Quintilian writes that the speaker's own excellent character "will make his pleading all the more convincing and will be of utmost service to the cases which he undertakes" (*Inst.* 6.2.18).

There were certain stylistic features that were recommended for the *peroratio* in order to arouse the emotions. We note four that are particularly relevant to Hebrews. First, asyndeton was regularly discussed as a particularly forceful and effective style for stirring the emotions. Aristotle writes, "To the conclusion of the speech the most appropriate style is that which has no connecting particles, in order that it may be a peroration, but not an oration: 'I have spoken, you have heard, you know the facts; now give your decision'" (*Rhet.* 3.19.6 [Freese, LCL]). When discussing arousing the emotions via amplification in the *peroratio*, Cicero notes that "in sentences the words must be disconnected – *asyndeton* as it is called – so as to make them seem more numerous" (*Part. or.* 54 [Rackham, LCL]). Longinus writes of the emotional effectiveness of asyndeton by considering what happens when asyndeton is abandoned for connecting particles: "For just as you deprive runners of their speed if you tie them together, emotion equally resents being hampered by connecting particles and other appendages. It loses its freedom of motion and its effect of coming like a bolt from a catapult" ([*Subl.*] 21 [Heinemann, LCL]). Finally, Apsines affirms that emotional expression in the *peroratio* can be created via asyndeton, though he

differs from Cicero in stating that amplification is achieved through figures of separation or conjunctions, "*Well then* (τοίνυν), this alone was not enough, *but* (ἀλλά) that happened which was worse than this" (*Rhet.* 10.55 [Dilts and Kennedy], emphasis our own).

Second, vivid description (ἐνάργεια), metaphorical language, and examples were recommended for emotional appeals in the *peroratio*. Both Cicero (cf. *Inv.* 1.104) and Rhetorica ad Herennium (cf. 2.49) recommend stirring the emotions of the audience by describing the action as vividly as possible as though the action was unfolding before the audience's very eyes. Quintilian instructs that through vivid description "[e]motions will ensue just as if we were present at the event itself" (*Inst.* 6.2.32 [Russell, LCL]). Again, Apsines remarks, "Among those things that arouse the most pity are vivid description of the unfortunate and ethopoeia and characterization of them" (*Rhet.* 10.32 [Dilts and Kennedy]). In conjunction with vivid description, we also point to Cicero's recommendation that to arouse the emotions "[w]ords must be employed that are powerfully illuminating ... and above all used metaphorically" (*Part. or.* 54 [Rackham, LCL]). We further note that examples could be fittingly portrayed by vivid and metaphorical descriptions. Moreover, Rhetorica ad Herennium states that examples from the past are preferable in the *peroratio* of a deliberative speech. (cf. 3.9). Similarly, Quintilian advises that when speaking of what is likely to happen (e.g., when counseling a specific course of action) historical examples are preferable (cf. *Inst.* 5.11.8). Current examples were sometimes desirable because they were not as easily refuted (cf. *Inst.* 5.13.24).

Third, exhortations were recommended for the *peroratio* in an effort to stir emotions. Cicero writes, "[T]he greatest part of a [deliberative] speech must occasionally be directed to arousing the emotions of the audience, by means of exhortation ... to either hope or fear or desire or ambition" (*De. or.* 2.337 [Sutton and Rackham]).

Fourth, as a way to stir the emotions through amplification, Cicero recommends the "repetition, iteration, doubling of words, and the gradual rise from lower to higher terms" (*Part. or.* 53 [Rackham, LCL]).

In Hebrews

Returning to Heb 13:1–25 and 12:14–17, do we find emotional appeals typical of *peroratio*? We first take note of the range of emotions that the author attempts to stir. In 12:14–17 the author

evokes the emotions for peace instead of retaliation (v. 14). He warns against community defiling bitterness that would result from compromise or defection (v. 15). Also he stirs up fear over the impossibility for repentance that would result from community defecting (v. 17). The focus of these emotions is to encourage community survival and solidarity amidst a hostile pagan culture.

The author of Hebrews also excites a range of emotions in 13:1–19. He calls for love (vv. 1–2), compassion (v. 3), fear (v. 4), emulation (v. 7, 13), hope (v. 14), and especially courage (v. 6).[28] In his summons to particular expressions of community solidarity and nonassimilation, the author of Hebrews makes a strong appeal to courage. Such appeals can be found in battle exhortations.[29] When Alexander marshals his commanders for battle against the Persian forces of Darius, Arrian's account summarizes Alexander's speech as an exhortation to courage (παρεκάλει θαρρεῖν; *Anab.* 2.7.3). The author of Hebrews uses the same language when he calls his audience courageously (θαρροῦντας) to put their hope in God and not to fear what other humans can do to them. Again, one particular aim of deliberative pleading was to arouse courage or fortitude in the auditors so that they undertake the course of action which is recommended (cf. *Rhet. Her.* 3.3).[30] Cicero lists four parts to courage: high-mindedness (imagining great projects), confidence, patience, and perseverance (cf. *Inv.* 2.163). The author of Rhetorica ad Herennium describes the summons to courage in the following way:

> Again, from an honorable act no peril or toil, however great, should divert us; death ought to be preferred to disgrace; no pain should force an abandonment of duty; no man's enmity should be feared in defense of truth; for country, for parents, for guest-friends, intimates, and for the things justice commands us to respect, it behooves us to brave any peril and endure any toil. (3.5 [Caplan, LCL])

[28] For various emotions discussed in rhetorical treatises, see Aristotle, *Rhet.* 2.2–11 (especially 2.5.16–22 on θαρρεῖν which is used by the author of Hebrews in 13:6), and Cicero, *De or.* 2.205-11. See also Cicero, *Part. or.* 56, who lists three broad topics for arousing the emotions: love of God, country, and parents; affection for one's household; and moral considerations. All of these topics are present in Heb 13:1–25.

[29] Some rhetorical theorists, like Dionysius of Halicarnassus (*Thuc.* 42), consider battle exhortations to be deliberative or political speeches (δημηορίαι). Cf. Juan Carlos Iglesias Zoido, "The Battle Exhortation in Ancient Rhetoric," *Rhetorica* 25 (2007): 152–3.

[30] Cf. Aristotle, *N.E.* 3.6–9; *Rhet.* 2.5.16–22 (1383a–b).

Identifying with the community and its confession of Jesus Christ has resulted in both shame and potential danger for its members (e.g., Heb 10:32–39). The author continues to exhort his audience to the costly, even dangerous, activities that require courage, namely, to identify with those who are imprisoned and tortured, to confess its loyalty to God through Jesus Christ, and to follow the example of its former leaders who were likely martyred.[31] Moreover, the audience is to endure the shame that identification with Jesus brings and to eschew the pursuit of wealth and advancement. The audience then is to endure patiently these toils, persevering in their faith while they fix their hopes on the great project of God (a coming eternal city) and confident that he who promised is both able and faithful.

In Heb 13:1–25, we also see the author making emotional appeals concerning the three primary groups often targeted in the *peroratio*. The basic structure of Heb 13:1–19 addresses the audience about themselves in verses 1–17. The cryptic, derogatory statement in verses 9–10 briefly touches on the community's opponents.[32] In verses 18–19 the author then addresses the audience about himself and those with him. The author asks, even urges, for prayer from his audience while both confessing that he has sought to live honorably and desiring that he be restored to them soon. He has thereby asserted his good character and his goodwill towards his audience.[33] Furthermore, in 13:20–21, he includes himself in the prayer for the necessary enablement from God. He thus recognizes his own need alongside his audience's need for divine empowerment to live according to the very exhortations and admonitions he has given throughout the discourse. In verses 22–25, the author concludes by mentioning his intention to visit his audience with Timothy "who has been released" and, thus, has presumably suffered for his confession of Jesus Christ. He sends greetings and ends with a grace wish. Such a self-presentation is in line with what Cicero writes, "[the orator] will plead and entreat and soothe the audience; ... he will put himself on terms of intimacy with his audience" (*Or. Brut.* 138 [Harmon, LCL]).

---

[31] For further discussion of this point see Whitlark, *Resisting Empire*, 116–18.

[32] Cf. Übelacker, *Der Hebräerbrief als Appell*, 223.

[33] Cf. Übelacker, *Der Hebräerbrief als Appell*, 221, 223; ibid., "Hebrews and the Implied Author's Rhetorical Ethos," in *Rhetoric, Ethic, and Moral Persuasion in Biblical Discourse: Essays from the 2002 Heidelberg Conference* (ed. Thomas H. Olbricht and Anders Eriksson; ESEC; London: T&T Clark, 2005), 331–4.

Stylistically, we find the four characteristic methods discussed above for developing emotional appeals in the *peroratio*. First, in both 12:14–17 and 13:1–25, the author makes use of asyndeton. Asyndeton is most apparent in 12:14–17 in the three successive μή τις constructions (vv. 15–16) that head each exhortation to "see to it." In Heb 13:1–25, asyndeton is especially noticeable in his opening exhortations in 13:1–7 where he begins with a grammatically unconnected exhortation and rapidly moves from one exhortation or statement to the next without employing any connective particle or conjunction:

> Let "brotherly" love remain ... (v. 1)
> Do not neglect ... (v. 2)
> Remember ... (v. 3)
> Marriage is to be honored and sex is to be undefiled ... (v. 4)
> Your manner of life is to be free from the love of money ...
>   (v. 5)
> Remember your leaders ... (v. 7)
> Jesus Christ is the same ... (v. 8)
> Do not be carried away ... (v. 9)
> We have an altar ... (v. 10)
> Let us offer ... and do not neglect ... (vv. 15–16)
> Obey . . and submit ... (vv. 17)
> Pray for us ... and I urge ... (vv. 18–19)
> You know ... (v. 23)
> Greet all your leaders ... (v. 24a)
> Those from Italy greet you ... (v. 24b)
> Grace be with you all. (v. 25)

The only place where asyndeton is significantly dropped is in the digressionary unit of verses 10–14.[34] The author connects the main clauses of 10–14 together by conjunctions (v. 12, διό; v. 13, τοίνυν):

> We have an altar ... (v. 10)
> For (γάρ) the bodes are burned ... (v. 11)
> Therefore (διό) Jesus also suffered ... (v. 12)
> So then (τοίνυν) let us go out ... (v.13)
> For (γάρ) we do not have here a city that remains
> but (ἀλλά) we look for one to come. (v. 14)

---

[34] The καί in vv. 4 and 17 and the δέ in vv. 16 and 19 closely link the pair of exhortations and contribute to the doubling effect in 13:1–19. The variant reading with οὖν in v. 15 should be considered secondary. See also Koester, "Rhetoric," 118–19.

The style is similar to Apsines's description of amplification in the *peroratio* when asyndeton is dropped in favor of connecting particles or conjunctions (cf. *Rhet.* 10.55). This is precisely what the author of Hebrews has done in vs. 10–14, making this section a distinct, amplification of the succinct exhortations he has just offered in 7–9.

Additionally, asyndeton effects a sudden shift from *argumentatio* to the *peroratio* in 12:14 and 13:1. The style then predominates, as we have seen, in the exhortations or statements that follow. The shift is further accentuated by a sudden change in topic and emotional tone – from courageously engaging in divine training through suffering to the unexpected exhortation to seek peace with all, and from final judgment and the apocalyptic upheaval of the cosmos that ends with reverent awe towards God who is a consuming fire to the unexpected exhortation to let "brotherly" love remain.[35] This stylistic, topical, and emotional shift then provides further reasons for beginning the secondary *peroratio* at 12:14 and the primary at 13:1.

Second, in both Heb 12:14–17 and 13:1–25, the author makes use of vivid description, metaphorical language, and examples to heighten the emotional appeal. In fact, these three characteristics are conjoined in both *perorationes*. In 12:17, the author puts forward the example of Esau as a warning against apostasy. The author both vividly portrays Esau's selling of his birthright for "one meal," and he pathetically describes Esau seeking the blessing "with tears." Additionally, he describes Esau's decision metaphorically as sexually immoral and worldly. Sexual immorality could be used to identify covenant faithlessness in an attempt to describe emotively the nature of idolatry.[36] The author also draws upon the Deuteronomistic metaphor of the "root of bitterness" to describe the harm that idolatrous defection would do to the whole community.

In Heb 13:1–25, the author of Hebrews again supplies examples that are recommended for a deliberative *peroratio*. These examples are ideal because they are recent historical examples relative to the community. The author first mentions the past leaders of the com- munity and exhorts his audience to imitate their faith by considering the outcome of their lives (13:7). If this cryptic reference is to leaders'

---

[35] Some interpreters have recognized a change in emotional tone and topic at the beginning of each section, especially between 12:25–29 and 13:1–25. Cf. Harold W. Attridge, *The Epistle to the Hebrews* (Hermeneia; Philadelphia: Fortress, 1989), 284–5; Lane, *Hebrews 9–13*, 496; O'Brien, *Hebrews*, 502.

[36] See note 25.

martyrdom, then they have joined the faithful cloud of witnesses who are awaiting a better resurrection and will be a part of the joyful assembly in the heavenly Jerusalem. This then is the advantageous outcome of imitating such courageous examples of faith. Second, the author points to the central example of Jesus who suffered outside the city. The author uses a vivid description of the disposal of the animal carcasses from the Day of Atonement that he then relates metaphorically to Jesus's own suffering outside Jerusalem. Based upon this provocative metaphorical, even figured, association, the author summons his audience to bear the same reproach (even a shameful death) that Jesus himself endured for the benefit of God's people (13:12–13).[37] The outcome of such identification is articulated in the following verse. The audience is looking for a coming city that will endure, a place where Jesus is already enthroned (cf. 2:5–9). Other metaphors and cryptic, figured references occur in verse 10 with the mention of the community's "altar" and "those who serve in the tent." There is also the evocative language in verse 3 of remembering those who are tortured "because you yourselves are in the body." Also the community's confession of Jesus Christ and the call to do good are metaphorically expressed in terms of the priestly activity of offering sacrifice.

We would add that the metaphorical language, which is often cryptic, in Heb 12:14–17 and 13:1–25 is characteristic of forceful (δεινότης) speaking according to Demetrius. He writes:

> For this reason, symbolic expressions are forcible, as resembling brief utterances. We are left to infer the chief of the meaning from a short statement as though it were a sort of riddle. Thus saying "your cicalas shall chirp from the ground" is more forcible [δεινότερον] in this more figurative form than if your sentence had simply run "your trees shall be hewed down." (*Eloc.* 243 [Roberts, LCL])

Such suggestive language can also function as covert allusion or figured speech (ἐσκηματισμένον ἐν λόγῳ) which is subsequently discussed by Demetrius as part of the forceful style (*Eloc.* 287–98). These symbolic and figured references are more emotionally evocative. In fact, Quintilian affirms that there is no more effective method for exciting the emotions than when a speaker

---

[37] Cf. Koester, "Rhetoric," 119.

uses such figures in a speech (cf. *Inst.* 9.1.21). Similarly, in Hebrews, there is emotional force in "a root of bitterness" as a symbolic and allusive description of one who defects from the community to identify with pagan society (12:15). Also there is emotive power in referring to such covenant infidelity as "sexual immorality" similar to Esau selling his birthright for a single meal (12:16). From chapter 13, we would note the cryptic reference to remember the past leaders' "outcome of their manner of life" as a way of talking about their martyrdom. Additionally, there is the metaphorical and cryptic references to the community's "altar," to "those who serve in the tent," to "going outside the camp," and to "a city that does not remain." Most of these references are symbolic and elliptical and heighten the emotional appeal in the two identified *perorationes*.[38]

Third, both Heb 12:14–17 and 13:1–25 use numerous explicit exhortations which, as we discussed above, evoke emotions. "Seek peace ... and holiness" (12:14). "See to it that no one ... that no one ... that no one" (12:15–16). "Let 'brotherly' love remain" (13:1); "do not neglect" (13:2; 16); "remember" (13:3, 7); "imitate" (13:7); "do not be carried away" (13:9); "let us go out" (13:13); "let us offer up" (13:15); "obey ... and submit (13:17); "pray" (13:18); and "I urge you" (13:19, 22). The numerous, brief, and, in many cases, grammatically unconnected exhortations heighten the emotional appeal in both *perorationes*.

Fourth, in Heb 13:1–25, the author employs doubling of words similar to what Cicero recommended concerning amplification. This doubling is characteristic of the exhortations in verses 1–9 and 15–19. Some interpreters have already noted the doubling that typifies the exhortations in verses 1–5:[39]

φιλοδελφία—φιλοξενία
τῶν δεσμίων—τῶν κακουχουμένων
γάμος—κοίτη
πόρνους—μοιχούς
ἀφιλάγυρος—ἀκρουμενοι τοῖς παροῦσιν

---

[38] For further discussion of figured speech and how these figured references function in Hebrews to encourage the audience not to (re)assimilate to its pagan Roman society, see Whitlark, *Resisting Empire*, passim.

[39] E.g., Michel, Vanhoye, and McCown. Their observations are summarized and discussed in William L. Lane, *Hebrews 9–13* (WBC 47B; Nashville: Thomas Nelson Publishers, 1991), 501–2.

We can extend this observation to include verses 7– 9:

μνημονεύετε—μιμεῖσθε
ποικίλαι—ξέναι

Doubling is resumed in verses 15–19 where additional topics are addressed:

ἀναφέρωμεν—μὴ ἐπιλανθάνεσθε
τῆς εὐποιΐας καὶ κοινωνίας[40]
πείθεσθε—ὑπείκετε
μετὰ χαρᾶς—μὴ στενάζοντες
προσεύχεσθε—παρακαλῶ

Again, that leaves verse 10–14 as a distinctive but significant digressionary section where doubling has been dropped.

In sum, Heb 12:14–17 ad 13:1–25 are characterized by significant emotional appeal that was typical of a *peroratio*.[41] The author uses several stylistic features to stir up the emotions. Longinus points to the power of using a combination of apt stylistic figures: "The combination of several figures often has a supremely moving effect, when two or three cooperate as it were together to contribute force, conviction, and beauty. Thus, for instance, in [Demosthenes's] speech against Meidias, the asyndeta are interwoven with the figures of repetition and vivid presentation" ([*Subl.*] 20 [Heinemann, LCL]). The emotional appeals, especially in 13:1–25, also might help to address the difficulty of its arrangement. The UBS[4] notes potential paragraph and section breaks after every verse among translations and critical editions.[42] Longinus states that emotional appeal "being a violent upheaval of the soul, demands disorder." He then notes the appeals in Demosthenes's speech against Meidias where strategic uses of repetitions and asyndeta make the speech's "very order disordered and equally his disorder implies a certain element of order" ([*Sub.*] 20 [Heinemann, LCL]). Apsines states that emotional expressions do not need careful arrangement (cf. *Rhet.* 10.55). Thus, Heb 13:1–25 defies rigid structural organization because of its appeal to the emotions and a strategic use of stylistic figures common to

---

[40] Note how the two words are governed by one article which establishes their close connection.

[41] Cf. Übelacker, *Der Hebräerbrief als Appell*, 222: "U. E. dient das ganze Kapitel der Affekterregung."

[42] Noted also by Cockerill, *Hebrews*, 673 n. 1.

such appeal. There do appear, however, to be some broad contours that imply a certain element of order. The appeals in 1–19 may be arranged as those concerning the audience about itself (1–17) and those concerning audience about the author (18–19). There then is a benediction (20–21) followed by a final urging with comments typical of a letter's ending (22–25).[43] Again, the emotional appeals reinforce the deliberative focus of Hebrews by encouraging both community solidarity and courageous resistance to community defection.

The Length of the *Peroratio* and Hebrews

One final consideration for our discussion of the *peroratio* is its length. Both in regard to recapitulation and emotional appeal, theorists universally recommended that that both elements of the *peroratio* be brief. Concerning recapitulation, Rhetorica ad Herennium states that recapitulation is to be made "briefly" (2.47). Anonymous Seguerianus instructs that "[o]ne should recapitulate briefly" (219 [Dilts and Kennedy]).[44] Similarly, Cicero writes,

> As a general principle for summing up, it is laid down that since the whole of any argument cannot be given a second time, the most important point of each be selected, and that every argument be touched on as briefly as possible, so that it may appear to be refreshing the memory of the audience, rather than a repetition of the speech. (*Inv.* 1.100 [Hubbell, LCL])

Quintilian also affirms, "The points to recapitulate must be treated as briefly as possible and ... we must run quickly through all 'headings,' for if we spend too much time, it will become almost a second speech rather than an 'enumeration'" (*Inst.* 6.1.2 [Russell, LCL]). Concerning emotional appeals, Cicero advises not to linger over emotions once aroused because "[n]othing dries more quickly than tears" (*Inv.* 1.109 [Hubbell, LCL]). Likewise, Quintilian states,

---

[43] There appear to be three basic parts to the *peroratio* in Heb 13:1–25. These parts are set off by the δέ in vv. 20 and 22, often translated "now":

"Let love remain ..." (v. 1)
"Now (δέ) may the God of peace ..." (v. 20)
"Now (δέ) I urge you ..." (v. 22)

[44] Cf. Anaximenes of Lampsacus, *Rhet. Alex.* 21 (1434a); 36 (1444b).

"Appeals to pity, however, must never be long. There is good reason for the saying that nothing dries more easily as tears" (*Inst.* 6.1.27 [Russell, LCL]).[45] Hebrews 12:14–17 and 13:1–25 are appropriately brief both with regard to recapitulation and the emotions stirred. It would have taken less than four minutes to read aloud 13:1–25 whereas to read Hebrews aloud from beginning to end takes approximately forty-five minutes.[46] Thus, the primary *peroratio* of Heb 13 occupies less than one-tenth of the discourse and Heb 12:14–17, even less.[47]

Conclusion

The examination of Heb 12:14–17 and 13:1–25 demonstrates that both passages qualify as *perorationes* in Hebrews, the former secondary and the latter primary. First, and above all, both passages occur at the end. Hebrews 12:14–17 ends the two sections (5:1–6:20 and 7:1–12:13) that developed the topics related to the pursuits of the new covenant and old covenants via their priestly representatives and ministries. Hebrews 13:1–25 ends the whole discourse. Second, they both can be characterized by the dual functions that were often attributed to *peroratio*. They recapitulate and appeal to a range of emotions. They also have characteristic stylistic elements often recommended for arousing the emotions in the *peroratio*: asyndeton, vivid descriptions, metaphorical language, doubling of words, and exhortations. The sudden topical, stylistic, and emotional shift that begins both passages further marks them off as distinctive concluding units in Hebrews. They both also employ strategic examples (Esau, community leaders, Jesus), which were recommended for the *peroratio* of deliberative speeches. Finally, they are brief, occupying less than one-tenth of the whole sermon when read aloud.

Both *perorationes* support the overall deliberative aim of Hebrews. As just mentioned, they use examples, which were recommended for deliberative *peroratio*. The examples support the deliberative aim to persevere and not to apostatize. The *perorationes* are dominated by numerous exhortations strung together by asyndeton. Many of these

---

[45] Cicero attributes the often-quoted aphorism to the rhetorician Apollonius. Cf. Rhet. Her. 2.50, Cicero, *Part. or.* 57.

[46] Cf. Koester, "Rhetoric," 118.

[47] This also is an argument against beginning the *peroratio* in Heb 10. In such a case the *peroratio* would have been almost twenty minutes and dominated nearly half the discourse turning it into a second speech.

exhortations seek to strengthen community identity and thus to enable perseverance. Hebrews 13 especially attempts to stir up courage – a distinctive emotion engaged in deliberation, especially of battle exhortations where the recommended course of action is dangerous. In Heb 13 there is the attempt of the author to favorably identify with his audience and buttress his authority, which was essential to be persuasive in deliberative matters. All of these considerations demonstrate that Heb 12:14–17 and 13:1–25 are integral to the deliberative aims of the whole sermon. Thus, Heb 13:1–25 should not be considered a secondary addition appended to the original sermon. It strategically and eloquently fulfills the expectations associated with *peroratio*.[48]

---

[48] We earlier mentioned scholars who challenged the authenticity of Heb 13, e.g., Wedderburn, "Thirteenth Chapter," 391–405. There are many facets to this challenge but some typical evidence brought forward fails to recognize the rhetorical conventions associated with *peroratio* that we discussed above. For example, some point to the sharp break in topic and tone between Heb 12:29 and 13:1 or the stylistic elements of asyndeton and the lack of argumentation as evidence that demonstrates the secondary nature of Heb 13. As we have argued, all these elements are typical of rhetorical conclusions. Instead of being a mark against the author's rhetorical skill (or even an awkward addition by a second author, so Wedderburn, "Thirteenth Chapter," 394), these elements actually demonstrate the author's rhetorical skill in crafting a sophisticated but appropriate conclusion. We would add, as well, that since both Heb 12:14–17 and 13:1–25 share the rhetorical features of *peroratio* (and the authenticity of Heb 12:14–17 is without question), then Heb 13 is not an exceptional case in the speech.

9

PUTTING IT ALL TOGETHER

The Rhetorical Arrangement and Aim of Hebrews

What then may we reasonably conclude from our arguments to this point of our study of Hebrews? There are two key ideas that we will highlight from our findings. First, the arguments presented in the previous chapters show the conventional nature of Hebrews's arrangement in light of classical rhetorical expectations. Second, this arrangement in all its aspects suggests a deliberative aim for the speech. We will consider each of these conclusions in turn.

The Rhetorical Arrangement of Hebrews

What is Hebrews's place among the rhetorical practices of the first-century CE? In Chapters 5–8 we have demonstrated that its arrangement is wholly conventional. This arrangement entails an essentially twofold rhetorical move, from epideictic *narratio* to deliberative *argumentatio* where amplificatory praise of a new covenant subject in comparison with an old sets the stage for the theses concerning perseverance and their main proofs.

Within this twofold movement, the *narratio* appears wholly conventional in form and function. Likely because of its length and complexity, the *narratio* is arranged in the widely attested (though little discussed in biblical scholarship) "disjointed" form. Specifically, it is divided into five units, each of which is paired with corresponding and related materials of *argumentatio*. Each of these units, moreover, performs the conventional function of παραδιήγησις or "incidental *narratio*" in that it sets the stage for the argumentation with which it is paired by establishing the comparative premise (that a particular new covenant representative is superior to an old) upon which the argumentation proceeds. These units, moreover, are arranged by standard search topics prescribed for developing the order and contents of *narratio* – at the macro-level, governing the

five units themselves, origin, birth, education, deeds, and death and posthumous events. Perhaps most significantly, these units are wholly made up of epideictic amplification and syncrisis, materials commonly prescribed for *narratio*.

One of the key insights of this study, in our view, is the interpretation of these materials, long acknowledged as central to Hebrews, as *narratio* in accordance with conventional rhetorical standards of arrangement. As we have argued, epideictic amplification was among the most commonly prescribed forms of παραδιήγησις or "incidental *narratio*." Furthermore, comparison, a natural companion to epideictic amplification, was one of the five major *schemas* of exposition commonly prescribed for *narratio*. Also, the temporal juxtaposition of past and present experience seen within every one of Hebrews's many comparisons belongs to a specific comparative schema prescribed for *narratio*, ἀντεξέτασις – the contrast of "what happened before and what has happened now." Simply put, the epideictic syncrises of old and new covenant experience that recur throughout Hebrews are the conventional "stuff" of *narratio*.

Similarly, within the essential twofold movement of Hebrews's arrangement, the *argumentatio* appears wholly conventional in form and function. Like the *narratio*, it is divided into five units, each following logically on its counterpart from the *narratio* per the convention of disjointed arrangement. Each of these units, too, is governed by the same five *topoi* used to order the *narratio*: origin, birth, education, deeds, and death and posthumous events. Such dual usage of headings is not novel, as the theorists prescribe the same search *topoi* for *argumentatio* as for *narratio*. Most significantly, each of these units consists predominantly, if not wholly, of proof and proposition. The proofs are expressed, as the theorists advise, both deductively through enthymemes and inductively through examples. Frequently they take a comparative "from the lesser" form, arguing that if perseverance was advantageous and/or apostasy disadvantageous in the lesser case of old covenant experience, then it is all the more so in the greater case of new covenant experience. In these instances, the proofs proceed on the comparative premise (that new covenant experience is superior to old) established in the preceding, corresponding unit of narration.

Throughout these units, too, inductive and deductive proofs are consistently enlisted in logical support of clearly stated *propositiones*,

which most often take the form of exhortations – a form fitting for deliberative rhetoric. These occur, as convention allows, both at the transition from *narratio* to *argumentatio* and interspersed in restated form throughout the *argumentatio*. They are stated, moreover, in single, double, and multiple forms, and usually in connection with a supporting reason, per rhetorical custom. In our estimation, the identification of proof and proposition within the body of Hebrews is one of the key insights of the study. Such material was considered essential to the *argumentatio* (indeed, it is by definition *argumentatio*), and its concentration in the body of the speech within the five deliberative units, together with its absence in the five epideictic units, serves as the clearest indication of where the *argumentatio* lies and how it is delineated.

Completing the arrangement of Hebrews are primary and secondary *exordia* and *perorationes* displaying conventional materials and aims. Both *exordia* win favor for the cause: the primary *exordium* (1:1–4), by garnering goodwill and attentiveness at the opening of the speech through hymnic praise of Christ expressed in highly stylized periodic prose; and the secondary exordium (4:14–16), by garnering receptivity for the complex and centrally important "priestly pursuits" unit through the enumeration of its major ideas. Both *perorationes* (12:14–17 and 13:1–21) effectively recapitulate the hortatory message of the preceding materials with which they are associated and arouse emotions, particularly on behalf of community life, through characteristic stylistic elements: asyndeton, vivid descriptions, metaphorical language, doubling of words, and exhortations. Both also employ the kind of concluding examples commonly prescribed for *perorationes* of deliberative speeches: the minor *peroration*, the negative example of Esau; and the primary *peroration*, the positive examples of both the community leaders and Jesus.

In sum, though Hebrews's content is unique, Hebrews is comprehensively conventional in its rhetorical arrangement. The traditional "parts of speech" do not have to be forced upon Hebrews as something alien to its organization. When properly understood, Hebrews exhibits the anticipated categories of classical rhetorical arrangement from beginning to end. There is little doubt that the authorial audience would have recognized and admired the rhetorical artistry of this early Christian sermon even if the audience was both encouraged and disturbed by its forceful summons to persevering courage.

Using the classical rhetorical categories discussed in Chapters 5–8, we may represent the arrangement of Hebrews in outline form as follows:[1]

Exordium	**Heb 1:1–4**
Disjointed *narratio* with *argumentatio*	**Heb 1:5–12:29**
I. Covenant origins	
Incidental *narratio*	Heb 1:5–14
Deliberative *argumentatio* with *propositio*	Heb 2:1–18
Amplificatio	*(Heb 2:5–18)*
II. Covenant births	
Incidental *narratio*	Heb 3:1–6
Deliberative *argumentatio* with *propositiones*	Heb 3:7–4:13
Secondary *exordium* (for III.–IV.)	Heb 4:14–16
III. Covenant education	
Incidental *narratio*	Heb 5:1–10
Deliberative *argumentatio* with *propositiones*	Heb 5:11–6:20
Digressio (amplification-blame)	*(Heb 5:11–14)*
IV. Covenant deeds	
Incidental *narratio*	Heb 7:1–10:18
Deliberative *argumentatio* with *propositiones*	Heb 10:19–12:13
Secondary *peroratio* (for III.–IV.)	Heb 12:14–17
V. Covenant death/events beyond death	
Incidental *narratio*	Heb 12:18–24
Deliberative *argumentatio* with *propositio*	Heb 12:25–29
Peroratio	**Heb 13:1–25**

The Deliberative Aim of Hebrews

If Hebrews is conventional in its rhetorical arrangement, then its primary rhetorical purpose should also be identifiable by the traditional genres of rhetoric, that is, judicial, epideictic, or deliberative. In the present state of the question, the debate turns on whether Hebrews is essentially an epideictic speech designed to praise Jesus in comparison with others, or a deliberative speech designed to encourage perseverance and discourage apostasy. All scholars agree both kinds of materials are present: the question concerns which are central and which are ancillary. In Chapter 3, we made a preliminary

---

[1] We note here that at each of the major seams there is an inferential conjunction or adverb: 1:5 (γάρ); 2:1 (διὰ τοῦτο); 3:1 (ὅθεν); 3:7 (διό); 4:14 (οὖν); 5:1 (γάρ); 6:1 (διό; start of *argumentatio* III proper); 7:1 (γάρ); 10:19 (οὖν); 12:18 (γάρ); 12:25 (γάρ). As previously mentioned in Chapter 6, the traditional γάρ marks the transition to most of units of *narratio*. Again, 12:14 and 13:1 lack the conjunction because of the use of asyndeton that is recommended for a *peroratio*.

case based on the relationship of epideictic and deliberative comparison for a primarily deliberative thrust in Hebrews. Deliberative syncrises, we observed, consistently proceed in Hebrews on the basis of premises established in preceding epideictic syncrises. Thus epideictic is ancillary, and deliberative, central. In Chapters 5–8, our analysis of arrangement has confirmed the preliminary verdict at every turn. We summarize presently several indicators of the conclusion that emerged in this analysis.

First, there is the very mixture itself of epideictic and deliberative rhetoric in equal measures. This is itself telling, since "epideictic is only seldom employed by itself independently," and "in judicial and deliberative causes extensive sections are often devoted to praise or blame" (Rhet. Her. 3.15 [Caplan, LCL]). Ironically, the very factor that has given rise to the debate concerning whether Hebrews is deliberative or epideictic – the presence of both materials – is, in fact, compelling evidence for an overall deliberative aim. Epideictic's most common use was in service to deliberative and judicial causes; deliberative, by contrast, is never prescribed for ancillary service to epideictic.

Second, there is the evidence from *narratio*. In the body of Hebrews, the epideictic materials have all the expected characteristics of *narratio*, including location, structure, subtypes of *narratio* employed, schemas employed, topics employed, etc. Correspondingly, these units lack the materials essential to the *argumentatio* – namely, enthymeme and *exemplum* employed in support of proposition. The very identification of these materials as *narratio*, and the corresponding disqualification of these materials as *argumentatio*, speaks directly to the question concerning what is central in Hebrews, as the *argumentatio* is always the center of the speech, and the *narratio* always ancillary to it. More specifically, the epideictic materials have all the expected characteristics of παραδιήγησις or "incidental *narratio* " – which suggests they are incidental to the cause and not reflective of its central question. Additionally, each of the five sections takes the form of amplification, a common subtype of παραδιήγησις, and precisely the kind of material Aristotle recommends for use as *narratio* in deliberative speeches (cf. *Rhet.* 3.16.11 [1417b]). Thus all considerations point consistently to an ancillary purpose for the five epideictic units. Far from reflecting the speech's main claim, these units "set the stage" by establishing the comparative premise on which the deliberative proofs "from the lesser" proceed.

Third, there is evidence from the *argumentatio*, the heart of the speech. Unlike the epideictic sections, the five deliberative units

all feature the material essential to *argumentatio*, enthymeme and *exemplum* enlisted in support of *propositio*. This is, perhaps, the clearest indication that the speech is deliberative in genre. Moreover, in the body of Hebrews all *propositiones* fall *only* within these units, and they only express deliberative claims. Similarly, all enthymemes and *exempla* in the body of Hebrews fall *only* within these units, and they only prove deliberative claims. In other words, all thesis and logical proof in Hebrews align consistently in support of a deliberative aim. Many of the *propositiones*, too, are expressed as exhortations, a form typical of deliberative *propositio*.[2] Most also arouse the emotions either to hope or fear, a function typical of *propositio* in deliberative speeches (cf. Cicero, *De or.* 2.337). Lastly, many of the *exempla* are historical, the subtype that theorists believed to be the most persuasive in deliberative cases (cf. Aristotle, *Rhet.* 1.9.40 [1368a]; 3.17.5 [1418a]; Quintilian, *Inst.* 3.8.66; 5.11.8).

Additionally, the disjointed nature in which the discourse is presented enhances the deliberative focus. The author essentially has a singular deliberative appeal (i.e., to persevere in the faith) that is developed from various topical perspectives (i.e., covenant origins, births, education, deeds, death/events after death). The disjointed style enables the author to quickly get to the appeal (2:1–18), and thereafter return to it repeatedly (4×) over the course of the speech (3:7–4:13; 5:11–6:20; 10:19–12:13; 12:25–29). Repeating the primary advice in one's speech is an effective strategy for getting one's main purpose across to an audience. It also happens to put on display repeatedly the recurring logic of the speech, wherein epideictic praise is in service to the author's deliberative exhortations.

Fourth, there is the evidence of the *exordia*. All evidence from both the major (1:1–4) and minor (4:14–16) *exordia* in Hebrews is consistent with a deliberative purpose. The primary *exordium* opens with epideictic praise and comparison, but is silent with regard to the deliberative appeal of the *argumentatio*. Both factors are telling, as Quintilian advises refraining from stating the major claim of the speech in the *exordium* (*Inst.* 4.1.1–5). Moreover, epideictic *exordia* were prescribed *in particular* for deliberative speeches (cf. Aristotle, *Rhet.* 3.14.12 [1415b]; Quintilian, *Inst.* 3.8.8), and especially those

---

[2] Gilbert Highet in his analysis of speeches in the *Aeneid* has proposed that the *propositio* is an essential element of deliberative oratory and is typically a compact proposal (or proposals) that urges the audience to follow a suggested course of action. See Gilbert Highet, *The Speeches in Virgil's* Aeneid (Princeton: Princeton University Press, 1972), 51–2.

speeches (like Hebrews) where the audience potentially "attaches too little importance" to the author's "idea." Far from suggesting an epideictic cause, the strict use of epideictic in 1:1–4 actually points instead to a deliberative aim.

Also, the secondary exordium is illuminating, as it is engaged in *enumeratio* of the unit's main ideas because of the complexity of the "priestly pursuits" unit that follows. Because of its summative aim, this *exordium* puts on display in brief the essential logical move of the section to come (and, for that matter, of the entire speech), wherein epideictic premise leads to deliberative thesis:

EPIDEICTIC PREMISE	"Since, then, we have a great high priest who has passed through the heavens, Jesus, the Son of God,"
DELIBERATIVE THESIS	"let us hold fast to our confession."
EPIDEICTIC PREMISE	"For we do not have a high priest who is unable to sympathize with our weaknesses, but we have one who in every respect has been tested as we are, yet without sin."
DELIBERATIVE THESIS	"Let us therefore approach the throne of grace with boldness, so that we may receive mercy and find grace to help in time of need."

Thus in its own way the secondary exordium highlights deliberation as the ultimate end of Hebrews's rhetoric.

Fifth, there is the evidence from the *perorationes*. One of the major tasks of the *peroratio* according to the theorists was recapitulation of the central message. As we saw, both the primary (13:1–25) and secondary (12:14–17) *perorationes* feature exhortations with a clear deliberative function, namely, to encourage nonassimilation and thus persevering fidelity to Jesus and his followers. This is strong structural evidence that the speech is, as the primary *peroratio* asserts, a "word of exhortation" (13:22) rather than a "word of praise." Also, the other primary function of *peroratio* according to the theorists was the arousal of emotion, and the primary *peroratio* especially accomplishes this through its consistent appeal for courage. Such an appeal is revealing, as courage was the emotion commonly associated by the theorists with deliberative rhetoric. Furthermore, the theorists recommend the use of examples for *perorationes* of deliberative speeches, and this is precisely what we find in Hebrews. Vivid, deliberative examples that encourage fidelity and

discourage apostasy are offered in both 12:14–17 (Esau) and 13:1–25 (former leaders, Jesus, the author).

Finally, there is the future orientation of Hebrews that is the *sine qua non* of deliberative oratory (cf. Quintilian, *Inst.* 3.4.8).[3] That orientation is evident in almost all aspects of the arrangement of Hebrews. First, what do we find when we consider the units of *argumentatio* in Hebrews? The propositional exhortations in the deliberative units all force the audience to consider the outcome of their actions. The audience is to consider the future consequences of perseverance or apostasy. All the proofs, both enthymeme and example, in support of these *propositiones* supply warrants for the members of the community to hope in God's promises and fear God's coming judgment. The one major argumentative amplification at the beginning of the discourse in 2:5–18 enlarges upon the "so great salvation" for which the audience hopes. Second, what do we find when we consider the units of *narratio*? Again, the chronological ordering of topics within many of the syncritical, incidental *narrationes* continue to emphasize the future focus of Hebrews. The first *narratio* unit in 1:1–14 concludes with the *topos*, "events beyond death," in its depiction of the anticipated, final eschatological victory of the Son over all his enemies. Similarly, the third *narratio* unit in 5:1–10 concludes with the same *topos*, depicting the perfecting of Christ and his exaltation into the world to come as the source of eternal salvation for which the audience presently hopes. The fourth unit of *narratio* in 7:1–10:18 also concludes with "events after death," giving consideration to what Jesus does (action, place, time, manner, cause) as Melchizedekian high priest once he enters the heavenly realm upon his resurrection. The perfected Son is able to perfect God's worshippers so that they can presently approach God and experience of foretaste of their ultimate, eschatological approach to God when they will be made perfect with all the people of God through a "better" resurrection. The emphasis in these central units of *narratio* is that Jesus is the enabler of the audience's achievement of its future hope – a hope Jesus has already experienced. Third, what do we find if we consider the structure of

---

[3] Quintilian discusses why speeches should be limited to the three traditional genres (epideictic, judicial, deliberative). He states that questions that do not come before a judge must either relate to the past (praise or denunciation) or the future (deliberation). Cf. Walter G. Übelacker, *Der Hebräerbrief als Appell: Untersuchungen zu Exordium, Narratio und Postscriptum (Hebr 1–2 und 13, 22–25)* (ConBNT 21; Stockholm: Almquist & Wiksell, 1989), 216.

all the units of *narratio* and *argumentatio*? As we demonstrated in Chapter 2, the chronological ordering of the topical comparisons of the covenants points the audience to their future hope by concluding with the *topos* of death and events beyond death. The audience is thus oriented through the progression of topics structuring the sermon to the eschatological outcome of new covenant life in the heavenly Jerusalem of the heavenly fatherland (i.e., the world to come). Fourth, if we consider the *perorationes*, what do we find? Again, the future orientation comes to the fore. The audience is not to be like Esau who sold his birthright but to be like Jesus and endure his shame by considering that they have an eternal city that is to come. Additionally, the members of the community are to consider the outcome of their martyred leaders' lives and imitate their faith. They are to consider God's judgment against the sexually immoral and God's faithfulness to his promises. They are to embrace a community ethic that discourages becoming a "root of bitterness" and, instead, encourages perseverance and nonassimilation to their former pagan lives. Thus, at all points in Hebrews's arrangement, the audience is continually led to contemplate the eschatological future and whether they will choose to participate in the world that God has promised his faithful people.

Conclusion

If Acts 14:22 is any indication, deliberative speeches were not uncommon among Christian communities that faced all levels of pressure and persecution from their pagan society. In a summary of Paul's and Barnabus's message to the Christ-followers whom they revisited in Lystra, Iconium, and Antioch, Luke writes that "they strengthened the souls of the disciples and encouraged them to continue in the faith, saying, 'It is through many persecutions that we must enter the kingdom of God.'" As we have argued, this is precisely, in brief, the message of Hebrews. All evidences point to Hebrews being a conventional deliberative speech, "a word of exhortation," that conforms to expectations and instructions outlined in rhetorical education of the ancient Mediterranean world, and prevalent in the early Roman imperial context of Christian origins.

Additionally, if the rhetorical framework of Hebrews is, in fact, as our analysis suggests, primarily deliberative, how may the comparison of covenants be seen to function within this framework? In other words, what is one rationale for making a syncritical analysis of

covenants the basis of a deliberative discourse on perseverance? We suggest that throughout Hebrews the promises of God are held out as the goal of God's actions and the motivation for ongoing perseverance on the part of the faithful (cf. 2:3, 5, 10; 4:1; 6:12; 10:34; 11:13–16; 12:28). The new covenant mediated by Jesus and his priestly ministry (as anticipated in the old covenant and its priestly ministry) deals with the problem of human sin and faithlessness, which would otherwise keep God's people from inheriting God's eschatological promise (cf. 9:14–15).[4] The members of the audience addressed in Hebrews are exhorted and enabled to faithfulness in their pressing circumstances in view of the new covenant realities inaugurated by Jesus. The covenant syncrises amplify these reasons, providing both greater encouragement and certainty concerning the soteriological foundation for present perseverance, so that the audience may be equipped and inspired to press on to the eschatological resting place, the world-to-come, the heavenly Jerusalem which God has promised to the faithful.

---

[4] Koester, *Hebrews*, 112. See also Jason A. Whitlark, *Enabling Fidelity to God: Perseverance in Hebrews in Light of the Reciprocity Systems of the Ancient Mediterranean World* (PBMS; Milton Keynes, Paternoster Press, 2008), 127–71.

10

EXAMINING IMPLICATIONS

Early Christian Sermons and Apostasy in Hebrews

This study has demonstrated the structure and genre of Hebrews on the basis of the classical rhetorical tradition of the ancient Mediterranean world. Given its conclusions, the study has important implications for at least two related questions. The first, emerging from the classical rhetorical arrangement Hebrews displays, concerns the presence of rhetorical training among the early Christian communities and its relationship to Christian preaching in the first four centuries. The second, emerging from the comparative rhetoric of Hebrews, concerns the type of the apostasy faced by Hebrews's audience and opposed by Hebrews's rhetoric.

Rhetoric and Early Christian Sermons

As discussed in Chapter 1, scholarship has long speculated about the emergence of the Christian homily or sermon in the first two centuries CE. It has often been noted that there are no extant, self-described early sermons that are not embedded in another text (e.g., Acts 13:15–41).[1] It is clear that prophetic addresses and exhortations were occurring within the earliest Christian communities (e.g., 1 Cor 14:26–33; 1 Tim 4:11), but the form of these addresses remains a conundrum. Some form-critical studies have attempted to reconstruct the earliest shape and content of Jewish and Christian homilies, but as Alistair Stewart-Sykes concludes from his brief survey of form-critical studies, "[t]hese recent form-critical efforts fail on the basis of circularity. No self-confessed homily is extant, and so the critic is left to determine for her or himself the form or forms which

[1] Alistair Stewart-Sykes, *From Prophecy to Preaching: A Survey for the Origins of the Christian Homily* (VCSup 59; Leiden: Brill, 2001), 4.

one might expect for a homily, and then so to label any document in which they might be found."[2]

Hebrews as Our Earliest Self-confessed Christian Speech

What we put forward is that Hebrews is our earliest self-identifying Christian speech (or sermon) to an assembly of Christ-followers.[3] The author, in fact, refers to his discourse as a λόγος τῆς παρακλή-σεως.[4] The term λόγος can refer to a speech (cf. Aristotle, *Rhet.* 1.2.3 [1355b]; 1.2.22 [1358a]; Anonymous Seguerianus 1). This seems the best understanding of this term in Heb 13:22. Thus, the author thinks that what he has written to his audience is a speech, a λόγος, that will be delivered via proxy similar to a Pauline letter. Indeed, many early Christian letters, like Paul's, were read orally to the gathered community of Christ-followers (cf. 1 Thess 5:27; Col 4:16), and Paul's letters were rhetorical events that were meant to teach and to persuade his audiences. Paul's letters, however, self-identify as letters with opening addresses and thanksgivings, and concluding travel plans, prayer wishes, and greetings. There are also a combination of typical epistolary *topoi* found in the bodies of the letters such as self-conscious letter writing (e.g., 1 Cor 4:14; 5:9; 7:1), health of companions (e.g., Phil 2:25–30), business affairs (e.g., 2 Cor 9:1–5); domestic matters (e.g., 1 Cor 5:1–6:11), and reunion with addressees (1 Thess 2:17–3:13).[5] Various combinations of these topics can also

---

[2] See the brief survey of these studies by Stewart-Sykes, *From Prophecy to Preaching*, 24–39.

[3] Broad definitions for a sermon are offered by scholars such as "oral communication of the word of God in the Christian assembly" (Stewart-Sykes, *From Prophecy to Preaching*, 6) or "public explanation of a sacred doctrine or a sacred text with its *Sitz im Leben* being worship" (Folker Siegert, "Homily and Panegyrical Sermon," in *Handbook of Classical Rhetoric in the Hellenistic Period, 330 B.C.–A.D. 400* [ed. Stanley Porter; Leiden: Brill, 1997], 421). Again, we consider Hebrews, like other interpreters, to be a sermon because it was a speech (though written down and sent to its audience) that would likely have been delivered in the context of a worshipping Christian community, and because the author attempts to relate sacred text and doctrine to the needs of the community. Hebrews, however, does not appear to be a sermon that is delivered after a liturgical reading of Scriptures or to mark a particular time on the liturgical calendar when the community gathered (e.g., Melito's *Peri Paschal*). The urgency for perseverance in the *argumentatio* seems to argue against both possibilities.

[4] This phrase eventually came to describe the bishop's sermon by the end of the fourth century (cf. *Apos. Con.* 8.5.12, though here it is in the plural—λόγοι παρα-κλήσεως).

[5] For this list of topics see David E. Aune, *The New Testament in Its Literary Environment* (LEC 8; Philadelphia: Westminster Press, 1987), 189.

be found among the epistolary papyri. Hebrews, however, opens like a speech and not like a letter. There is no opening address identifying the author and recipients. There is no doubling of introductory periods typical of Paul's letters in which thanksgiving is expressed (or condemnation in the case of Galatians). Additionally, the author makes frequent use of the hortatory subjunctive, "let us" (2:1; 4:1, 11, 14, 16; 6:1; 10:22, 23, 24; 12:1, 28; 13:13, 15). More telling, the author does not refer to his act of writing but of speaking throughout the discourse: "The main point about which we are speaking ..." (8:1; cf. 2:5, 5:11; 6:9) and "What further can I say? For time fails me to give a detailed account concerning ..." (11:32; cf. 9:5).[6] Up until the final verses, Hebrews is written and arranged like a piece of classic oratory. It is only with the final verses that the reader is aware that this speech was delivered, like a letter, by proxy. Also, only at this point do characteristic letter closings and topics appear such as letter writing, travel plans, a hoped-for-reunion, circumstances surrounding a companion, secondary greetings, and a final grace wish.

Hebrews and the Implications of the Practice of Rhetoric among Early Christians

There are three implications to consider if Hebrews is, in fact, our earliest independent, self-identifying speech, even sermon, from Christians (and Jews). First, as we indicated at the end of Chapter 9, there was a need among the early Christian communities for deliberative sermons as Acts 14:22 illustrates where Paul exhorts (παρακαλέω) the disciples to endure in the faith through affliction. Such language was associated with deliberative oratory. Anaximenes of Lampsacus states that protreptic or deliberative speech is παρά-κλησις and may be used in public or private deliberations (*Rhet. Alex.* 1 [1421b]). Thus, it is no argument against Hebrews's deliberative thrust that Hebrews is not delivered before a public assembly but amidst a private gathering of Christ-followers. In view of the arguments made in this study, we should then understand the self-identification of Hebrews in 13:22 as a λόγος τῆς παρακλήσεως to

---

[6] Hebrews 11:32 with the verses that follow is also a stylistic figure where the speaker intends to omit certain subjects or evidence but then proceeds to state them in passing. Cf. Isocrates, *Or.* 1.11; *Rhet. Her.* 4.37; Cicero, *De or.* 3.202; Quintilian, *Inst.* 8.3.82; 9.2.47; 9.3.50.

refer to a speech of exhortation or a deliberative speech.[7] Some discussions limit the function of the Christian sermon to the believing community as epideictic with some deliberative elements.[8] Hebrews, however, is a deliberative sermon with supporting epideictic elements. Such a blend of rhetorical genres, as we have seen, is not anomalous but in line with the rhetorical expectations and instructions for deliberative rhetoric.

Deliberative rhetoric among Christians did not just focus on conversion of outsiders.[9] The precarious situation of many Christian communities in the first and second centuries, like that of Hebrews, still called for the daring rhetoric and the compelling persuasion of deliberative oratory. It is worth noting that Tacitus wrote his *Dialogus de oratoribus* in Flavian Rome, where, as we think, the community of Hebrews lived. In Tacitus's *Dialogus de oratoribus*, Maternus attributes the decline in oratorical display and eloquence to the safety and security that the Roman Empire had achieved under its emperor (cf. 41). Maternus introduces this explanation by stating, "Great oratory is like a flame: it needs fuel to feed it, movement to fan it, and it brightens as it burns" (36 [Peterson, LCL]). Thus the need for bold and impressive rhetorical displays had apparently diminished in Rome. The Christian subculture, however, did not always enjoy such safety and security, especially, in the latter half of the first-century in Rome. We see the conditions of chaos and real or perceived danger – conditions that, according to Maternus, fuel the flame of oratory in the late Republic – present among Christian communities like that of Hebrews. The informant culture of Rome in the latter part of the first century was described by Tacitus as "the gain-getting rhetoric now in vogue, greedy for human blood" (*Dia.* 12 [Peterson, LCL]). Some in the community addressed by Hebrews had been the target of this gain-getting rhetoric by which they were "made a public spectacle" that led to shame, imprisonment, the confiscation of their property (cf. Heb 10:33–34).[10] Some had even

---

[7] On the broad range of meaning of παράκλησις denoting, among other things, encouragement, comfort, or exhortation, see BDAG. The unrelenting deliberative focus and the forcefulness with which the author has called his audience to persevere leads us to place emphasis on the notion of exhortation.

[8] Cf. Stewart-Sykes, *From Prophecy to Preaching*, 38, 80, 86.

[9] Cf. Stewart-Sykes, *From Prophecy to Preaching*, 4, 80, who limits deliberative oratory to missionary preaching.

[10] For further discussion, see Jason A. Whitlark, *Resisting Empire: Rethinking the Purpose of the Letter to "the Hebrews"* (LNTS 484; London: T&T Clark, 2014), 37–43.

quit meeting with the community (cf. Heb 10:25).[11] The sermon of Hebrews confronts the precarious situation of its audience with its own powerful oratory and rhetorical artistry in order to deliberate on a matter of utmost importance – perseverance in the faith.

Second, Hebrews points to the high level of rhetorical training of some early Christians. Rhetorical studies of the New Testament have demonstrated that the widespread rhetorical practices of the Greco-Roman world were shared by early Christians. Hebrews, however, appears to be an exceptional case of rhetorical artistry, not just in its style but in its invention of arguments and in its arrangement of its discourse (cf. Origen's comments in Eusebius, *Hist. eccl.* 6.25.11–13). The author thus adapted what appears to be sophisticated Greco-Roman rhetorical training to communicate his exhortation grounded in the gospel of Jesus Christ. Hebrews also demonstrates that good rhetorical skill was appreciated – even valued – among some Christians. The author of Hebrews then develops existing and attractive cultural offerings from rhetoric to communicate his hope in God through Jesus Christ.[12]

Third, Hebrews is a conventional speech by classical rhetorical standards that develops its content from the unique and distinctively Christian convictions of the author and his audience. In fact, rhetorical artistry and anticipated arrangement finds a trajectory from Hebrews in the second half of the first century, to Melito of Sardis's *Peri Pascha* in the second half of the second century,[13] and eventually to Augustine's own adaptation of Cicero for "Christian Rhetoric," *De doctrina christiana*, in the early fifth-century.[14] Pagan rhetorical canons seemed to guide the form of some of the earliest extant Christian sermons we have. Thus Christians adopted forms of communicating in their gatherings that were readily and widely

---

[11] These former members of the community could have proven problematic to the other members of the community, especially in Rome. These defectors could potentially become informants looking to gain favor with social superiors or to gain the possessions of some in the community. Thus, these former members could stir up and intensify trouble for the community.

[12] Cf. Udo Schnelle "Das frühe Christentum und die Bildung," *NTS* 61 (2015): 113–43.

[13] Cf. Alistair Stewart-Sykes, *The Lamb's High Feast: Melito, Peri Pascha and the Quartodeciman Paschal Liturgy at Sardis* (VCSup; Leiden: Brill, 1998), 72–92, 113–39 (esp. 114).

[14] Cf. George A. Kennedy, *Classical Rhetoric and Its Christian and Secular Tradition from Ancient to Modern Times* (Chapel Hill: University of North Carolina Press, 1980), 156–7.

identifiable in the Greco-Roman world. In sum, when considering the question of Christian preaching among Christians, we must say that Hebrews stands out as a shining example of rhetoric in the first century among Jews, Christians, and pagans. Certainly the author of Hebrews exhibits much care in crafting his "word of exhortation." His rhetorical skill could be equally recognized and appreciated by all in the Greco-Roman world.

Rhetoric and Relapse in Hebrews

The second question for which our study has important implications concerns the nature of the apostasy envisioned in Hebrews. Clearly the audience is tempted to relapse into the social and religious milieu from which it was converted. But what is that milieu? Our analysis of the comparative rhetoric of the speech suggests that Hebrews's antilapsarianism is directed against imperial pagan culture, and not non-Christian forms of Judaism.[15] Thus Hebrews's rhetoric is not targeting "Judaism" or "the Jews," and properly understood, should not be too quickly placed in the stream of a developing *adversus Judaeos* tradition.[16] In support of this thesis are four key considerations.

First, the covenant comparison that spans Hebrews in its disjointed *narratio* does not have in view two different faiths of two different peoples as we might expect if a lapse into non-Christian forms of Judaism was the concern. Rather, the covenant comparison has in view a *single* people, running from "our fathers/elders" to the present generation, and a *single* faith shared by this people with a single trajectory – a people who will be perfected together in the heavenly Jerusalem (cf. 11:39–40; 12:22). The author frames the audience as members of the same "house of God" in which Moses was a servant, and over which Christ is a son (cf. 3:2–6). Their models of faith are those of the Jewish scriptures beginning with

---

[15] This lapsarianism that threatens the community is especially pertinent if we take the audience in Hebrews to be primarily Gentile Christians.

[16] See the survey by Jody A. Barnard, "Anti-Jewish Interpretations of Hebrews: Some Neglected Factors," *Melilah* 11 (2014): 29–34. This is not to say that Hebrews could not be offensive to Jews who did not believe the Christological claims articulated in the discourse or in the manner which the community is included in the identity of God's people (cf. Philip Esler, "Collective Memory and Hebrews 11: Outlining a New Investigative Framework," in *Memory, Tradition and Text: The Uses of the Past in Early Christianity* [ed. Alan Kirk and Tom Thatcher; SemeaSt 52; Leiden, Brill, 2005], 163).

Abel, running through Moses, and including the Maccabean martyrs (though the reference is muted; cf. 11:35b).[17]

Second, the individual covenant comparisons throughout Hebrews are double encomiums and not encomium-invectives as we might expect if reversion to Judaism was the problem. Though obsolete, the old covenant as Hebrews describes it nonetheless has heavenly origins with angels who mediate it as a message from God (1:5–2:4); it is inaugurated by the faithful servant Moses who spoke of Christ and God's future and thus can even be said to preach the gospel (3:1–4:13, cf. 4:2); it is mediated by a high priest "chosen" and "called by God" to deal gently with the wayward and ignorant and to offer sacrifice for sins (5:1–10); it is mediated, too, by a Levitical priesthood that through its sacrifices "sanctifies those who have been defiled so that their flesh is purified," and as a revelatory foreshadowing of the even greater new covenant realities to come through which salvation is accomplished (even for the transgressions committed under the first covenant, cf. 9:15).[18] Such a positive characterization of the old covenant is essential to the writer's syncritical goal of heightening the audience's appreciation of its own new covenant experience. Comparison to something utterly negative could not have this effect. As Theon (112) puts the matter, "syncrises are not comparisons of things having a great difference between them; for someone wondering whether Achilles or Thersites was braver would be laughable." If Hebrews was targeting non-Christian forms of Judaism, we might expect what Daniel Sheerin observes in some later patristic writers. When these patristic authors engaged in a

---

[17] Even for a Gentile audience, such a perspective is hardly unprecedented. First Peter describes its Gentile recipients unproblematically in terms borrowed from Exod 19 and pertaining to Israel – as a chosen race, a royal priesthood, a holy nation, a people who have become God's own possession (cf. 1 Pet 2:9). So, too, Paul summons Gentile converts to see themselves as grafted into Israel (Rom 11:17) and to view the wilderness generation as their "fathers" (1 Cor 10:1). New kinship or ethnic identities could also be rooted in certain ancestral figures by emphasizing behaviors or patterns of life that could be adopted and imitated. See David H. Horrell, "Ethnicisation, Marriage, and Early Christian Identity: Critical Reflections on 1 Corinthians 7, 1 Peter 3 and Modern New Testament Scholarship," *NTS* 62 (2016): 439–60. See also Isocrates, *Paneg.* 50; Josephus, *C. Ap.* 2.210; Philo, *Virt.* 195 (cited in Horrell, "Ethnicisation," 456–7).

[18] Cf. Mary D'Angelo, *Moses in the Letter to the Hebrews* (SBLDS 42; Atlanta: Scholars Press, 1979), 201–58. The new covenant thus vindicates God's faithfulness to his promises even to those before Christ (under the old covenant); cf. Ole Jakob Filtvedt, *The Identity of God's People and the Paradox of Hebrews* (WUNT 2/400; Tübingen: Mohr Siebeck, 2015), 121.

polemic against their Jewish heritage, they would employ the rhetorical device of a negative syncrisis – the encomium of the Christian fulfillment accompanied by an invective of its Old Testament or Jewish type.[19] Were the writer intending such a comparison, he would hardly have related old covenant experience of the wilderness generation as "good news" as he does in 4:2, nor would he have framed faithfulness to it as exemplary.

Third, Hebrews's deliberative argument does not pit new covenant faith against old covenant faith as we might expect if reversion to non-Christian Judaism was the issue, but rather, pits covenant faithfulness past and present against a common apostasy. The first occurrence of this deliberative rhetoric (Heb 2:1–4) is typical of all five units and, because of its brevity, illustrates the underlying logic clearly: "For if the message declared through angels was valid, and every transgression or disobedience received a just penalty, how can we escape if we neglect so great a salvation, which was declared at first through the Lord." Here the writer does not frame "the message declared by angels" in negative terms as a symbol of "Judaism" and then warn against heeding that message *instead of* the "salvation ... declared by the Lord."[20] Rather, he frames the angel's message as "valid" or "firm/secure," and highlights the *failure to heed* that message as an example of what happens in the case of apostasy. The lesser to greater logic only heightens the urgency of the example: if apostasy was punished under the lesser covenant mediated by angels, how much more will it be punished in the case of "so great a salvation" announced by the Lord himself?

---

[19] "Rhetorical and Hermeneutic *Synkrisis* in Patristic Typology," in *Nova & Vetera Patristic Studies in Honor of Thomas Patrick Halton* (ed. John Petruccione; Washington D. C.: Catholic University Press, 1998), 35.

[20] The old covenant in Hebrew should not be taken as a metonym for Judaism. Cf. Jesper Svartvik, "Stumbling Block or Stepping Stone? On the Reception History of Hebrews 8:13," in *Hebrews in Contexts* (ed. Gabriella Gelardini and Harold W. Attridge; AJEC 91. Leiden: Brill, 2016), 336; Ekkehard W. Stegemann and Wolfgang Stegemann, "Hebrews and the Discourse of Judeophobia," in *Hebrews in Contexts* (ed. Gabriella Gelardini and Harold W. Attridge; AJEC 91; Leiden: Brill, 2016), 363. Charles H. Talbert (*Romans* [Macon: Smyth & Helwys, 2002], 270) also notes that all forms of Judaism did not make Moses or the Mosaic covenant central to Jewish identity. Indeed, *1 Enoch* and Paul represent Jewish identities that are not centered upon the Mosaic covenant precisely because that covenant was viewed as soteriologically deficient. Cf. Gabriele Boccaccini, "The Evilness of Human Nature in *1 Enoch, Jubilees,* Paul, and *4 Ezra*: A Second Temple Jewish Debate," in Fourth Ezra *and* Second Baruch: *Reconstruction After the Fall* (ed. Matthias Henze and Gabriele Boccaccini; JSJSup 164; Leiden: Brill, 2013), 67–9.

Fourth, Hebrews's comparative rhetoric not only makes the old covenant's summons *to* faithfulness paradigmatic for new covenant experience, but also the old covenant's historic summons *away from* pagan imperial culture. This summons is succinctly expressed in Joshua's ultimatum to the people: "Now if you are unwilling to serve the Lord, choose this day whom you will serve, whether the gods your ancestors served in the region beyond the River or the gods of the Amorites in whose land you are living; but as for me and my household, we will serve the Lord" (24:15 [NRSV]; cf. Deut 6:13–15).[21] In Hebrews the same summons as it relates to new covenant experience is evident from at least four telling indicators:

(1) Many citations of and allusions to the Septuagint in the appeals of Hebrews are taken from contexts that warn against idolatry and assimilation to the way of life under pagan nations (e.g., Heb 10:28, 30, 37–38; 12:15, 29).[22]

(2) The phrase, "repentance from dead works and faith in God" (Heb 6:1) suggests an opposition between idolatry and covenant faithfulness. Idols were commonly regarded as "dead" and as "works of the hands" – and in contrast to the "living" God. Wisdom of Solomon speaks of pagans who put their hope in "dead things" (νεκρά; 13.10), and who take "works of human hands" (ἔργα χειρῶν ἀνθρώπων; 13.10) as their gods. It also polemicizes against the mortal (one subject to death) who "makes a dead thing with lawless hands" (νεκρὸν ἐργάζεται χερσὶν ἀνόμοις; Wis 15.17).[23] Similarly, the Shepherd of Hermas says of the doubleminded, who commit idolatry out of fear, that their "works are dead" (τὸ δὲ ἔργα αὐτῶν νεκρά ἐστιν; Sim. 9.21.1–4).[24] The opposition in Heb 6:1, then, between "dead works" and "faith in God" is key evidence of the audience's background in pagan idolatry. So, too, the phrases, "cleanses our/your conscience from dead works so that we might

---

[21] Cf. John Barclay (*Jews in the Mediterranean Diaspora: From Alexander to Trajan 323 BCE–117 CE* [Edinburgh: T&T Clark, 1996], 429–39) points out that abstention from all pagan cults was one of the key distinguishing features of Jewish identity in the Diaspora.

[22] Cf. Whitlark, *Resisting Empire*, 61–75, for further discussion of these texts.

[23] Cf. David A. deSilva, *Perseverance in Gratitude: A Socio-Rhetorical Commentary on the Epistle 'to the Hebrews'* (Grand Rapids: Eerdmans, 2000), 216–17.

[24] In Did. 6.3, pagan idolatry is described as "service to dead gods" (λατρεία θεῶν νεκρῶν). Cf. 2 Clem. 3.1.

serve the *living* God" (9:14);[25] and "an evil heart of unbelief that turns away from the *living* God" (3:12).[26]

(3) In the key examples of the wilderness generation and Moses, the threat envisioned to faithfulness is assimilation to pagan imperial society. In the Numbers narrative, the wilderness generation is remembered both for its failure to believe the promise of God and its contemplation of a return to pagan Egypt and its idols (cf. Num 14:4). This same narrative is operative in the background of Heb 3–4, and is explicitly invoked in Heb 3:17 ("whose bodies fell in the wilderness"), which recalls the curse from Num 14:33 ("and you shall suffer for your faithlessness, until the last of your dead bodies lies in the wilderness").[27] The wilderness generation's choice contrasts with that of Moses, who according to Heb 11:24–26 chose solidarity in suffering with the people of God over and against the status, power, and wealth of the pagan imperial culture of Egypt. That is, he "refused to be called a son of Pharaoh's daughter," he chose "to share ill-treatment with the people of God rather than to enjoy the fleeting pleasures of sin," and he "considered abuse suffered for the Christ to be greater wealth than the treasures of Egypt."

(4) The author's addition of καὶ τῶν ἀνομιῶν αὐτῶν to the quotation from Jer 38:34 (LXX) in Heb 10:17 recalls the golden-calf incident. The phrase echoes the language used to narrate the episode in Exod 34:9 (LXX).[28] Its addition by the author suggests that the

---

[25] There are some similarities with Ezek 36:25–27 where God will cleanse Israel from her idols, which is followed by a new heart and the indwelling Spirit given to the people to enable their faithfulness.

[26] Cf. Alan C. Mitchell (*Hebrews* [SP 13; Collegeville: Liturgical Press, 2009], 89), who cites "doing evil in the sight of the Lord" as a potential parallel to 3:12. As Mitchell notes, this language from the Old Testament is associated with Israel turning away from God and to idols.

[27] It is also worth noting that the wilderness generation is not critiqued by the author for turning to the "ineffective" old covenant for salvation – something we might expect if a relapse to a Judaism that made central the old covenant and its practices was the issue. The rhetoric is also similar to Paul's in 1 Cor 10. There Paul treats the wilderness generation as both "our fathers" and a cautionary tale for the current generation. The wilderness generation, he argues, in an anticipatory and inferior sense was baptized and ate the Eucharist, just as the present generation does – and yet, that did not protect them from the consequences of idolatry; so how much more will it not protect the present generation? This is the essence of Hebrews's own argument.

[28] This potential allusion was pointed out by Madison N. Pierce, "Intra-Divine Discourse and the New Covenant in Hebrews: Subtext(s) in Hebrews 8–10" (paper presented at the annual meeting of SBL, San Antonio, TX, 21 November 2016). Paul alludes to the incident in 1 Cor 10:7.

new covenant brings the forgiveness of, and even deliverance from, idolatry (golden-calf-like rebellion).

In sum, the comparative rhetoric of Hebrews as we have described it in this volume is intended to heighten resistance to pagan imperial culture and is in no way aimed at other forms of Judaism. This rhetoric invokes the "old covenant" not as a negative metonym for deficient Judaism, but rather, as a past model of relationship with God that is made paradigmatic – and with the "all the more" urgency of *a minore ad maius* argumentation – for the present generation, both in its summons to covenant fidelity and in its opposition to imperialist idolatry. That Hebrews's rhetoric came to be read in the Patristic period and beyond as an attack on Judaism and the Jewish people is, therefore, in our view a tragic development in the history of interpretation. In point of fact, Hebrews targets pagan imperial culture as the great threat to faithfulness and, ironically enough, regards old and new covenant forms of fidelity as historically *allied*, not only in their allegiance to the same God, but also, therefore, in their resistance to this culture.[29]

---

[29] If we place Hebrews in a late first-century (or even early second-century) Roman context, our considerations might lend support to Pamela M. Eisenbaum's observation, following Judith Lieu, that "Hebrews represents a unique form of Judeo-Christian religiosity that perhaps existed briefly when Rome was the common enemy of Jews and believers in Jesus"; see "Locating Hebrews within the Literary Landscape of Christian Origins," in *Hebrews: Contemporary Methods—New Insights* (ed. Gabriella Gelardini; Atlanta: Society of Biblical Literature, 2005), 236–7. Also see the interesting proposal by Giorgio Jossa, "Jews, Romans, Christians: From the *Bellum Judaicum* to the *Antiquitates*," in *Josephus and Jewish History in Flavian Rome and Beyond* (ed. Joseph Sievers and Gaia Lembi; JSJSup 104; Leiden: Brill, 2005), 331–42, who argues that Josephus's portrayal of Jesus and John the Baptist represents "something more than a neutral attitude many scholars have often ascribed to him: it expresses an awareness of a solidarity between Jews and Roman Christians as representatives of a wisdom alien to the tyrannical sovereign" (342).

BIBLIOGRAPHY

Secondary Sources

Allen, David M. "Who, What, Why? The Worship of the Firstborn in Hebrews 1:6." Pages 159–75 in *Mark, Manuscripts, and Monotheism: Essays in Honor of Larry Hurtado*. Edited by Chris Keith and Dieter Roth. The Library of New Testament Studies 528. London: T&T Clark, 2015.

Aletti, Jean-Noël. "La présence d'un modèle rhétorique en Romains: Son role et son importance." *Biblica* 71 (1990): 1–24.

Alexander, Philip S. "Quid Athenis et Hierosdolymis? Rabbinic Midrash and Hermeneutics in the Graeco-Roman World." Pages 97–115 in *A Tribute to Géza Vermès: Essays on Jewish and Christian Literature and History*. Edited by Philip R. Davies and Richard T. White. Journal for the Study of the Old Testament Supplement Series 100. Sheffield: JSOT Press, 1990.

Amador, J. D. H. "Revisiting 2 Corinthians: Rhetoric and the Case of Unity." *New Testament Studies* 46 (2000): 92–111.

Anderson, Kevin L. *Hebrews: A Commentary in the Wesleyan Tradition*. New Beacon Bible Commentary. Kansas City: Beacon Hill Press, 2013.

Attridge, Harold W. "Paraenesis in a Homily (λόγος παρακλήσεως): The Possible Location of, and Socialization in, the 'Epistle to the Hebrews.'" *Semeia* 50 (1990): 211–226.

The Epistle to the Hebrews. Hermeneia. Philadelphia: Fortress, 1989.

"The Psalms in Hebrews." Pages 197–212 in *The Psalms in the New Testament*. Edited by Steve Moyise and Maarten J. J. Menken. New Testament and the Scriptures of Israel. London: T&T Clark, 2004.

Aune, David E. "The Use and Abuse of Enthymeme in New Testament Scholarship." *New Testament Studies* 49 (2003): 299–320.

Backhaus, Knut. *Der Hebräerbrief*. Regensburger Neues Testament. Regensburg: Verlag Friedrich Pustet, 2009.

"How to Entertain Angels: Ethics in the Epistle to the Hebrews." Pages 149–175 in *Hebrews: Contemporary Methods – New Insights*. Biblical Interpretation Series 75. Edited by Gabriella Gelardini. Atlanta: Society of Biblical Literature, 2005.

Der Neue Bund und das Werden der Kirche: die Diatheke-Deutung des Hebräerbrief im Rahmen der frühchristlichen Theologiegeschichte. Neutestamentliche Abhandlungen 29. Münster: Aschendorff, 1996.

Barclay, John. *Jews in the Mediterranean Diaspora: From Alexander to Trajan 323 BCE–117 CE*. Edinburgh: T&T Clark, 1996.

Barnard, Jody A. "Anti-Jewish Interpretations of Hebrews: Some Neglected Factors." *Melilah* 11 (2014): 29–34.

——. *The Mysticism of Hebrews*. Wissenschaftliche Untersuchungen zum Neuen Testament 2/331. Tübingen: Mohr Siebeck, 2012.

Bauckham, Richard. "The Divinity of Jesus Christ in the Epistle to the Hebrews." Pages 15–36 in *The Epistle to the Hebrews and Christian Theology*. Edited by R. Bauckham, Daniel R. Driver, Trevor A. Hart, and Nathan MacDonald. Grand Rapids: Eerdmans, 2009.

Baugh, S. M. "Hyperbaton and Greek Literary Style in Hebrews." *Novum Testamentum* 59 (2017): 194–213.

Berry, D. H., and Andrew Erskine. "Form and Function." Pages 1–17 in *Form and Function in Roman Oratory*. Edited by D. H. Berry and Andrew Erskine. Cambridge: Cambridge University Press, 2010.

Betz, Hans Dieter. "The Literary Composition and Function of Paul's Letter to the Galatians." *New Testament Studies* 21 (1975): 353–379.

Black, C. Clifton II. "The Rhetorical Form of the Hellenistic Jewish and Early Christian Sermon: A Response to Lawrence Wills." *Harvard Theological Review* 81 (1988): 1–18.

Boccaccini, Gabriele. "The Evilness of Human Nature in *1 Enoch, Jubilees, Paul,* and *4 Ezra*: A Second Temple Jewish Debate." Pages 63–79 in *Fourth Ezra and Second Baruch: Reconstruction after the Fall*. Edited by Matthias Henze and Gabriele Boccaccini. Supplements to the Journal for the Study of Judaism 164. Leiden: Brill, 2013.

Bornkamm, Günther. "Das Bekenntnis im Hebräerbrief." Pages 188–203 in *Studien zu Antike und Urchristentum: Gesammelte Aufsätze, Volume 2*. Edited by Günther Bornkamm. Beiträge zur evangelischen Theologie 28. Munich: Kaiser, 1963.

Bovon, François. "Names and Number in Early Christianity." *New Testament Studies* 47 (2001): 267–288.

Brauw, Michael de. "The Parts of the Speech." Pages 187–202 in *A Companion to Greek Rhetoric*. Edited by Ian Worthington. Malden: Blackwell, 2007.

Bruce, Frederick F. *The Epistle to the Hebrews*. New International Commentary of the New Testament. Grand Rapids: Eerdmans, 1990.

Büschel, F. "Hebräerbrief." Pages 1669–1673 in vol. 2 of *Religion in Geschichte und Gegenwart: Handwörterbuch für Theologie und Religionswissenschaft*. Edited by H. Gunkel and L. Zscharnack. 2nd ed. Tübingen: J. C. B. Mohr (Paul Siebeck), 1928.

Byron, John. "Living in the Shadow of Cain: Echoes of a Developing Tradition in James 5:1–6." *Novum Testamentum* 48 (2006): 261–274.

Caird, George B. "Son by Appointment." Pages 73–81 in vol. 1 of *The New Testament Age: Essays in Honor of Bo Reicke*. Edited by W. C. Weinrich. Macon: Mercer University Press, 1984.

Caneday, Ardel B. "The Eschatological World Already Subjected to the Son." Pages 28–39 in *A Cloud of Witnesses: The Theology of Hebrews in Its Ancient Context*. Edited by Richard Bauckham, Trevor Hart, Nathan MacDonald, and Daniel Driver. The Library of New Testament Studies 387. London: T&T Clark, 2008.

Catto, Stephen K. *Reconstructing the First-Century Synagogue: A Critical Analysis of Current Research.* The Library of New Testament Studies 363. London: T&T Clark, 2007.

Cockerill, Gareth Lee. *The Epistle to the Hebrews.* New International Commentary on the New Testament. Grand Rapids: Eerdmans, 2012.

Conley, Thomas A. "Philo of Alexandria." Pages 695–713 in *Handbook of Classical Rhetoric in the Hellenistic Period, 330 B.C.–A.D. 400.* Edited by Stanley Porter. Leiden: Brill, 1997.

"The Enthymeme in Perspective." *Quarterly Journal of Speech* 70 (1984): 166–187.

D'Angelo, Mary. *Moses in the Letter to the Hebrews.* Society of Biblical Literature Dissertation Series 42. Missoula: Scholars Press, 1979.

Daube, David. "Rabbinic Methods of Interpretation and Hellenistic Rhetoric." *Hebrew Union College Annual* 22 (1979): 239–64.

Deichgräber, Reinhard. *Gotteshymnus und Christushymnus in der frühen Christenheit.* Studien zur Umwelt des Neuen Testaments 5. Göttingen: Vandenhoeck & Ruprecht, 1967.

DeSilva, David. A. *Despising Shame: Honor Discourse and Community Maintenance in the Epistle to the Hebrews.* Society of Biblical Literature Dissertation Series 152. Atlanta: Scholars, 1995.

Perseverance in Gratitude: A Socio-Rhetorical Commentary on the Epistle "to the Hebrews". Grand Rapids: Eerdmans, 2000.

Duff, Tim. *Plutarch's Lives: Exploring Virtue and Vice.* Oxford: Clarendon Press, 2000.

Eisenbaum, Pamela. *Jewish Heroes of Christian History: Hebrews 11 in Literary Context.* Society of Biblical Literature Dissertation Series 156. Atlanta: Scholars, 1997.

Ellingworth, Paul. *The Epistle to the Hebrews: A Commentary on the Greek Text.* New International Greek Testament Commentary. Grand Rapids: Eerdmans, 1993.

Ellis, E. E. *The Old Testament in Early Christianity: Canon and Interpretation in the Light of Modern Research.* Tübingen: J. C. B. Mohr (Paul Siebeck), 1991.

Erbse, Hartmut. "Die Bedeutung der Synkrisis in den Parallelbiographien Plutarchs." *Hermes* 84 (1956): 398–424.

Eskola, Timo. *Messiah and the Throne.* Wissenschaftliche Untersuchungen zum Neuen Testament 2/142. Tübingen: Mohr Siebeck, 2001.

Esler, Philip. "Collective Memory and Hebrews 11: Outlining a New Investigative Framework." Pages 151–171 in *Memory, Tradition and Text: The Uses of the Past in Early Christianity.* Edited by Alan Kirk and Tom Thatcher. Semeia Studies 52. Leiden, Brill, 2005.

Filson, Floyd V. *"Yesterday": A Study of Hebrews in the Light of Chapter 13.* Studies in Biblical Theology 4. Naperville: Allenson, 1967.

Filtvedt, Ole Jakob. "Creation and Salvation in Hebrews." *Zeitschrift für die neutestamentliche Wissenschaft* 106 (2015): 280–303.

The Identity of God's People and the Paradox of Hebrews. Wissenschaftliche Untersuchungen zum Neuen Testament 2/400. Tübingen: Mohr Siebeck, 2015.

Filtvedt, Ole Jakob, and Martin Wessbrandt. "Exploring the High Priesthood of Jesus in Early Christian Sources." *Zeitschrift für die neutestamentliche Wissenschaft* 106 (2015): 96–114.

Fowler, R. A. "Aristotle on the Period." *The Classical Quarterly* 32 (1982): 89–99.

France. R. T. "The Writer of Hebrews as Biblical Expositor." *Tyndale Bulletin* 47 (1996): 246–276.

Frankowski, Janusz. "Early Christian Hymns Recorded in the New Testament: A Reconsideration of the Question in Light of Heb 1, 3." *Biblische Zeitschrift* 27 (1983): 183–194.

Gäbel, Georg. *Die Kulttheologie des Hebräerbriefes: Eine exegetisch-religionsgeschichtliche Studie.* Wissenschaftliche Untersuchungen zum Neuen Testament 2/212. Tübingen: Mohr Siebeck, 2006.

Geiger, Joseph. "Nepos and Plutarch: From Latin to Greek Political Biography." *Illinois Classical Studies* 13 (1988): 245–256.

Gelardini, Gabriella. "From 'Linguistic Turn' and Hebrews Scholarship to *Anadiplosis Iterata*: The Enigma of Structure." *Harvard Theological Review* 102 (2009): 51–72.

"Hebrews, Homiletics, and Liturgical Scripture Interpretation." Pages 121–144 in *Reading the Epistle to the Hebrews: A Resource for Students.* Edited by Eric F. Mason and Kevin B. McCruden. Resources for Biblical Study 66. Atlanta: SBL, 2011.

"Rhetorical Criticism in Hebrews Scholarship: Avenues and Aporias." Pages 213–236 in *Method and Meaning: Essays on New Testament Interpretation in Honor of Harold W. Attridge.* Edited by Andrew B. McGowan and Kent Harold Richards. Resources for Biblical Study 67. Atlanta: SBL, 2011.

"Verhärtet eure Herzen nicht": Der Hebräer, eine Synagogenhomilie zu Tischa Be-Aw. Biblical Interpretation Series 83. Leiden: Brill, 2007.

Gill, Christopher. "The Ethos/Pathos Distinction in Rhetorical and Literary Criticism." *The Classical Quarterly* (1984): 149–166.

Goodspeed, Edgar J. *The Epistle to the Hebrews.* New York: Macmillan, 1908.

Gräbe, Peter "The New Covenant and Christian Identity in Hebrews." Pages 118–127 in *A Cloud of Witnesses: The Theology of Hebrews in Its Ancient Context.* Edited by Richard Bauckham, Trevor Hart, Nathan MacDonald, and Daniel Driver. The Library of New Testament Studies 387. London: T&T Clark, 2008.

Gräßer, Erich. *An die Hebräer: Hebr 1–6.* Evangelische-Katholischer Kommentar zum Neuen Testament 17/1. Zürich: Benziger Verlag/ Neukirchener Verlag, 1990.

Griffiths, Jonathan I. *Hebrews and Divine Speech.* The Library of New Testament Studies 507. London: T&T Clark, 2014.

Grillo, Luca. *Cicero's De Provinciis Consularibus Oratio.* New York: Oxford University Press, 2015.

Guthrie, George H. "Hebrews in Its First-Century Contexts: Recent Research." Pages 413–443 in *The Face of New Testament Studies: A Survey of Recent Research.* Edited by Scot McKnight and Grant R. Osborne. Grand Rapids: Baker, 2004.

The Structure of Hebrews: A Text-Linguistic Analysis. Supplements to Novum Testamentum 73. Leiden: Brill, 1994.

Guzmán, Ron, and Michael W. Martin. "Is Hebrews 5:11–6:20 Really a Digression?" *Novum Testamentum* 57 (2015): 295–310.

Gyllenberg, Rafael. "Die Komposition des Hebräerbriefs." *Svensk Exegetisk Årsbok* 22–23 (1957–1958): 137–147.

Hahn, Scott. "A Broken Covenant and the Curse of Death: A Study of Hebrews 9:15–22." *Catholic Biblical Quarterly* 66 (2004): 416–436.

Hearing, Theodor. "Gedankengang und Grundgedanken des Hebräerbriefs." *Zeitschrift für die neutestamentliche Wissenschaft* 18 (1917–1918): 145–164.

Heath, Malcolm. "Codifications of Rhetoric." Pages 59–74 in *The Cambridge Companion to Ancient Rhetoric*. Edited by Erik Gunderson. Cambridge: Cambridge University Press, 2009.

"Invention." Pages 89–119 in *Handbook of Classical Rhetoric in the Hellenistic Period (330 B.C.–A.D. 400)*. Edited by Stanley E. Porter. Leiden: Brill, 1997.

"Theon and the Progymnasmata." *Greek, Roman, and Byzantine Studies* 43 (2002): 129–160.

Heil, John Paul. *Hebrews: Chiastic Structures and Audience Response.* Catholic Biblical Quarterly Monograph Series 46. Washington D. C.: Catholic Biblical Association of America, 2010.

Highet, Gilbert. *The Speeches of Vergil's Aeneid.* New Jersey: Princeton University Press, 1972.

Horton, Fred L. *The Melchizedek Tradition: A Critical Examination of the Sources to the Fifth Century A.D. and in the Epistle to the Hebrews.* Society for the Study of the New Testament Monograph Series 30. Cambridge: Cambridge University Press, 1976.

Horrell, David H. "Ethnicisation, Marriage, and Early Christian Identity: Critical Reflections on 1 Corinthians 7, 1 Peter 3 and Modern New Testament Scholarship." *New Testament Studies* 62 (2016): 439–460.

Hughes, Philip E. *A Commentary on the Epistle to the Hebrews.* Grand Rapids: Eerdmans, 1977.

Huizenga, Leroy A. *The New Isaac: Tradition and Intertextuality in the Gospel of Matthew.* Supplements to Novum Testamentum 131. Leiden: Brill, 2009.

Hurst, L. D. "The Christology of Hebrews 1 and 2." Pages 151–164 in *The Glory of Christ in the New Testament: Studies in Christology in Memory of George Bradford Caird.* Edited by L. D. Hurst and N. T. Wright. Oxford: Clarendon Press, 1987.

Isaacs, Marie E. *Reading Hebrews and James: A Literary and Theological Commentary.* Macon: Smyth and Helwys, 2002.

Jamieson, R. B. "Hebrews 9.23: Cult Inauguration, Yom Kippur and the Cleansing of the Heavenly Tabernacle." *New Testament Studies* 62 (2016): 569–587.

Jipp, Joshua W. "The Son's Entrance into the Heavenly World: The Soteriological Necessity of the Scriptural Catena in Hebrews 1.5–14." *New Testament Studies* 56 (2010): 557–575.

Johnson, Luke Timothy. *Hebrews: A Commentary.* New Testament Library. Louisville: Westminster John Knox, 2006.

Joslin, Barry C. "Can Hebrews Be Structured? An Assessment of Eight Approaches." *Currents in Biblical Research* 6 (2007): 99–129.

Karrer, Martin. *Der Brief an die Hebräer: Kapitel 5,11–13,25*. Ökumenischer Taschenbush-Kommentar zum Neuen Testament 20/2. Gütersloh: Gütersloher Verlagshaus, 2008.

Kennedy, George A. *Classical Rhetoric and its Christian and Secular Tradition from Ancient to Modern Times*. Chapel Hill: University of North Carolina Press, 1980.

"Historical Survey of Rhetoric." Pages 3–41 in *Handbook of Classical Rhetoric in the Hellenistic Period (330 B.C.–A.D. 400)*. Edited by Stanley Porter. Leiden: Brill, 1997.

Progymnasmata: Greek Textbooks of Prose Composition and Rhetoric. Atlanta: SBL, 2003.

Koester, Craig R. *Hebrews: A New Translation with Introduction and Commentary*. Anchor Bible 36. New York: Doubleday, 2001.

"Hebrews, Rhetoric, and the Future of Humanity." Pages 99–120 in *Reading the Epistle to the Hebrews: A Resource for Students*. Edited by Eric F. Mason and Kevin B. McCruden. Resources for Biblical Study 66. Atalnta: SBL, 2011.

Kraus, Manfred. "Theories and Practice of Enthymeme in the First Centuries B.C.E. and C.E." Pages 95–111 in *Rhetorical Argumentation in Biblical Texts: Essays from the Lund 2000 Conference*. Edited by Anders Eriksson, Thomas H. Olbricht, and Walter Übelacker. Emory Studies in Early Christianity 8. Harrisburg: Trinity Press International, 2002.

Kümmel, W. G. *Introduction to the New Testament*. Translated by H. C. Kee. Nashville: Abingdon, 1975.

Laansma, Jon. *"I Will Give You Rest": The Rest Motif in the New Testament with Special Reference to MT 11 and Heb 3–4*. Wissenschaftliche Untersuchungen zum Neuen Testament 2/98. Tübingen: Mohr Siebeck, 1997.

Lampe, Peter. "Rhetorical Analysis of Pauline Texts—Quo Vadit?" Pages 3–24 in *Paul and Rhetoric*. Edited by J. Paul Sampley and Peter Lampe. New York: T&T Clark, 2010.

Landgraf, Paul David. "The Structure of Hebrews: A Word of Exhortation in Light of the Day of Atonement." Pages 19–27 in *A Cloud of Witnesses: A Theology of Hebrews in its Ancient Contexts*. Edited by Richard Bauckham, Trevor Hart, Nathan MacDonald, and Daniel Driver. The Library of New Testament Studies 387. London: T&T Clark, 2008.

Lane, William L. *Hebrews 1–8*. Word Biblical Commentary 47A. Nashville: Thomas Nelson, 1991.

Larmour, David H. J. "Making Parallels: Synkrisis and Plutarch's 'Themistocles and Camillus'." *ANRW* 33.6: 4154–4200. Part 2, *Principat*, 33.6. Edited by H. Temporini and W. Haase. New York: de Gruyter, 1992.

Lausberg, Heinrich. *Handbook of Literary Rhetoric: A Foundation for Literary Study*. Edited by David Orton and R. Dean Anderson. Translated by Matthew Bliss, Annemiek Jansen, and David Orton. Leiden: Brill, 1998.

Lehne. Susanne. *The New Covenant in Hebrews*. Journal for the Study of the New Testament Supplement Series 44. Sheffield: Sheffield Academic Press, 1990.

Levenson, Jon D. *The Death and Resurrection of the Beloved Son: The Transformation of Child Sacrifice in Judaism and Christianity*. New Haven: Yale University Press, 1993.

Lincoln, Andrew. *Hebrews: A Guide*. London: T&T Clark, 2006.

Lindars, Barnabas. "The Rhetorical Structure of Hebrews." *New Testament Studies* 35 (1989): 382–406.

Lindsay, William. *Lectures on the Epistle to the Hebrews*. Edinburgh: William Oliphant, 1867.

Loader, William R. G. *Sohn und Hoherpriester: Eine traitionsgeschichtliche Untersuchung zur Christologie des Hebräerbriefes*. Wissenschaftliche Monographien zum Alten und Neuen Testament 53. Neukirchen-Vluyn: Neukirchener, 1981.

Löhr, Hermut. "Reflections of Rhetorical Terminology in Hebrews." Pages 199–210 in *Hebrews: Contemporary Methods—New Insights*. Edited by Gabriella Gelardini. Biblical Interpretation Series 75. Atlanta: SBL, 2005.

Long, Frederick J. *Ancient Rhetoric and Paul's Apology: The Compositional Unity of 2 Corinthians*. Society for New Testament Studies Monograph Series 131. Cambridge: Cambridge University Press, 2004.

Longenecker, Richard N. *Biblical Exegesis in the Apostolic Period*. Grand Rapids: Eerdmans, 1975.

Lünnemann, Gottlieb. *Handbuch über den Hebräerbrief*. Göttingen: Vandenhoeck and Ruprecht, 1864.

Martin, Michael. *Judas and the Rhetoric of Syncrisis in the Fourth Gospel*. Sheffield: Sheffield Phoenix, 2010.

———. "The Poetry of the Lord's Prayer: A Study in Poetic Device." *Journal of Biblical Literature* 134 (2015): 347–372.

———. "Progymnastic Topic Lists: A Compositional Template for Luke and Other *Bioi*?" *New Testament Studies* 54 (2008): 18–41.

Martin, Michael, and Bryan Nash. "Philippians 2:6–11 as Subversive *Hymnos*: A Study in Light of Ancient Rhetorical Theory." *Journal of Theological Studies* 66 (2015): 90–138.

Martin, Michael, and Jason Whitlark. "Choosing What Is Advantageous: The Relationship between Epideictic and Deliberative Syncrisis in Hebrews." *New Testament Studies* 58 (2012): 379–400.

———. "The Encomiastic Topics of Syncrisis as the Key to the Structure and Argument of Hebrews." *New Testament Studies* 57 (2011): 415–439.

Martin, Troy W., ed. *Genealogies of New Testament Rhetorical Criticism*. Minneapolis: Fortress, 2014.

———. "Invention and Arrangement in Recent Pauline Studies: A Survey of the Practices and the Problems." Pages 48–118 in *Paul and the Ancient Letter Form*. Edited by Stanley E. Porter and Sean A. Adams. Pauline Studies 6. Leiden: Brill, 2010.

Mason, Eric F. *"You Are a Priest Forever": Second Temple Jewish Messianism and the Priestly Christology of the Epistle to the Hebrews*. Studies on the Texts of the Desert of Judah 74. Leiden: Brill, 2008.

Meier, J. P. "Symmetry and Theology in the Old Testament Citations in Heb 1,5–14." *Biblica* 66 (1985): 504–533.

Michel, Otto. *Der Brief an die Hebräer. Übersetzt und erklärt*. Kritisch-exegetischer Kommentar über das Neue Testament 12. Göttingen: Vandenhoeck & Ruprecht, 1966.

Mitchell, Alan C. *Hebrews*. Sacra Pagina 13. Collegeville: Liturgical Press, 2009.

Moffatt, James. *A Critical and Exegetical Commentary on the Epistle to the Hebrews*. International Critical Commentary. Edinburgh: T&T Clark, 1979.

Moffitt, David M. *Atonement and the Logic of Resurrection in the Epistle to the Hebrews*. Supplements to Novum Testamentum 141. Leiden: Brill, 2011.

"But We Do See Abel: Hebrews and the Depiction of Abel's Sacrifice in Some Mosaics of Ravenna." Paper presented at the annual meeting of SBL, San Antonio, TX, 21 November 2016.

Murphy, James Jerome. *Rhetorical Theory from Saint Augustine to the Renaissance*. Berkeley: University of California Press, 1974.

Murphy-O'Connor, Jerome. *Paul the Letter Writer: His World, His Options, His Skills*. Good News Studies 41. Collegeville: Michael Glazier, 1995.

Nauck, Wolfgang. "Zum Aufbau des Hebräerbriefes." Pages 199–206 in *Judentum, Urchristentum, Kirche, Festschrift für Joachim Jeremias*. Edited by Walter Eltester. Beihefte zur Zeitschrift für die neutestamentliche Wissenschaft 26. Berlin: Alfred Töpelmann, 1960.

Neeley, Linda L. "A Discourse Analysis of Hebrews." *Occasional Papers in Translation and Textlinguistics* 3–4 (1987): 1–146.

Neyrey, Jerome H. "Encomion Versus Vituperation: Contrasting Portraits of Jesus in the Fourth Gospel." *Journal of Biblical Literature* 126 (2007): 529–552.

Nissilä, Keijo. *Das Hohepriestermotiv im Hebräerbrief: Eine Exegetische Untersuchung*. Schriften der Finnischen Exegetischen Gesellschaft 33. Helsinki: Oy Liiton Kirjapaino, 1979.

O'Brien, Peter. *The Letter to the Hebrews*. Pillar New Testament Commentary. Grand Rapids: Eerdmans, 2010.

Olbricht, Thomas H. "Anticipating and Presenting the Case for Christ as High Priest in Hebrews." Pages 355–372 in *Rhetorical Argumentation in Biblical Texts: Essays from the Lund 2000 Conference*. Edited by Anders Eriksson, Thomas H. Olbricht, and Walter Übelacker. Emory Studies in Early Christianity 8. Harrisburg: Trinity Press International, 2002.

"Hebrews as Amplification." Pages 375–387 in *Rhetoric and the New Testament: Essays from the 1992 Heidelberg Conference*. Edited by Stanley E. Porter and Thomas H. Olbricht. Journal for the Study of the New Testament Supplement Series 90. Sheffield: Sheffield Academic Press, 1993.

Oliver, J. H. "The Ruler Power: A Study of the Roman Empire in the Second Century after Christ through the Roman Oration of Aelius Aristides." *Transactions of the American Philosophical Society* 43/4 (1953): 871–1003.

Parsons, Mikeal C. *Acts*. Paideia. Grand Rapids: Baker, 2008.

Pelling, Christopher. *Plutarch and History: Eighteen Studies*. London: Duckworth, 2002.

Perlman, S. "The Historical Example, Its Use and Importance as Political Propaganda in the Attic Orators." Pages 150–166 in *Studies in History*. Edited by Alexander Fuks and Israel Halpern. Scripta Hierosolymitana 7. Jerusalem: Magnes, 1961.

Perry, Peter S. *The Rhetoric of Digressions: Revelation 7:1–17 and 10:1–11:13 and Ancient Communication.* Wissenschaftliche Untersuchungen zum Neuen Testament 2/268. Tübingen: Mohr Siebeck, 2009.

Peterson, David. *Hebrews and Perfection: An Examination of the Concept of Perfection in the 'Epistle to the Hebrews.'* Society for New Testament Studies Monograph Series 47. Cambridge: Cambridge University Press, 2005.

Pierce, Madison N. "Intra-Divine Discourse and the New Covenant in Hebrews: Subtext(s) in Hebrews 8–10." Paper presented at the annual meeting of SBL, San Antonio, TX, 21 November 2016.

Rissi, Mathias. *Die Theologie des Hebräerbriefs: Ihre Verankerung in der Situation des Verfassers und seiner Leser.* Wissenschaftliche Untersuchungen zum Neuen Testament 41. Tübingen: J. C. B. Mohr, 1987.

Robertson, John C. *The Gorgianic Figures in Early Greek Prose.* Baltimore: Friedenwald, 1893.

Rothschild, Clare K. *Hebrews as Pseudepigraphon: The History and Significance of the Pauline Attribution of Hebrews.* Wissenschaftliche Untersuchungen zum Neuen Testament 2/235. Tübingen: Mohr Siebeck, 2009.

Russell, D. A. *Plutarch.* New York: Charles Scribner's Son, 1973.

"On Reading Plutarch's Lives." Pages 73–98 in *Essays on Plutarch's Lives.* Edited by B. Scardigli. Oxford: Clarendon Press, 1995.

Sanders, Jack T. *The New Testament Christological Hymns: Their Historical Religious Background.* Society for New Testament Studies Monograph Series 15. Cambridge: Cambridge University, 1971.

Schaff, Philip, ed. *A Select Library of the Nicene and Post-Nicene Fathers of the Christian Church.* 14 vols. Grand Rapids: Eerdmans, 1889.

Schenck, Kenneth L. "A Celebration of the Enthroned Son: The Catena of Hebrews 1." *Journal of Biblical Literature* 120 (2001): 469–485.

Cosmology and Eschatology in Hebrews: The Settings of Sacrifice. Society for New Testament Studies Monograph Series 143. Cambridge: Cambridge University Press, 2007.

"Keeping His Appointment: Creation and Enthronement in Hebrews." *Journal for the Study of the New Testament* 66 (1997): 91–117.

"The Worship of Jesus among Early Christians: The Evidence from Hebrews." Pages 114–126 in *Jesus and Paul: Global Perspectives in Honor of James D. G. Dunn on His 70th Birthday.* Edited by B. J. Oropeza, C. K. Robertson, and Douglas C. Mohrmann. The Library of New Testament Studies 414. London: T&T Clark, 2009.

Schnelle, Udo. "Das frühe Christentum und die Bildung." *New Testament Studies* 61 (2015): 113–143.

Schunack, Gerd. *Der Hebräerbrief.* Zürcher Bibelkommentare Neuen Testament 14. Zürich: Theologischer Verlag Zürich, 2002.

Seid, Timothy W. "Synkrisis in Hebrews 7: Rhetorical Structure and Analysis." Pages 322–347 in *The Rhetorical Interpretation of Scripture: Essays from the 1996 Malibu Conference.* Edited by Stanley E. Porter and Dennis L. Stamps. Sheffield: Sheffield Academic Press, 1999.

Siegert, Folker. "Homily and Panegyrical Sermon." Pages 421–443 in *Handbook of Classic Rhetoric in the Hellenistic Period (330 B.C.–A.D. 400)*. Edited by Stanley Porter. Leiden: Brill, 1997.

Sheerin, Daniel. "Rhetorical and Hermeneutic *Synkrisis* in Patristic Typology." Pages 22–39 in *Nova & Vetera Patristic Studies in Honor of Thomas Patrick Halton*. Edited by John Petruccione. Washington D. C.: Catholic University Press, 1998.

Small, Brian C. *The Characterization of Jesus in the Book of Hebrews*. Biblical Interpretation Series 128. Leiden: Brill, 2014.

Solmsen, Friedrich. "The Aristotelian Tradition in Ancient Rhetoric." *American Journal of Philology* 62 (1941): 35–50, 169–190.

Son, Kiwoong. *Zion Symbolism in Hebrews: Hebrews 12:18–24 as a Hermeneutical Key to the Epistle*. Paternoster Biblical Monographs. Milton Keys: Paternoster, 2005.

Spicq, Ceslas. *L'Épître aux Hébreux*. 2 vols. Echter Bibel. Paris: J. Gabalda, 1952-1953.

Standaert, Benoît. *L'évangile selon Marc: Composition et genre littéraire*. Nijmegen: Stichting Studentenpers, 1978.

Stanley, Steve. "The Structure of Hebrews from Three Perspectives." *Tyndale Bulletin* 45 (1994): 245–71.

Steel, Catherine. "Divisions of Speech." Pages 77–91 in *A Cambridge Companion to Ancient Rhetoric*. Edited by Erik Gunderson. Cambridge: Cambridge University Press, 2009.

Stegemann, Ekkehard W., and Wolfgang Stegemann. "Hebrews and the Discourse of Judeophobia." Pages 357–69 in *Hebrews in Contexts*. Edited by Gabriella Gelardini and Harold W. Attridge. *Ancient Judaism and Early Christianity 91*. Leiden: Brill, 2016.

Stegner, William Richard. "The Ancient Jewish Synagogue Homily." Pages 51–69 in *Greco-Roman Literature and the New Testament*. Edited by David E. Aune. Society of Biblical Literature Sources for Biblical Study 21. Atlanta: Scholars, 1988.

Stermberger, Gunter. "Response." Pages 45–48 in *Preaching in Judaism and Early Christianity: Encounters and Developments from Biblical Times to Modernity*. Edited by Alexander Deeg, Walter Homolka, and Heinz-Günther Schöttler. Studia Judaica 41. Berlin: De Gruyter, 2008.

"The Derashah in Rabbinic Times." Pages 7–21 *Preaching in Judaism and Early Christianity: Encounters and Developments from Biblical Times to Modernity*. Edited by Alexander Deeg, Walter Homolka, and Heinz-Günther Schöttler. Studia Judaica 41. Berlin: de Gruyter, 2008.

Stewart-Sykes, Alistair. *From Prophecy to Preaching: A Survey for the Origins of the Christian Homily*. Vigiliae Christianae Supplements 59. Leiden: Brill, 2001.

The Lamb's High Feast: Melito, Peri Pascha and the Quartodeciman Paschal Liturgy at Sardis. Vigiliae Christianae Supplements 42. Leiden: Brill, 1998.

Svartvik, Jesper. "Stumbling Block or Stepping Stone? On the Reception History of Hebrews 8:13." Pages 316–342 in *Hebrews in Contexts*. Edited by Gabriella Gelardini and Harold W. Attridge. Ancient Judaism and Early Christianity 91. Leiden: Brill, 2016.

Swetnam, James. *Jesus and Isaac: A Study of the Epistle to the Hebrews in the Light of the Aqedah*. Analecta Biblica 94. Rome: Biblical Institute, 1981.

Talbert, Charles H. *Reading Corinthians: A Literary and Theological Commentary*. Rev. ed. Macon, GA: Smyth & Helwys, 2002.

Reading John: A Literary and Theological Commentary on the Fourth Gospel and the Johannine Epistles. Rev. ed. Macon: Smyth & Helwys, 2005.

Romans. Macon: Smyth & Helwys, 2002.

"The Way of the Lukan Jesus: Dimensions of Lukan Spirituality." *Perspectives in Religious Studies* 9 (1982): 237–49.

Talbert, Charles H., and Jason Whitlark. *Getting "Saved": The Whole Story of Salvation in the New Testament*. Grand Rapids: Eerdmans, 2011.

Thiessen, Matthew. "Hebrews 12.5–13, the Wilderness Period, and Israel's Discipline." *New Testament Studies* 55 (2009): 366–379.

Thompson, James W. "Argument and Persuasion in the Epistle to the Hebrews." *Perspectives in Religious Studies* 39 (2012): 361–377.

The Beginnings of Christian Philosophy: The Epistle to the Hebrews. Catholic Biblical Quarterly Monograph Series 13. Washington D.C.: Catholic Biblical Association of America, 1982.

Hebrews. Paideia. Grand Rapids: Baker, 2008.

Thurén, Lauri. "The General New Testament Writings." Pages 587–607 in *Handbook of Classical Rhetoric in the Hellenistic Period, 330 B.C.– A.D. 400*. Edited by Stanley Porter. Leiden: Brill, 1997.

Thyen, Hartwig. *Der Stil der jüdisch-hellenistischen Homilie. Forschungen zur Religion und Literatur des Alten und Neuen Testaments*. Göttingen: Vandenhoeck & Ruprecht, 1955.

Übelacker, Walter G. *Der Hebräerbrief als Appell: Untersuchungen zu* exordium, narratio, *und* postscriptum *(Hebr 1–2 und 13, 22–25)*. Coniectanea Biblica: New Testament Series 21. Stockholm: Almqvist & Wiksell International, 1989.

"Hebrews and the Implied Author's Rhetorical Ethos." Pages 316–334 in *Rhetoric, Ethic, and Moral Persuasion in Biblical Discourse: Essays from the 2002 Heidelberg Conference*. Edited by Thomas H. Olbricht and Anders Eriksson. Emory Studies in Early Christianity 11. London: T&T Clark, 2005.

Usher, Stephen. "Symbouleutic Oratory." Pages 220–235 in *A Companion to Greek Rhetoric*. Edited by Ian Worthington. Blackwell Companions to the Ancient World. Malden: Blackwell, 2007.

Vaganay, Leon. "La plan de l'Épître aux Hébreux." Pages 269–277 in *Memorial Lagrange*. Edited by L.-H. Vincent. Paris: J. Gabalda, 1940.

Vanhoye, Albert. *A Structured Translation of the Epistle to the Hebrews*. Translated by James Swetnam. Subsidia Biblica 12. Rome: Pontifical Biblical Institute, 1964.

La Structure littéraire de l'Épître aux Hébreux. 2nd ed. Paris: Desclée de Brouwer, 1976.

La Structure littéraire de l'Épitre aux Hébreux. Paris: Desclée de Brouwer, 1963.

Visotzky, Burton L. "Midrash, Christian Exegesis and the Hellenistic Hermeneutic." Pages 111–131 in *Current Trends in the Study of Midrash*. Edited by C. Bakhos. Supplements to the Journal for the Study of Judaism 106. Leiden: Brill, 2006.

von Soden, Hermann. *Hebräerbrief, Briefe des Petrus, Jakobus, Judas*. Hand-Commentar zum neuen Testament 3. Tubingen: Mohr, 1899.

von Stockhausen, Annette. "Christian Perception of Jewish Preaching in Early Christianity?" Pages 49–70 in *Preaching in Judaism and Early Christianity: Encounters and Developments from Biblical Times to Modernity*. Edited by Alexander Deeg, Walter Homolka, and Heinz-Günther Schöttler. Studia Judaica 41. Berlin: de Gruyter, 2008.

Wardman, A. *Plutarch's Lives*. Berkeley: University of California Press, 1974.

Wedderburn, A. J. M. "The 'Letter' to the Hebrews and Its Thirteenth Chapter." *New Testament Studies* 50 (2004): 390–405.

Weiss, Hans-Friedrich. *Der Brief an die Hebräer*. Kritisch-exegetischer Kommentar über das Neue Testament 15. Göttingen: Vandenhoeck & Ruprecht, 1991.

Westfall, Cynthia L. *A Discourse Analysis of the Letter to the Hebrews: The Relationship between Form and Meaning*. The Library of New Testament Studies 297. London: T&T Clark, 2005.

Whitfield, Bryan J. *Joshua Traditions and the Argument of Hebrews 3 and 4*. Beihefte zur Zeitschrift für die neutestamentliche Wissenschaft 194. Berlin: De Gruyter, 2013.

Whitlark, Jason A. "Cosmology and the Perfection of Humanity in Hebrews." Pages 117–130 in *Interpretation and the Claims of the Text: Resourcing New Testament Theology*. Edited by Jason A. Whitlark, Bruce W. Longenecker, Lidija Novakovic, and Mikeal C. Parsons. Waco: Baylor University Press, 2014.

Enabling Fidelity to God: Perseverance in Hebrews in Light of the Reciprocity Systems of the Ancient Mediterranean World. Paternoster Biblical Monographs. Milton Keyes: Paternoster Press, 2009.

"Fidelity and New Covenant Enablement in Hebrews." Pages 72–91 in Charles H. Talbert and Jason A. Whitlark, *Getting "Saved": The Whole Story of Salvation in the New Testament*. Grand Rapids: Eerdmans, 2011.

"The God of Peace and His Victorious King: Hebrews 13:20–21 and Its Roman Imperial Context." Pages 155–178 in *Hebrews in Contexts*. Edited by Harold W. Attridge and Gabriella Gelardini. Ancient Judaism and Early Christianity 91. Leiden: Brill, 2016.

Resisting Empire: Rethinking the Purpose of the Letter to "the Hebrews." The Library of New Testament Studies 484. London: T&T Clark, 2014.

"The Warning against Idolatry: An Intertextual Examination of Septuagintal Warnings in Hebrews." *Journal for the Study of the New Testament* 34 (2012): 382–401.

Wills, Lawrence. "The Form of the Sermon in Hellenistic Judaism and Early Christianity." *Harvard Theological Review* 77 (1984): 277–283.

Windisch, Hans. *Der Hebräerbrief: Handbuch zum Neuen Testament*. Tübingen: J.C.B. Mohr (Paul Siebeck), 1931.

Witherington, Ben. *Letters and Homilies for Jewish Christians: A Socio-Rhetorical Commentary on Hebrews, James, and Jude.* Downers Grove: InterVarsity Press, 2007.

The Indelible Image: The Theological and Ethical Thought World of the New Testament, Vol. 2: The Collective Witness. Downers Grove: Inter-Varsity Press, 2010.

Wuellner, Wilhelm. "Arrangement." Pages 51–87 in *Handbook of Classical Rhetoric in the Hellenistic Period (330 B.C.–A.D. 400).* Edited by Stanley E. Porter. Leiden: Brill, 1997.

Zimmerman, Heinrich. *Das Bekenntnis der Hoffnung: Tradition und Redaktion im Hebräerbrief.* Boner biblische Beiträge. Koeln: Peter Hanstein Verlag, 1977.

Zoido, Juan Carlos Iglesias. "The Battle Exhortation in Ancient Rhetoric." *Rhetorica* 25 (2007): 141–158.

SCRIPTURE INDEX

Genesis
  2, *120*
  4:10, *70*
  14:17–20, 164
  15:4–5, 63
  21:12, 63
  22, *65*
  22:16–17, *62*, 63
  22:17, 65

Exodus
  15, *50*
  15:17–18, *50*
  19, *266*
  24:8, *172*
  25:40, 169
  34:9, 269

Leviticus
  2:1, *64*
  2:4, *64*
  2:11, *64*
  2:14, *64*
  7:8, *64*
  7:29, *64*
  7:33, *64*
  21:6, *64*

Numbers
  12:7, 38, 161
  14:4, 269
  14:33, 269
  19:1–6, *232*

Deuteronomy
  4:11, 50
  5:22, 50
  6:13–15, 268
  17:2–6, *66*

28:17, *236*
32:35–36, *124*

Joshua
  24:15, 268

1 Maccabees
  4:56, *64*
  7:33, *64*
  12:11, *64*

Psalms
  2:7, 36
  8, *6*, *61*, 110–11
  8:5–7 (LXX), 37
  18:49 (LXX), *231*
  39:7–9 (LXX), 175, 179
  94 (LXX), *118*, *120*
  94:7b–11 (LXX), *9*
  96 (LXX), *35*
  109 (LXX), 164
  109:1 (LXX), *2*, 169, 176
  109:4 (LXX), *2*, *62*, 63, 65, 165
  109:4b (LXX), 166

Wisdom of Solomon
  13:10, 268
  15:17, 268

Isaiah
  26:20, *125*
  53:12, 175

Jeremiah
  38 (LXX), 169
  38:31–34 (LXX), *2*, *9*, 33, 169
  38:33–34 (LXX), 176
  38:34 (LXX), 269
  38:38–40 (LXX), 169

Ezekiel
  36:25–27, *269*

Habakkuk
  2:3–4, *125*

Matthew
  3:11–12, *39*
  10:32, *231*

Mark
  1:7–8, *39*

Luke
  2:40–52, 42
  3:16–17, *39*
  12:8, *231*

John
  1:15, *39*
  1:26–34, *39*
  5:19–21, 42
  7:16–18, 42
  12:47–50, 42

Acts
  5:42, *61*
  13, 11
  13:6b, 11
  13:6b–41, 11
  13:14–41, 11
  13:15–41, 260
  13:17–25, 11
  13:26–27, 11
  13:33, 36
  13:38–41, 11
  14:22, 258, 262

Romans
  11:17, *266*

1 Corinthians
  4:14, 261
  5:1–6:11, 261
  5:9, 261
  7:1, 261
  10, *269*
  10:1, *266*
  10:7, *269*
  14:26–33, 260

2 Corinthians
  3:1–18, 33
  9:1–5, 261

Philippians
  2:6, 214
  2:6–11, 214
  2:25–30, 261

Colossians
  1:15, 214
  4:16, 261

1 Thessalonians
  2:17–3:13, 261
  5:27, 261

1 Timothy
  3:16, 214
  4:11, 260

Hebrews
  1–2, *198*, 214
  1:1–2, *61*
  1:1–4, 3, 16, *17*, 18, *75*, 138, 191, 193,
    197–99, 201, *201*, 207, 214, 217–18,
    220, 252, 255
  1:1–14, 257
  1:1–2:4, 17–18
  1:1–2:18, 3, 17–18
  1:1–4:13, 2, 15, 18
  1:2b, 214
  1:3, 210, 212, 214
  1:3–4, 210, *210*, 211, 213–14
  1:4, *107*, 201, 212, 214
  1:4–2:4, 201
  1:5, *36*, 138, 149, 151, 161, 210, 214, *253*
  1:5–14, 30, *35*, 36–37, 51–52, 60–61,
    68, 75, 107, 109, 111–13, 117,
    129–30, 133, 149, 151, 160, 191, 201,
    207, 209, *210*
  1:5–2:4, 266
  1:5–2:9, 48
  1:5–2:18, 3, 16, 18, *138*
  1:5–4:13, 17–18, *138*
  1:5–6:20, 16, 18
  1:5–12:17, *17*, 18
  1:5–13:16, *17*, 18
  1:6, *35–36*, 36, 110, 149, 161
  1:7, 151
  1:7–8, *209*
  1:7–9, 149, 161
  1:10–12, 149, 161, 230
  1:13, 151
  1:13–14, 149, 161
  1:14, 151
  2:1, 61, 109, 113, 115–17, *127*, *253*,
    262

Hebrews (cont.)
2:1–4, *14*, 17, 35, 37, 70, *107*, 109–12, 114, *127*, 201, 230, 267
2:1–18, 76, 86, 106–7, 109, 114, 117, *127*, 129, 255
2:2, 112
2:2–3, 60, 107
2:2–3a, 109
2:2–4, 58, 60, 107–8, 111, 114, 117
2:3, 113, *198*, 259
2:3–4, 35, 37, 111, 114
2:5, 35, 111, 259, 262
2:5–8, 110
2:5–9, *6*, *14*, 17–18, 112, 244
2:5–16, *138*
2:5–18, 18, 37, 110–13, 117, 257
2:6, 35, *164*
2:7–9, 36
2:9, 111–12
2:10, 61, 110, 259
2:10–12, 36
2:10–13, 111
2:10–5:10, 17
2:10–6:20, *32*
2:10–12:27, 17–18
2:13–14, 37
2:14–15, 111
2:16, 110
2:17–18, 16, 18
2:18, 201
3, *6*
3:1, 138, 152, *253*
3:1–6, 16, 30, 38, 51–52, 60–61, 68, 76, 117, *127*, 129–30, 133, *151*, 151, 160, 191
3–4, 269
3:1–4:13, 18, 218, 266
3:1–4:14, 3
3:1–6:20, 3
3:1–12:29, 16–18
3:2, 38, *152*, 161
3:2–6, 265
3:3, *152*, *161*
3:3–4, 38, 161
3:4a, *152*
3:4b, *152*
3:5, *50*, 61, 161, 184
3:5–6, *162*
3:6, *152*, 162
3:7, 71, 109, 115, *198*, *253*
3:7–4:1, *58*
3:7–4:11, 71, 76

3:7–4:13, 86, 106, 114–15, 117, *127*, 129, 255
3:7–8, 71
3:7a, 117
3:7b–11, 118, *118*
3:8, 71
3:11, 114
3:12, 71, 115, *118*, 269
3:12–13, 116, 118, 234
3:13, 71, 115, *118*, 231
3:14–15, *107–8*, 114, 119
3:15, 71, 114
3:16, 61
3:16–19, *107*, *118*, 118
3:17, 269
3:18, 114
4, *6*
4:1, 61, 71, 114–15, 118, *120*, 259, 262
4:1–2, 71
4:2, *50*, 58, 60–61, *61*, 71, *107*, 108, 119, 266–67
4:2–3, *58*
4:2–3a, *118*
4:2–10, *118*
4:3, *61*, *107*, 114
4:3–6, 48
4:3a, *119*, 119
4:3b–5, *120*
4:3b–10, *118*, *120*
4:4, 114
4:5, 114
4:6–8, *120*
4:6–10, *120*
4:7, 114
4:9–10, *120*
4:11, 71, 115, 118, 262
4:12–13, *107*, 119
4:13, 201
4:14, 262
4:14–5:10, *41*
4:14–6:20, 15, 18
4:14–10:18, 17–18
4:14–10:31, 2, 18
4:14–16, 2, 17–18, 39, 72, *75*, *116*, 193, 215, *216*, 217–20, 225, 233–34, 252, 255
4:14a, 216
4:14b, 216
4:15, 65, 73, 216
4:15–5:10, 3
4:16, 216, 219, 262
5–6, 187–88
5:1, 41, 138, *253*

5:1–3, 41, *162*, 220
5:1–10, 30, 40–41, 51–52, 60, 62, 68,
  72, 76, 120, 129, 133, 152, 160,
  186–88, 191, 215–16, 219–20, 257,
  266
5:1–11, 232
5:1–6:20, 225, 248
5:1–10:18, *41*
5:1–12:13, 215, 225
5:1–12:29, 232
5:4a, 41, *162*
5:4b, 41, *162*
5:5, 42, 162
5:5–6, 64
5:5–7, 65
5:5a, 41, *162*
5:5b, 41, *162*
5:6, 41–42, *63*, 65, 162, *162*
5:6–10, 65, 73
5:7, 41, 65, 162
5:7–10, 31, 41, *162*
5:7a, 41, *162*
5:7b, 41, *162*
5:8, 41, 43–44, *162*, 162
5:8–10, 43, 220
5:9, 44
5:9–10, 41–42, *162*, 163
5:10, 44, 188
5:11, 5, *191*, 262
5:11–14, 72, *120*, 185–88
5:11–6:1, 31
5:11–6:12, *72*
5:11–6:20, 3, *14*, 16–17, *16*, 40, 71, *71*,
  76, 86, 106, 114, 116, *127*, 129–30,
  188, 215–16, 219, 255
5:11–6.20, 120
6:1, 230, *253*, 262, 268
6:1–2, 109, 115, 120
6:1–10, 187
6:1–20, 73, 186
6:4–6, *107–8*, 121, 186, 231, 235
6:7–8, *107*, 121
6:9, 262
6:9–12, 116, 121
6:10, *110*, 231
6:11–12, 59
6:11–20, 187
6:12, 62, 73, 230, 259
6:13–14, 65
6:13–15, 65
6:13–15a, 65
6:13–16, *63*
6:13–18, 108, 114

6:13–20, 58–60, 62, *107*, 122
6:15, 62
6:15b, 65
6:17, *62*
6:17–18, 65
6:18, *62*
6:19–20, 48, 234
6:20, *63*
7, 46
7:1, 138, *253*
7:1–2a, 164
7:1–10, 45, 64, 164
7:1–24, 163, 166
7:1–28, 3, *41*
7:1–9:10, 173
7:1–9:23, 176
7:1–10:18, 3, 16, 19, 30, 40, 44, 51–52,
  60, 66, 68, 76, 122, 129–30, 133, 152,
  160, 163, 191, 215–16, 232, 257
7:1–10:25, 17
7:1–10:39, *32*
7:1–12:13, 16, 19, 225, 248
7:2b–3, 164
7:4–10, 165
7:5, 164–65
7:6, 164–65
7:8, 184
7:8a, 164–65
7:8b, 164–65
7:11, 48, 152, 165
7:11–12, 184
7:11–14, 165
7:11–19, 45, 164, *165*
7:11–25, 65
7:14, 165
7:15–17, 165
7:16, *176*
7:16–21, 184
7:17, 184
7:17–25, 65
7:18, 164
7:18–19, 165
7:19, 164
7:20, 164
7:20–21, 166
7:20–22, 45, 164
7:21, *63*, 164
7:22, *69*, 166, 184
7:23, 164
7:23–24, 45, 166
7:24, 164
7:25, 166–67
7:25–28, 45, 163, 166–67

Hebrews (cont.)
7:25–10:18, *44*, 45, 163, *176*
7:26, *167*
7:26–28, 166
7:26a, 167
7:26b, 167
7:27a, 168
7:27b, 168
7:27c, 168
7:27d, 168
7:27e, 168
7:27f, 168
7:27g, 168
7:28, 66, *167*, 168, 184, 230
8, *3*, 34, 169
8:1, *167*, 169, 262
8:1–2, 168
8:1–5, 168, 170
8:1–10:18, *41*, 167, *167*
8:1–13, 45, 163, 168, 170, *176*
8:1–9:28, 3
8:1a, 170
8:1b, 170
8:1c, 170
8:2a, 170
8:2b, 170
8:3, 168, 170
8:3–5, 168
8:4–5, 168, 170
8:4–6, 169
8:6, *38*, *69*, 184
8:6–13, 168, 170, 184
8:7, 168, *171*, 173
8:7–13, *4*
8:7–9, *171*
8:8–12, 33
8:9, 184
8:13, *171*
8:15, 184
9, 232
9:1, *170–71*, *173*, 184
9:1–7, 171, *173*
9:1–5, 171
9:1–8, *171*
9:1–10, 45, 163
9:1–10:18, 170
9:2–3, *171*
9:5, 262
9:6, *171*
9:6a, 171
9:6b, 172
9:6c, 172
9:6d, 172
9:7, *168*, *171*

9:7–8, 171
9:7a, 172
9:7b, 172
9:7c, 172
9:7d, 172
9:8–10, *171*, 171, 172
9:9, 173
9:9–10, 171
9:10, *170*, 173
9:11, *61*, *171*, 173
9:11–10:18, 171
9:11–12, *173*
9:11–14, 100, *171*, 172–73
9:11–23, 45, 163
9:12, *168*
9:12a, 173
9:12b, 173
9:12c, 173
9:12d, 173
9:12e, 173
9:13–14, 172, 184
9:13a, 173
9:13b, 174
9:14, *58*, 66, *176*, 269
9:14a, 174
9:14b, 174
9:15, *38*, *171*, 184, 259, 266
9:15–23, 172, 174
9:16–21, 184
9:18, *171*
9:18–21, *38*, *69*
9:19–22, 184
9:20, 66
9:22, 173
9:23, *174*
9:24–25, *168*
9:24–26, 175
9:24–28, *174*
9:24–10:14, 176
9:24–10:18, 45, 163, 173–74, 176
9:24a, 176
9:24b, 176
9:24c, 176
9:25a, 177
9:25b, 177
9:25c, 177
9:25d, 177
9:25e, 177
9:25f, 177
9:25g, 177
9:26, 174
9:26a, 175, 177
9:26b, 177
9:26c, 177

9:26d, 177
9:26e, 177
9:27–10:14, 175
9:27a, 177
9:27b, 177
9:27c, 177
9:27d, 177
9:28, *61*, 174–75
9:28a, 177
9:28b, 177
9:28c, 178
9:28d, 178
10, *248*
10:1, 39, *61*
10:1–3, *178*
10:1–4, 184
10:1–14, 175
10:1–18, 3
10:1a, 178
10:1b, 178
10:1c, 178
10:2a, 178
10:2b, 179
10:2c, 179
10:2d, 179
10:3, 174
10:3a, 179
10:3b, 179
10:4, 174
10:4–10, *178*
10:4a, 179
10:4b, 179
10:5–10, 175
10:5a, 179
10:5b–9, 179
10:10a, 179
10:10b, 179
10:11, 174
10:11–14, *178*
10:11a, 180
10:11b, 180
10:11c, 180
10:11d, 180
10:11e, 180
10:12, 174
10:12–13, 176
10:12a, 180
10:12b, 180
10:12c, 180
10:12d, 180
10:12e-13, 180
10:13, *180*
10:14a, 180
10:14b, 180

10:14c, 180
10:15–17, *176*, 184
10:15–18, 176, 180, 184
10:16, 184
10:17, 269
10:18, 174, *176*
10:19, *253*
10:19–20, 73
10:19–23, 2, 40, *216*
10:19–25, 116, 122, 216
10:19–39, 3
10:19–12:3, 3
10:19–12:13, 73, *116*, 116, 122, 129,
   215, 223, 225, 255
10:19–12:17, 76, 86, 106, 114, 216
10:19–13:21, 16–17, 222
10:19–13:21/25, 19
10:19–13:25, 18, 222
10:22, 73, 109, 115, 262
10:23, 73, *110*, 115, 262
10:24, 74, 262
10:24–25, 231
10:24–31, 234
10:25, 74, 115, 264
10:26, 66, 74
10:26–27, 74, *107–8*, 124
10:26–31, *124*
10:26–39, *14*, 17, *127*
10:28, 114, 268
10:28–29, 58–60, 66, 108, *124*, 124
10:28–30, 74
10:29, 58, 114
10:30, 114, *124*, *198*, 268
10:30–31, *107*, 124
10:31, *124*
10:32, *17*
10:32–34, 123, 230, 234
10:32–39, 74, *217*, 241
10:32–12:3, 232
10:32–13:17, 2
10:32–13:25, 19
10:33–34, 263
10:34, 259
10:35, 115, 123
10:36, 114
10:37–38, *125*, 268
10:37–39, *107*, 125
10:39, *125*
11, 234
11:1, 74, 125
11:1–39, 50
11:1–40, 3, 74, *217*
11:1–12:24, 17
11:1–12:27, *32*

Hebrews (cont.)
11:2, 114
11:2–38, *107*, 123
11:4, 114, *234*
11:8, *169*
11:8–22, *234*
11:9, 114
11:13, 114
11:13–14, 48
11:13–16, 48, 259
11:15–16, 50
11:16, 232
11:17, 65, 114
11:17–19, 63–65
11:18, 65
11:19, 63, 65
11:24–26, 269
11:26, 230
11:32, 262
11:35, 64
11:35b, 266
11:35–38, 230
11:36–37, 234
11:38, *234*
11:39–40, *125*, 265
11:40, 50
12:1, 114–15, 262
12:1–2, 123
12:1–3, *217*
12:1–13, 3, 74
12:2, 65
12:2–3, 74
12:3, *107*, 124
12:4–13:25, 3
12:5–6, 43, 115, *198*
12:5–7, 116
12:5–7a, 123
12:5–11, 67
12:5–13, 74
12:7, 115
12:7–8, 42
12:7b–11, *107*, 124
12:8–9, 43
12:9, 58–59, 67
12:12–13, 115, 123
12:14, 234, 240, 243, 245, *253*
12:14–13:19, 3
12:14–17, 39, *72, 75, 116*, 193, 219,
    223, 225, 233, 235, 239, 242–46,
    248–49, 252, 256–57
12:14–29, 16, 19
12:14a, 233
12:14b, 233
12:14c, 233

12:15, 233, *233*, 240, 245, 268
12:15–16, 242, 245
12:16, 230, 234, 245
12:17, *169*, 234, 240, 243
12:18, 138, *253*
12:18–21, 181
12:18–24, *4*, 30, 46, 51–52, 60, 66, 68,
    76, 125, 129–30, 133, 152, 160, 191,
    223
12:18–29, *4, 17,* 19
12:21, 50
12:22, 169, 232, 265
12:22–24, 48, 181
12:24, *38, 69–70*
12:24–29, 223
12:25, 58–60, 66, 100, *107*, 108–9, 115,
    125–26, *253*
12:25–27, *14*, 17, *127*
12:25–29, 74, 76, 86, 106, 114, 116,
    125, *127*, 129, 223, *243*, 255
12:26, 114
12:26–27, 49, 126
12:28, 115, 231, 259, 262
12:28–29, 126, *127*
12:28–13:21, 18–19
12:29, *110, 127, 249*, 268
13, *230*, 248–49
13:1, 228, 242–43, 245, *249, 253*
13:1–2, 240
13:1–5, 245
13:1–7, 242
13:1–9, 245
13:1–17, 241, 247
13:1–19, 16, 228–30, 233, 235, 240–41,
    242, 247
13:1–21, 16, *17*, 223, 228, 230, 252
13:1–21/25, 19
13:1–25, 17, *75*, 193, 223–25, 228, 230,
    235, 239, *240*, 241–42, 243–46, *243,
    247*, 248–49, 256–57
13:2, 242, 245
13:2a, 228
13:2b, 228
13:3, 228, 230, 240, 242, 244–45
13:4, 240, 242
13:4a, 228
13:4b, 228
13:5, 230, 242
13:5a, 228
13:5b–6, 228
13:6, 240
13:7, 228, 240, 242–43, 245
13:7–9, 231, 243, 246
13:8, 228, 242

13:9, 242, 245
13:9–10, 241
13:9a, 228
13:9b, 229
13:10, 229, 231, 242, 244
13:10–14, 231–32, 242–43, 246
13:10–16, *232*
13:11, 242
13:11–12, 229, 231
13:11–14, 235
13:12, 242
13:12–13, 244
13:13, 229, 231–32, 240, 242, 245, 262
13:14, 48–49, 229, 240, 242
13:15, *242*, 245, *245*, 262
13:15–16, 242
13:15–16a, 229
13:15–19, 245
13:16, *217*, *242*, 245
13:16b, 229
13:17, 242, 245
13:17–25, *17*
13:17a, 229
13:17b, 229
13:17c, 229

13:18, 245
13:18–19, 241–42, 247
13:18a, 229
13:18b, 229
13:19, *242*, 245
13:19a, 229
13:19b, 229
13:20, *35*, 36, *247*
13:20–21, 3, 228–29, 232, 241, 247
13:20–25, 16
13:22, 104, *198*, *223*, 228, 245, *247*,
  256, 261–62
13:22–25, 16, *17*, 18, *223*, 241, 247
13:23, 242
13:23–25, *223*
13:24a, 242
13:24b, 242
13:25, *17*, 242

1 Peter
  2:9, *266*

2 Peter
  2:4, 50
  2:17, 50

ANCIENT SOURCES INDEX

1 Clement
  36.1, *189*
  63.3, *189*
  64.1, *189*
2 Clement
  3.1, *268*

Aelius Aristides
  Roman Oration
    32–3, *30*
    36, *30*
    69, *48*
    72, *30*
    89, *48*
    90, *30*
    94–99, *48*
    103, *48*
    106, *48*
Aeschylus
  Ag.
    177, *43*
Aesop
  Fab.
    370, *43*
Alexander
  Fig.
    3.20.30, *205*
    3.29, *205*
Anaximenes of Lampsacus
  Rhet. Alex.
    1 [1421b], *87*, 262
    7 (1428a), *89*
    10 [1430a], *93*
    20 [1433b], 36
    20 [1434a], 235
    21 [1434a], *247*
    26 [1435b], 203
    26–28 [1435b–1436a], *201, 202*
    27 [1436a], *203*
    28 [1436a], *204*
    29, 193

29 [1436a–1438a], 195
30 [1438a], 152
31 [1438b.14–29], 137, 190
36 [1444b], 225, 227, *247*
Anonymous Seguerianus
  1, *126*, 261
  10–12, 195
  10–13, 196
  10–18, 193
  14–15, 196
  16–18, 195
  46, 140
  48, 140
  49, 140
  50, 140–41
  55, 145
  63, 188
  88, 189
  89–93, 158
  124–131, 136
  132–33, 137, 190
  145, *89*
  146, *90*
  157, 92
  160, 99, 132
  160–1, *83*
  163, 101
  171, 95
  174, *98*
  180, 97
  186, *81*
  198–99, 224
  203, 226
  210, 226
  211, 224
  214, 227
  219, 227, 247
  221, 227
  224, 237
  228, 237
  230, 98, 110, 130

Antiphon
On the Murder of Herodes
  85, *223*
Aphthonius
  22, 141
  35–36, *33*
  35–44, *212*
  36, *34*, *40*
  38, 30
  38–40, *33*
  39, 30
  40, *33*
  42, *33*, 46, *56*, *98*
  43, 25, 29
  44, 46
Apos. Con.
  8.5.12, *261*
Apsines
Rhet.
  2.1, 188
  2.3, *118*, 135, *151*
  2.7–8, 154
  2.28, *152*
  3.1, 141
  3.7, *161*
  3.10, *161*
  3.26, 143
  8.1 (285), *90*
  8.2 [285], 94
  8.10–24 [288–91], 94
  10.1, 225
  10.2, *226*
  10.3, 224
  10.4–13, 227
  10.32, 239
  10.55, 239, 243, 246
Apthonius
  22, 156
Aristotle
N.E.
  3.6–9, *240*
Rhet.
  1, *184*
  1.2.2 [1355b], 89
  1.2.3 [1355b], 261
  1.2.3–6 [1356a–b], 89
  1.2.8 [1356b], *93*
  1.2.8–9 [1356a–b], *90*
  1.2.13 [1357a], 93
  1.2.18 [1357b], 93
  1.2.22 [1358a], 261
  1.3.3 [1358b2], *143*
  1.3.5 [1358b], 55
  1.4.2 [1359a], *87*

1.5.5 [1360b], 29
1.5.6 [1360b], 29
1.9.40 [1368a], 94, 131, 255
1.15.2–3 [1375a], 89
1.15.13 [1375b], 108
2.1.2–3 [1377b], 238
2.1.3–4 [1377b], 238
2.2–11, *240*
2.2.11 [1379a], 186
2.5.16–22 [1383a–b], *240*
2.18.2–2.19.27 [1391b–1393a],
  95
2.18.5 [1392a], *95*
2.19.26 [1398a], 99
2.20.3–4 [1393a–b], 94
2.20.4 [1393b], 94
2.20.5 [1393b], 94
2.21.2 [1394a], *102*
2.21.2 [1394b], *93*
2.22.1–2 [1395b], 93
2.22.3 [1395b–1396a], 91
2.23.1–30 [1397a–1400b], 95
2.23.4 [1397b], 58, 97
2.23.4–6 [1397b], 56
2.23.5 [1397b], 93
2.26.1–2 [1403a], 99–100, *130*, *183*
3, *184*
3.1.1 [1403b], *89*
3.1.8–10 [1404a], *210*
3.3.4 [1407a], *210*
3.9 [1409a–1410b], *201*
3.9.1–2 [1409a], *202*
3.9.3–4, 20
3.9.5–6 [1409b], 206
3.9.7–10 [1409b–1410a], *202*
3.9.9 [1410a], *203–4*, 204–5
3.9.9 [1410b], 204
3.13.2–4 [1414a–b], *81*, *84*
3.13.3 [1414b], 224
3.13.4 [1414b], *80*, 223
3.13.4–5 [1414b], 81, 89
3.14.7 [1415a–b], 195
3.14.8 [1415b], 193
3.14.12 [1415b], 194, 196, *199*, 200,
  220, 255
3.16.1–2 [1416b], 136, 190
3.16.3 [1417b], *88*
3.16.11 [1417b], 14, 136, 143,
  254
3.17.1–16 [1417b–1418b], 89
3.17.3 [1417b], 131
3.17.5 [1418a], 94, 255
3.19.1 [1419b], 237
3.19.1–4 [1419b], 225

Aristotle (cont.)
    3.19.3 [1419b], 237
    3.19.4 [1419b], 226
    3.19.5 [1420a], 227
    3.19.6 [1430a], 224, 238
Arrian
  Anab.
    2.7.3, 240
    2.7.3–9, 105
Augustine
  De docrtina christiana, 264

Cicero
  Brut.
    33–34, *201, 202*
    149, *201*
    162, *201*
  Cael.
    3–69, 127
  Cat.
    1.10, 103
  De or.
    1.142, *5*
    1.143, *84*
    1.145, 12
    1.146, *7*
    2.114–15, *90*
    2.116, *89*
    2.128, *90*
    2.162–72, *96*
    2.167–72, 93
    2.172, 97
    2.178, 237
    2.307, *81*
    2.307–8, 12, 82
    2.310, *90*
    2.311–12, *126*, 236
    2.313–14, *5, 113*
    2.333, 238
    2.334, 55
    2.336, *87*
    2.337, 239, 255
    2.40.172, *56*
    2.79, *80*
    3.37, *5*
    3.184–7, 209
    3.184–92, *201*
    3.202, *262*
    3.205, *233*
  Dom.
    144–5, *233*
  Inv.
    1.19, *80*, 101
    1.20, 193–95

1.21, 193
1.22, 195
1.23, 196
1.23–25, 196
1.24.34, *29*, 46
1.27, 140, *141, 143*, 145, 157
1.28.41, *56*
1.28–29, 188
1.30, 137
1.34, 95, 157
1.34–36, *96, 212*
1.37–43, *96*
1.41, 97
1.49, *98*
1.51, 94
1.51–53, *118*
1.51–77, *89*, 90, *184*
1.57, 91–92
1.67, 92
1.68, 103
1.78, *81*
1.96, *87*
1.97, 111
1.98, 224–27
1.100, 99, 247
1.104, 239
1.109, 247
2.17.55, *56*
2.32–34, *96*
2.59.177, *29*, 39, 46
2.146, 55
2.156–76, *87*
2.163, 240
2.177, *96*
Leg. man.
  51–68, 126
Mil.
  32–91, 126
  72, 98
Or. Brut.
  108–211, *218*
  131, *237*
  138, *233*, 241
  174–6, *210*
  198–211, *206*
  198–221, *201*
  221–5, 206
Part. or.
  4, *80*
  11–15, 82
  27, 99, 132
  31, 140
  31–32, 188
  32, *184*

52, 224
52–57, 225
53, 98, *130*, *183*, 239
54, 238
55, 99
56, *240*
57, *248*
59, 228
71, 98–99, *130*,
　183
74, 5, 46
74–75, *29*
75, *167*
83–90, 55
Pro Caecin.
　1, *203*
Pro Cluentia
　117–8, 197
Pro Murena
　7, 197
Top.
　23, 56, 97, 107
　71, *96*
　97–8, *80*
　98, 237
Verr.
　5.26–8, *142*, 146

Demetrius
Eloc.
　1–2, 206
　1–35, *201*
　9, 206
　10–11, *202*
　12, *202*
　12–15, *210*
　15, *202*
　16–17, 206
　18, 209
　19–21, *206*
　22–3, *203*
　25, *203–4*
　30–3, *93*
　32, *93*
　243, 244
　287–98, 244
Demosthenes
2 Philip.
　16, *235*
Didache
　6.3, *261*
Dio Chrysostom
Or.
　4.26–31, 43

38.18, *234*
38.51, *233*
Diodorus Siculus
　12.53.4, *210*
Dionysius of Halicarnassus
Comp.
　2, *201*
　9, *201*
　22–23, *201*
　22–3, *218*
　23, *210*, *218*
　33, *202*
Dem.
　25, *210*
Is.
　19, *210*
Lys.
　2–3, *210*
Thuc.
　42, *240*

Epictetus
Diatr.
　1.4.1, 44
　1.4.4, 44
　1.4.18–21, 44
Eusebius
Hist. eccl.
　6.25.11–12, *83*
　6.25.11–13, 264

Fortun.
　2.20 [113, 25], 197

Homer
Il.
　9.526, *204*
Od.
　9.159–60, *47*
　20.356, *50*

Ignatius
Mag.
　4.1, *189*
　7.2, *189*
Phld.
　9.1, *189*
Isocrates
Or.
　1.11, *262*
Paneg.
　50, *266*
Soph.
　16–17, *5*

John Chrysostom
  Heb. Hom.
    1.2, *34*
    5.1–3, *34*
    8.1, *34*
    12.1, *34, 138*
    13.1, *34*
    13.5, *34*
    32.1, *34*
Josephus
  C. Ap.
    2.210, *266*
Jubilees
  17:16–17, *73*
  19:8, *73*
Justin Martyr
  Dia.
    33, *189*
    34, *189*
    36, *189*
    42, *189*
    86, *189*
    96, *189*
    113, *189*
    115, *189*
    116, *189*
    118, *189*

Libanius
  Prog., *33*
    249, *48*
Longinus
  [*Subl.*]
    20, 246
    21, 238
Lysias
  14.46, *223*

Martianus Capella
  45–54, 185
Melito
  Peri Pascha, 264
    1–10, *10*
    11–45, *10*
    34–43, *10*
    46–65, *10*
    66–105, *10*
Menander Rhetor
  346.26–367.8, *33*
  346–7, 29, *160*
  368, 212
  368–70, *34*
  368–77, 29, 38, 46, *212*
  373, *167*

Nicolaus
  11, 141
  11–12, 155
  13–14, 158
  15–16, *118*, 134,
    151
  15–17, 148
  47–63, *212*
  50, 28, *34*
  51, *28*, 29
  51–2, *38*, 38
  52, 39, *40*, *167*
  57, *33*
  59, 25
  60, *56*, *98*
  60–61, *33*
  61, 29

Philo
  Abr.
    168, *65*
  Fug.
    138, *43*
  Her
    73, *43*
  Leg.
    3.159, 44
  Mos.
    2.280, *43*
  Post.
    132, 44
  Somn.
    2.107, *43*
    2.234–5, 44
  Spec.
    4.29, *43*
  Virt.
    195, *266*
  Vita Pachomii
    2, 44
    28, 44
    43, 44
Polycarp
  Phil.
    12.2, *189*
Ps. Dionysius of Halicarnassus
  [*Rhet.*]
    8.9, *52*
Ps. Hermogenes
  4, 140, 155
  5, 147
  11, *87*
  15, *34*, 38, *38*
  16, 39, *40*, 44

16–17, *46*
16–19, 29, *160*
17–19, *33*
18–20, *212*
19, 29, 38, *46*, *56*, *98*
83, 29

Quintilian, *Inst.*
2.4.21, *25*
3.4.8, 257
3.7, 38, *160*
3.7.1–3, 144
3.7.1–6, 88, 131
3.7.1–7, 184
3.7.2, *143*
3.7.6, 130
3.7.7–9, 212
3.7.9, 212
3.7.10, *28*, *34*, 46, *46*
3.7.10–18, *29*
3.7.17–18, 46, *46*
3.7.24, *143*
3.7.26, *33*
3.7.26–28, 29
3.8.1–3, 55
3.8.8, 200, 220, 255
3.8.12, 237
3.8.12–13, 238
3.8.22–25, *87*, *109*
3.8.26–27, *87*
3.8.66, 94, 255
3.9.1, *80*
3.9.2–3, 80–81
3.9.5, *81*, *84*
3.9.6, 84
4–6, *5*
4.praef.6, *81*
4.1, 219
4.1.1, 194
4.1.1–5, 194, 255
4.1.2, *194*
4.1.5, 80, 193, 195
4.1.6–7, 195, 238
4.1.6–33, 195
4.1.8, *110*
4.1.25, 195
4.1.30, 196
4.1.31, 196
4.1.33, 199
4.1.33–9, 196
4.1.34, 196
4.1.40–41, 194
4.1.42, 195
4.1.44–50, 196

4.1.73–5, 197
4.1.75, *197*
4.1.76–77, 214
4.2.1, 139
4.2.2–3, 157
4.2.3, 153, 155
4.2.17–18, 145
4.2.19, 146
4.2.24–30, 136
4.2.31, 139
4.2.31–33, 188
4.2.36, 157
4.2.53–54, *126*
4.2.54–56, 182
4.2.79, 182
4.2.82, 137
4.2.85, 138
4.2.85–87, 137
4.2.86, 138
4.2.101, 137
4.2.108, 182
4.2.108–9, *126*
4.2.109–10, 183
4.3.1–13, 185
4.3.4–5, 187
4.3.5–6, 187
4.3.6, 185
4.3.9, 186
4.3.9–11, 197
4.3.11–12, 224
4.3.13–14, 185
4.3.14, 185–86
4.3.16, 186
4.3.129–131, 159
4.4.1, 80, 101–2
4.4.1–4.5.28, 83
4.4.5, 116
4.4.5–6, 116
4.4.5–7, 102
4.4.8, 102, 109, 115
5.praef.1–5, 90
5.praef.3–5, 131
5.praef.5, *81*, 84
5.1.1, *89*
5.1.1–7.37, *90*
5.1.2, *89–90*
5.7.35, 108
5.8.2, 84
5.8.5, 95
5.8.33, 97
5.10.1, *90*, *93*, 182
5.10.1–3, *184*
5.10.1–8, *93*
5.10.3, *93*

Quintilian, *Inst.* (cont.)
  5.10.8, 91
  5.10.11–12, 91
  5.10.12–14, 92
  5.10.23, 95
  5.10.23–31, *96*
  5.10.32, 96
  5.10.54, *125*
  5.10.73, *119*
  5.10.83, 93
  5.10.87–88, 97
  5.10.88, 98
  5.10.94, 96
  5.10.119–25, *7*
  5.11.1–2, *98*
  5.11.1–29, *94*
  5.11.3–5, *118*
  5.11.6, 94
  5.11.8, 94, 239, 255
  5.11.8–10, 57
  5.11.9, 58
  5.11.9.12, 98
  5.11.36–44, 108
  5.12.2, *120*
  5.12.14, 5, *113*
  5.13.24, 239
  5.14.1, *93*
  5.14.24, *93*
  6.1.1, 226
  6.1.1–2, 226
  6.1.2, 247
  6.1.2–3, 227
  6.1.9–52, 237
  6.1.11, 237
  6.1.12, 238
  6.1.18, 227
  6.1.27, 248
  6.1.51–52, 236
  6.1.54–55, 224
  6.1.55, 224
  6.2.1, 237
  6.2.2, 236
  6.2.5, 237
  6.2.8–9, 236
  6.2.18, 238
  6.2.32, 239
  7, *5*
  7.3.19, *125*
  7.10.11, 137
  8–11.1, *5*
  8.1.1, *5*
  8.3.82, *262*
  8.4.3–14, 130
  8.4.11, 100

  8.4.12, 99, *130*, *183*
  8.5.9–11, *100*
  8.9.10, *94*
  9.1.21, 245
  9.2.47, *262*
  9.2.63, 6
  9.3.30, *205*
  9.3.36–7, *205*
  9.3.50, *262*
  9.3.77, *204*
  9.3.80, 203
  9.3.91, *208*
  9.4.19–22, *201*
  9.4.122–30, *201*
  9.4.125, 206
  9.4.127, 206
  9.4.128, 206
  10.1.48, 199
  12.1.28, *104*

Recognitions
  1.60, *39*
  3.3, *39*
Res ges. Divi Aug.
  10.1, *212*
Rhetorica ad Herennium
  1.3, *80*
  1.4, *80*, *84*, 101, *126*
  1.5–11, 194
  1.6, 193, 195
  1.7, 196, 199
  1.8, 195
  1.9–11, 196
  1.10, 197
  1.12, 145–46
  1.12–13, 157
  1.14, 188
  1.15, 189
  1.18, *81*, 84
  2.28, *102*, 102
  2.28–30, 132
  2.47, 224–26, *226*, 247
  2.49, 239
  2.50, *248*
  3.2, 55
  3.3, 240
  3.5, 240
  3.6.10–11, *29*, *46*, 46
  3.8, *81*
  3.9, 239
  3.15, *88*, 131, 144, 254
  3.17, 82
  3.18, *5*, *113*
  4.19, 205, *205*

4.25, *93*
4.26–32, *201–2*
4.28, *203–4*
4.31, *150*
4.37, *262*

Seneca
Prov.
  1.5, 43
  2.5, 43
Shepherd of Hermas.
  Sim.
    9.21.1–4, 268

T. Ben.
  9.3, *36*
Tacitus
  Dia.
    12, 263
    36, 263
    41, 263
Theon
  5, *93*
  11, *87*, *98*
  16, *40*
  70, 25
  70–1, *73*
  74–75, 151
  78, *46*, 140, *141*, 155, *160*
  79–85, 188
  81, 189
  85, 150
  88, *149*
  89–91, 148
  90, *152*

91, 149
108, 57–58
109–12, *212*
110, *34*, 39, *46*
111, 29
112, 260
112–5, *212*
112–13, *33*
113, 39
113–14, 29, *160*
114, *31*
Thucydides
  2.87.7–9, 222
  4.10.1, 105
  4.10.2–5, 105

Virgil
  Aen.
    1.525–26, 103
    1.551–52, 103
    2.353, 105
    4.347–50, *93*
    10.279–84, 105
    11.252–93, 103
    11.252–54, 104
    11.255–77, 104
    11.278, 104
    11.279–82, 104
    11.292–93, 104
    11.296–335, 104
    11.300–4, 104
    11.305–13, 104
    11.321–22, 104
    11.326–29, 104
    11.330–34, 104

MODERN AUTHORS INDEX

Aletti, Jean-Noël, 83, 271
Alexander, Philip, 56, 271
Allen, David M., 36, 271
Amador, J. D. H., 14, 271
Anderson, Kevin L., 2, 4, 14, 18, 112,
127, 138, 201, 222, 271
Attridge, Harold W., 2–3, 8–9, 15, 24, 49,
53, 61 62, 70, 72, 82, 129, 243, 271
Aune, David E., 91, 93, 261, 271

Backhaus, Knut, 2, 4, 17–18, 24, 41, 53,
72, 112, 116, 127, 138, 201, 222, 235,
236, 271
Barclay, John, 268, 272
Burnard, Jody A., 33, 265, 272
Bauckham, Richard, 211, 272
Baugh, S. M., 208, 272
Berry, D. H., 82, 127, 272
Betz, Hans Dieter, 8, 272
Black, C. Clifton, 11–12, 272
Boccaccini, Gabriele, 267, 272
Bornkamm, Günther, 210, 272
Bovon, François, 47, 272
Brauw, Michael de, 80, 137, 139, 272
Bruce, F. F., 1, 62, 72, 272
Büschel, F., 13, 272
Byron, John, 70, 272

Caird, G. B., 211, 272
Caneday, Ardel B., 35, 272
Catto, Stephen K., 10, 273
Cockerill, Gareth Lee, 2, 4, 16, 138, 230,
233, 246, 273
Conley, Thomas A., 9, 91–93, 273

D'Angelo, Mary, 61, 266, 273
Daube, David, 56, 273
Deichgräber, Reinhard, 210, 273
DeSilva, David A., 2, 8, 12, 15, 43, 50,
52, 53–54, 62, 72, 82, 171, 228, 232,
236, 268, 273

Dilts, M. R., xiii–xiv
Duff, Tim, 26

Eisenbaum, Pamela, 53, 130, 270,
273
Ellingworth, Paul, 3, 62, 72, 119, 273
Ellis, E. E., 56, 273
Erbse, Hartmut, 26
Erskine, Andrew, 82, 127, 272
Eskola, Timo, 167, 273
Esler, Philip, 265, 273

Felten, Joseph, 25, 273
Filson, Floyd V., 115, 273
Filtvedt, Ole Jakob, 49, 120, 189, 266,
273
Fowler, R. A., 202, 274
France, R. T., 1, 274
Frankowski, Janusz, 210, 274

Gäbel, Georg, 174, 274
Geiger, Joseph, 26
Gelardini, Gabriella, 1–4, 3, 6, 6, 8–9, 24,
72, 274
Gill, Christopher, 236, 274
Goodspeed, Edgar J., 72, 274
Gräbe, Peter, 34, 274
Gräßer, Erich, 53, 274
Griffiths, Jonathan I., 1, 274
Grillo, Luca, 144, 274
Guthrie, George H., 1–2, 3, 4, 6, 8, 24,
72, 82, 219, 274
Guzmán, Ron, 71, 81, 121, 185, 185,
275
Gyllenberg, Rafael, 13, 275

Hearing, Theodor, 15, 275
Heath, Malcolm, 25, 80, 137, 148, 275
Heil, John Paul, 3, 275
Highest, Gilbert, 103, 104, 255, 275
Horrell, David H., 266, 275

Horton, Fred L., *165*, 275
Hughes, Philip E., *1*, 275
Huizenga, Leroy A., *65*, 275
Hurst, L. D., *35*, *211*, 275

Isaacs, Marie E., *72*, 275

Jamieson, R. B., *174*, 275
Jipp, Joshua W., *35*, 275
Johnson, Luke Timothy, 4, *15*, *72*, *111*, *167*, *211*, 275
Joslin, Barry C., *1*, *3*, 275

Karrer, Martin, *2*, *4*, *223*, *235*, 276
Kennedy, George A., xiii, 7, *25*, *141*, *148*, *264*, 276
Koester, Craig R., *4*, *6*, *14–15*, *17–19*, *24*, *32*, *61–62*, *72*, *110*, 112, *116*, *127*, *170–71*, *174*, 201, *210–11*, *219*, *231*, *235*, *242*, *244*, *248*, *259*, 276
Kraus, Manfred, *91*, *93–94*, 276
Kümmel, W. G., *2*, 276

Laansma, Jon, *119*, 276
Lampe, Peter, *7*, 276
Landgraf, Paul David, *71*, 276
Lane, William L., *3*, *8*, *12*, *15*, *62*, *82*, *243*, *245*, 276
Larmour, David J., *26*
Lausberg, Heinrich, *87*, *130*, *139*, *143*, *197*, 199, *200*, *205–6*, 276
Lehne, Susanne, *34*, 276
Levenson, Jon D., *65*, 276
Lincoln, Andrew, *2*, *15*, *17*, *18–19*, *46*, *182*, 201, 277
Lindars, Barnabas, *4*, *15*, *53*, 277
Lindsay, William, *72*, 277
Loader, William R. G., *210*, 277
Löhr, Hermut, *15*, *82*, 277
Long, Frederick J., 14, *134*, *136*, *223*, 277
Longenecker, Richard N., *1*, 277
Lünnemann, Gottlieb, *71*, 277

Martin, Michael Wade, *30*, *42*, *56*, *71*, *81*, *121*, *148*, *150*, 185, *185*, *202*, *208–9*, *211*, *213*, 275, 277
Martin, Troy W., *8*, *95*, 277
Mason, Eric F., *165*, 277
Meier, J. P., *37*, 277
Michel, Otto, *2*, *46–47*, *72*, *245*, 277
Mitchell, Alan C., *3*, *8*, *269*, 277
Moffatt, James, *35*, 278

Moffitt, David M., *41*, *49*, *65*, *70*, *167*, *174*, *176*, 278
Murphy, James Jerome, *90*, 278
Murphy-O'Connor, Jerome, 83, 278

Nauck, Wolfgang, 2–4, *5*, 40, *216*, 278
Neeley, Linda L., *72*, 278
Neyrey, Jerome H., *43*, 278
Nissilä, Keijo, *13*, *16*, 16, 18–19, *112*, *127*, 201, 223, 278

O'Brien, Peter, *3*, *8*, *62–63*, *66*, *72*, *223*, *243*, 278
Olbricht, Thomas H., *15*, *17*, 18, 23, 52–53, *115*, *129*, *183*, 201, 278
Oliver, H., xiii
Oliver, J. H., *30*, 278

Parsons, Mikeal C., 11, 278
Pelling, C. B. R., *26*
Perlman, S., *94*, 278
Perrin, Bernadotte, *26*
Perry, Peter S., *72*, 279
Peterson, David, *48*, *50*, 279
Pierce, Madison N., *269*, 279

Rabe, Hugo, *25*, 279
Rissi, Mathias, *119*, 279
Robertson, John C., *202*, *204*, *208*, 279
Rothschild, Clare K., 279
Russell, D. A., *26*, *195*, *212*

Sanders, Jack T., *210*, 279
Schaff, Philip, *34*, 279
Schenck, Kenneth L., *6*, *35–37*, *110*, 112, *171*, *211*, 279
Schnelle, Udo, *264*, 279
Schunack, Gerd, *2*, 279
Seid, Timothy W., 23, *46*, 53, *129*, 279
Sheerin, Daniel, *266*, 280
Siegert, Folker, *9*, *261*, 280
Small, Brian C., *24*, *83*, *138*, *182*, 280
Solmsen, Friedrich, *89*, 280
Son, Kiwoong, *50*, 280
Spicq, Ceslas, 16, *18–19*, *82*, *112*, *127*, 201, 223, 280
Standaert, Benoît, 83, 280
Stanley, Steve, *72*, 280
Steel, Catherine, *5*, 280
Stegemann, Ekkehard W., *267*, 280
Stegemann, Wolfgang, *267*, 280
Stegner, William Richard, *10*, 280
Stermberger, Günter, *10*, 280

Stewart-Sykes, Alistair, *9–10*, 10, 12, *260*, 260, *263–64*, 280
Svartvik, Jesper, *267*, 280
Swetnam, James, *8*, *63*, *65*, 281

Talbert, Charles H., *33*, *36*, *44*, *176*, *233*, *267*, 281–82
Thiessen, Matthew, *43*, 43, 281
Thompson, James W., *2*, *4*, *17*, 18–19, *72*, 115, *115–16*, *138*, *140*, *183–84*, 201, *210*, 281
Thurén, Lauri, 17–19, *127*, 201, 223, 281
Thyen, Hartwig, *9*, 281

Übelacker, Walter G., 16, *53–54*, *232*, *241*, *246*, *257*, 281
Usher, Stephen, *87*, 281

Vaganay, Leon, *72*, 281
Vanhoye, Albert, 2–3, 5–6, *8*, *174*, *245*, 281
Visotzky, B., *56*, 282

von Soden, Hermann, 8, *15*, 19, *52*, 201, 222, 282
von Stockhausen, Annette, *10*, 282

Wardman, A., *26*
Wedderburn, A. J. M., *228*, *230*, *249*, 282
Weiss, Hans Friedrich, *2*, *4*, *17*, *174*, 282
Wessbradt, Martin, 189, 274
Westfall, Cynthia L., *1*, 3, *4*, *8*, *71*, 282
Whitfield, Bryan J., *6*, 282
Whitlark, Jason A., *111*, *120*, *124*, *176*, *200*, *232–33*, *236*, *241*, *245*, *259*, *263*, *268*, 277, 281–82
Wills, Lawrence, *1*, 11, 282
Wilson, N. G., *212*
Windisch, Hans, *15*, 282
Witherington, Ben, *15*, *17*, 53, *130*, *182*, *193*, *210*, *214*, 283
Wuellner, Wilhelm, *80*, 283

Zimmermann, Heinrich, *210*, 283
Zoido, Juan Carlos Iglesias, *104–5*, *240*, 283

SUBJECT INDEX

Aaron, 30, *41–42*, 51, 62–65, 69, 76, 120,
    162–63, 166, 175, 187, 215,
    219–20
Abel, 48, *70*, 181, *234*, 266
Abraham, 45, 59, 62–65, *62*, *65*, 73–76,
    110–11, 121–22, 164–65, *217*
Amplification, 218, 225, 238–39, 243, 245
    in *argumentatio*, 37, 86, 88, 98–101,
        108, 110–14, *130*, *183*, 257
    in *narratio*, *88*, *95*, *107*, 129–34,
        141–42, 145–46, 167–68, 173–78,
        183–84, 191, 215, 251, 254
apostasy, 15, 54, 59–62, *66–67*, 74–75,
    79, 101, 106–7, 109, 115–17,
    117–19, *118*, 121–24, *124*, 125–27,
    186, 234–35, 243, 251, 253, 257,
    260–70
argumentatio, 18–19, 79–81, 84–128,
    132–33, 250–52, 254–55
    aims, 86–88, 106, 116
    proofs, 80, 84–94, 99, 102–3, 105–16,
        127, 135–36, 225–26, 230, 250–52,
        257
        artistic, 89, *89*, 108, *184*
        artless, 89, *90*, 108, 114–15, 164,
            167, 168, 184
    propositions, 14, *81*, 86, *95*, 101–5,
        109, 115–18, 120–23, 125–26,
        229–30, 251–52, 255
    topics, 86, 94, 99–100, 104–5, 114, 157,
        175
asyndeton, 147–49, 231, 238–39, 242–43,
    248–49, *249*, 252, *253*

Christian homilies, 260–64
Christian rhetoric, 264–65
Christology, *35*, *41*, *211–12*, 211–12
confirmatio, 80–82, 90, *126*, 128, 134
covenant, 3, 13, 15, 23–24, *24*, 29–30, *30*,
    33–34, *38*, 38–42, 44–51, *46–48*,
    50, 60–67, *61*, *66–69*, 68–71,

74–76, 114, 117, 120, 122, *124*,
    125, 129, *138*, 142, 153, 160,
    168–70, *171*, 172–73, *174*, 175–76,
    176, *178–79*, 184, 191, 198–99,
    215, 218–19, 225, *231–33*, 248,
    250–51, 257–59, 265–70, *266–67*,
    269

defensibility of cause, 194–95
    genus admirabile / turpe, 194–95
    genus anceps, 194–95
    genus honestum, 194–95
    genus humile, 194–96, 199–200, 221
    genus obscurum, 194–96, 216
    genus turpe, 196
deliberative, 9, 13–15, *14*, 52–55, *52–54*,
    57, 58–67, 70–76, 86, 87–88,
    87–88, 93–94, *95*, 99, 101–6, *107*,
    108–9, 112, 115–26, *118*, *121*, *123*,
    126, 130–33, 136, *140*, 143, 146,
    151, 153, 194, 198, 200–1, 211,
    216, 220–22, 232, 235, 237–38,
    240, 247–49, 252–59, *255*, 262–64,
    263, 267
digressio, 10, *81*, *120*, *126*, 145, 185–88,
    188, 192
disjointed structure, 14, 132–34, *136*,
    136–39, *138–39*, 146, 160, *187*,
    190–91, 224, 250–53, 255, 265

enthymeme, 14, 89, 90–94, *90–95*, 97–98,
    100–2, 106, 107–8, *107–8*, 114,
    119–20, *124*, *126–28*, 132, 182–85,
    184, 251, 255, 257
epainos, 211–12
epideictic, 9–10, 13–14, *15*, *17*, 23–24,
    26–30, *30*, *33*, 33, 46, *48*, *52–53*,
    52–54, 60–76, *87–88*, 87, *95–96*,
    107, 111–13, 129–44, *129*, *143*,
    146, 148, 159, 183–86, 191, *210*,
    216, 220–21, 227, 250–56, 266–67

epilogue, 16, 27, 89, 224, 236–37
Esau, 230, 234–35, *236*, 243, 245, 252,
    257–58
ethos, 89, *90*, 184, *184*, *236*
example, 57–58, 89–90, 94, *98*, 105–6,
    107, 114, 118–21, *118*, 123–24,
    126–28, 132, 134–35, *145*, *151*,
    182, *184*, 234–35, 239, 243–44,
    248, 251–52, 256–57, 269
exhortation(s), 2, 4, 7, 14, 35, 37, 40, *52*,
    54, 75, 87–88, 103–6, *104*, 109,
    113, 115–16, *118*, *121–23*, *126*,
    127, 142, 216–17, *217*, 222, *223*,
    228, 228–36, *232*, 239, *240–43*,
    240–43, 245–46, 248–49, 252,
    255–58, 260, 263–65
exordium, 10–11, 18, 80, 89, *126*, 134,
    193–221, *208*, *210*, 255–56
    deliberative *exordium*, 200
    primary *exordium*, 195–214, *216*, 252,
        255
    purpose, 80, 193–97
    secondary *exordium*, *39*, *72*, *116*,
        215–20, 225, 234, 252, 255–56
    subtypes, 194–95
exposition, 4, 39–40, 54, 80, 112–13,
    139–42, 144–46, 148, 153, 156,
    160, 191–92, 226, 251

favor, 139, 193–200, 215–17, 225–26,
    237, 249, 252
    attentiveness, 196, 199–200, 217
    goodwill, 195–96, 198–99, 216–17
    receptivity, 185, 196, 215–16
funeral oration, *17*, 52–53

Gorgianic figures, 202–3, *206–10*, 217 18
    antithesis, 202–3, 207
    parisosis, 202–3, 209, *210*, 218
    paromoiosis, 202, 204

hymnos, *210–11*, 210–14, 218, 220
hyperbaton, 208, *218*

idolatry, *66*, *124*, *236*, 243, 268–70,
    268–69
imperial culture, 268–70
incidental *narratio*, 88, 104, 133, *140*,
    143, 144–46, 184, 191, 196, *198*,
    250–51, 254, 257

Joshua, *6*, *120*, 268
Judaism, 9–11, *65*, 265–70, *267–69*

judicial (forensic), 9, *14*, 56, 80, 84,
    87–88, *88*, *95*, *139–40*, 139, *143*,
    144, *155*, *223*, 227, 237, 254

Levitical, 24, 30, 44–46, 51, 62, 66, 69,
    76, 101, 122, 163–80, *165*, 215,
    232, 266
logos, 89–90, *90*, *184*, 185–86

Melchizedek, 24, 30, *41–46*, 41–46, 51,
    62, 64–66, 69, 73, 76, 101, 122,
    130, 163–74, *165*, *167*, 215, *217*,
    257
Moses, 30, 38–39, *50*, 51, 61–62, *61*,
    66, 68, *69*, 71, 76, 117, *152*, 162,
    219, 230–32, 234, 265–66, *267*,
    269

narratio, 10–11, 14, 18, 80, *95*, 109, 112,
    129–92, 201, *210*, 219, 224,
    250–51, 254, 257–58
    definition of, 80, 142
    degrees of completion, 156
    elements of, 155, 158
    functional types, 144–46
    location, 134–36, 138–39
    persuasion appropriate for, 182–85
    relation to epideictic, 142–44, 251,
        254
    schemas of, 146–53, 160, 173, 251
    structure, 136–39
    temporal classifications, 152–54,
        257–58
    topoi, 156–82
    virtues of, 188–91

pathos, 89, *90*, 184–86, *184*, *236*
perfection, 42–44, 47–49, *48*, *50*, 64, 69,
    100, 120, 163, *165*, 168, 174,
    185–88, *217*, 220, 257, 265
period, 201–10, *201–10*, 217–18, 252, 262
peroratio, 8, 10, 19, *46*, 81, *126*, 219,
    222–49, *223–26*, *233*, *247*, *249*,
    252, 256–58
    asyndeton, 231, 238–39, 242–43, *253*
    concluding exhortations, 231, 235–36,
        239
    doubling, 231, 239, 245–46
    functions, 248
    length, 247–48
    location, 225, *248*
    metaphorical language, 239, 243–45
    primary *peroratio*, 224–25, 228–33

secondary *peroratio*, *39*, *72*, 219, 225, 233–35
vivid description, 239, 243–45
perseverance, 54, 59, 63, 65, 74–75, 79, 111, 115–16, *118*, 119–28, *121–22*, *125*, 142, 185, 197–200, 216, 235, 240, 249–51, 253, 257–59, *261*, 264
prayer, *41*, 104, 232–33, 241, 261
principium, 80, 82, 194–96, 198, *201*
probatio, 10–11, *17*, 81, 85, 108, 114, *140*
progymnasmata, 25, *25*, 29, 146–48, *148*, 155–56, 181
prooemium, 16, 131, 200, 214, 219, 236
propositio, *6*, 14, *17*, 18, 79, 81, 83, *84*, 101–6, *102*, 109–10, *110*, 112–13, 115–27, *118*, *121–23*, *132*, 134, *139*, 254–55, *255*
prose style
continuous, 201–2, *202*, 206–7, 209–10
periodic, 202–9, *202–10*, 252

Rahab, 232
resurrection, *35–37*, *41*, *47*, *49*, 63–64, *65*, 164, *167*, 244, 257
rhetorical arrangement, 4, 10–18, 79–82, 250–53, 260
rhetorical handbooks, 7–9, 12–13, 23, 54–58, *56*, 68, 82, *82*, 86–106, *90*, *136*, 157, 182, 188–89, 193–97, 206, 211
rhetorical *topoi*, 26 30, 32–33, 96, 114, 127, 149, 157, 160, 181–82, 190, 250–51
  action, 166–68, 181
  birth, 32, 38–39, 68, 71, 161–62, 164–65, 215
  cause, 174–80
  death/events beyond death, 32, 46–50, 69, 74–75, 164, 166 ·
  deeds, 32, 39–40, 44–46, 69, 73–74, *96*, 166, *191*, 215
  education, 32, 39–44, 68, 71–73, 162–63, 215
  manner, 172–74
  origins, 32, 34–37, 68, 70–71, 164–65, 215

place, 168–70, 181
time, 170–72
Rome, 25–26, *30*, *48*, 232, 235, 263, *264*, *270*

structure(s) of Hebrews, *1–3*, 1, 6–9, *6*, 13, 15–19, 24, 30–53, *31*, 60, 75–76, 138–39, 160
suffering, 37, 41, 43, *44*, 69, 73–74, *113*, 123, *167*, 187, 217, 220, 230, 232–33, 243–44, 269
synagogue homily, 9–12
syncrisis, 23–34, *31*, *33–34*, 52–76, *56*, 198, *211*, 251
  Jesus/Aaronic high priest, 30, 40–44, 62–65, 69, 76, 219
  Jesus/Angels, 30, 34–37, 60–61, 68, 75–76, 106–8, 214
  Jesus/Moses, 30, 38–39, 61–62, 68–69, 76
  Melchizedekian/Levitical priestly ministries, 30, 40–46, 66, 69, 76
  old covenant/new covenant, 39–50, 66–67, 76
  Zion/Sinai, 30, 46–50, 66–67, 69–70, 76

topos, 70, *96*, 97, *130*, 155, 158–61, 166, *167*, 168, 170–75, *178–80*, 183–84, 187, 212–14, *213*, 219, 257–58

wilderness generation, 43, *58*, 61–62, 71, 101, 114, *118*, 142, 219, 231, 234, *266*, 267, 269, *269*

ἀντεξέτασις, 133, 154, 191–92, 251
ἀφήγησις, *118*, 134–35, *151*
διήγημα, 133, 156
διήγησις, 80, *84*, 133–35, 154–56
ἐπίλογος, *80*, *84*, 223–24
παραδιήγησις, 133, 142, 144–46, 191, 250–51, 254
παράκλησις, 262
πίστις, *80*, 80–81, 84, 89, 223
πρόθεσις, 81, 84, 223
προοίμιον, 80, *84*, 223